Communities of Practice

Creating Learning Environments for Educators, Volume 2

edited by

Chris Kimble
University of York, United Kingdom

Paul Hildreth
K-Now International, United Kingdom

and

Isabelle Bourdon
Montpellier University of Sciences, France

Information Age Publishing, Inc.
Charlotte, North Carolina • www.infoagepub.com

Library of Congress Cataloging-in-Publication Data

Communities of practice : creating learning environments for educators /
edited by Chris Kimble, Paul Hildreth.
    v. <1> ; cm.
  Includes bibliographical references.
  ISBN-13: 978-1-59311-864-8 (paperback.)
  ISBN-13: 978-1-59311-865-5 (hardcover)
  1. Teachers—Training of. 2. Teachers—Professional relationships.
3. Communities of practice. I. Kimble, Chris. II. Hildreth, Paul M., 1959-
  LB1707.C66 2007
  370.71'5—dc22

                                          2007043205
Volume 1 ISBNs:
ISBN 13: 978-1-59311-862-4 (paperback)
ISBN 13: 978-1-59311-863-1 (hardcover)

Volume 2 ISBNs:
ISBN 13: 978-1-59311-864-8 (paperback)
ISBN 13: 978-1-59311-865-5 (hardcover)

Set ISBNs:
ISBN 13: 978-1-59311-866-2 (paperback)
ISBN 13: 978-1-59311-867-9 (hardcover)

Printed in the United States of America

THE UNIVERSITY OF WINCHESTER

Martial Rose Library
Tel: 01962 827306

CONTENTS

Acknowledgments   *vii*

Introduction and Overview
    Chris Kimble and Paul Hildreth   *ix*

1. Designing for Growth: Enabling Communities of Practice to
Develop and Extend Their Work Online
    Melissa Koch and Judith Fusco   *1*

2. Holding the Virtual Space: The Roles and Responsibilities of
Community Stewardship
    Brenda Kaulback and Debbie Bergtholdt   *25*

3. Education Leadership for a Networked World
    Diana D. Woolis, Susan Restler, and Yvonne Thayer   *45*

4. Virtual Problem-Based Learning Communities of Practice for
Teachers and Academic Developers: An Irish Higher Education
Perspective
    Roisin Donnelly   *67*

5. Exploring the Potential of Online Communities of Practice for
Distance Tutors
    Janet Macdonald and Anne Hewling   *89*

6. Supporting a Dispersed Community: CoP Development in The
Caribbean
    Sabine Little   *107*

7. Virtual Communities of Practice: A Vehicle for Meaningful
Professional Development
    Kathy Hibbert   *127*

8. Distributing Teaching Presence: Engaging Teachers of English to
Young Learners in an International Virtual Community of Inquiry
    Joan Kang Shin and Beverly Bickel   *149*

9. Communites of Practice Across Learning Institutions
   Thérèse Laferrière and Fernand Gervais   *179*

10. Teacher-Librarian Communities: Changing Practices in
    Changing Schools
    Eric M. Meyers, Lisa P. Nathan, and Matthew L. Saxton   *199*

11. Communities of Practice at the Math Forum: Supporting
    Teachers as Professionals
    Wesley Shumar and Johann Sarmiento   *223*

12. Heads Together: A Professional Online Community of Practice
    for Scottish Headteachers
    Kevin Thompson and Michael Hartley   *241*

13. Graduate Professional Education from a Community of Practice
    Perspective: The Role of Social and Technical Networking
    Linda Polin   *267*

14. Learning Communities Are Not Mushrooms—or —How to
    Cultivate Learning Communities in Higher Education
    Mélanie Bos-Ciussi, Marc Augier, and Gillian Rosner   *287*

15. Enabling Duality in Teaching and Learning Environmental
    Decision Making: A Role for Communities of Practice?
    Chris Blackmore   *309*

16. The Adult Literacy Education Wiki as a Virtual Community of
    Practice
    Erik Jacobson   *327*

17. Implications of a Virtual Learning Community Model for
    Designing Distributed Communities of Practice in Higher
    Education
    Richard Schwier and Ben Daniel   *347*

18. Online CoPs: Towards the Next Generation
    Leonie Ramondt   *367*

19. Gender and Moderation: The Style's The Thing!
    Valentina Dodge and Sheila Vine   *395*

About the Contributors   *417*

ACKNOWLEDGMENTS

First, the editors would like to thank the authors of the chapters in this book. The process of creating the book was very much a collaborative effort and would not have been possible without the patience, under-standing, and commitment of all involved.

Second, although most of the authors also served as referees for chap-ters submitted by other authors, we would also like to acknowledge the help of all those other people who were involved in the review process. We are sure that this has helped to ensure the high quality of chapters that form the finished version of the book. We must also thank the staff at Information Age Publising for their guidance and support through the 18 months of work on the book.

Finally, we would like to reiterate our thanks to all of the authors for their excellent contributions and thank our friends and families without whose ongoing support we would never have been able to complete this project.

INTRODUCTION AND OVERVIEW

Chris Kimble and Paul Hildreth

INTRODUCTION

Many of the current notions of communities of practice (CoP) originated in the late 1980s and early 1990s from the Institute for Research on Learning (IRL) at the Xerox Palo Alto Research Center (PARC). The research in IRL at PARC brought together ideas from several different academic disciplines and occupational backgrounds that included Lucy Suchman, Jean Lave, Etienne Wenger, John Seely Brown, and Paul Duguid. Together they worked on projects that spanned disciplines from computer science to anthropology employing a number of what were then novel techniques and theoretical frameworks such as ethnographic studies and social constructivism.

For many years, what were termed behaviorist models of learning had been dominant. Essentially these models held that learning was concerned with the transmission of knowledge from the teacher to the learner. Knowledge was viewed as an object that could be clearly defined, abstracted, codified, and "transferred" from one person to another. However, during the 1970s and 1980s there began to be an increasing interest in "social constructivist" models of learning. These saw learning not as a process of transmission of abstract and decontextualized knowledge to an individual but as a process that is situated in a particular context where knowledge is mutually "constructed" by the participants in that process.

Much of the conceptual basis for these theories, can be found in the work of Vygotsky (1978). Vygotsky was concerned with the ways in which individuals learn within communities. He believed that knowledge was constructed through collaboration and interaction in activities and used the notion of a zone of proximal development (ZPD) to describe the way in which a learner interacts with others in a particular activity. Lave and Wenger (1991) in particular built upon Vygotsky's notion of social constructivism and ZPD in order to develop a different understanding of learning that moved away from seeing learning as the product of an individual mind mastering abstract tools and techniques, to one that saw learning as a process of social transformation as part of a collective.

The aim of Lave and Wenger's (1991) book was to explore an alternative theory of learning to that of the dominant behaviorist models; their work was concerned with colocated communities and drew on previously conducted studies of tailors in Goa, Mayan midwives, nondrinking alcoholics, butchers in supermarkets, and navy quartermasters. At this point, they were content to leave the definition of a CoP as a largely intuitive notion (Lave & Wenger, 1991, p. 26) considering the value of their description of a CoP to be primarily as a heuristic device that could highlight issues that had previously been overlooked. Thus, their goal was not to provide us directly with a new theory of learning, but to change our way of thinking about how learning might take place.

By the end of the 1990s things had changed somewhat. There was a premillennium sense of optimism that the economy and perhaps society in general, was undergoing a fundamental shift. The stock market was in the grip of "dot-com fever" so that speculation and hype had inflated the value of hi-tech start-up companies (known colloquially as dot-com companies), to astronomical levels. It seemed that the relentless growth of computer and telecommunications technology had finally reached a point where the "revolution" that authors such as McLuhan and colleagues (1964; 1989), Ellul (1964), Toffler (1972; 1980), Bell (1974) and (Hiltz & Turoff, 1978) had been predicting for the last 30 years was about to happen.

In his work from this period, Wenger (1998a, 1998b) is keen to put the concept of a CoP on a firm footing for the new millennium. In the opening pages of *Communities of Practice: Learning, Meaning, and Identity,* Wenger (1998a) makes it clear that he wishes to establish a new intellectual foundation of his work (p. 11). In this book and the associated papers, Wenger introduces several new concepts, elaborates some of the terms used in his earlier work (Lave & Wenger, 1991) with Lave (e.g., identity and participation) and also abandons some (e.g., LPP). It is in this book (Wenger, 1998a) and the articles that preceded it (Wenger, 1998b), that we begin to see the first links being made between CoP and virtual or distributed working (e.g., Wenger, 1998a, p. 131) which form the basis for this second volume of papers.

For example, in an echo of Brown and Duguid's (1991) notion of the organization as a "collective of communities," Wenger (1998a, p. 127) develops his view of an organization as a "constellation of communities," carrying this idea further than Brown and Duguid's passing reference to cultivating "connections throughout the corporation" (p. 47) and making an explicit link between this and the capacity of an organization to be "effective." Similarly Wenger now begins to highlight the importance of the boundaries between communities (e.g., Wenger, 1998a, p. 106) and uses the notion of "boundary objects" (Star & Griesemer, 1989) to describe how artifacts, having been produced by one CoP, can then act as a link to other geographically distinct groups (cf. Kimble & Hildreth, 2005).

OVERVIEW OF THE BOOK

The of this book is to combine current academic research in CoP in education with "hands on" practitioner experience in order to provide teachers and academics with guidance and an incentive to develop and work in their own CoP.

The result is a wide mix of authors from around the world who relate their experiences in their own words. The chapters and styles range from reports into research to very personal accounts and thus provide a fascinating view of CoP in Education.

This book is divided into two volumes with volume one addressing issues associated with "colocated" CoPs. This volume deals with CoP in a distributed (virtual) environment and like volume one, is divided into three sections. A brief description of each section and each chapter follows.

The aim of the first section is to introduce some of the motivations for encouraging the development of virtual communites of practice (vCoPs) in educational settings and to reflect on some of the practical problems of doing so.

In chapter 1, "Designing for Growth: Enabling Communities of Practice to Develop and Extend their Work Online," Melissa Koch and Judith Fusco describe how a CoP for teaching professionals can affect professional growth through informal collegial interactions. In line with the theme of this volume, they provide a series of examples to show how CoP can become vCoP using specialist software such as Tapped In® and CLT-

Net. This chapter introduces some of the themes in the book and the use of "professional" software provides an interesting contrast to Bos-Ciussi, Augier, and Rosner's approach in chapter 14.

Then, in chapter 2, "Holding the Virtual Space: The Roles and Responsibilities of Community Stewardship," Brenda Kaulback and Debbie Bergtholdt examine the ways in which a specialist team in the U.S. Department of Education for the state of Virginia, provided support for a vCoP of educational leaders, administrators, and instructors. The focus of the chapter is on adult education and it is concerned with issues of leadership; in particular, it examines the need to maintain a delicate balance between various competing factors in order to "hold a space" where the members to do their work.

Diana D. Woolis, Susan Restler, and Yvonne Thayer continue the theme of leadership in chapter 3, "Education Leadership for a Networked World," and describe a "distributed" leadership model based on vCoP. Their argument is that since the late 1980s, educational leaders have faced a burgeoning array of new initiatives and that only leaders with the skill to harness networks of vCoP will be capable of responding to this reform agenda. The use of the model is illustrated by case studies drawn from the author's work in developing and facilitating vCoPs for educational leaders.

The second section focuses on the use of vCoPs for continuing professional development and as a medium for teaching. Although most chapters deal with both issues, chapters 4 to 7 are primarily concerned with the problems of continuing professional development while chapters 8 to 12 focus more on issues relating to teaching.

Roisin Donnelly introduces some of the broad issues of professional development for educators from an Irish perspective in chapter 4, "Virtual Problem-Based Learning Communities of Practice for Teachers and Academic Developers: An Irish Higher Education Perspective." She looks at the experiences of a group of staff in Irish higher education who shared an interest in designing e-learning courses and shows how a group of people taking a postgraduate diploma in "Designing E-Learning" became a vCoP. The chapter concludes with an examination of practical implications for teacher-practitioners and the developers of academic courses.

In chapter 5, "Exploring the Potential of Online Communities of Practice for Distance Tutors," Janet Macdonald and Anne Hewling look at a more specific example of the problems of continuing professional development: support and development of so called "distance tutors" who rarely have the opportunity for ongoing support and informal development enjoyed by campus based staff. The chapter describes the work of such tutors at the United Kingdom's Open University and gives examples of the ways in which a variety of platforms—from online forums to Wiki based environments—have been used to support CoP between them.

Chapter 6, "Supporting a Dispersed Community: CoP Development in the Caribbean" continues the theme of supporting personal and professional development, but in a very different setting. In this chapter, Sabine Little describes how technology has helped support a CoP that brings together practicing teachers and educationalists from several islands in the Caribbean that has enabled practitioners to build on local resources and expertise, rather than being reliant on first-world countries for literature and input. The chapter contains a number of observations on facilitating such a community and provides a valuable insight into the inner workings of the community.

In chapter 7, "Virtual Communities of Practice: A Vehicle for Meaningful Professional Development," Kathy Hibbert offers us a chapter that combines the two strands of this section of the book: teaching and professional development. The chapter describes how the use of a virtual learning environment designed for professional development combined with some strategies for discussion to lead to the evolution of a vCoP. She describes how this in turn helped to shift the emphasis in training program from one where those undergoing professional development were seen as "knowledge receivers" to one in which they became "knowledge producers."

Then, in chapter 8, "Distributing Teaching Presence: Engaging Teachers of English to Young Learners in an International Virtual Community of Inquiry," Joan Kang Shin and Beverly Bickel describe an online course to train teachers of English to young learners which leads to the creation of an international CoP and several more localized spin-off communities (cf. chapter 12, volume 1). Shin and Bickel use a community of inquiry framework to analyze the modes of interaction in the course and show how teaching presence became more distributed as participants took on leadership roles in the distributed community, which later helped them to build their own local CoP.

Thérèse Laferrière and Fernand Gervais look at what happens when people move in the opposite direction in chapter 9, "Communities of Practice across Learning Institutions," and cross the boundary from a small-scale local CoP to a constellation of communities as found in virtual CoP. The chapter examines three different cases based on school-university partnerships for teacher education and professional development and presents a set of sociotechnical design principles that stress the dynamics of change. The chapter concludes with some lessons that have been learnt from attempting to build that CoP cross institutions.

Chapter 10, "Teacher-Librarian Communities: Changing Practices in Changing Schools," describes how such a CoP developed when six isolated teacher-librarians joined university researchers in a project studying high schools undergoing reform. In this chapter Eric M. Meyers, Lisa P. Nathan, and Matthew L. Saxton also look at crossing the boundaries between different communities. They argue that CoP are a powerful means of supporting new roles and professional identities among education specialists such as teacher-librarians. The chapter also contains some interesting observations on the potential pitfalls of using virtual CoP in this way.

Chapter 11, "Communities of Practice at the Math Forum: Supporting Teachers as Professionals," by Wesley Shumar and Johann Sarmiento, describes how the math forum, an interactive digital library that aims to provide opportunities for individuals to talk and work with others on mathematics, has become the focus for multiple overlapping CoPs among mathematics teachers and others. The chapter argues that opportunities to build knowledge collaboratively are often not as open to teachers as they are to other professions where the daily practice is more visible to peers that initiatives such as the math Forum could provide a model for online professional development for teachers.

Finally, chapter 12, "Heads Together: A Professional Online Community of Practice for Scottish Headteachers," Kevin Thompson and Michael Heartly describe the "Heads Together" project—an online community of head teachers within primary, secondary, nursery and special educational needs sectors in Scotland—that originated from ULTRALAB at Anglia Polytechnic University. The chapter describes a number of the tools and techniques used in the project and like many of the other chapters in this section, it is concerned with professional development and crossing boundaries, although this example is concerned specifically with head teachers and operates on a national scale.

The final section of the book looks at some of the emerging tools and techniques that are applicable to virtual CoP. The section contains a mix of practical chapters and chapters that attempt to address some of the more theoretical issues.

Linda Polin, in chapter 13, "Graduate Professional Education from a Community of Practice Perspective: The Role of Social and Technical Networking," describes the "revisioning" of graduate professional education as an activity that occurs at the intersection of three related areas: communities of practice, pedagogy, and digital culture. Using illustrations from her own work, she shows how social computing applications enable the use of the CoP model in graduate professional education. The chapter contains a number of examples of how so-called Web 2.0 applications, such as blogs, podcasts, and Wikis, have been used in two graduate level programs.

In chapter 14, "Learning Communities Are Not Mushrooms—or—How to Cultivate Learning Communities in Higher Education," Mélanie Bos-Ciussi, Gillian Rosner, and Marc Augier continue the theme of innovative approaches to working in the digital world. In an interesting contrast to Melissa Koch and Judith Fusco in chapter 1, Bos-Ciussi, Rosner, and Augier describe a "self build" approach to VLE's using open source software. The focus of the chapter is on information and communication technologies and their effect on learning processes. It contains three case studies, the building of a VLE, a participative EFL course and an intern follow up scheme, all of which are based in a French business school.

Chris Blackmore takes a slightly more theoretical approach and considers teaching and learning as a duality in chapter 15, "Enabling Duality in Teaching and Learning Environmental Decision Making—A Role for Communities of Practice?" Using a case study of an open university course on environmental decision making, she examines what is meant by a CoP in this context, the design of supportive learning systems to support this type of course and finally looks at how teaching and learning are conceptualized.

In chapter 16, "The Adult Literacy Education Wiki as a Virtual Community of Practice," Erik Jacobson asks whether a large Wiki, the Adult Literacy Education (ALE) Wiki, can be considered a virtual CoP. The chapter examines the limited opportunities available for professional development opportunities for adult literacy practitioners, the role the ALE Wiki plays in this and the multilayered nature of participation in the Wiki. The conclusion is that while the ALE Wiki as a whole cannot be considered a CoP, the concept itself does provide a useful way of analyzing different aspects of the functioning of the Wiki.

Richard A. Schwier and Ben K. Daniel present a model of virtual learning communities in chapter 17, "Implications of a Virtual Learning Community Model for Designing Distributed Communities of Practice in Higher Education." The central premise of their argument is that virtual learning communities are closely to CoP, particularly when they distributed. The chapter discuses both the theoretical background of the model and offers advice of a more practical nature about how such communities might be nurtured, how to deal with the changes that take place over time and how to take advantage of the individual elements that the model identifies.

Like Kevin Thompson and Michael Heartly (chapter 12), Leonie Ramondt also describes work from ULTRALAB. In chapter 18, "Online CoPs—Towards The Next Generation" she describes her experiences of the facilitation of vCoP at the National College of School Leaderships in England. She presents a highly practical, step-by-step methodology for establishing online CoP that is illustrated by case studies and observations. The chapter concludes also includes a discussion of how CoP can leverage the "next generation" of technology and how the performance of these online communities might be measured.

Finally, Valentina Dodge and Sheila Vine return to the theme of teaching English as a foreign language in chapter 19, "Gender and Moderation: The Style's The Thing!" Like the previous chapter, the focus here is on the facilitation of vCoP but in this case, the focus is on the differences between male and female styles of discourse. Dodge and Vine present the results of research based on the case-history analysis of four selected virtual CoP to illustrate the importance of recognizing the different effects that male and female styles of moderating can have on the long term success of a vCoP.

REFERENCES

Bell, D. (1974). *The coming of the Post-industrial Society: A venture in social forecasting.* Portsmouth, NH: Heinemann.

Brown, J. S., & Duguid, P. (1991). Organizational learning and communities of practice: Toward a unified view of working, learning, and innovation. *Organization Science, 2*(1), 40-57.

Ellul, J. (1964). *The technological society*: Random House.

Hiltz, S. R., & Turoff, M. (1978). *The network nation: Humman communication vai computers.* Cambridge, MA: MIT Press.

Kimble, C., & Hildreth, P. (2005). Dualities, distributed communities of practice and knowledge management. *Journal of Knowledge Management, 9*(4), 102-113.

Lave, J., & Wenger, E. (1991). *Situated learning: Legitimate peripheral participation.* London: Cambridge University Press.

McLuhan, M. (1964). *Understanding media: The extensions of man.* New York: McGraw-Hill.

McLuhan, M., & Powers, B. R. (1989). *The global village: Transformations in world life and media in the 21st century.* New York: Oxford University Press.

Star, S. L., & Griesemer, J. R. (1989). Institutional ecology, translations and boundary objects: Amateurs and professionals in Berkeley's Museum of Vertebrate Zoology, 1907–1939. *Social Studies of Science 19*, 387-420.

Toffler, A. (1972). *The futurists* (1st ed.). New York: Random House.

Toffler, A. (1980). *The third wave*: London: Pan.

Vygotsky, L. S. (1978). *Mind in society: The development of higher psychological processes.* London: Cambridge University Press.

Wenger, E. (1998a). *Communities of practice: Learning, meaning, and identity.* London: Cambridge University Press.

Wenger, E. (1998b). Communities of practice: Learning as a social system. *Systems Thinker, 9*(5), 1-10.

CHAPTER 1

DESIGNING FOR GROWTH

Enabling Communities of Practice to Develop and Extend Their Work Online

Melissa Koch and Judith Fusco

A teaching professionals' community of practice (CoP) can affect professional growth through informal collegial interactions. The desire to support professional growth through community has led scores of teacher education, induction, and professional development providers and educators to seek online virtual spaces to meet their CoP needs. This chapter provides examples of using a phased approach to help CoPs become virtual communities of practice (vCoPs) in Tapped In®, a Web-based virtual environment for professional development providers and educators, and CLTNet, an online network; CLTNet supports the United States National Science Foundation's Centers for Learning and Teaching in graduate training, research, and practitioner development. As many organization leaders and users have noted, the greatest value to the organization and its CoP is the phased assistance that CoP community developers provide to CoP leaders and participants. This phased approach enables leaders to articulate their CoP vision, understand what is possible online, support and scaffold their initial online activities, and gradually remove the scaffolding as the organization's capacity to use the online environment to sustain and scale its CoP's activities

Communities of Practice: Creating Learning Environments for Educators,
Volume 2, pp. 1–23
Copyright © 2008 by Information Age Publishing

grows. Through this phased approach, leaders gain an understanding not only of what is possible online, but also of what is possible in growing vCoPs.

INTRODUCTION

> Communities of practice ... cannot be legislated into existence or defined by decree. They can be recognized, supported, encouraged and nurtured, but they are not reified, designable units. (Wenger, 1998, p. 229)

Wenger and others who develop online learning environments state that communities of practice (CoPs) cannot be designed (Barab, Kling, & Gray, 2004; Schwen & Hara, 2004), but that they can be designed for (Schlager & Fusco, 2003). This chapter reports experiences in developing online environments that support existing, emerging and new CoPs. Specifically, it describes Tapped In (http://tappedin.org) as a Web-based virtual environment for professional development providers and educators, and CLTNet (http://cltnet.org), as an online network developed to support the work of the United States National Science Foundation's (NSF's) Centers for Learning and Teaching (CLTs) in graduate training, research, and practitioner development.

In creating support strategies and infrastructure for educators, the Tapped In community developers have been guided by the theoretical CoP framework (Brown & Duguid, 1991; Lave & Wenger, 1991; Wenger, 1998). The framework suggests that a teaching professionals' CoP can provide professional growth through informal collegial interactions (Barab & Duffy, 2000; Brown & Duguid, 2000; Schlager & Fusco, 2003; Schlager, Fusco, & Schank, 2002). This desire to support professional growth through community has led scores of teacher education, induction, and professional development providers and educators to seek online or virtual spaces to meet their CoP needs. More than 60,000 have joined Tapped In for this reason. Many organization leaders and users have noted that the organization and its CoP benefit most from the phased assistance that community developers provide to the CoP leaders and participants, and early adopters of the system.

The phased approach used in Tapped In and CLTNet enables leaders to articulate their CoP vision, to understand what is possible online and start moving the work of their CoP to a virtual environment, to model and scaffold their initial online activities, and to gradually remove the scaffolding as the organization matures in using the online environment to sustain and scale CoP's activities. In preparation for the focus of this chapter—a description and examples of this three-phase approach of bringing a CoP online: Getting Started, Modeling and Scaffolding, and

Maturing—CoPs are defined and an approach for designing their virtual environments is presented.

Defining CoPs and Their Virtual Environments

CoPs are defined here as self-reproducing, emergent and evolving entities that frequently extend beyond formal organizational structures (Schlager & Fusco, 2003). Individual members focus on learning through practice to improve their own practice and that of the CoP as a whole. Riel and Polin (2004) distinguish a CoP from other learning communities that focus solely on completing specific tasks or gaining knowledge about something specific. Although CoP members certainly complete tasks and acquire knowledge, their collective mission of engaging in and improving joint practice is what fuels the CoP.

CoPs, as Wenger (1998) states, must be recognized and understood but must not be artificially created in the real or virtual world. Schwen and Hara (2004) in their review of the CoP research literature conclude, "all the fully functioning CoPs we have observed in our work and have read about in the literature were not designed. Instead, they evolved quite naturally over several years" (p. 163). Work with education CoPs supports that conclusion (Schlager & Fusco, 2003): we cannot design virtual CoPs (vCoPs) per se; instead, we must design the social and technological aspects of the virtual environments (Kim, 2000; Preece, 2000) that vCoPs can use for learning and for improving their practice.

In designing online community infrastructure, we have studied the social aspects of existing CoPs to create fertile online environments in which mature CoPs coming to a virtual environment will flourish and in which emerging CoPs—both in the physical and virtual worlds—will grow. A CoP's social aspects are the artifacts and dynamics of the CoP members interacting with the CoP mission, structured activities, resources, other members within the CoP, the community manager and other CoPs. The technical structures consist of the online tools (e.g., chat, discussion board, group creation and management, member management, event management) that support these artifacts and communications.

The social aspects of physical and vCoPs inform the initial design and ongoing refinement of the technology structure (Farooq, Harris, Schank, Fusco, & Schlager, in press). In turn, the technology, or more precisely its affordances, influences the interactions and artifacts of the vCoPs using the system. Orlikowski (1992) calls these ongoing exchanges between the technical and the social the "duality of technology." To let vCoPs evolve naturally this duality or dynamic between the social and the technical has been reinforced.

Designing the Virtual Environment: Focus on the Social

This chapter focuses on two online environments, Tapped In and CLTNet. Tapped In is an open online environment that has supported the online activities of diverse educator communities worldwide since 1997. Although not every member of Tapped In is in a CoP, some are and some of the communities in Tapped In meet the above definition of a CoP. In 2003, the Tapped In team extended the Tapped In infrastructure to develop CLTNet, an online network to support the NSF's CLTs. CLTNet is a closed community limited to CLTs. Each center is a multiinstitutional consortium focused on research and graduate training in science, technology, engineering, and mathematics education. Members of these interdisciplinary centers may belong to several CoPs, including their centers, their existing home institutions, and other CoPs in the education community.

For both CLTNet and Tapped In, it was found to be important to start designing the technology in cooperation with representatives from existing physical and vCoPs rather than with emerging CoPs. There were two reasons for doing so: (1) members of existing CoPs have accumulated experience about their needs in an online environment to share with developers; and (2) emerging CoPs need to focus on getting started (see below) and to have a technology (and active community management team) in place to support their emergence. For these reasons, we first highlight the technological design process for an online environment that will support existing CoPs and encourage the growth of new vCoPs.

It is easy to begin thinking about technology features when designing an online environment; indeed, many organizations start with a list of online tools or features that they want. However, focusing first on users' needs, practices, and social dynamics is key to developing an online community environment (Carroll, 2000; Cooper, 1999). We use a scenario-based participatory design approach guided by theory-informed principles derived from the broader literature on communities (Koch, 2000; Schlager & Fusco, 2003). The following guiding principles serve as a designer's checklist of fundamental elements required in the online environment. The needs and characteristics of the CoP members being designed for dictate the specific form and interplay of these principles:

- Learning process and practice: Each CoP can easily share its approach and commitment to a specific practice within and across the CoP.

- Identity and trust: Everyone's identity in the online environment is consistent and persistent. We know with whom we are dealing and that it is safe to do so.
- Communication: We have ways to share information and ideas.
- Groups: We can relate to each other in smaller groups, including separate CoP and smaller groups within a CoP.
- Environment, tools, and artifacts: We interact in a shared space that is appropriate to our goals.
- Boundaries: We know who belongs and who does not.
- Governance: We regulate and moderate behavior according to shared or stated values.
- Exchange: We have a system of exchange or barter, and can trade knowledge, support, goods, services, and ideas.
- Expression: We have a group identity and know what other members are doing. We can easily indicate our preferences and opinions.
- History and culture: Both new and veteran members can develop, reproduce and review cultural artifacts, norms and values over time.
- Community reproduction and evolution: We can grow and evolve the CoP.

Phases of Bringing a CoP Online: Becoming a Virtual CoP

When the technology features are ready, new and existing CoPs can be brought online. The focus here is on organizations that have an existing or emerging CoP they plan to bring online. This focus has been chosen, rather than ad hoc communities that contact us or that start using the online system on their own, because we have found that the case studies of these organizations have a great deal to tell us about "recogniz[ing], support[ing], encourag[ing], and nurtur[ing]" CoPs (Wenger, 1998). These formal organizations are distinct from the CoPs—the CoP is a part of the organization, but not limited to the organization—and frequently have leaders who are not members of the CoP. However, the leaders of the organization are in a position to recognize the need for the CoP and encourage its development.

Helping an organization move its CoP to an online venue occurs in phases with the assistance of a community developer—a member of the technology development team who works with an organization to bring its CoP online—or a designated community manager from the organization who has experience in working with online communities. In the first phase, Getting Started, the organization focuses on defining its goals and vision for a CoP, learns to use the online features, and undertakes an initial online activity. Next, in the Modeling and Scaffolding phase, CoP members identify their community leaders and carry out a range of activities to see what works for them. In this process, they consult with the community developer and gain confidence in working online. Finally, in the Maturing phase, the new CoP leaders bring in new members and manage the overall health of the CoP (see Figure 1.1 for a visual representation of this process.)

THE GETTING STARTED PHASE

The Tapped In community developer works first with the organizational leaders and a few initial participants to begin training online leaders and to move one or two of the CoP's activities online. Throughout all three phases in the CoP's membership cycle, the online leaders, in turn, work with all the CoP members through this same Getting Started phase to bring them online.

Identify Goals and Needs

It is important to spend some time talking with different members of the organization and CoP to ascertain their goals for their organization and for a CoP, as well as members' needs. This process helps members articulate their goals for their CoP—both online and off—and gives the community developer some ideas for activities they may want to start with online. Differences and similarities between the goals of the organization and CoP are noted. The community developer fosters activities that have immediate value for both entities.

Demonstrating the immediate value of an online CoP is crucial: the majority of people will not spend time now if a CoP only has future value.

Meeting an immediate need for an existing CoP or an organization's vision for a CoP works well to bring an organization online. However, some organizations may have only immediate needs to fulfil and no vision for the practice; a community of purpose is not a CoP. They may view the online venue as a way to create a CoP rather than a means to support its work. If an organization has conflated CoP with community of purpose and views an online option as the answer to its problems, the community developer should provide examples of communities of purpose as well as

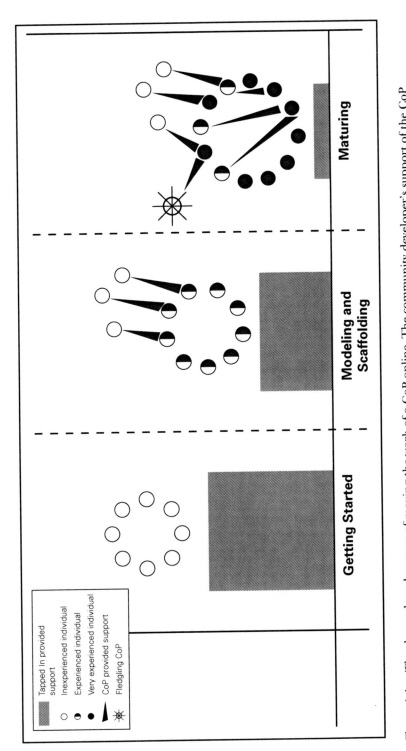

Figure 1.1. The three-phased process of moving the work of a CoP online. The community developer's support of the CoP decreases as individual CoP members' online, CoP, and community support experience increases. This process enables the CoP to support themselves.

CoPs and their work (see Connect With Other CoPs below in this phase for details).

Identify Online Leaders and Initiators

Once the community developer has interviewed organization leaders about prospective members and online leaders to understand needs, vision and existing community elements, identifying potential initiators, and working with these individuals must begin immediately. Often, the online leaders identified are too busy to address online CoP needs immediately. It thus may be better to work with individuals who are ready to get started (i.e., the initiators) and draw the online leaders of the organization in through the online activities. To determine who is ready for online work one-on-one phone conversations can be conducted with each potential initiator. Talking with these individuals also helps build relationships with them and the organization.

Identify Level of Experience

Learning what experience the initiators and organization have with online technologies and the CoP aids the community developer in planning how to get them online to participate in activities that matter to them and their CoP. A two-dimensional chart is useful in depicting initiators and the organization as a whole in planning technology training, CoP discussions and online activities (see Table 1.1).

For example, if many of the initiators are inexperienced with online technologies, online training with audio capabilities can be held to provide basic guidance in using the system. All initiators should be in the same room, with the person who has been working with the community

Table 1.1.   Mapping Both individuals' and the Organization's CoP and Online Technology Experience

		CoP Experience		
		High	Medium	Low
Online Technology Experience	High			
	Medium			
	Low			

Note: The mapping helps the community developers focus their efforts.

developer. The community manager is online. If the members are experienced in using online technologies, the members could be in different locations and meet in a specific room online. A phone number for the community manager serves as a backup if anyone has trouble getting online.

If CoP experience is limited, the community developer can provide examples of other CoPs online, including their goals and activities. The community developer may contrast these CoPs with communities of purpose that focus on tasks or gaining knowledge about specific areas.

Table 1.1. Mapping both individuals' and the organization's CoP and Online Technology Experience, helps the community developers focus their efforts.

Introduce the Technology Space

The initiators first meet online in the technology space that the group will use. Once the initiator or other leaders are comfortable, they should organize a face-to-face training session with other CoP members who have access to the online environment. The community manager coleads the training with the initiator online. The training session introduces the tools needed in the planned CoP use. Another online meeting or activity, but this time with members not in the same room, should be scheduled a week or 2 after the initial training session.

Establish Trust

Building members' trust—both in organization leaders and with other CoP members—is key to CoP success (Carlson, 2006). Going online adds two new dimensions of trust. Two-way trust must develop among the community builder, organizational leaders, and online initiators. That is, the leaders and initiators must trust the advice of the community builder, and the community builder must trust the commitment of the leaders and initiators to enact the agreed-upon strategies. The second dimension of trust is between the CoP members and the system itself. Community members must trust that the system will meet their needs, overcome constraints, and match their capacity. The trust, established with the community builder, must be reinforced by the tools available in the online environment.

Along each dimension, trust among members is based largely on multiple positive interactions, comprehensive understanding of each member's identity, and concurring opinions of other trustworthy members (Buskens, 1998). Trust-building encounters among the community builder, organization's leaders, and initiators may begin offline, but eventually moves online. Online interactions frequently allow people to get to know each other in new ways. Online tools such as discussion boards and chat tools that enable and capture conversations and profiles that indicate members' online activities and connections with others in the community make members' activities visible over time to each other.

Initiate an Activity

Working with the initiator(s), community developers form a plan for implementing an activity online as soon as possible with the CoP members who are ready. Getting started involves translating activities regularly conducted face-to-face into a form that works well online and serves a purpose. As noted, starting with an activity that connects to an immediate need and is comfortable for the organization is important. Planning often involves choosing a motivating activity that cannot be accomplished face to face (e.g., collaboration between two classes of geographically distant students) or a face-to-face activity that can be accomplished more effectively, accessibly, or cost-effectively online (e.g., engaging students who are quiet when face to face in reflective discussion online).

Frequently, Tapped In community developers begin working with the initiators online as a group so that they can interact online with their peers before bringing others online. If possible, the new leaders are also introduced to leaders from other CoPs who have mastered the online environment. Such interactions are illustrative of the power of the constellations of CoPs: another CoP in the online system is supporting the new organization.

Not every organization successfully progresses past the Getting Started phase; initiating an activity takes time and investment. On average, 4-5 hours of one-on-one work are required with the community developer for initiators to reach the point of being ready to work online.

Encourage Collaboration

Some CoP members may struggle with collaboration. An individualistic approach to practice is deeply ingrained in the U.S. cultural psyche and specifically in the teaching culture (Hofstede, 1991; Lortie, 1975). In fact, some view sharing and collaborating as a loss rather than a gain (Toole &

Louis, 2002). The community developer thus often needs to work with the organization leaders and the initiators to find ways to demonstrate to CoP members the benefits of collaborating and sharing information to further CoP work.

Connect With Other CoPs

Educators have referred to Tapped In as a "network of communities" or a "constellation of practices" (Schlager & Fusco, 2003; Wenger, 1998). Tapped In members can participate in more than one CoP within Tapped In or elsewhere. Tapped In facilitates the sharing of expertise and ideas across CoPs in forums such as After School Online (ASO), a weekly series of hour-long real-time discussions on topics suggested by Tapped In community members, led by volunteers recruited from the community, and available to any member of Tapped In (Schlager, Fusco, & Schank, 1998). The virtual reception room of Tapped In is also a gathering place for members of different CoPs to connect and a place to meet with experts who are part of the Help Desk (volunteers in the chat system who help with problems) (Schlager, Fusco, & Schank, 2002). The members who belong to multiple CoPs act as bridges between CoPs, helping with the flow of information among CoPs (Kossinets & Watts, 2006). ASO and places like reception allow interactions among members that encourage the growth of existing, emergent, and new CoPs. These gathering places are built into the social-infrastructure of Tapped In (Schlager, Fusco, & Schank, 2002).

Case Study: Organizations Getting Started

In 2006, the Tapped In team began working with six university teacher education programs whose common mission was to support teacher candidates in the field and graduates during their induction into teaching. Each organization had received a 5-year grant to help improve the way new teachers are prepared and to help graduates of the programs thrive during and beyond their first years of teaching. The six organizations, with faculty and preservice teachers, had formed internal CoPs. However, they were reaching a point in their work at which their candidates were graduating and the faculty needed a way to keep in touch and support these teachers as they began to teach.

Faculty, administrators, and preservice teachers from the six programs reviewed many technology options and chose to use Tapped In primarily because it would enable them to create an umbrella CoP for all of the organizations, in addition to meeting the needs of each organization (see Figure 1.2). Tapped In was the only system that made it easy to communicate across organizations and among their existing CoPs. Members could make the spaces as open to others or as private as they needed. To promote cross-institution sharing, common virtual spaces (e.g., reception rooms, conferences rooms, cross-institution group rooms) were provided for collaboration.

During the Getting Started phase, Tapped In community developers talked with leaders from each of the institutions, usually on the phone, to identify their goals and needs as well as with the online leaders and initiators who would start working online. The community developer encouraged collaboration among the six organizations and promoted the idea of sharing resources rather than having each organization duplicate the same activities. The community developer also spent time putting cross-institution supports in place (e.g., a panel of Tapped In experts from different CoPs in Tapped In that the six institutions could call on for help). A managers group room kept everyone informed of the activities across institutions. In the managers group room, the community developer modeled online facilitation strategies, such as posting articles for people to read and discuss, offering starting prompts and raising questions. The community developer modeled the types of posts that encourage participation and discussed with the initiators and leaders how to use these facilitation strategies in their own groups.

The community developer introduced the organizations to the technology space after talking with the leaders and inviting eight of the initiators to an initial technology training and brainstorming session. This session provided an understanding of the initiators' technology experience and some insight into the initial activities that might work well. The initiators needed to see the technology, its capabilities, affordances and limitations to visualize their initial activity. Two months passed before an initiator, a professor working with preservice teachers, developed her first online activity to bring other participants online. The community developer's goal was to integrate the online activities into existing, timely projects. Making the activities immediately relevant to the CoP was important. For the preservice teachers, introducing the online activity early in the course (the professor did so in the first class period) was crucial so that they knew it was an important part of their whole course experience, not a peripheral activity.

The community developer and the professor discussed ideas for the initial activity and considered how best to use the technology space. The community developer identified the professor's level of experience in regard to both the technology and CoP dimension. From this information, the community developer knew that they needed to focus on

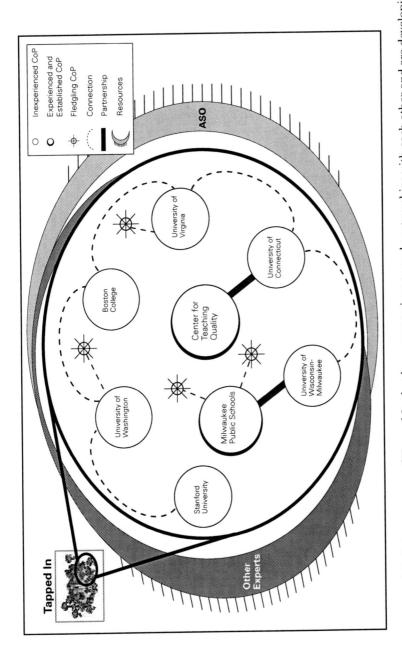

Figure 1.2.   Several CoPs in a segment of Tapped In that have connections to and partnerships with each other and are developing new CoPs. These CoP connections and resources embedded in the Tapped In environment enhance the work of each CoP.

making sure the professor gained experience with the online system. The professor had 3 weeks to prepare for the class and integrate the Tapped In system into her curriculum. The community developer and professor used the course syllabus as a collaboration point: the community developer suggested online activities, and the professor reviewed these suggestions.

Because the initial activity went well, the community developer, and the professor began to work with a second group of preservice teachers, with focus on getting them comfortable with the technology, encouraging them to collaborate with each other, and connecting with other CoPs members. The community developer was able to point out experts and public discussion sessions that would be of use to the professor and pre-service teachers. Through experiences in their CoP and the larger Tapped In community, the community developers worked to build their trust in the Tapped In tools, community, and members of their CoP.

After the initial activity where leaders and participants began to see the possibilities of a vCoP, they moved into the second phase of Modeling and Scaffolding. In this phase, with the community developer they focused on building the capacity in the organization to lead and manage the online CoP itself.

THE MODELING AND SCAFFOLDING PHASE

At first, the organization's leaders may have had only a theoretical understanding of an online CoP and may have wondered if it actually could be implemented. The Getting Started phase has created a successful experience for several CoP members online. The community developer may have worked with them to create a class experience, a mentoring relationship or a dialog among organization leaders that demonstrates to them the value of working online. With that experience, they now know that they can do work online. The initiators and leaders of the organization are also experiencing or envisioning specific benefits for themselves resulting from the online CoP. These benefits may take the form of a professor learning that her students have more questions about the materials than she realized, indicating a need for further clarification, or a professional development leader realizing that teachers will go online at all hours to use the discussion boards to discuss a pedagogical issue.

In the Modeling and Scaffolding phase, these experiences enable the community developer to move from modelling community management behaviors to making those behaviors explicit and scaffolding them for the identified CoP leaders.

Try Different Types of Activities

Once they have seen how it works, CoP members should be encouraged to try out different types of activities on their own. Community developers can encourage members to view themselves and other members as resources for reflecting with them on the activities and developing ways to assess what has happened.

Engage in Ongoing Reflection on Online Activities

Reflective dialog may be the most important process during the creation of the CoP. In this intermediate stage, the participants and leaders in the CoP are gaining a deep understanding of how collaboration works. They are learning strategies and starting to adapt these strategies for use in their organization.

In this phase, the community developer helps groups assess their progress and shows them some of the functionality built into the system to help with this assessment. For example, the "About Us" area in group rooms is a quick way for a leader of a group to see how active all of the participants have been. It shows the last login and the number of discussion board posts, and it provides posters' e-mail addresses and a way to e-mail from the About Us area. Tapped In community developers emphasize the importance of communicating with their members who "go missing" to find out why they have done so. Are they missing because they cannot remember their passwords, are they shy about participating, or do they not feel it is important to interact online? The CoP leaders need to "take the pulse" of their nascent community frequently to determine what is happening in their CoP.

Make Online Facilitation Explicit

Throughout the Getting Started phase of bringing the CoP online, the community developers model best practices in online facilitation. As the new CoP leaders do more facilitating, the community developer introduces resources such as *Facilitating Online Learning: Effective Strategies for Moderators* (Collison, Elbaum, Haavind, & Tinker, 2000) or the article

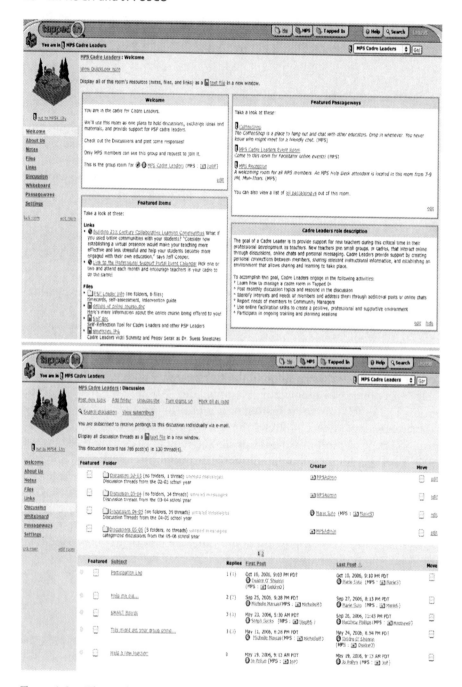

Figure 1.3.   The Cadre Leaders Group Room of the Milwaukee Public Schools. Shown here are the Welcome page and the Discussion board.

"Facilitating Deepened Online Learning" (Haavind, 2005) from the E-Learning 2005 conference to increase their understanding.

Help CoP Leaders Define Specific Roles for Online Leaders

In a new vCoP, the organization needs to define the specific roles and responsibilities for CoP staff and facilitators so that new members understand where to go for help. Typical roles include community manager, cadre facilitators, help desk staff and discussion leaders. Those in the defined roles should have associated ongoing tasks and responsibilities, and should report CoP development progress regularly to the CoP leaders. Identifying a community manager from the organization or existing CoP is a critical step in moving from community developer modelling and support of the community to a sustainable model that the CoP itself can support.

The CoP leaders also need their own group room in which to meet (see Figure 1.3). As critical resources for one another, the leaders need a place to share their collective wisdom. An essential leadership role is the community manager, who conceives of and manages the activities and services that keep people engaged, connected, and feeling supported.

Nonparticipation of the Community Developer

In Wenger's (1998) writing about CoPs, he discusses the concept of nonparticipation that helps define identity as much as participation. In part, we are defined by what we are not. As CoP members become CoP leaders, the outside community developer must stop participating. Even though the community developer led the initial online effort, she has been facilitating the participation of the CoP members, not her own. The community developer helps the new community leaders engage in legitimate peripheral participation (LPP) (Lave & Wenger, 1991) in the Getting Started and Modeling and Scaffolding phases. As a result, they can become full participants and can take on more responsibility for managing the community. Transition to nonparticipation by the community developer is thus necessary. Bruckman (2000) argues that if this transition does not occur, the community is in danger of withering when the leader leaves.

Plan for Growth and Sustainability

In this phase, the organization and CoP members develop a plan for CoP growth and sustainability by answering questions such as who are the online leaders, facilitators, and technical supports? What are their roles? How will facilitators learn to facilitate? What is the plan for the types of activities we will offer? How and when will we check in with each other to reflect on how the CoP is going? How will we know we are meeting our goals? Having a flexible but concrete plan in place aids in the transition from the community developer's leading the effort to the CoP leaders' providing leadership.

Case Study: Modeling and Scaffolding for Milwaukee Public Schools

In 2002, the Tapped In team began working with Milwaukee public schools (MPS). This public school district for the city of Milwaukee, Wisconsin has more than 200 schools and 6,000 education professionals. This 1-year pilot program was mounted to determine if an online CoP could help support beginning teachers during their induction years. In addition, MPS was looking for a way to support teacher retention and continued professional growth at all stages of the teaching career continuum. MPS had immediate needs it wanted to achieve with its CoP, but it also had a long-term vision for the CoP to which many areas of the district were committed. MPS established a professional support portal (PSP) of which Tapped In was a part.

During most of the first year of the project, MPS was in the Getting Started phase. The community developers worked with PSP leadership to create community leadership positions, and recruit and train MPS teachers to fill those positions (as cadre leaders to support new teachers online). MPS assigned a full-time staff member to the role of community manager. The community manager, who conceives of and manages the activities and services that keep people engaged, connected, and feeling supported, then recruited a part-time trainer and five part-time help desk staff to serve as the core support team.

After the leadership decided what it wanted to accomplish and how to do so, the community developers worked with cadre leaders to initiate activities. They helped the core team, cadre leaders, and district experts develop their own competence with online facilitation strategies by being with them online in real time to model community norms and conduct, such as introducing themselves to and assisting new users, encouraging and assisting new community volunteers, and being respectful of multiple points of view. To help new teachers develop a sense of ownership in the network and competence with online discourse strategies, the community developers instituted a series of weekly online colloquia on topics suggested by the community and led by experts recruited by PSP staff. The

Tapped In community developers worked with the guest speakers to help them prepare for their sessions and as moderators during sessions (via telephone and online private messaging), to help speakers model and foster appropriate norms of online discourse.

By the end of the school year 2003, 332 MPS staff members had established Tapped In accounts and formed 40 groups. From January 1 to May 31, 2003 this first year, 237 members logged into Tapped In.

MPS was dedicated to making the transition to managing its CoP itself. The district moved quickly through the Modeling and Scaffolding phases on to the Maturing phase. Early in the second year, the MPS community manager, MPS help desk staff, and cadre leaders were leading the CoP online, and the community developers had transitioned from central participants to peripheral participants. The district encouraged these leaders through compensation and recognition within the CoP and the larger organization.

MPS's online CoP and PSP continue to thrive. In September 2006, 890 MPS education professionals had Tapped In accounts, and there were 49 groups. Between January 1, 2006 and May 31, 2006, a total of 587 MPS members logged into Tapped In. Their active participation in the online CoP more than doubled from their first year.

THE MATURING PHASE

In this phase, the leaders of the CoP, including the community manager, are central participants, leading the efforts of the CoP online, including bringing new members online and taking responsibility for CoP health. The initial outside community developer is now mostly a nonparticipant, but is available to take questions, make links to other CoPs, and serve as a strategic advisor whenever needed. New developments that sometimes occur during the Maturing phase include a branching of CoP members' work that connects with an existing CoP or other organizations. New CoPs may develop.

Bring New Members and Institutions Online

The community manager and other online leaders are now in charge and continue to iterate on the Getting Started phase to bring new members and institutions online. The leaders help new members come online by setting up online trainings, with face-to-face trainings if necessary. They also determine whether facilitators have the resources they need to be effective.

Check the Health of the CoP

Online leaders and facilitators use leadership group rooms to reflect on what is and what is not working in order to make improvements. Leaders know how to use community management tools—both technical and social—for assessing CoP health of and addressing its needs.

Keep In Touch With Related CoPs

Online leaders keep in touch with other CoPs that have similar interests to mine their expertise and to share resources.

Encourage the Emergence of New CoPs

Sometimes groups within a CoP develop into their own CoP, or a member of a CoP may connect with others to form their own CoP. Often these new CoPs retain connections to the original CoP. The Tapped In online environment supports communication among these multiple, interwoven CoPs.

Encourage Stakeholders to Participate

Other stakeholder organizations within or connected to the organization now online may benefit from coming online in connection with the CoP to work together more effectively.

Case Study: Pepperdine University Maturing

Pepperdine University's Graduate School of Education and Psychology, located in Malibu, California, has used Tapped In for its master's and doctoral programs in education, working groups, and professional development opportunities for practitioners since 1998. Alumni and students participate in online activities and discussions; the community manager and instructors check the health of this community by seeing how many people are attending the events and participating in the discussions. The graduates of Pepperdine go on to be leaders in education in other settings, frequently bringing new members and institutions that they belong to into Tapped In. For example, two graduates who are now faculty at two other universities used Pepperdine's master's program as a model for their own programs. Both universities incorporated Tapped In into the work of their CoPs. Often these organizations have CoPs that are beginning to form. A vCoP may emerge as a result of the connection to Pepperdine and the organization's efforts to support a CoP. These new vCoPs may share activities and resources with faculty who are at Pepperdine, and with the CoP of Pepperdine alumni, allowing them to encourage stakeholders to participate and providing a means for keeping in touch across CoPs.

CONCLUSIONS

VCoPs can start from existing or emerging physical CoPs that move online, or they may get their start online from the collaboration of another vCoP or group and then grow into their own vCoP. The phased approach of bringing CoPs online encourages sustainable growth of the vCoP by developing an organization's internal capacity to use the system and provides a forum for them to further define and refine their vision for their virtual CoP: we provide the soil and the water while the organizations, such as Milwaukee public schools, bring the seeds. Some vCoPs also sprout new vCoPs (e.g., Pepperdine University).

It is important to note that not all online groups or CoPs that attempt to work online become vCoPs. For example, the CLTNet community mentioned earlier in this chapter has all the tools to support a CoP. Many CLTNet members who may belong to a CoP make use of CLTNet resources for various activities such as courses, working groups and events, but no CoP has specifically moved into CLTNet to do its work. Why? It may be that the main users of CLTNet (university faculty and graduates students participating in a CLT) have CoPs that are not entirely defined by the CLT. For example, many university professors in education belong to a CoP through the network of professionals that they or their university has developed. Given the technologies available to them, they may not see a need to move their existing CoP to a specific online environment. It also may be that their vision for their CoP is still being defined.

In our work with organizations and their CoPs, we have noted that the organizations with a vision for their CoPs and the role of online interaction in that vision are the ones that succeed. As noted in the description of the Getting Started phase, work can be undertaken with them to articulate their vision and move forward online, but that vision be created for them nor their CoP designed for them. They can be helped to connect an immediate need that they have to their vision so that members who might be reluctant to invest the time will have their immediate needs met while contributing to the growth of the CoP. However, an organization with many immediate needs that hopes that a vision will result from addressing those needs is likely to be disappointed.

Because vision is so important, time should be spent at the outset in a phased approach to help an organization articulate its vision. The phased approach helps leaders understand not only what is possible online, but also what is possible in growing vCoPs.

ACKNOWLEDGMENT

This material is based upon work supported by the National Science Foundation under Grant No. 0314484.

REFERENCES

Barab, S. A., & Duffy, T. M. (2000). From practice fields to communities of practice. In D. Jonassen & S. Land (Eds.), *Theoretical foundations of learning environments* (pp. 25-56). Mahwah, NJ: Erlbaum.

Barab, S. A., Kling, R., & Gray, J. H. (2004). *Designing for virtual communities in the service of learning.* London: Cambridge University Press.

Brown, J. S., & Duguid, P. (1991). Organizational learning and communities-of-practice: Toward a unified view of working, learning, and innovation. *Organization Science, Special Issue: Organizational Learning: Papers in Honor of (and by) James G. March, 2*(1), 40-57.

Brown, J. S., & Duguid, P. (2000). *The social life of information.* Cambridge, MA: Harvard Business School Press.

Bruckman, A. (2000). Situated support for learning: Storm's weekend with Rachael. *Journal of the Learning Sciences, 9*(3), 329-372.

Buskens, V. (1998). The social structure of trust. *Social Networks, 20,* 265-289.

Carlson, C. (2006). *Innovation: The five disciplines for creating what customers want.* New York: Crown.

Carroll, J. M. (2000). *Making use: Scenario-based design of human-computer interactions.* Cambridge, MA: MIT Press.

Collison, G., Elbaum, B., Haavind, S., & Tinker, R. (2000). *Facilitating online learning: Effective strategies for moderators.* Madison, WI: Atwood.

Cooper, A. (1999). *The inmates are running the asylum: Why high-tech products drive us crazy and how to restore the sanity.* Indianapolis, IN: Sams.

Farooq, U., Schank, P., Harris, A., Fusco, J., & Schlager, M. (in press). Sustaining a community computing infrastructure for online teacher professional development: A case study of designing Tapped In. *Journal of Computer Supported Cooperative Work.*

Haavind, S. (2005). Facilitating deepened online learning. In G. Richards (Ed.), *Proceedings of world conference on e-learning in corporate, government, healthcare, and higher education 2005* (pp. 696-708). Chesapeake, VA: Association for Advancement in Computing Education.

Hofstede, G. (1991). *Cultures and organizations: Software of the mind*. London: McGraw-Hill.

Kim, A. J. (2000). Community *building: Secret strategies for successful online communities on the Web*. Berkeley, CA: Peachpit Press.

Koch, M. (2000). *Learning from civilization. LiNE Zine*. Available from http://www.linezine.com/3.1/features/mklic.htm

Kossinets, G., & D.J. Watts. (2006). Empirical analysis of an evolving social network. *Science, 311*, 88-90.

Lave, J., & Wenger, E. (1991). *Situated learning: Legitimate peripheral participation*. London: Cambridge University Press.

Lortie, D. (1975). *Schoolteacher*. Chicago: University of Chicago Press.

Orlikowski, W. J. (1992). The duality of technology: Rethinking the concept of technology in organizations. *Organization Science, Focused Issue: Management of Technology, 3*(3), 398-427.

Preece, J. (2000). *Online communities: Designing usability, supporting sociability*. New York: Wiley.

Riel, M., & Polin, L. (2004). Online learning communities: Common Ground and critical differences in designing technical environments. In S. Barab, R. Kling, & J. Gray (Eds.), *Designing for virtual communities in the service of learning* (pp. 16-50). London: Cambridge University Press.

Schlager, M. S., & Fusco, J. (2003). Teacher professional development, technology, and communities of practice: Are we putting the cart before the horse? *The Information Society, 19*, 1-18.

Schlager, M., Fusco, J., & Schank, P. (1998). Cornerstones for an on-line community of education professionals. *IEEE Technology and Society Magazine, Special Issue: Wired Classrooms: The Internet in K-12, 17*(4), 15-21, 40.

Schlager, M., Fusco, J., & Schank, P. (2002). Evolution of an online education community of practice. In K. A. Renninger & W. Shumar (Eds.), *Building virtual communities: Learning and change in cyberspace* (pp. 129-158). New York: Cambridge University Press.

Schwen, T. M., & Hara, N. (2004). Communities of practice: A metaphor for online design? In S. Barab, R. Kling, & J. Gray (Eds.), *Designing for virtual communities in the service of learning* (pp. 154-178). London: Cambridge University Press.

Toole, J. C., & Louis, K. S. (2002). The role of professional learning communities in international education. In K. Leithwood & P. Hallinger (Eds.), *Second international handbook of educational leadership and administration*. The Netherlands: Kluwer.

Wenger, E. (1998). *Communities of practice: Learning, meaning, and identity*. London: Cambridge University Press.

CHAPTER 2

HOLDING THE VIRTUAL SPACE

The Roles and Responsibilities of Community Stewardship

Brenda Kaulback and Debbie Bergtholdt

As educational leaders turn increasingly to virtual communities of practice (vCoPs) in the design, implementation, and management of educational programs, the issue of how to design, launch, and support them arises. This chapter examines how one governmental education department provided support for a vCoP over a 3-year period. Through the use of a team that stewarded the knowledge and the community, this virtual community engaged over 400 educational leaders, administrators, and instructors in creating, capturing, and disseminating the knowledge necessary to develop and advance education programs for adults seeking high school equivalency diplomas. Based on this experience, the roles and responsibilities of these stewards are defined and described. This chapter also identifies the balances needed between competing factors of community and knowledge, members and organizations, and ownership and time demands in order to hold a space for the members to do their work. Finally, some lessons learned are offered.

Communities of Practice: Creating Learning Environments for Educators,
Volume 2, pp. 25–43

INTRODUCTION

Educational leaders wanting to drive organizational change and administrators and instructors seeking to improve their programs are turning to virtual communities of practice (vCoPs) to help them accomplish their goals. Effective and successful vCoPs, however, do not happen without attention to their design, launching, and support. As in face-to-face communities, simply providing a room and inviting people in does not create an engaged community; putting up shelves and filling them with books does not produce knowledge. The knowledge that moves a practice forward and the collaboration and exchange that grows and disseminates that knowledge requires stewardship—a person or a group of people who are creating and holding a space for the community to engage and the knowledge to thrive. This stewardship helps professionals to do their work and to derive benefit from it. When it is done well, the organization also profits, with improved performance, outcomes and insight.

This chapter looks at stewardship of a vCoP in an educational setting, based on a vCoP that was launched and supported by a stewardship team. This vCoP was a state-supported community for managers and educators of adults returning to school to acquire the equivalent of a high school diploma[1] and/or learning English as speakers of other languages.

We first define vCoPs and describe the vCoP in question. Second, the four roles of community stewardship that were employed in supporting this community (knowledge leader, facilitator, event coordinator, and librarian) are considered and tasks related to each of these roles are described. Three tensions are then suggested that have to be balanced in order to hold the space for the members to do their best work: relationship building and task accomplishment, the needs of the members and those of the organization, and the desire for ownership with the demands on the time of the members. Finally, the basic lessons learned in the stewarding of this vCoP are articulated.

BACKGROUND

Definition of Community of Practice

Wenger, McDermott, and Snyder (2002) define communities of practice (CoPs) as "groups of people who share a concern, a set of problems, or a passion about a topic, and who deepen their knowledge and expertise in this area by interacting on an ongoing basis." We further define vCoPs as CoPs with a geographically dispersed membership utilizing primarily online collaborative technologies to communicate.

Wenger, McDermott, and Snyder (2002) further explain that, while CoPs exist as a natural part of organizational life, they flourish with cultivation. They advise finding the middle ground between those who would argue that there is nothing one can do to cultivate CoPs and those who believe that anything organizations do gets in the way of their development and health. Our experience of cultivating the vCoP described in this chapter supports their conclusion—an active stewardship team can assist in the building of a vital and engaged vCoP, and, at the same time, what happens in a community is driven by the members and their work together.

Our Role

The design and support of a vCoP for adult educators in the state of Virginia, in the United States, was started in 2004 by a stewardship team, under the sponsorship of the Virginia State Department of Education. To date over 34 virtual events on various adult education topics have been facilitated and supported for the 400 plus members of this vCoP. These virtual events have included information sharing and dissemination, identification of best practices, planning, surfacing of issues, team building, professional development, and expert briefings. Members of this team have also supported the development of numerous subcommunities and additional activities that have occurred as the community has grown. The vCoP has accumulated nearly 1,500 artifact (documents, manuals, marketing materials, news articles, videos, presentations) which were organized and highlighted by the stewardship team. This team also produced periodic management reports for the sponsor with management recommendations for the state leadership.

From this experience, we have learned the basic roles of a team providing support to a vCoP, articulated three tensions that require balancing, and identified a number of lessons learned. The following section begins with a description of the purpose and composition of this vCoP.

DESCRIPTION OF THE vCoP

Overview

In response to an initiative of then United States Governor Mark Warner of Virginia, to increase the number of adults obtaining a general educational development certificate (the equivalent of a high school diploma), the Virginia Department of Education funded a team of professionals to launch and support a vCoP using a Web-based collaborative technology. This vCoP was to be used to engage educators across the state in supporting and implementing the initiative. With the aid of the vCoP, these educational leaders implemented the changes that the governor envisioned and increased the numbers of adults enrolling and successfully obtaining their GED[2] certificates. Once the governor's initiative was launched, the vCoP evolved into an ongoing space for educators at the state and local levels to communicate, plan, and learn.

Purpose

The primary purpose of this community was to create, capture, and disseminate the knowledge of members as they engaged in the launching of this initiative and in their ongoing work. Wenger, McDermott, and Snyder (2002) identify stewarding knowledge as a valid purpose for CoPs and describe these knowledge-stewarding communities as "host(ing) forums for members to connect, develop and verify practices, but their main intent is to organize, upgrade, and distribute the knowledge their members use every day" (pp. 76-77).

This is an apt description of the adult education vCoP. It should be noted however, that this vCoP served other purposes as part of the key purpose of stewarding knowledge. The vCoP offered members opportunities to accomplish work together (for example, a work group on developing standards), to reflect on their practice (for example, dialogues about best practices in implementing the governor's initiative), and to learn (for example, a mentoring space where experienced managers offered insights and answered questions from newly appointed managers). As in any thriving community, members of a vCoP come with a variety of intentions and pursue a range of activities.

In describing the opportunity to reflect, one member of the Virginia vCoP noted a:

> key benefit (of the community) is the reflection the discussions prompt me to do. They make me stop and consider what our program does. The jam (as the online dialogue events were called—a term borrowed from IBM) forces me to pause and do program evaluation—considering the pros and cons of everything we do here before I offer it up to colleagues.... Without this forum, I would not likely do the systematic review and evaluation that has occurred.

Composition

Fontaine (2001) notes that roles in these communities may emerge naturally or may be deliberately created. The Virginia vCoP was created with initial roles established and the community staffed from the outset. The membership in this vCoP was by invitation only, with the invitations provided by the State Department of Education to adult educators (program managers, instructors, assessment specialists, state leaders) working in local programs or at the state level. It was a geographically dispersed community that operated across organizational boundaries with members reporting to local school divisions or to the State Department of Education. The stewardship team was selected and supported by the State Department of Education.

With a geographically dispersed membership, the members of this vCoP communicated primarily through the use of a Web-based collaborative technology. It should be noted, however, that many of the members of the vCoP did have opportunities to interact face-to-face with other members in regional and statewide meetings, trainings, and conferences. Also, the community was launched with a face-to-face meeting of a few local managers who agreed to play a role in initiating dialogue and participating as core members of the virtual community.

The stewardship team for this vCoP included a liaison from the State Department of Education, a technology support person, a trainer/facilitator from a university resource center that provides professional development to adult educators in the state and a consultant/coach from a knowledge consulting firm.

The experience in launching and supporting this vCoP identified the basic roles necessary to support such a community: knowledge leader, facilitator, event coordinator, and librarian (see Figure 2.1). In performing these roles, three tensions that had to be balanced to maintain the viability of the community were also identified. These roles and tensions have been set out and described below. Finally, some basic lessons learned from the work in this vCoP are set out.

THE ROLES OF STEWARDSHIP

The goal of stewardship of a vCoP is to engage members and to create and hold a space where they can interact, learn, and create the next iteration of their practice. It is a role that can be compared to that of a midwife. The stewards do the work of analyzing, facilitating, coordinating, and developing an inventory while enabling the birthing of knowledge. We look first at the various roles played by those engaged in

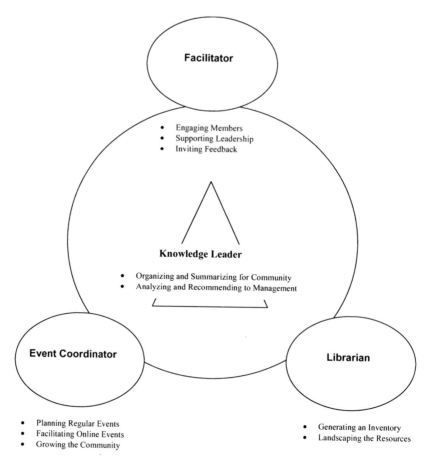

Figure 2.1.   Roles of the stewardship team.

stewarding a vCoP: knowledge leader, facilitator, event coordinator, and librarian.

Knowledge Leader

When the purpose of the vCoP is to create, capture, and disseminate knowledge, a critically important role of stewarding is that of analyzing, translating, organizing, highlighting, summarizing, and reporting on the meaning created out of the knowledge that the members generate. As community members engage in dialogue about their work, they identify best practices, surface differences of interpretations of policy and protocols, propose solutions to dilemmas, and post resources related to the topic of discussion, but these are embedded in the conversation and, in order to be useful, often must be organized and prioritized. The stewards' role in this regard involves reviewing and summarizing the dialogue, culling the postings, identifying main themes, analyzing the discourse, and assessing and sorting the data into forms that the members can reflect on and use in their common work.

The stewardship team for adult educators in Virginia posted reports after each online conversation, using a variety of formats depending on the nature of the conversation and the purpose of the event. These reports included "verbatims" or quotes from the members that documented or validated the points and identified the "speaker." Members commented that they did not know how much they knew, or understand what use to make of it, until they saw it reorganized into the reports prepared by the team and posted on the site.

The dialogue of the community also offers information that could be instrumental in furthering the management agenda. While the leadership may read or even participate in the dialogue of the community, it can benefit from another perspective, which distills the salient points from the conversation, identifies potential actionable items, and makes recommendations for further decisions. Stewards who understand the work and the issues can advise the leadership in this regard. They can use the knowledge culled from the dialogue and make management recommendations to the sponsor based on that knowledge. In this way, the knowledge extracted by the stewards informs the next iteration of the work both for the community members and for the administration and the state level agenda.

Facilitator

A second role played by community stewards relates to facilitating members' use of the community space.

> Knowledge brokering is about bringing people together, to help them build relationships, uncover needs and share ideas and evidence that will let them do their jobs better. It is the human force that makes knowledge transfer (the movement of knowledge from one place or group of people to another) more effective. (Canadian Health Services, 2003)

Knowledge development depends on community engagement. The stewards' role, therefore, is to develop strategies to spark initial interest as well as maintain commitment. As Kimble, Hildreth, and Wright (2001) point out: "Participation is central to the evolution of a community and ...

essential to the creation of the relationships that help to build trust" (pp. 220-234).

Stewardship efforts relating to community engagement revolve around the following three areas:

- Engaging members
- Supporting leadership
- Inviting reflection and feedback

Engaging Members

Engaging members is an issue of gaining the trust of the members in the community and also of the stewards being ambassadors for the work of the community. Having a plan for launching the community that engages widening circles of members and invites each wave in to support the next is a way of building that trust in members.

The stewards in the Virginia community started small and built deliberately. The five program mangers who had been selected by the state director to develop pilots for the governor's initiative assisted with the planning and the initial steps. These five became the core membership of the community, which grew as the initiative was extended, 6 months later, to 10 additional leaders, and then, 6 months subsequently, to the remaining approximately 80 program managers in the state. The first events, 2-day dialogue "Jams" got the word of mouth campaign operating and drew potential members into the fold. The stewardship team was responsible for extending the invitation, orienting the members, welcoming their participation, and assisting them in navigating.

The outreach was successful in that increasing numbers of potential invitees joined and became active participants in the community, with a membership of over 400 at the end of 3 years. As the communities and subcommunities grew, word of mouth spread that the vCoP was a place to go to learn and shape events in the state. Because of time constraints of the stewardship team, occasionally limits had to be placed on the number of invitations that could be extended so that the team could continue to provide adequate monitoring, landscaping, planning, and technical assistance. It can be seen as a sign of success that the team was sometimes unable to respond immediately to the desire for new membership.

In addition to building trust, the stewards saw members' own confidence in their ability to access and use the site as a factor in their successful engagement. New members had varying familiarity with technology and the team used several strategies in orienting new members: face-to-face trainings, phone conferences, online tutorials, help desk instructions, and one-on-one phone or face-to-face orientations. As potential members became more adept at Internet navigation, instructions posted on the site seemed to satisfy most newcomers; nevertheless, the stewardship team made a practice of being available through phone calls to anyone who wanted assistance.

Supporting Leadership

Ongoing participation and engagement may be encouraged when active members have an opportunity to play more substantial roles in the community, as hosts of events, as members of advisory teams, or in mentoring new members, for example. Some of the strategies that produce successful events offer opportunities to develop and support leadership as well. Stewards may enlist members who sign into the community but do not post in the dialogues to play leadership roles in future events or in subcommunities and thus secure their more active participation. Acknowledging members' contributions in reports adds to their status as leaders in the state and makes their work more visible to peers and to state leadership.

Promoting work that is happening in other venues in the online community also may serve to promote leadership. When a member in the Virginia community offered a workshop on how to use data to manage an adult education program at a statewide conference that inspired wide interest, the stewardship team worked with her to develop a video tutorial and posted it on the site. The member introduced it and led a discussion about the workshop during one of the Jams.

Inviting Reflection and Feedback

A final function of stewardship related to engaging members is obtaining and analyzing feedback from the community members, both about process and about content. The Virginia adult education team employed online surveys, online focus groups, one-on-one phone calls and input from advisory panel members to identify needed changes. Additionally, team members were alert to word-of-mouth messages that came through off-line conversations. The team responded to feedback, making changes in both access and content issues.

Event Coordinator

While the mission of engaging community participation is a major one, creating a comfortable rhythm of activity once the community is launched is equally challenging. Wenger, McDermott, and Snyder (2002) point out, "There are many rhythms in a community—the syncopation of familiar and exciting events, the frequency of private interactions, the ebb and flow of people from the sidelines into active participation, and the pace of the community's overall evolution" (pp. 76-77).

The beginning activity in the Virginia vCoP was around the 2-day dialogues, or Jams, that were held approximately once a month, on a topic of interest to the whole community. These created the initial engagement and became the heartbeat of the community, with the activity of subcommunities and other work groups being added and falling into more temporary, faster-paced, or more intense beats around this main one. The following sections will look at three aspects of coordinating the activity of the community.

- Planning regular activities
- Facilitating online
- Growing the community

Planning Regular Activities

Wenger, McDermott, and Snyder (2002) point out that communities need both activities that are familiar and regular as well as opportunities for fresh perspectives that bring an element of challenge and excitement. This advice was important in supporting the vCoP for adult educators. In planning regular activities, the team sometimes focused on expertise within the community and sometimes invited outside guests. Members of the stewardship team or the advisory panel in the Virginia community often knew which community members were engaged with a particular topic, so that when a dialogue topic was agreed upon, one of the team might say,

Oh, if we are going to talk about retention, make sure to get our Hampton representative to host part of the discussion, because she has been really successful at creating a tracking system that we want to know more about.

This type of planning brought the latest field expertise into the practice and gave the members an opportunity to dialogue about practices that they had heard about and also to showcase their own work.

The Virginia vCoP typically included state-level and local perspectives, but the team also strove to maintain interest by stretching the boundaries of the community through inviting stakeholders from various perspectives into the room. Each summer, for example, the vendors from the publishing companies that published texts relevant to the adult education programs were invited to participate in a Jam, where they could discuss their products and where members could ask questions about latest developments. In the summer as the state was beginning the implementation of standards for the adult education programs, the members had many questions about the relationship of the various products to the new state expectations for their programs.

Another example of the cross-fertilization offered by crossing the boundaries into other arenas is the Jam that was held with representatives from programs that offer workforce training to residents. Program managers who were particularly successful with developing partnerships with the workforce boards in their areas were invited to host the dialogue with the executive director of a local workforce investment board and with the director of operations for the One-Stop Centers, which offer job placement services. Program managers were asked to be responsible for sharing their practices, explaining their philosophy or challenges and asking questions of these guests.

Facilitating the Dialogue

Supporting the dynamics of an active community involves facilitating the conversations taking place in the community. Here the issue of trust goes in two directions. The members must be able to trust that the facilitator will provide a space where their comments will be welcomed and listened to respectfully, and also where it is possible to make statements that involve taking a risk when it is appropriate. Equally, the facilitator must trust and encourage the members to identify the critical issues and create the space for them to share their perspectives.

The facilitation, therefore, does not require a subject matter expert, but rather someone to help the community sharpen the focus and clarify the intentions of its work, deepen the dialogue, and push the envelope at the edges of the community knowledge. Facilitating events involves acknowledging and welcoming participation, setting a tone that the community operates within a culture of respect, and modelling appropriate community behavior. This role demands that the person be able to assess the group and determine what it needs next to create and maintain momentum towards achieving its goals (Collison, Elbaum, Haavind, & Tinker, 2000). In the Virginia vCoP, the online facilitator was is the chief learner, modeling, learning, and helping members attend to what they themselves are saying.

Effective facilitation involves genuinely inviting everyone into the conversation and ensuring that members have the opportunity to hear what each person has to say. Facilitation also is about working to engage the members in what Collison et al. (2000, pp. 29-30) calls pragmatic dialogue. The "intention of pragmatic dialogue" is that it is "time-limited, product-driven dialogue that is critically sensitive to collaboration and the use of each participant's personal resources."

The opening of the dialogue events tends to be at the level of social dialogue, with members greeting each other and getting their footing for the work ahead. "Chat fosters an important sense of belonging and that is an essential step in establishing a learning community," suggests Collison et al. (2000, p. 20). It is the job of the online facilitator to shift participants into the work of the day, to move the conversation to a deeper level, through the early stages of social dialogue, past argumentative dialogue, or advocating for a particular position, and toward pragmatic dialogue. During the dialogue, the goal of the facilitator is to move them to examining long-held beliefs and to transition from position-taking to inquiry, and, hopefully, to move to pragmatic dialogue, whose goal is not to persuade, but rather to inquire. "Participants in pragmatic dialogue value the tough questions and the importance of the unknown" (Collison et al., 2000, p. 29).

Moderating in the sense of ensuring that members do not violate guidelines for community behavior is theoretically a facilitation function of stewardship. In the Virginia professional community, however, this function was not utilized. Members willingly and obligingly maintained a professional demeanor and produced a sense of safety for members.

Growing the Community

In order to appreciate where the work of the community is headed, make decisions about future events and develop work plans, those supporting the community need input both from the members and from the organization sponsoring the vCoP. Members of the Virginia stewardship team met every 6 months with a group of active members, either face-to-face, or through a phone conference or Web meeting. The purpose was to identify the major strategic issues of the community and to surface opportunities for improving the vCoP. In building the work plan for each year for the vCoP, the stewardship team also considered state department plans, priorities, and the agenda of the leadership. In this way, the community grew from its original format, incorporating new opportunities to dialogue, new members, new subcommunities and new activities—always maintaining the original heartbeat of the monthly Jam.

Librarian

The stewards perform two main functions related to the artifacts or knowledge objects of the community: generating an inventory of resources and landscaping the resources. The stewards thus perform the tasks that historically, in a face-to-face context, might have been considered tasks of the librarian: identifying the knowledge to be kept on the shelves and acting as the keeper of that knowledge by organizing the books and documents in a way that will entice readers and make the knowledge accessible.

Generating an Inventory

While stewarding the vCoP, there was the question of how to generate an inventory or build the resources that might benefit the community and attract members to the site through their use. One option was to identify the current knowledge objects used by the community—the manuals, papers, Web sites, and articles that were related to adult education. This could be done through requests to or a survey of the initial core group of members, through a literature search, or through developing an inventory of resources available at the state department. Alternately, a more organic approach could be used to let the inventory build as the community grew.

David Snowden (Barth, 2000), a proponent of approaching knowledge management (KM) organically, describes the organization as a complex ecology, in which one tries to "understand the underlying values and rule sets around which that ecology is organizing" (p. 22).

In the Virginia vCoP it was decided to follow the more organic course, attending to the resources that the practitioners were using as they did their work, rather than trying to anticipate what might be needed or inventory knowledge documents currently in use. Knowledge objects were therefore posted as members referred to them in the course of their conversations or when other members requested resources that they had heard about that had proved helpful in the field, for example, forms that they had developed, formats for tracking systems, and curricula that had been developed for particular target audiences. Other knowledge objects were offered by guest experts who posted resources that they wanted to use as a basis for their dialogue or by state department officials who wanted to disseminate important documents to the field and seek feedback on them.

When the governor's initiative was getting underway, marketing the new services was a topic of much interest to local program managers, who were trying to creatively implement new ideas for reaching out to residents who did not have a high school diploma. A two-day Jam, as the monthly dialogues were called, on marketing surfaced a multitude of creative ideas for the outreach efforts that had been successful in different geographic areas of the state. In addition to the ideas for approaches to marketing, a host of materials—copy for billboards, news articles, success stories, editorials and flyers—was offered by members. Through these postings from program managers, teachers, instructors, state level staff, and guests, the community amassed a rich and relevant resource inventory.

The role of the stewardship team, therefore, was not to compile a huge collection of resources, but to elicit from the members the documents, forms, and articles, the names of potential guest "speakers," the Web pages, the media links, and other resources that were informing their work in the field.

Landscaping the Resources

The second aspect of the library work involves managing, classifying and organizing the community materials—all activities described by the term "landscaping." Here again, the philosophy was to let the needs of the community drive the classification, or taxonomy, by generating it out of knowledge that was posted. In the beginning of the Virginia vCoP, as the site was prepared for launch, the stewardship team organized the topics or categories on the site based on the input of a user focus group. This had the advantage of engaging core members in thinking about the community and provided an initial framework for the resources that were being used by members.

During the Virginia community's first year, in surveys of member satisfaction or in incidental face-to-face meetings, members consistently brought up their difficulties in finding materials and information. This ebbed in the second year, partly due to improvements in the technology, and partly because members became more familiar with the organization of the site. Also, importantly, the stewardship team began to understand how to better arrange and highlight materials so that members could locate them easily.

Many of the original topics or categories proposed by the pilot members had garnered no resources and had not been the subject of any of the dialogues that had been hosted. A few of the topics, notably marketing and outreach, were congested with postings. It seemed clear that a more organic approach was preferable and we began to let the order be driven by the material. We eliminated most of the topics in the original classification, maintained a few of the topics which were rich with materials, and opened new classifications as the current ones became unwieldy due to an overabundance of knowledge objects. In other words, rather than anticipating a hierarchy, all the knowledge objects were posted in one general category under the community until the number of postings made it difficult to access and then divided that topic into two or more topics or subtopics, based on the items that had already been posted. Thus, the hierarchy grew out of the knowledge objects that the community posted.

Additionally, since most of the inquiries for knowledge objects were related to topics that were currently the subject of dialogues or special initiatives that were taking place in the community, the team highlighted links to those on the top page of the community. This meant that one of the tasks of the stewardship team in their landscaping efforts was to attend to the activity of the members so as to know what to highlight and what to archive. Both the inventory of knowledge objects and the organizing of them evolved naturally from the activity and needs of the community.

BALANCES

In performing the roles that were identified, it was found that there were three crucial tensions that the stewardship team balanced in order to "hold the space" optimally for community members: (1) community and knowledge, (2) the needs of the members and the needs of the organization, and (3) community ownership with the time demands of the members.

BALANCING COMMUNITY AND KNOWLEDGE

In thinking about the function of the stewardship team, the question had to be asked, is the team stewarding knowledge or stewarding the community? The team understood the stewardship role to provide both—support for the community and a focus on knowledge, as well as being the catalyst that brought these two together. The stewardship team attended to both the relationship—the building and supporting of the members (facilitation/host), and to the task—the building and supporting of knowledge (librarian/knowledge leader) (see Figure 2.2).

If the community's energy shifts too far in the direction of the task, the organization will achieve only a hierarchical library of data and information, a collection of postings of knowledge objects or artifact that few people access and use. If the attention shifts too far toward relationship, the organization has only an online water cooler, a community where colleagues may socialize and chat together, but gain little in the way of new information to incorporate into their thinking and the growing of their community.

To the extent that the stewardship team is able to balance the tension between knowledge and relationship, the practice of adult educators and the work of the organization are better able to advance and thrive.

Balancing the Needs of the Organization and of the Members

In a community such as the Virginia adult education vCoP, the impetus for the existence of the community is the organizational agenda. The vCoP provides a forum for this agenda as well as the opportunity to learn

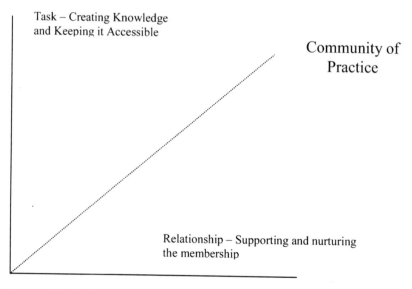

Figure 2.2.   Task and relationship balance.

from those implementing it. Simultaneously, the vCoP provides an opportunity for members to improve their practice. Members also have individual motivations, such as enhancing recognition of their professional leadership and gaining resources for their own programs that extend beyond the sponsor's initiative.

The balance between keeping the organization or agency's overall agenda in the forefront and in meeting other community needs must be taken into account in all aspects of stewarding the vCoP. Fortunately, these are often overlapping and what serves the organization's purpose also serves that of the members. If the needs of members are not served by the community, then they will not be engaged in the community. If the vCoP is not supporting the agenda of the sponsoring organization, it fails to serve its essential purpose.

Balancing Ownership and Time Demands of Members

The stewardship team also attends to finding a balance between giving the members responsibility for their own community and understanding that the members have many demands on their time and not a great deal of time to devote to thinking about what will make this online community work. Members need to find what they are looking for and add what they have to offer without investing too much time. Once they perceive the value of active participation, they are much more likely to sign in again and become involved. While having members engaged in designing the site develops ownership, if the balance shifts too far toward ownership and too much work is involved in participating, membership will decline.

LESSONS LEARNED

There are four key points that inform work in stewarding that we have learned from supporting vCoPs.

It Takes a Team

While the tasks of stewardship may be arrayed in a variety of ways, having a team allows for coverage of the skills needed, for having people located in strategic places with the perspective of the various stakeholders, and for the extra synergy that group thinking offers. Having a team that works well together, that understands the purpose and the dynamics of the vCoP is high on the list of factors of success.

A vCoP is About the Work

People are busy and sometimes resist working in new ways, so the critical success factor is the value members derive from the work. It can be a challenge to get to the place where members see their participation as a new way of doing work, not an add-on to the work that they are already doing. Notably, however, value is often a function of giving as much as getting—that is, people who contribute to discussions feel the exchange is valuable.

Community Support Does Not Stop

A community is only as vital as its last piece of work. Stewardship involves consistently planning and preparing for the next goal while the current one is being addressed.

While it was clear to the team from the beginning that launching a virtual community such as the one that was envisioned would take planning, effort and support, it was expected that once the community was launched, the effort needed to support it would diminish. In reality, the opposite happened. As the membership grew, the tasks required to maintain it grew. As members saw the potential for its use, the interest in activities and subcommunities grew, and the chores related to planning activities and making accessible links to these events increased.

The Small Things Matter

Having the technology work, engaging newcomers effectively, helping members find what they are looking for—these are seemingly small issues which cannot be allowed to get in the way of the work. Finding ways to get feedback from members, listening to what they are saying, either through their words or through their actions, and then making changes to accommodate these needs make a difference in the ability of the community to pay attention to the tasks that they come to the community to accomplish.

FUTURE TRENDS

The use of virtual CoPs holds promise for adult education practitioners and for state departments coordinating, overseeing, or supporting their work. As educators at all levels of the system begin to see advantages and the potential for these vCoPs, it is possible that their use will become more widespread. While the case presented here began at the state level, there was growing interest in exporting the use to local and regional communities. With adult education instructors often hired on a part-time basis and working at different locations around the community, managers could see the advantages of asynchronous, virtual discourse.

As the use of vCoPs becomes more universal, the need for attention to their support is evident. Clearly, the level of support afforded the educational community presented here was instrumental in its success, but not all potential communities may have the resources to sustain this level of team support. Some developments may mean that the tasks involved in this support require less time and effort. For example, as more practitioners recognize the value of the work accomplished in these vCoPs, perhaps some of the level of work needed to engage people will level off or even decrease. Also, as collaborative technologies improve, the amount of time it takes knowledge stewards or community coordinators to accomplish tasks such as landscaping may decrease. More critically, however, may be the expectation that supporting a vCoP becomes an integral part of the work and the staff time needed to develop and maintain the vCoP is assumed in any endeavor where learning and moving forward the practice is involved.

What educators experience and learn from participating in an online community also translates into strategies and ways of operating that can impact their own instructional programs. As they realize how and what they learn as part of a learning community, perhaps they will be encouraged to make changes in the way the adult learners in their programs are engaged in learning, integrating opportunities for more situational learning and collaborative social interaction, both face-to-face and virtual.

NOTES

1. General Educational Development Certificate or GED Certificate.
2. In 2002, 14,981 tested and 11,602 passed; in 2006, 21,206 tested and 13,313 passed.

REFERENCES

Barth, S. (2000). The organic approach to the organization: A conversation with KM practitioner David Snowden. *Knowledge Management, 3*(10), 22-25.

Canadian health services research foundation, (2003). *The theory and practice of knowledge brokering in Canada's health system.* Retrieved September 12, 2006, http://chsrf.ca/brokering/pdf/Theory_and_Practice_e.pdf

Collison, G., Elbaum, B., Haavind, S., & Tinker, R. (2000). *Facilitating online learning: Effective strategies for moderators.* Madison, WI: Atwood.

Fontaine, M. (2001). *Identifying and selecting the roles needed to staff and support communities of practice.* Cambridge, MA: IBM Institute for Knowledge.

Kimble, C., Hildreth, P., & Wright, P. (2001). Communities of practice: Going virtual. In Y. Malhotra (Ed.), *Knowledge management and business innovation* (pp. 220-234). Hershey, PA: Idea Group.

Wenger, E., McDermott, R, & Snyder, W. (2002). *Cultivating communities of practice: A guide to managing knowledge.* Cambridge, MA: Harvard Business School.

CHAPTER 3

EDUCATION LEADERSHIP FOR A NETWORKED WORLD

Diana D. Woolis, Susan Restler, and Yvonne Thayer

This chapter describes an education leadership model based on virtual communities of practice (vCoPs) which is amplified using cases from the authors' professional practice. In this context, education leaders are those leading systems, institutions or programs. The model is explained, how it works, what it accomplishes, and why it represents a sea change. It is argued that leaders with the skill to harness networks of virtual communities of practice will be the only ones capable of carrying out a reform agenda. vCoPs are both method and medium, requiring a correlating set of new leadership competencies, defined in three broad areas: vision, networks, and knowledge ecology. The chapter concludes with five reasons why education leaders should invest in vCoPs: time, human capital, leader and organization development, policy and practice, and outcomes.

INTRODUCTION

the failure of recent reforms to accelerate student achievement in line with policy objectives has been widely documented ... and ... provides a strong argument for governments to embrace networks not only to assist in the implementation of their reform agendas, but also as an innovation in its

Communities of Practice: Creating Learning Environments for Educators,
Volume 2, pp. 45–65

own right. Without doing so, it is likely that the aspirations of educational reform, particularly in decentralized systems, will continue to rise beyond the capacity of the system to deliver. (Istance & Kobayashi, 2003, p. 162)

Leading all levels of education—systems, institutions, and programs—is daunting in the face of escalating but legitimate demands for measurable student achievement. There is an emerging consensus among researchers and practitioners that new leadership models are required. In particular models of "distributed" leadership that incorporate digital networks and communities into the work process hold great potential for education.

This chapter outlines a distributed leadership model as it is framed by a virtual community of practice (vCoP). We challenge those who lead education systems, institutions, and programs to harness vCoPs to achieve their broad leadership goals. This is, of course, an imperative for all leaders regardless of sector. The opportunity in the field of education is particularly compelling given the overwhelming pressure to improve outcomes in teaching and learning. To say that twenty-first century education leadership requires a paradigm shift understates the scope of transformation that is called for.

In this chapter, a vCoP leadership model is described, how it works, what it accomplishes, and why it represents a sea change in education leadership. The leadership requirements for a vCoP are presented and the specific competencies that an education leader must have to derive the full benefits of the model are outlined. This discussion is supported with case examples drawn from work developing and facilitating vCoPs for education leaders. The analysis and discussion rest on an amalgamated analytic foundation, including the ample literature on communities of practice (CoPs), organizational leadership, organizational learning, story telling, and narrative as an organizational resource, and knowledge management (KM), as well the emerging literature on vCoPs, distributed leadership, leading with technology, networks and social network analysis. These elements are connected to shape the leadership model.

THE CONTEXT OF EDUCATION LEADERSHIP IN THE UNITED STATES

the sheer number and variety of responsibilities facing school leaders, the emerging imperative to focus on learning improvement, and the multiple sources of expectations of school leaders' work, raise important issues about school leaders' roles, responsibilities, and authority to act. (Portin, Alejano, Knapp, & Marzolf, 2006, p. 14)

Since the late 1980s, education leaders have been pressed by a burgeoning array of demands and expectations. In the United States, the desire for accountability for what is taught and what is learned has driven states to develop standards for content and student performance that can be measured easily on statewide assessments. To the same end national and state policymakers have created legislative mandates for student achievement, and both public and private funding have become focused on making visible and measurable the intangibles of "good" educational programs. Successful learning, one infers, can and should be seen as following closely on the education intervention. While it is on the shoulders of leaders to implement the details of education reform, the ability to act thoughtfully and creatively is challenged as legislative guidelines and inflexible timelines force educators to respond quickly to new policies.

Additional burdens come in the form of calls for school choice, reconstitution of schools, and threats of state takeovers, to name a few. Indeed the frenzy of expectations and deliverables outstrip the capacity of even the most extraordinary education leader. Under any circumstances, these challenges cannot be faced effectively alone, or even with a great team, and certainly not within the economic constraints that often accompany the demands. Leadership's best hope for success is to consider a distributed leadership model,—one that reframes the role of the leader, requires new competencies to effect, and capitalizes on the capacity of technology to facilitate work and equip organizations to respond rapidly and flexibly to both internal and outside stimuli.

THEORETICAL FOUNDATIONS: VIRTUAL COMMUNITIES OF PRACTICE, NETWORKS, AND EDUCATION LEADERSHIP

School and district administrators need to think creatively about a variety of incentives for participation in communities of practice that can, over time, become part of the culture of accountability and how work gets done. A first step is for leaders to model this approach to learning and problem solving. (Wagner, 2002, p. 41)

communities ... involving active collaboration among researchers, teachers, and policymakers to develop insights about educational innovation are more powerful than simply transferring to educators the outcomes of research and evaluation studies conducted elsewhere. Shifting from communicating information to collaborating on extending knowledge, increases both the speed and the effectiveness of applying, refining, and generalizing research and evaluation findings. (Dede, 2004, Dede, 2004, http://thejournal.com/articles/16909_2)

Virtual Communities of Practice and Their Role in Education

vCoPs draw their shape from the work on CoP most identified with Wenger (1998). However, several writers have variously defined and discussed them (Brown, & Duguid, 1991; Lave & Wenger, 1991; Smith, 2003; Wenger, 1998; Wick, 2000) There is ample evidence in the literature of their value to organizations generally for improving practice, driving innovation, increasing value, managing knowledge, and creating knowledge networks (Allee, 2003; Hildreth & Kimble, 2004; Swan, Scarbrough, & Robetson, 2002). While still in its infancy, there is also a respectable body of work on virtual or online communities (Barab, Kling, & Gray, 2004; Dube, Bourhis, & Jacob, 2006; Ellis & Vasconcelos, 2004; Johnson, 2001; Kimble, Hildreth, & Wright, 2001; Dubé, Bouris, & Jacob, 2006; Siemens, 2005).

There is an emerging literature on vCoPs for improving various aspects of education (Wachter, Gupta, & Quaddus, 2000), with most focused on teaching and learning (Barab, 2004). Other areas of investigation include vCoPs for faculty development (Dede, 2004; Lock, 2006; Sherer, Shea, & Kristensen, 2003), for curriculum planning (Parr, 2006), for resource pooling to foster the scholarship of teaching and learning (Duffy, 2006), for developing, sharing and applying assessment standards (Price, 2005), for building community among people with common education interests (Storberg-Walker, 2006; Weiss, 2005).

Leadership and the Importance of Vision

Much has been written about the importance of a "shared vision" in leading organizations (Beckhard & Pritchard, 1992; Savage, 1990; Senge, 1990; Weisbord, 1992) as well as for leading education organizations (Buell, 1992; Kantabutra, 2005; Kenneth & Leithwood, 2003; Leithwood & Riehl, 2003; Roueche, 1989; Yimaki, 2006). The term shared vision is used here to mean

the organization's understanding of its major enterprise—its clarity, the extent to which it is shared by organization members, the understanding members at all levels have of it, especially in relation to their work; and members' latitude and authority to locally re-create the vision within their own spheres. (Woolis, 1994, p. 174)

Networks and Distributed Leadership

The literature has yet to offer a consensus on what specifically distributed leadership is. Universally, however, it interrogates the credulity of the "heroic leader" who stands atop an organization, bends it to his or her will and thereby achieves the desired organizational results. The research on distributed leadership amplifies this concept of leadership (Grubb & Flessa, 2006; Grunn, 2000; Harris, 2002; MacBeth, 2005; Portin et al., 2006; Rayner, 2005; Timperley, 2005). Moreover, the literature suggests that the education environment has become too complex, legislated, and multiple-outcome-driven, for any single individual to manage effectively.

Distributed leadership embraces the power of a diversity of ideas, prizes dialogue over mandate, expertise over authority, and promotes an understanding of context for improving decision making. The challenge before us then is "to think more systematically about how leadership can be productively distributed and how the distribution can be managed over time" (Portin et al., 2006, p. 15).

The research on vCoPs points towards their potential as a vehicle for distributed leadership and, conversely, the literature on distributed leadership make vCoPs a logical vehicle for advancing from theory to practice. The dynamics that connect the two can be found in the burgeoning literature on networks (Cross, Parker, Prusak, & Borgatti, 2001; Hildreth & Kimble, 2004; Krebs & Holley, 2002; Savage, 1990; Scott, 2000; Watts, 2004).

Networks can be defined as a constellation of nodes and links that form and disperse as a community interacts online in problem solving, decision making, or the making of meaning. In a vCoP, a node is defined as a collection of explicit knowledge captured in repositories of texts through such things as podcasts, learning management systems, written documents of academic exchanges, or other things that are characterized by a general sense of autonomy (Norris, Lefrere, & Mason, 2006). Links are defined as the action or connections made through dialogue, interactive work, or the exchange of knowledge artifacts, as well as the collective analysis of these.

One way in which vCoPs distinguish themselves from repositories of information, such as might reside on an organization's Web site, are the operations and actions that are reflected in the links. Organization Web sites typically broadcast information or "push" out information. While alone this type of information sharing has value, it is insufficient to spawn actionable knowledge. Rather it is the interaction through structured dialogue, including the discussion of relevant resources, which stimulates thinking and generates innovation. It is the analysis of these exchanges and the stewarding of the knowledge created that will prompt the transformative learning required for education reform.

The cultivation of networks of vCoPs is the key skill required of a leader in a distributed leadership model. Technology and facilitation must be harnessed in combination for value to be derived.

> Without an active leader who takes responsibility for building the network, spontaneous connections between groups emerge slowly, or not at all ... [the leader] actively creates new interactions between clusters ... and has the vision, energy, and social skills to connect diverse individuals and groups and start information flowing to and from them. (Krebs & Holley, 2002, para. 10)

Leading With Technology

vCoPs present a powerful imperative for a reconceptualization of the relationship between leader and technology. This change has been coming in stages, reflective of the evolution of technology itself and coincident with the political and performance demands made of education administrators. If early technological advances can be thought of as "back office" enhancements, most notably databases of various kinds, we now are experiencing the emergence of "front office" technologies that speak directly to the way in which core or mission-critical work is accomplished. While it is not incumbent on leaders to be schooled in the arcane aspects of software, it is vital that the leader consistently approach each new goal by asking the question—what technology is available that could enhance, support or change the way we tackle this challenge?

> managers who distance themselves from IT abdicate a critical responsibility.... They must help select technologies, nurture their adoption, and ensure their exploitation. However ... different types of IT result in different kinds of organizational change when they are implemented, so executives must tailor their roles to the technologies they are using. What's critical, though, is that executives stop looking at IT projects as technology installations and start looking at them as periods of organizational change that they have a responsibility to manage. (McAfee, 2006, p. 2)

Leadership and the Power of Story Telling and Narrative

Whether in the context of bridging the gap between research and practice, addressing the impact of turnover in organizations and the loss of human expertise, or the technology-spurred objective of managing organizational knowledge, education leaders have long appreciated the potential value of capturing the insights of deeply experienced professionals, be they teachers or administrators. Those who have looked at narrative analytically see it as a natural "knowledge medium" in organizations that can be capitalized on as a tool of change (Brown, 1999; Carey, Vredenburg, & Bizzoechi, 2001; Cross, et al., 2001; Senge, 1990) Leaders using vCoPs can maximize the power of story telling as a way of eliciting expertise from community members and ensure that community facilitators have the sophisticated competence to probe and encourage the sharing of substantive narratives. This particular approach to building network knowledge can sharply increase the value of vCoP data to a leader and serve beneficially to aid her in guiding the vCoP in its work.

LEADING USING VIRTUAL COMMUNITIES OF PRACTICE—A MODEL

This review of literature across a range of disciplines is intended to show that there is a foundation for seeing vCoPs as an organizational structure for implementing a new leadership model in education. That model requires active engagement by the leader and skills in exploiting technology, tapping narrative, building networks, and most importantly facilitating and evaluating vCoP work to produce actionable knowledge. The focus is simultaneously on achieving short-term goals and immediate applications and on cultivating a more global knowledge ecology for longer-term use.

The Model Defined—The Protocol for Establishing Effective Distributed Leadership Using Virtual Communities of Practice

This section rests on the premise that the role of the leader is to guide those with whom he works to move from point A to point B; from a current status to a future desired one. Generally, this requires the leader to articulate organizational or group goals, to determine time-frames and the makeup of teams, to assess progress and evaluate achievement, and to model the behavior and culture appropriate to the organization.

Getting Started
Whether working offline or online, the leader using a distributed leadership model must initiate any significant work effort by determining

whom to engage as the core team. S/he must then frame the specific goals to be worked on in the context of the larger organizational mission, set the timeframe for achieving these goals, and provide the resources to make the work possible. In sum,

- Develop the vision
- Formulate the goal(s)
- Identify the starting team
- Set the timeframe
- Delineate the deliverables in broad terms/the basis for assessment
- Select the software that suits both the work and the technology realities and experience level of community members
- Provide necessary human and other resources to support the team's work

Launching the vCoP

The next competency required of the leader of a vCoP is to foster the robust development of an active online working community. The prospective vCoP leader needs to realize that "if you build it they won't come." This is intended to make several points. First, technology is the medium—it is not the end in itself. While it is impossible to have a functioning vCoP without using a Web-based platform, and while the features of the software, or its perceived ease of use by community members, will have an impact on activity in the community, simply providing a "place" and a means for a group to work together will not cause the group to do so.

Second, the technology makes it relatively easy to collect the nodes of a network—a wide range of documentational resources—written materials of all kinds, podcasts, Web site links, and so forth. However, a place with resources and even answers to FAQs, calendar announcements, and so forth., will neither occasion member contributions over time nor will it, by itself, become a venue for members to accomplish work. Groups of busy educators will not alter the way in which they link, that is, the way in which they get work done, without a range of support and encouragement and the particular social context that motivates them to participate.

Fostering the nodes and links of an active vCoP begins with engaging the designated team in the work itself. If the group focuses first and deeply on the challenge and mission it has been assigned then the transition to using a technological interface to address it is easier and more compelling. Having said this, it is nonetheless vital to take a structured approach to vCoP engagement. Here both adapted offline engagement techniques and new methods, reflective of the medium, are beneficial.

Indeed a new profession is emerging in online facilitation of which engagement is the first component.

Getting the Work Done

Facilitation then becomes vital to pursuing the vCoP's agenda. As indicated earlier, engagement is first and foremost about the mission and the vCoP members must "own" their goals, priorities, and timetable. The leader and the facilitator(s) must support the group by creating the exchanges, eliciting, and contributing the resources that will enable the group to do its work. The primary medium of exchange in a vCoP is the asynchronous or quasi-synchronous discussion. IBM coined a term drawn from the jazz environment for these exchanges—Jams. Like a meeting, a Jam is publicized in advance as to its date, length, subject, and objective. Experts outside the group may be invited to participate for all or part of the discussion. Members may moderate discussions but always supported by a facilitator whose primary role is to make sure that the discussion remains focused, to encourage clarifications where appropriate, to draw in "lurking" members who are "in" the meeting but perhaps hesitant to contribute their thinking, and, of course, to assure that technology issues do not interfere with member participation.

Analyzing the Work/Capturing New Knowledge

The critical next step following a substantive exchange in a vCoP is for that exchange to be organized, summarized, and analyzed. The leader can read the discussion as it is unfolding and participate in it, if appropriate, but she will still require that this analysis be done because this reframing of the narrative uncovers issues and ideas that are not easily evident either in the moment or upon a cursory read of the discussion. The challenge, opportunity, and responsibility of the leader of a vCoP is to take this input, this data, and determine how to use it first and foremost to aid the vCoP in achieving its goal(s). This is how distributed leadership begins to manifest itself concretely. The vCoP has provided inputs to the leader. The leader uses and cites the inputs as the basis for comment and action. The vCoP responds to the response to its inputs and moves its work forward. What has been created has both the advantages of human psychology and the advantages of data driven decision making. The value of both the leader and the team are consistently reinforced with each cycle of exchange, analysis, and action.

Summary: Steps for Building an Active vCoP Network

- Convene the starting team (preferably face-to-face)

- Engage the team in delineating the elements of the goal and the path to reaching it—what needs to be done, in what sequence, by whom, with what resources
- Move the team from offline to online using appropriate engagement techniques
- Support active and professional facilitation of the work agenda online—scheduling of asynchronous and quasi-synchronous exchanges, eliciting and posting of documentational resources, tapping relevant experts, pushing for consideration of documentational and human resources beyond the group or organization's traditional circle
- Provide technical support to assure that technology issues do not disproportionately interfere with work
- Require the regular organizing, summarizing and analyzing of substantive exchanges in the community
- Ensure that competent resources regularly organize and prune the "landscape" of the community to maximize the ease with which community members can locate desired information
- Engage with the community sufficiently to both address its issues and impress upon it the importance of the work
- Utilize the data emerging from the exchanges to acknowledge challenges, clarify issues and reframe the goal(s) to both deepen and accelerate the work
- Celebrate outstanding contributions to the community whether of documentational resources, personal expertise, or of innovative ideas
- Guide the community to stay focused and to do effective work
- Respond to suggestions and expressions of need from the community, including recommendations of when and how to expand the community's membership and logically extend its work

Bridging Short and Medium Term Goals/Building a Knowledge Ecology

In the field of education, the pressure to achieve measurable change in student outcomes in 12-month or school year timeframes is enormous. Those leading education systems, institutions, and programs can most realistically respond to these demands by developing medium term goals that they plan to accomplish steadily, perhaps in 1-year increments. One of the potentially transformational benefits of using vCoPs to lead in education is the bridge they can form between short term and medium term objectives. This can occur in three ways. First, active and productive vCoPs will spawn related communities that take up aspects of the mission. This should be an explicit decision by the leader and when it is, progress towards various goals can occur rapidly. Second, active and productive vCoPs generate data that can be used to develop actionable knowledge for the leader and simultaneously knowledge for the organization or system. Here again technology is very useful in making it easy to take inputs residing in one area and share them more broadly. Third, the resources and outputs of an active and productive vCoPs may have much broader relevance for the organization or system's medium term goals and/or for the field at large. The leader now has the opportunity and responsibility to consider his assets and determine how to share them most advantageously.

Building a knowledge ecology therefore requires managing the spawning of new vCoPs and using the knowledge created there for multiple organizational purposes. In this way knowledge is not only "recycled" but knowledge "seeds" are used to grow knowledge created in one moment and context to grow more knowledge in a completely different context and/or a different time.

Summary: Steps for Building a Knowledge Ecology

- Encourage a community to identify those of its documentational resources that have wider organizational applicability
- Identify both documentational resources and the summary and analysis of exchanges that can be repurposed within the organization for related and potentially unanticipated benefit
- Share resources and work with others focused on similar issues
- Be intentional in supporting the growth of vCoPs within the organization

In sum, these steps allow a leader to establish and effectively use a vCoP to produce deep learning, effective problem solving, and to do so with an increased ability to capture the knowledge inherent in her educational system. We have outlined many important elements of an effective launch and implementation of a vCoP in an educational setting. The following section provides three case studies that give an overview of vCoPs in action.

CASES STUDIES

To illustrate how vCoPs really work and the process of establishing the community and implementing the process that unites the members into a community, the following sections describe the experiences of two vCoPs.

Case 1—Increasing the Capacity of Existing Instructional Programs for Adults, Launch Date: 2004, Current Status: Ongoing

Under a mandate from the governor of the Commonwealth of Virginia (United States) to double the number of general educational development (GED)[1] recipients in the state in 18 months, a vCoP was used to effect rapid program development and increase program capacity to a successively wider field of local program managers and instructors. Resistance was remarkably low, as were costs, and the nature of adult education programming in the state was dramatically changed.

Vision

Yvonne Thayer, Director of Adult Education and Literacy for Virginia at the time, saw the daunting mandate as a leadership opportunity. She recognized that this "crisis" could serve to facilitate implementation of a radically new model of GED programming—one that incorporated active student recruitment, new teaching techniques, and, a new mindset. Having served as state director for adult education since 2000, Thayer believed a cultural shift was needed, away from the traditional adult education worldview of "literacy as empowerment," to a transformative self-image—that of provider of practical skills for workplace advancement. Most importantly, from a change process point of view, she saw that if this new GED model could be developed and implemented with some in the field and be successful, she would have the leverage to bring both a changed programmatic approach and a changed mindset to the field as a whole.

The key to being able to move quickly in this case was the limited preparatory work done by the Virginia Department of Education itself. A small team was convened by Thayer and together they worked out the basic goals and parameters for the new accelerated GED program. For example, they stipulated the minimum score on a pretest that a program participant would require, and they decided that the GED preparation program would be 6 weeks in length. Five field program managers were selected to participate in developing the pilot program. A range of criteria for participation were considered, including competence and experience, influence among peers, geographic/demographic program diversity, and an openness to new ideas. With the parameters and people in place, the vCoP was launched in a face-to-face meeting in Richmond, Virginia.

Networks

Traditional program development thinking was shifted by asking the pilot program managers to work together to design the key program elements. The aim was to have everyone learn by doing so the pilot efforts could be launched within several months of the group's first convening. The vCoP became the venue for experiences and issues to be shared, discussed and resolved. Facilitated asynchronous online discussions were held on topics ranging from recruiting new learners via market segmentation, to building bridges to employers for both program funding and job placement. Rapid analysis of these exchanges enabled Thayer to endorse emerging better practices, clarify important areas of confusion and press the team to test the key components of the emerging model.

Approximately 10 months after taking the first steps to respond to the governor's mandate, it was felt that the pilot team's model was sufficiently robust and promising to allow them to widen the pilot circle from 5 to 15 programs. The new pilot program managers were exposed to the model in one face-to-face meeting and then engaged via the vCoP to learn more and position themselves for rapid rollout.

These two rounds of work-first with the initial pilot team and then with the additional 10 not only strengthened the model but taught everyone how to use the vCoP to engage new leaders with the model. Barely 4 months later, Thayer felt that the program was ready to scale statewide in approximately 80 local and regional adult literacy programs. The entire program rollout took place over 2 days via the vCoP with a succession of Jams held on each major program element and moderated by the 15 experienced program managers. The vCoP provided a twofold benefit. The first was in cost- and time-savings, as new managers were introduced to the program elements without having to leave their work sites. The second could be characterized as psychological—a peer-to-peer inculcation with the explicit message that new program managers were being offered the benefit of the experience of colleagues, which they could consider and adapt to their own environments. In this way, a degree of distributed leadership was achieved, controlled, and observable via the vCoP.

Knowledge Ecology

The immediate goal of the initial vCoP was achieved. A new accelerated model for GED preparation was developed and launched statewide, and it produced the desired results of greatly increasing the number of GED recipients in about 18 months. Thayer also achieved her goals of changing the mindset of GED program managers and their staffs and helping them to adopt many of the features of the accelerated program in their overall day-to-day work. It could be argued that buy-in came as a result of participation in the work of the vCoP, aided by the resources and peer support it afforded.

The initial work was continued by enabling subcommunities to form within the vCoP, each of which identified specific objectives for their work as communities. The overall Virginia GED vCoP has grown to exceed 300 members in five discrete subcommunities, ranging from instructors to test examiners to new program managers. Perhaps the best testament to the value created by the vCoP is that it has survived and flourished in the wake of leadership changes within the state.

Case 2—Content Standards Development, Launch Date: 2005, Current Status: Ongoing

After a brief experience with the program model vCoP, Thayer saw the advantage of using a similar structure to move the adult education English for speakers of other languages (ESOL) community rapidly through the development of content standards for English literacy. She sought to have the content standards emerge from collaboration among the field, the Department of Education and independent experts. She wanted written standards that would drive good teaching and improve student performance outcomes. Owing in part to the incorporation of a vCoP, draft content standards for ESOL were produced in a 5-month period. The vCoP has continued under new state leadership, serving as the primary vehicle for the stress testing and rollout of the standards statewide.

Vision

Virginia launched the vCoP on standards with a planning group made up of field program managers and state department personnel. This group had been given its mandate before being asked to work in this way, so the mandate was not altered but the team was asked to consider how a vCoP might accelerate and deepen the work.

Networks

The group's initial goal was to bring a group of field practitioners together for a 4-day writing session. They held onto this offline plan but used the vCoP to help them develop their premeeting work agenda and to move through it. The vCoP had a notable impact on the face-to-face session because participants worked in the vCoP before arriving at the physical location for the writing session. They met the experts on line, asked questions about process, clarified roles and goals, and bonded as working teams, so that by the time they met they were ready to work. Based on similar undertakings the department estimated that this vCoP prework saved at least ½-day of face-to-face meeting time and associated travel cost. The planning group and the draft writers returned to the vCoP to vet and discuss the draft after the meeting. The planning group used the vCoP to plan for and implement the initial field testing of the standards and is now in the process of using the vCoP to implement the standards statewide.

Knowledge Ecology

Adult education is an amorphous component of the educational field in the sense that programs are of differing size and priority, are funded by different sources, and are staffed by instructors of varied background. Yet both GED and ESOL are important factors on the landscape. In the case of Virginia, not only has a vCoP served to facilitate the development of content standards, but also because of the vision of the department leaders, the expertise of the field has been tapped in a stimulating and productive way. The net result of this effort is the evolution of practitioners who feel that they own the content standards and, rather than constraining their ability to help students learn, they are improving their capacity to do so. The vCoP has built connectivity among otherwise disconnected professionals and increased their sense of recognition for and commitment to their work. The overarching goal remains intact-improved outcomes for adult learners.

The Future

There are at least four areas of investigation that would advance the new work of education leaders as explained in this chapter: Leading with technology; metrics; knowledge ecosystems, collaborative technology.

Leading With Technology

This chapter has shown that new models of leading will require a new set of leadership competencies. First, leaders will need to understand how to make technology selection and application part of both strategy development, and of getting the work done. Second, they need to understand more deeply how to create and capitalize on rich networks of knowledge. Third, they will need proficiency in building a knowledge ecology. The investigation needed then is to establish the most effective ways for leaders to develop this skill set.

Knowledge Ecology

Virtual communities can become heavily populated, disorganized, messy places that waste valuable resources. Here then, in a sense, we are asking what "green" nonvirtual community planners ask, What are affordable, sustainable design, construction, and landscape practices? How do we teach them to leaders and community members? How can and should they be "enforced?" What is the relationship between vCoP governance and community sustainability?

Collaborative Technology

The collaborative tools available today are adequate but not more than that. There is a need for tools that are driven by the interests of the social sector. To begin, a comprehensive set of requirements must be laid out. This could be the first step in a larger agenda to build an extensible, open source platform that meets the changing demands of collaborative work for social good. The third leg of this investigation is mapping out the entire field of collaborative technologies—for example, blogs, Wikis, vblogs, and so forth, which ones are best for leading, and how so.

Metrics

We must improve our understanding of the characteristics of high performing vCoPs. At the community level, for example, it will be beneficial to document ways of understanding participation, the relative value of knowledge artifacts, the lifecycle of the community, community dynamics, the quality of facilitation, and of the online structure.

At the organization and systems level measures are needed to indicate when we should know and when we will know if a virtual community is,

- A good idea well executed
- A good idea poorly executed
- A bad idea well executed
- A bad idea poorly executed

In the final analysis, a leader needs to be able to say with confidence that the virtual community served teaching and learning well. A new set of dimensions will be required to ascertain this and it will include areas not yet well defined in this context, for example social network analysis.

FIVE GOOD REASONS WHY EDUCATION LEADERS SHOULD INVEST IN VIRTUAL COMMUNITIES OF PRACTICE

vCoPs are a rich medium and a sophisticated method for harnessing the socialness of knowledge. When well executed, vCoPs offer a powerful vehicle for distributing leadership. Education leaders who grasp, in a substantive way, the potential of vCoPs will be well positioned to cope with the perils and grasp the opportunities of a networked world (Rogers, 2000; Wagner, 2002). At this early juncture in their adoption, vCoP seem to have the unique quality of simultaneously serving individuals, practice fields, organizations and systems. Moreover, used as described here as an integral part of accomplishing mission-critical work, they generate ready value within a single space for practitioners and scholars, policymakers, and advocates.

Why should an educational leader invest in a vCoP? Here are five reasons leaders should look to vCoPs to maximize the productivity of the people who work within their organizations and the contribution they can make to improving educational services.

1. Time—Any technology that saves meeting, travel time, and is accessible from any location has great appeal to today's professional. The ability to learn and collaborate with colleagues and to have access to resources worldwide offers a highly effective use of work and personal time. The value of face-to-face meetings is not diminished as a result; however, the number of such meetings can be reduced and their productivity can increase significantly.

2. Human capital—Today's world requires the capacity building of human resources that extend and create knowledge. vCoPs provide a place for sharing resources and generating dialogue that pose dilemmas and innovative solutions to problems, which ultimately become knowledge. The vCoP offers an opportunity for growth and contribution among participants while generating valuable knowledge that sustains educational organizations through change, restructuring, and new opportunities. Educational institutions are challenged to attract human capital, so developing existing human resources is critical to meeting the changing demands of programs and services.

3. Organizational and leadership development—Changes in demands and restrictions on resources have limited the actions taken to develop the members of organizations and prepare them for leadership. When leaders are needed—especially in educational settings—and the pool of potential leaders seems weak, the question of leadership succession planning arises. The vCoP offers an organization the opportunity to engage members in thoughtful activities that do more than accomplish the organization's mission. VCoP activities allow leaders to emerge, develop and offer new knowledge for the next stage in the organization's journey to actualizing its vision. The work accomplished through the community becomes a series of staff development activities that allow potential education leaders to emerge. The history of vCoP activities-documented and archived-provides testimony that new leaders are being birthed

within their vCoPs and are ready to assume the responsibilities of leading an education organization.

4. Practice and policy—The identification, development, and implementation of best practice and policy are arduous, inelegant, and often unrewarding processes. Scaling up promising programs that sustain transitions of leadership and shifts in funding priorities are the exception rather than the rule. vCoPs offer a hospitable medium for good policy and practice to emerge and evolve. While not immune to conventional politics or problems, their structure makes their work less susceptible to being derailed or comprised by such vagaries. Finally, vCoPs are early and fast harbingers of resistance and resilience, bad ideas and good judgement, and resource potential. Enabling quick and data driven practice and policy adaptation, when well done they garner broad support that further reduces the barriers to implementing sustainable practice and policy.

5. Outcome—It is, in the end, all about outcomes—better, smarter, deeper, faster, sustainable outcomes for teaching and learning and the systems that provide them. VCoPs are currently one of the most promising vehicles for producing those desired outcomes.

NOTES

1. In the United States, GED certificates are issued as high school equivalency diplomas to individuals who have not graduated from high school but are able to complete equivalency requirements and pass a national examination.

REFERENCES

Allee, V. (2003). *The future of knowledge: Increasing prosperity through value networks.* Oxford, England: Butterworth-Heinmann.

Barab, S., Kling, R., & Gray, J. (Ed.). (2004). *Designing for virtual communities in the Service of Learning.* London: Cambridge University Press.

Beckhard, R., & Pritchard, W. (1992). *Changing the essence: The art of creating and leading fundemental change in organizations.* San Francisco: Jossey-Bass.

Brown, J. S. (1999, Spring). Sustaining the ecology of knowledge. *Leader to Leader, 12,* 3.

Brown, J. S., & Duguid, P. (1991). Organizational learning and communities-of-practice:Toward a unified view of working, learning, and innovation. *Organization Science, 2*(1), 40-57.

Buell, N. A. (1992). Building a shared vision—the principal's leadership challenge. *NASSP Bulletin, 76*(542), 88-92.

Carey, T., Vredenburg, K., & Bizzoechi, J. (2001). *Interactive narrative and knowledge stewardship*. Paper presented at the conference on Human Factors in Computing Systems, Seattle, Washington.

Cross, R., Parker, A., Prusak, L., & Borgatti, S. (2001). *Knowing what we know: Supporting knowledge creation and sharing in social networks*. Charlottesville: University of Virginia.

Dede, C. (2004). Enabling distributed learning communities via emerging technologies—Part Two. *T.H.E. Journal, 32*(3), 16.

Dube, L., Bourhis, A., & Jacob, R. (2006). Towards a typology of virtual communities of practice. *Interdisciplinary Journal of Information, Knowledge, and Management, 1*, 69-93.

Duffy, K. D. (2006). Copper: Commmunities of practice: Pooling educational resources to foster the schlorahip of teaching and learning. *Community College Journal of Research and Practice, 30*(2), 151-152.

Ellis, D. O., & Vasconcelos, A. (2004). Community and virtual community. *Annual Review of Information Science and Technology (ARIST), 38*(1), 145-186.

Grubb, W. N., & Flessa, J. (2006). "A Job Too Big for One": Multiple principals and other non-traditional approaches to school leadership. *Education Administration Quarterly, 42*(4), 518-550.

Grunn, P. (2000). Distributed properties: A new architecture for leadership. *Educational Management & Administration, 28*(3), 317-338.

Harris, A. (2002). Effective leadership in schools facing challenging contexts. *School Leadership & Management, 22*(1), 15-26.

Hildreth, P., & Kimble, C. (Ed.). (2004). *Knowledge networks: Innovation through communities of practice*. Hershey, PA: Idea Group.

Istance, D., & Kobayashi, M. (Ed.). (2003). *Networks of innovation: Towards new models for managing schools and systems*. New Milford, CT: OECD Distribution Center.

Johnson, C. (2001). A survey of current research on on-line communities of practice. *The Internet and Higher Education, 4*, 45-60.

Kantabutra, S. (2005). Improving Public school performance through vision-based leadership. *Asia Pacific Education Review, 6*(2), 124-136.

Kenneth A., & Leithwood, C. R. (2003). *What we know about successful school leadership*. Nottingham: National College for School Leadership.

Kimble, C., Hildreth, P., & Wright, P. (2001). Communites of practice: Going virtual. In *Knowldge managment and business model innovation* (pp. 220-234). Hershey, PA: Idea Group.

Krebs, V. H., & Holly, J. (2002). *Building sustainable communities through network building*. Retrieved from http://www.orgnet.com/BuildingNetworks.pdf

Lave, J., & Wenger, E. (1991). *Situated learning: Legitimate peripheral participation*. London: Cambridge University Press.

Leithwood, K. A., & Riehl, C. (2003). *What we know about successful school leadership*. Philidelphia: Temple University.

Lock, J. V. (2006). A new image: Online communities to facilitate teacher professional development. *Journal of Technology and Teacher Education, 14*(4), 663-678.

MacBeth, J. (2005). Leadership as distributed: A matter of practice. *School Leadership and Management, 25*(4), 349-366.

McAfee, A. (2006). Mastering the Three Worlds of Information Technology. *Harvadr Business Review*(November).

Norris, D., Lefrere, P., & Mason, J. (2006, September/October). Making knowledge services work in higher education. *Educause Review, 41*(5), 84-98.

Parr, J. W. (2006). Building on foundations: Creating online community. *Journal of Technology and Teacher Education, 14*(4), 775-793.

Portin, B., Alejano, C., Knapp, M., & Marzolf, E. (2006). *Redefining roles, responsibilties, and authority of school leaders.* Seattle: Center for the Study of Teaching and Policy, University of Washington.

Price, M. (2005). Assessment standards: The role of communities of practice and the scholarship of assessment. *Assessment & Evaluation in Higher Education, 30*(3), 215-230.

Rayner, S. G. H. (2005). Rethinking leadership: Perspectives on remodelling practice. *Educational Review, 57*(2), 151-161.

Rogers, J. (2000). Communities of practice: A framework for fostering coherence in virtual learning communities. *Educational Tecahnology & Society, 3*(3). Retrieved from http://ifets.fit.fraunhofer.de/periodical/vol_3_2000/e01.pdf

Roueche, J. E. (1989). *Shared vision: Transformational leadership in American community colleges.* Washington, DC: American Association for Community and Junior Colleges.

Savage, C. (1990). *5th Generation management: Integrating enterprises through hunman networking.* New York: Digital Equipment Corporation.

Scott, J. (2000). *Social network analysis: A Handbook.* London: Sage.

Senge, P. (1990). *The fifth discipline: The art and practice of the learning organization.* New York: Doubleday.

Sherer, P., Shea, D., & Kristensen, T. (2003). Online communities of practice: A catalyst for faculty development. *Innovative Higher Education, 27*(3).

Siemens, G. (2005). Connectivism: A learning theory for the digital age. *Journal of Instructional Technology and Distance Learning,* 3-10

Smith, M. K. (2003). *"Communities of practice": The encyclopedia of informal education.* Retrieved from www.infed.org/biblio/communities_of_practice

Storberg-Walker, J. (2006). *Exploring the role of communities of practice in judicial continuing education.* Unpublished manuscript.

Swan, J., Scarbrough, H., & Robetson, M. (2002). The construction of communities of practice in the management of innovation. *Management Learning, 33*(4), 477-496.

Timperley, H. (2005). Distributed leadership: Developing theory from practice. *Curriculum Studies, 37*(4), 395-420.

Wachter, R. M., Gupta, J. N. D., & Quaddus, M. A. (2000). Virtual communities in support of education. *International Journal of Information Management, 20*(6), 473-489.

Wagner, T. (2002). The challenge of change leadership: Transforming education through "Communities of Practice." *Education Week*. Retrieved from http://www.edweek.org/ew/articles/2004/10/27/09wagner.h24.html

Watts, D. J. (2004). The "New" Science of Networks. *Annual Review of Sociology, 30*, 243-270.

Weisbord, M. R. (1992). *Discovering common ground*: San Francisco: Berrett-Koehler.

Weiss, H. (2005, September). *Creating communities of parctice to support quality after school programming*. Paper presented at the The After School Evaluation Symposium, Washington, DC.

Wenger, E. (1998). *Communities of practice: Learning, meaning, and identity*. London: Cambridge University Press.

Wick, C. (2000). Knowledge management and leadership opportunities for technical communicators. *Technical Communication, 47*(4), 515-529.

Woolis, D. D. (1994). *Learning and change in government*. New York: Columbia University Press.

Yimaki, R. M. (2006). Toward a new conceptualization of vision in the work of educational leaders: Cases of the visionary archetype. *Educational Administration Quarterly, 42*(4), 620-651.

CHAPTER 4

VIRTUAL PROBLEM-BASED LEARNING COMMUNITIES OF PRACTICE FOR TEACHERS AND ACADEMIC DEVELOPERS

An Irish Higher Education Perspective

Roisin Donnelly

This chapter presents the results from research and experience in the field of higher education (HE) academic development in the Republic of Ireland. The objective of this chapter is to discuss an exploration of how a problem-based learning virtual community of practice (vCoP) was developed and supported within the context of academic development. The chapter is based upon the notion of "community"—a group of academic staff in HE with a shared interest in designing e-learning courses—and the use of problem-based learning (PBL) as a pedagogical approach supported by learning technologies. As the development and availability of online tools for communication has led to an associated rise in the concept of an online community, inherent in this is a discussion of the consideration of suitable technologies and media choices available. The chapter will describe a case study in which virtual problem-based learning as a vCoP was implemented

Communities of Practice: Creating Learning Environments for Educators,
Volume 2, pp. 67–88
Copyright © 2008 by Information Age Publishing

in a professional development module for academic staff. It is hoped that through an exploration of the work that has occurred on vCoP, the experiences shared through this chapter will shed further light on what academics can do when faced with developing virtual communities in the future.

INTRODUCTION

This chapter aims to address:

1. How can technology be used to support PBL as a vCoP and how can such a PBL vCoP support teacher-educators and educators in their work with students?
2. What problems emerge from participant interactions in the PBL vCoP?

Through an exploration of these questions, the chapter will provide a practical resource for both teachers in the field of HE and those educators or academic developers who support academic staff in universities and colleges, who have begun or are considering introducing either online or blended PBL as a vCoP. The term academic development will be used for the context of this chapter. While the chapter does take into account how theory has informed the development and sustenance of this PBL vCoP, woven throughout is consideration of the practical implications for teachers in HE and academic developers charged with their professional development.

By definition, PBL is an educational strategy that involves the presentation of significant, complex and "real world" problems to participants, which are structured so that there is not one specific correct answer or predetermined outcome. In this approach, and for the context of this chapter, the vCoP is a group of adult educators who want to learn about designing e-learning courses of their own and the module on which they are participating is run on PBL principles, virtually and face-to-face, in order to negotiate a common understanding of a problem. The chapter refers to the PBL vCoP, and in this case, it is this group of participants in any given year of the module. In order to keep up with rapid change and make the most of learning technologies as aids to this form of vCoP, a series of practical insights will be provided, supplemented with a variety of illustrations of learning technology being integrated into the PBL strategy. What makes this community of practice (CoP) virtual is the fact that 25% to 50% of the face-to-face PBL tutorials are replaced by leader-guided e-learning activities. The face-to-face sessions occurred once every 2 weeks.

The chapter is written from the perspective of an academic developer/ teacher-educator, and experiences are shared from the past 5 years of PBL vCoPs in relation to this module. The role of the academic developer was as a facilitator or tutor of the PBL vCoP.

There is recognition that some authors question the fact that communities can and do exist in a virtual mode, since for them the notion of community cannot be disassociated from a common physical space and from a history shared by its members. There are others who have experienced it, albeit, until this point in an unquestioning and uncritical way, who have since chosen to investigate its pedagogical potential and implementation.

Historically in education, there has been an assumption that learning "has a beginning and an end; that it is best separated from the rest of our activities; and that it is the result of teaching" (Wenger, 1998, p. 3). Within academic development, there has been a paradigm shift from models of education where knowledge and skills are transmitted through formal attendance at training sessions, to an approach that encourages groups of practitioners to work together to examine, evaluate, and construct knowledge and skills relevant to their current professional practice in the context of their particular workplace (Lewis & Allan, 2005). This trend in professional academic development in teaching indicates a shift from traditional approaches such as presenter-led workshops, to building communities of practice (CoPs) where teachers work together to embrace educational change. Heppell (2006) has argued that the main direction that universities can take is to sustain CoPs for learning. It is argued here that teachers in HE need CoPs as they are going to be central to teaching in the future.

For the context of this case study, CoPs are "groups of people who share a concern, a set of problems or a passion about a topic, and who deepen their knowledge and expertise in this area by interacting on an ongoing basis" (Wenger, McDermott, & Snyder, 2002, p. 4). They are understood to operate (and are developed) along three key dimensions: the problem domain to be considered, the community to engage in the problem domain, and the practice by which the community will learn of, and solve, domain problems. Taken together, these three elements make a CoP an ideal knowledge structure, a social structure that can assume responsibility for developing and sharing knowledge (Wenger, McDermott, & Snyder, 2002).

The concept of CoP has become a major theme of teacher professional development research and practice (Schlager, Fusco, & Schank, 2002), with the positive outcome being argued that such "CoPs can be powerful catalysts for enabling teachers to improve their practice" (p. 129). It is argued that the vCoP model for professional academic development illustrated in this chapter is transformative, sustainable, and scalable.

Introducing virtuality to this is through the integration of tools such as discussion boards and chatrooms; Henri and Pudelko (2003) regard these as devices to support the existence of social entities such as various shapes of gatherings, regrouped under the common designation of virtual communities. Bekkers (2004) has argued that the Internet itself can also be seen as an "archipelago of virtual communities" (p. 194); he has built upon Rheingold's illustration that there exists a close relationship between the Internet and the existence of all kinds of virtual communities, each different in nature, orientation, membership, and scale.

HE is littered with terminology that often finds its way into our day-to-day conversation without introduction or definition. While the terminology used here is virtual rather than distributed, the learning model encompasses technologies such as video or audio conferencing, and Web-based multimedia formats. Within the CoP, discussed in this chapter, learning is independent of time and place, and different students often absorb the material at different times.

To guide the reader through this chapter, the following sections are included the purpose of the PBL vCoP; the purpose and structure of the PBL vCoP; when the group became a vCoP and exploration of the type of support required and when it is most useful.

THE PURPOSE AND STRUCTURE OF THE PBL vCoP

The PBL vCoP was designed primarily to enable the participants to work and learn together on a specific e-learning design problem, and in doing so, bring them together to develop further understanding of their e-learning knowledge. This was to be achieved by providing a mechanism for the management of knowledge already known and the creation of new knowledge in that field. It was also designed to provide opportunities for them to share good practice, develop skills, and acquire technical knowledge. Ultimately, it was to provide an arena for networking and socializing with other participants who share an interest and focus.

As a member of the group, participants were afforded opportunities to develop knowledge about, and solutions for, the innovative use of e-learning technology appropriate to their subject discipline. Benefits of involving participants in the process of program design have been multilayered, and these have been perceived through the module evaluations: the learning outcomes were tailored to meeting those of the group, and there was an increased sense of ownership over the module.

While there was a clear start date for the module, the learning on the module extended beyond the end date as the participants continued their mutual support of each other as they designed e-learning courses in their own teaching contexts.

The participants were academic staff on a current real-word module in a postgraduate diploma in HE entitled "Designing E-Learning." This module has been in existence since 2001. It was designed to be 10 weeks in duration, but the continuation of the learning from the module is discussed later in the chapter. The program is located within a faculty of academic affairs in an institute of technology in the Republic of Ireland. Each year, the module participants while drawn from very diverse disciplines, have a common background in that they are all lecturers in HE in the Republic of Ireland, and share a common interest in wanting to learn more about designing and integrating e-learning into the curriculum. Their common goal is to design an e-learning component to their courses and this formed the basis of their motivation. Throughout the chapter, quotations from the participants' summative evaluations are included to illustrate issues experienced:

> Our group worked on the design of a mathematical online module that could be used to support students. This decision was based on the fact that group members felt they had this element in common in their teaching practice. This proved to be an excellent strategy because everyone had a shared interest in the task. (2004-05 participant evaluation)

> Once we had agreed on the problem we all saw how our individual contributions could be input into the overall goal of the group. (2005-06 participant evaluations)

> Having a group project was instrumental in keeping us collaborating online and maintaining a strong bond. (2005-06 participant evaluations)

The participants were offered the choice of sharing and working on a common problem or they could take turns in working together on a colleague's workplace problem on integrating e-learning. Through the PBL process, they identified what aspects of e-learning to integrate into their courses, and why. The participants were all at different stages in their professional lives, from newly appointed staff to the institution, to those who had been teaching between 5 and 25 years. Networking with other academics and academic developers internationally has been a strong feature of this module and practice in designing e-learning has been enhanced by the multiple perspectives this collaboration can bring. In recent years, through this module, the participants become part of a wider community of e-learning practitioners and this has been developed and maintained with colleagues in England, Europe, and Australia. Experienced educators in e-learning and PBL were invited to the vCoP, to visit the participants both synchronously (two-way communication that requires participants to communicate at the same time, though they may be separated geographically) and asynchronously (participants are not available at the same time in order to communicate) initially for a set period of time. The purpose of this was to introduce specialist knowledge to the discussions and offer an opportunity to explore different perspectives about was happening in these different countries. It provided a "breath of fresh air" to the dialogue, alongside additional ideas and experiences on how to integrate e-learning with the HE curriculum.

> The part of the problem that provided us with an opportunity to collaborate with colleagues both in Finland and Australia in developing and implementing our work were to be the best experiences of the module for me. This was very exciting and when one of the tutors responded to me in the form of a personalized MP3 message. I thought this was truly amazing. (2005-06 participant evaluation)

> Having the international guest tutors ignited a brainstorming session with the group members, which showed us the true benefit of this technology. (2004-05 participant evaluation)

> Throughout the module we as a group used WebCT as a communication tool. We literally had hundreds of postings many of which included attachments. WebCT proved to be an excellent means of communication not just between the participants but also with our tutor and "guest lecturers." These guests were from Scotland, Finland, and Australia. It was wonderful to be able to communicate with such knowledgeable academics from halfway round the world. (2004-05 participant evaluation)

> It was an excellent idea to involve international guest tutors; every online module should use outside experts to demonstrate different software and perspectives. (2005-06 participant evaluation)

The type of e-learning facilities to which all the module participants had access were through the virtual environment, WebCT, online conferencing through the Marratech platform, and audio conferencing through MP3 software. All technologies allowed a range of key facets of the PBL CoP to develop, including pedagogical richness, allowing access to knowledge (e.g., international guest speakers), fostering social interaction, giving participants control of what they were doing, and by providing access to easy-to-revise/maintain/update materials. Using different forms of media such as video conferencing made the experience more interesting and exciting.

A wide variety of teachers and lecturers come on the module each year. In terms of their subject disciplines, they are an eclectic mix, with many subject disciplines being represented in the fields of apprentice education, undergraduate and postgraduate education. Participants also included librarians, IT trainers, graduate students, administrators, educational consultants, and other academic support staff who have a teaching role. Their common purpose was to problem-solve instructional design issues and through the creation and expansion of knowledge in e-learning, to turn scrutiny onto their professional practice The small number of participants, 10 per module, shared a vivid interest in learning technologies and e-learning, and were held together by this enthusiasm.

What did the PBL vCoP produce in a 10-week period? The participants built up an agreed set of communal resources in e-learning. The participants used the technology for representing and expressing what they knew about e-learning. They themselves functioned as designers, using the technologies as tools for analyzing the world, accessing information, interpreting, and organizing the personal knowledge and representing what they knew to others in the vCoP. The virtual environment seemed to be conducive to enabling the participants to build a project and a body of knowledge in e-learning.

Initially, working collectively on the negotiated PBL problem required the whole group to be involved in a series of brainstorming ideas about what disciplines and contexts would benefit from an e-learning course, pooling these ideas and resources and developing, agreeing, and implementing an action plan from week to week. In the first 2 weeks of the module, individuals were testing out ideas on which e-learning approaches would be best for their course and asking for feedback from the teacher. From week 3 onwards, whole group synchronous discussions in the WebCT chat facility was introduced with the purpose of producing new knowledge and expanding the collective understanding of what they were doing. The asynchronous discussion boards were used for the production of draft ideas, reports, and products, and these were complemented by a series of face-to-face tutorials, where the work was consolidated.

It became clear that e-learning infrastructures could offer CoPs a wide range of benefits: first, by offering new possibilities in supporting more flexible channels of communication; second, by contributing greater opportunities of information sharing and third, by stimulating collaborative approaches to knowledge construction and management.

WHEN THE GROUP BECAME A vCoP

The groups of participants who came together on this module to share information, insight, experience and tools about their area of common interest in designing e-learning evolved into a CoP as the module progressed. However, this CoP was not just a celebration of common interest. It focused on practical aspects of the practice of designing e-learning in HE, everyday problems, new tools, developments in the field, things that work and do not work for educators. So the academic staff participated because the community provided value to them. From week 4 of the module onwards, the community members frequently turned to each other to help solve technical problems, rather than using the tutor.

> While I knew the tutor was there in the background as a support, I had a security blanket in a way as my peers were with me in the online environment to help me with technical and content queries; they coached me just as much as the tutor. (2004-05 participant evaluation)

Horan and Wells (2005), in discussing the university campus as the local community, have reported that education is based on mentoring, internalization, identification, role modeling, guidance, socialization, interaction, and group activity. They argue that in these processes, physical proximity plays an important role. While acknowledging this, it is argued that if designed carefully and with attention to detail, the lack of physical human contact in a virtual environment can, to some degree, be compensated for by a strong emphasis on online socialization. Salmon's (2000) five stage model was used to support the participants in the module. The first stage of this model relates to access and developing a welcoming and encouraging atmosphere for learners. Figure 4.1 illustrates how the vCoP integrates the diversity of needs of the participants while maintaining the central learning outcomes of the module. Social awareness is a key point here. Online community space needs to support users and their social activities. It was important to provide a safe environment for participation in the online communications and activities. The participants may not engage fully unless the environment is nonthreatening and they feel it is safe to do so.

Social interaction can contribute to learner satisfaction and frequency of interaction in an online learning environment. Grabinger and Dunlap (2000) argue that without the opportunity actively to interact and exchange ideas with each other and the facilitator, learners' social as well as cognitive involvement in the virtual learning environment (VLE) is diminished. The importance of increasing the social aspect of learning is a recurring theme in this PBL vCoP. Dialogue, interaction, and shared

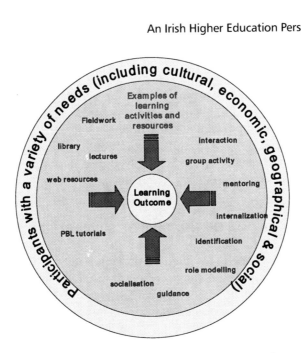

Figure 4.1.   Diversity of teacher needs integrated
with module learning outcomes via a range of
activities and resources.

narratives were key for the participants to maximize the learning opportunities available in the CoP:

> Learning activities that lack social interaction usually fail to evoke emotional
> involvement from learners and thus deny engagement with culture in the
> "community of practice." (Lave & Wenger, 1991, p. 24)

The social interaction that took place between the participants
throughout the module was key to their engagement. One example of this
was the members taking it upon themselves to organize an online book
club to review resources both related to the work they were doing and
other fictional texts that they had enjoyed.

The intention was to use the online discussion boards as both a social
network and a learning community. This involved the participants interacting frequently and feeling at ease to engage in academic discourse
based on their developing understanding of the module readings and
tasks. Virtual communities involve a combination of physical and virtual
interaction, social imagination, and identity (Renninger & Shumar, 2002).
The multilayered quality of the online communication space allowed for
the mingling of different conversations about e-learning and PBL and the

linking of these conversations through the WebCT site. Online technologies often enable traditionally effective instructional techniques to be used more efficiently. For example, the virtual PBL tutorial discussions were more easily saved to form a knowledge bank or archive for reference in future. The facility to archive the online discussions permitted social exchange around site resources at a future time. At any stage of the module, the participants had access to archived discussions and could revisit the postings if they so wished.

EXPLORATION OF THE TYPE OF SUPPORT REQUIRED

The PBL vCoP participants enjoyed the interactive environment that gave them the chance to engage with each other through the electronic tools available, at any time and from any place, work, home, or abroad on field trips with their own classes. Through an observation and analysis of activity and learning in the PBL vCoP, a number of key issues emerged for the teacher or academic developer. These are structured under induction, nurturing a conducive learning environment, handling conflict, the blended environment, participation and PBL group efficiency and finally the quality of conversations in the vCoP.

Nurturing a Conducive Learning Environment

Through the modeling of behavior, the teacher also had a role in letting everyone know that the online discussion board, like the face-to-face PBL tutorial, was a nonjudgmental, tolerant space. Relationships are a key aspect of any vCoP. They determine the motivation and the legitimization of the members, which in turn determine the identity and trust and confidence of the members. For the healthy growth of the PBL vCoP, specific conditions that were present were commitment and trust, with the participants feeling that their open and honest contributions were valued and accepted. An interesting aspect of the vCoP was the more senior members taking on a mentoring role of the newer members of academic staff when it came to discussions about learning and teaching, and the younger members mentoring the senior participants in using the technology.

> What I found the most use to me as a teacher of twenty odd years was how willing the younger members of our group were to take me under their wing when any sense of frustration with the technology was setting in, which it

did on a regular basis in the first few weeks. Looking back on it now I don't think I would have carried on without this. (2005-06 participant evaluation)

The acknowledgement of comfort zones both about the content of discussion on e-learning, and on the process of learning through PBL, enabled the participants to take risks and follow learning paths that led them beyond the sanctuary offered by their comfort zone. Embedded with this, a sense of fun enhanced the shared understanding and the good working relationships. However, these conditions were not fixed states for the entire duration of the module. Building the relationships and trust necessary to support shared actionable knowledge creation within the PBL CoP, on occasion proved difficult in the virtual environment. At times, the social processes (trust and relationships) were negatively affected in the virtual environment.

> The size of the group, 7, instead of working to our advantage, was too large in the virtual environment; I did feel a bit remedial at times, and I held back, but because of the large size if I was not determined I could have easily slipped away. (2005-06 participant evaluations)

> The face-to-face sessions were a life-line that was needed to clarify the online experience and to put any feelings of fear into perspective. (2005-06 participant evaluations)

A number of communication strategies have been tried out for effectiveness in the vCoP. Moore, Winograd, Lange, and Moore (2001) stress that first impressions are crucial, and that a timely, personal response that praises the participant is crucial in the first week. Alongside this, making the learning as accessible as possible might mean explaining acronyms, and with nonnative English speakers, avoiding complex grammatical sentence structures and idioms.

Trying to make personal connections and easy, informal conversation online is important. Participants were more tolerant of longer messages in the early stages of the module so content was limited to a few paragraphs in later online postings. It is useful to think about how messages might be received by other participants who will not know if you have read their messages, quickly deleted them, laughed aloud or burst into applause. Is silence angry, disinterested, bored, or impressed?

Typing skills (or lack of) may prove problematic; it may be necessary to provide extra training outside of the vCoP. To assist with typing at speed, it may be useful to encourage the participant to compose offline and take time to look over and reflect upon their compositions. Other participants should be encouraged to have patience and allow for inaccuracies in written communication. As long as the material makes sense, minor typos and grammatical errors should not detract from the quality of the contribution.

> Sometimes if you cannot type fast enough your point can get made for you or the discussion moves on. (2005-06 participant evaluation)

Handling Conflict

> There were difficulties with our group dynamics that mitigated against genuine trusting collaboration. (2004-05 participant evaluation)

> Our group was too large, with some members having strong personalities. Some individuals dominated while others were happy to plod along. (2005-06 participant evaluations)

> The group project works very well when everyone is committed to it. It is possible for one or two people to feel as if they are being left behind by those who are very competent at the tasks involved. (2005-06 participant evaluations)

One of the main reasons participants can be disruptive is that they either think they know too much or too little and as a result, usually frustration, panic, or boredom sets in. One approach to counter this is to increase or decrease the level of activities with the particular participants. If it is the former, grouping a few individual interactive tutorials helps get them in control and they feel part of the wider vCoP again; if the latter, increasing the online task challenge can help. Again sufficient competency assessment before a group begins helps here in terms of pitching the subject at the right level and knowing some of the participants' backgrounds is extremely helpful. If disruption persists it is important to question their motivation for being on the module and check if learning difficulties, background, or peer issues are contributing to the problem.

In identifying valid complaints and responding to them with the vCoP, it was important for all participants to acknowledge negative comments but reformulate them positively and constructively in the virtual space. The teacher also had a role here by constructively showing appreciation of real difficulties participants were experiencing early on in adapting to the virtual environment. Dealing with difficulties amongst participants tactfully, constructively and promptly was a key feature of the teacher's role. It was important to address any key contentious issues by providing rationale for changes. All message postings needed to be well thought out and by adhering to specific, time-limited discussion topics, participant focus could be facilitated.

Those participants that were lacking in confidence as well as time needed some direct reassurance throughout. Rather than forcing the participants to keep pace with the module, it was more a case of trying to pace the module around them. Clearly, there is a balance to be struck in having clear expectations, and by remaining flexible, the needs of most of the group members will be met.

If there are conflicts between members Juwah (2002) suggested dividing these people into different groups, otherwise if possible, let both parties be open and try to iron out their difficulties face-to-face. An option is for the group to revisit the ground rules and if participants are breaking these, it can be helpful to make them aware of their infringement of the rules. In addition, it may be necessary to consider including additional ground rules. It can be worthwhile to relate any conflict in the group to real-life experience and emphasize that not everything in the real world is perfect and compromises may need to be made.

There is little doubt that it can be difficult to assess emotions of participants online and therefore a good interaction in a face-to-face tutorial can be essential. There can be many virtual problems in a PBL CoP but once awareness is created, a face-to-face session can help resolve them.

Blended Environment

Lewis and Allan (2005) note that many virtual learning communities do not carry out all of their activities using technology; research has shown "participants rating a blended learning approach more highly than 'pure' online communications" (p. 11). In this module, an array of approaches were blended including virtual, face-to-face and resource-based activities. Figure 4.2 depicts a typical blended interaction in the PBL CoP of the classroom event and the online activities.

Blending a classroom event with relevant online activities can extend the learning experience over a longer period of time for the participants in the CoP. One of the most salient features of e-learning is that it allows learning to be place and time independent (Vrasidas & McIsaac, 2000). Adult learners, such as the participants on this module, can arrange their learning around their professional lives without being constrained by time and place.

A vCoP can quickly make decisions, or rapidly change course. Having the option of face-to-face discussions offer the benefit that requests and promises made of, and by, participants are less easily ignored than online messages. In stimulating and structuring a meaningful interaction for the group, a certain amount of face-to-face interaction is important, as there are certain communications that the computer cannot interpret. Face-to-

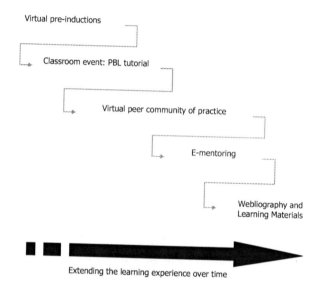

Figure 4.2.   An example of the virtual PBL CoP blended with face-to-face interaction.

face contact contains the familiar "smiles," "pats on the back" and other physical manifestations of support, encouragement, and approval that are so necessary for an effective CoP to function. These things are far less easy to manifest online than face-to-face, and the participants need help and support in coping with the differences. However, it would be a mistake to assume that because groups can meet face-to-face that they will do so, or that participants will know how to use this ability to good effect. They will need advice about how to "blend" effectively and efficiently their online and face-to-face meetings.

If face-to-face discussions are not available then synchronous online discussion may serve a similar organizational benefit in group work. However, chat was not without its problems. There were things of importance about expectations, about writing styles, about knowing people and trusting them—not necessarily the same thing—and about feeling watched and judged. Alleviating the trepidations of those participants who feel anxious is another important role for the leader or teacher. Operating in a vCoP can be both inspiring and frustrating. Discussions can be involving and interesting as you read and relate to others' comments. However, enthusiasm can wane quickly when a problem is encountered online (this could be a minor technical difficulty, being unable to add an attachment or more major, such as the computer not working, or could be a personal issue such as feeling daunted by expertise of other participants or just not relating to what they are saying). Participants may not expect to experience highs and lows in this way. They can be motivated by the tasks, and perhaps by wanting to achieve a tangible goal. However, frustration can set in when a group of participants cannot use the chat facility at the same time. Some may try to contribute, but others can find a "void"—was there anyone out there? It is at this point that they can be surprised that the teacher does not contribute more. Frustration can be magnified by feeling held back at times by the obvious expertise of some peers.

> Maybe I would have gone in online more deeply if we didn't meet face-to-face every week; I might have been forced to discuss issues even more deeply then. (2004-05 participant evaluations)

> I am unsure as to the consistency of depth to which our group used the discussion board to really "discuss" topics but when debate and discussion was generated it was clear that learning was a strong possibility through this medium. (2004-05 participant evaluations)

> The balance between face-to-face and virtual sessions was fine for me. I would not like to go for longer then two weeks without human contact in meetings. (2005-06 participant evaluation)

Participation and vCoP Group Efficiency

How can problems of participation in asynchronous discussions be overcome? Participation will flow if there is a need to impart knowledge through shared experience, or to engage in specific social relations. All CoPs include individuals who participate in different ways and at different rates. Some members participated much more vociferously and more frequently than others both face-to-face and online did. There was a sense that some participants felt that they did not know enough to contribute and this required a discussion on the quality and standard of responses required. Examples of the correct depth of engagement were useful so that expectations could be defined. Private e-mails to support and guide deeper input helped, provided the participant was responsive.

> Group work often has a competitive element which, in our situation and context, we harnessed in a positive way. (2004-05 participant evaluation)

> The team work was excellent. I learned how to approach group work and, I hope, how to make a team work better together. Some of the very active members promoted critical thinking, which gave confidence to others to do the same. The members were good at solving problems and more importantly, accepting solutions from each other. (2005-06 participant evaluation)

In terms of participation, as an educator of teachers, it was important to be aware of different approaches to using the technology and the learning material, which may reflect personal preferences rather than real problems, that is, some participants needed more reflection time, more research, or preferred different presentation formats (drawings rather than text) to understand issues. In addition, mature participants may react differently to the technology than the younger participants. It would be important to have as much background information as possible to help build up an e-personality for each participant. Building up a profile of the participant ages, background, expectations, and technical experience can help with understanding why certain behavior is present.

To encourage participation in the PBL vCoP, it can be useful to ask slow contributors to reply on simple points to "break the ice" with their peers. Some may require extra time to understand the material. This may result from different learning styles, different material presentation formats, too much text or too few diagrams.

Figure 4.3 illustrates the structure, context, and learning process vital for the efficient operation of the vCoP.

There are a number of requisites for having a clear structure for the vCoP. First, the culture of the group of participants can be significant in how the group will operate. Second, having clear and common goals and a motivating task, is key to participation; third, support needs to be provided to the group in defining individual roles and norms for how the group will function; fourth, sufficient time should be allowed for the group to complete the work and finally, the provision of a blended communal meeting place is important. The context of the vCoP can also have a strong influence on its effectiveness and the group can benefit greatly from having a shared history, clear mission, and mutual vision. The facilitator or leader of the vCoP can play a role in its effectiveness by providing a supportive culture in tone and purpose, formative feedback, and a coherent blend of technological and material resources. The process of the PBL vCoP informs the end product or performance of the group. Inherent in this is the administration of boundaries in the group, allowance for conflict management and support in decision making and problem solving.

Quality of Conversations

The research by Chapman, Raymond, and Smiley (2005) has identified elements in online conversations that describe a learning community and these include informality, familiarity, honesty, openness, heart, passion,

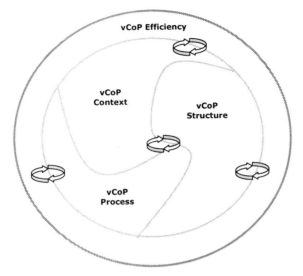

vCoP Efficiency:
- **Structure** is important for the individual participants to experience growth and development
- **Context** is important for the enhancement of participants' ability to work together
- **Process** informs the performance/product of the vCoP

vCoP Structure:
- Effective culture
- Clear & common goals
- Motivating task
- Clearly defined roles
- vCoP norms
- Sufficient time
- Blended communal meeting place

vCoP Context:
- Clear mission and shared vision
- Shared history
- Supportive culture: tone and purpose
- Rewards consistent with outcomes & design
- Formative feedback
- Blend of physical and online environment
- Technological and material resources

vCoP Process:
- Problem solving
- Decision making
- Conflict management: social construction of rules and behaviors
- Coherent communication
- Boundary management

Source: Schwarz, 1994.

Figure 4.3.   Towards efficiency in a virtual PBL CoP.

dialogue, rapport, empathy, trust, authenticity, disclosure, humor, and diverse opinions. Bekkers (2004) suggests that it is important to have a clear, rather narrow focus leaving enough room for discussion and deliberation. Involving past participants of a PBL vCoP to comment and post in the module, not just as content but also as part of examples in a discussion, has proved helpful.

One possibility with the online discussions is too much contribution coming from one source, compared with others. As in face-to-face discussions, some people can talk too much at the expense of their peer's contributions. Some may feel "others are doing so much that it is difficult to keep up." This can simply result from the flow and ebb of the conversations. For newcomers to the vCoP, a useful idea is to allow participants at the induction stage to work through exercises that are examples of a mock discussion, illustrating what to do. For example, include a title for the message, ensure the messages are in the right conference and ensure that one person is not dominating a discussion. They could reflect on these by exploring how well the messages contribute to the flow of a discussion.

The participants were working with an understanding of diversity in learning style, culture, and personal styles of each other. With this in mind, it is important to provide a choice of tasks to stimulate the discussion in order to accommodate different learning styles (Honey & Mumford, 1986). Effective facilitators must feel comfortable using the media and communication tools. Ideally, using a variety of media (text, graphics, audio, and video) to present material may accommodate individual learning styles and provide approaches for both visual and auditory learners. Activists should have a range of different activities to keep them engaged, and have the opportunity to brainstorm ideas. Pragmatists need a structure that will allow them to see an obvious link between the discussions and what they are learning, in order to evaluate its practical use and value. Theorists will need sufficient time to explore links between ideas and situations; the asynchronous nature of WebCT and other VLEs will support this. Reflectors, should be given time to reflect and give considered responses.

> Having people thinking the same way about education/e-learning, as you do, from different parts of the world allows you to break free from your bubble. It is very easy to believe that your educational system and methods are the only ones available. (2005-06 participant evaluation)

POTENTIAL PROBLEMS IN A PBL vCoP

Over the 5 years of the PG diploma module and its PBL vCoP being in operation, a number of problems emerged which had implications for the teacher involved:

- Procrastination by participants, which caused them later to experience difficulty in managing their time and requirements
- Problems with technology at the start (and as a result, the teacher overcompensated by trying to do too much). Instead, it is recommended to encourage those participants with good online skills to support those others who are less confident in using the technology
- The vCoP could be overwhelming (involving too much work for the teacher and participants) or it could be too novel an environment

- There could be little thought given to the integration of technology to the CoP or low levels of planning by the teacher which can result in confusion for participants
- Resistance to change by the participants
- Unequal relationships developing; trying to avoid the domination by one or two individuals
- Surface level of learning occurring; important to provide opportunities for reflection on the process of e-learning and how participants could improve, develop, and progress using this type of learning environment
- An unstimulating environment could occur occasionally; to overcome this it is important to use questions in discussion that will challenge the participants as well as provide interesting material and leave ownership of the problem to the participants

CONCLUSION

This final section includes recommendations for teacher-educators wishing to develop a PBL vCoP in the future. While contributing online and working in a community has its recognized problems, detailed induction, practice tasks, formative feedback and ongoing IT and pedagogic support by the teacher has been found to be crucial to success. Participants need to be able to use online techniques properly before they can feel comfortable using it in a real situation. Also, they have to be aware of etiquette and what is acceptable to the teacher and their peers in terms of communicating online. The area of what is expected of them is also key—they need to know how often they should log on/contribute, what tasks are a requirement, what IT they need, and when/how feedback is available. Any uncertainty or failure to access the vCoP/module can lead to a sense of isolation, which is not helpful in a virtual context.

Participants should reflect on their processes and progress in the vCoP; guidelines should be given to support this. Encouragement of everyone to participate and share their experience in the online discussion board can be very helpful, as participants relate to real life experiences quickly; this can then be combined with the recommended literature in the area. A study guide for each week with recommended materials should be laid out to match the objectives of each week. Evaluation details should be given in soft and hard copy formats, indicating participation, and attendance.

vCoPs are being increasingly used in initiatives seeking to enhance teaching in the HE sector (Churchill, 2006). In the Irish context discussed in this chapter, a number of important lessons have been learned by the academic developer and the participants in the vCoP. First, there is a need to be explicit initially about the purpose of the PBL vCoP, and how vital it is to invest time and effort into planning the structure of the PBL vCoP. Second, and from a technical perspective, coherence about the e-learning infrastructure is required and from a pedagogical viewpoint, it is important to take cognizance of the learning process within the PBL vCoP, particularly in how the participants work and learn together. Finally, it is useful to explore the type of support required and when this is most useful.

Having an initial predefined lifespan and a specific problem to mobilize its energies, the PBL vCoP developed well. Given the fact that the module was initially designed for a duration of 10 weeks, as Henri and Pudelko (2003) have noted, the learning community in it is born, grows and dies at the rhythm of the stages of an educational program. However, due to the process of reification occurring, the individual productions and the common achievements of the participants were published on the Web site, and the vCoP did not expire at the close of the module. For such a community of professional academic staff, involvement in the vCoP through this module was a means to make practice explicit, to improve and even to transform it. Virtual discussions with each other and the international guest tutors continued many weeks after the close of the module; a testimony to the strength of the CoP.

In a final contemplation of practical implications for teacher-practitioners and academic developers both now, and for the future, it can be useful to highlight some considerations:

- Educators have a longstanding tradition of pursuing professional academic development through various levels of collaboration within CoPs—the emergence of online versions, such as virtual learning communities, is a natural extension of the strategy.
- By taking a phased approach to community building in virtual asynchronous discussions, traffic can be increased and loyalty built over time: through such a phased approach, community can build naturally, while valuable participant information can be gathered that can be used to increase the relevance of the discussions. With a move towards an active community, participation, and engagement grows, resulting in a richer learning experience.
- Both opportunities and challenges arise in this form of problem-based learning community: it is important to induct the participants as part of their professional development as teachers in HE. Building a virtual learning community involves developing content mastery as well as facilitating interaction among the participants to

learn and share experiences; emerging technology such as tools, media, and virtual environments offer opportunities for creating new types of learning communities for these teachers.

- One of the most satisfying aspects within the PBL virtual community is the nurturing of long-distance professional relationships and local ties.

REFERENCES

Bekkers, V. (2004). Virtual policy communities and responsive governance: Redesigning online debates. *Information Policy, 9*, 193-203.

Chapman, C., Ramondt, L., & Smiley, G. (2005). Strong community, deep learning: Exploring the link. *Innovations in Education and Teaching International, 42*(3), 217-230.

Churchill, T. (2006, September). *E-communities of practice?* Paper presented at *ALT-C*, Heriot Watt University.

Grabinger, R. S., & Dunlap, J. C. (2000). Rich environments for active learning: A definition. In D. Squires, G. Conole, & G. Jacobs (Eds.), *The changing face of learning technology* (pp. 8-38). Cardiff: University of Wales Press.

Henri, F., & Pudelko, B. (2003). Understanding and analysing activity and learning in virtual communities. *Journal of Computer Assisted Learning, 19*, 474-487.

Heppell, S. (2006, September) *E-learning in the 21st century.* Keynote presentation at *ALT-C*, Heriot-Watt University, Edinburgh.

Honey. P., & Mumford, A. (1986). *Using your Learning Styles.* Maidenhead, England: Peter Honey.

Horan, T., & Wells, K. (2005). Digital communities of practice: Investigation of actionable knowledge for local information networks. *Knowledge, Technology & Policy, 18*(1), 27-42.

Juwah, C. (2002). *Using communication and information technologies to support problem-based learning.* Aberdeen, Scotland: The Robert Gordon University.

Lave, J., & Wenger, E. (1991). *Situated learning: Legitimate peripheral participation.* London: Cambridge University Press.

Lewis, D., & Allan, B. (2005). *Virtual communities of practice. A guide for practitioners.* Maidenhead, England: The Society for Research into Higher Education and Open University Press.

Moore, G. S, Winograd, K., Lange, D., & Moore, G. (2001). *You can teach online: The McGraw-Hill guide to building creative learning environments.* London: McGraw-Hill.

Renninger, K., & Shumar, W. (Eds.). (2002). *Building virtual communities: Learning and change in cyberspace.* London: Cambridge University Press.

Salmon, G. (2000). *E-moderating: The key to teaching and learning online.* London: Kogan Page.

Schlager, M., Fusco, J., & Schank, P. (2002). Evolution of an online education community of practice. In K. A. Renninger & W. Shumar (Eds.), *Building virtual communities. Learning and change in cyberspace.* London: Cambridge University Press.

Schwarz, R. M. (1994) *The skilled facilitator: Practical Wisdom For Developing Effective Groups.* San Francisco: Jossey-Bass.

Vrasidas, C., & McIsaac, M. (2000). Principles of pedagogy and evaluation for Web-based learning. *Education Media International, 37*(2), 105-111.

Wenger, E. (1998). *Communities of practice.* London: Cambridge University Press.

Wenger, E., McDermott, R., & Snyder, W. (2002). *Cultivating communities of practice.* Boston: Harvard Business School Press.

CHAPTER 5

EXPLORING THE POTENTIAL OF ONLINE COMMUNITIES OF PRACTICE FOR DISTANCE TUTORS

Janet Macdonald and Anne Hewling

As the name implies, distance tutors commonly work away from campus and rarely have the opportunity for ongoing support and informal development such as that enjoyed by campus based staff. In this context there is much potential in making provision for the development of online communities. This chapter describes three case studies of the establishment and evaluation of online communities of practice (CoPs) at the Open University (UK). CoPs are in use both as a central part of course related professional development, and for wider pedagogical issues. Platforms in use include online forums, which support online discussion, and new Wiki environments, which also offer the potential for extending the use of CoPs to the development and sharing of resources. The variety of ways in which CoPs are in use are described, the major factors which contribute to their success, and the social and institutional challenges to sharing and developing resources within a community.

Communities of Practice: Creating Learning Environments for Educators,
Volume 2, pp. 89–105
Copyright © 2008 by Information Age Publishing
All rights of reproduction in any form reserved.

INTRODUCTION

The planning and provision of staff development and support for distance learning tutors has always been a challenge. Tutors may be widely dispersed geographically, and therefore have few opportunities to meet face-to-face. Opportunities for interactions with colleagues from their own course are often limited and the chance to meet colleagues from other subject areas within their university can be rare. At the same time, they can benefit, as their campus based colleagues do, from the kind of ongoing support and informal development enjoyed by those who are able to share an office with fellow academics, or perhaps "know someone who knows" just down the corridor.

Online networks offer the potential to provide an informal context in which distance tutors can work with their peers. They can offer a space to meet others and exchange ideas on good practice where no alternative opportunity exists. CoPs may develop within or across subject or discipline areas, whether for sharing and developing teaching resources, or alternatively for moderation of marking or discussion of marking criteria; even for exploring issues that affect all staff—like dealing with learners' special needs. Such support may be of particular value to new staff members who are just beginning to find their way in the academic environment.

This chapter describes the roles, remits, and environments inhabited by part-time tutors who work at the Open University (UK). It gives examples of ways in which online networks have been used to support CoPs among these tutors by describing three case studies. It goes on to provide guidance on establishing good practice for the development of such virtual communities and sustaining activity within them.

BACKGROUND

This chapter discusses the role of informal learning as a part of professional development, and therefore it is relevant to consider how that relates to other forms of learning which staff might need to undertake in order to do their job effectively. Eraut (2002) refers to three different types of learning which really depend on the intention of the learner. He calls them:

- Implicit (learning which takes place almost unconsciously, taken for granted)
- Reactive (learning in response to a recent need for information)
- Deliberative (learning when time is deliberately set aside for study)

Using this framework, it is easy to see how reactive learning might take place in a campus environment, where staff are in constant contact with each other, and can turn to each other for help and assistance. Similarly, many of us have experience of implicit learning, a kind of wisdom about the nature of the institution and its working practices that develops over time. Finally, deliberative learning is probably the area which institutions are most practiced at addressing, through staff development workshops or seminars, or perhaps a distance or online course. In fact, it is the area most commonly associated with professional development. However, professional development which addresses the other two aspects is more problematic for institutions with distance tutors, because it cannot simply be assumed to take place without some kind of deliberate intervention. Institutions may need to consider how to plan and make provision for implicit learning, or how to facilitate reactive learning within the community.

Online CoPs have an important role in enhancing our provision of professional development for reactive and implicit learning among distance tutors. According to Wenger (1998), CoPs are groups of people who share a concern or a passion for something they do and who interact regularly to learn how to do it better. There is an established literature on the effectiveness of learning achieved within CoPs and their impact on levels of personal engagement for the individuals involved. Although used originally in the context of professional and social practice in "real-world" settings, the concept of the community of practice (CoP) is now increasingly used in relation to virtual environments. For example, research in this field has focused both on the use of online environments as an additional support to existing CoPs, such as the potential of an online forum for a university faculty learning community (Sherer, Shea, & Kristensen, 2003), and on the emergence of CoPs in online environments, such as the support of continuing professional development among teachers (Leach, 2002; Barab, MacKinster, & Scheckler, 2003). Bowskill, Foster, Lally, and McConnell (2000) review instances of their use as a means to support the process of networked learning and to promote collaboration among colleagues.

ABOUT DISTANCE TUTORS AT THE OPEN UNIVERSITY (UK)

The Open University is the United Kingdom's biggest provider of distance learning, with 580 courses offered to 150,000 undergraduate students and 30,000 studying at postgraduate level. The university employs 8,000 part-time tutors, who act as the human interface between the university and its students. The university operates in all parts of the United

Kingdom, including Scotland, where much of the work described here has taken place and where the university has 15,000 students and over 600 tutors. Each tutor is responsible for the support of a group of around 20 students, although the group may vary in size depending on the geographical distribution of students. While some staff work for the university part-time, and provide support to one group on one course, others have a portfolio of courses, and effectively work full time. Their role is to deal with students as identifiable individuals, marking assignments with detailed formative feedback, and providing support to students as appropriate. Tutors are not concerned with the delivery of content, since that is provided by central academic staff and delivered in the form of printed or Web-based course materials. The nature of their support will vary to some extent with the faculty and course, and some online courses run with low tutor input, but broadly speaking there is a standard remit.

Tutors are distributed throughout the United Kingdom, traditionally with responsibility for students who live locally, although this varies for low population courses. They work from home, and rarely have the opportunity to meet fellow tutors on the course that they tutor, or indeed to meet the course writers who have designed the course and its assessment strategy. They frequently have a variety of other work-related experiences they bring to the job. They might be working full-time in other institutions, or perhaps have a portfolio career across several institutions. It is likely that these varied backgrounds and motivations will influence tutors' needs for staff development in addition to their attitudes to drivers such as accreditation, job satisfaction or the enhanced ability to support students effectively.

Professional Development Initiatives

Professional development for the part-time tutors focuses on improving and extending their professional knowledge and skills as supporters of student learning. The university has pioneered the use of online media for learning and teaching, which has brought additional requirements on professional development. Since 2004, all tutors must have access to the Internet for administrative purposes, but also increasingly for supporting learners. Each tutor has a personalized home page, called TutorHome, which gives them access to their student details, and to news and other Web-based resources, including the library.

Presently, tutors are given an account on FirstClass, the Open University (UK) online forum system, which provides them with an official university e-mail to use for any communication with students or the university, as well as access to a wide range of forums for keeping in touch with both students and fellow staff. From 2007, tutors will be expected to use the electronic assignment submission system for most courses. From 2008, the university moves to a virtual learning environment (VLE) which will integrate all online tools and resources within one interface.

Since the end of 2004, there has been a mandatory 2 year induction program for tutors and an allowance within the contract for up to 2 days per year of continuing development activities for those who are more experienced. The responsibility for professional development for tutors is shared among a variety of units within the university. At the outset of a new course, faculties provide induction into course concepts and approaches to learner support through an initial compulsory course briefing, which is normally conducted in a day's workshop. For ongoing staff development needs, the university has a range of distance learning materials, which are both paper and Web-based. Opportunities for generic professional development, and some faculty associated briefings, are provided through optional, face-to-face seminars and workshops: such ongoing professional development is commonly the responsibility of locally situated staff such as those at the Open University (OU) in Scotland.

At the OU in Scotland, a number of initiatives have promoted professional development in the use of online media. The SOLACE (Supporting Open Learners in a Changing Environment) project pioneered the use of an online community for shared reflection on supporting learners across disciplines (Macdonald & Hills, 2005; Macdonald, 2006). A team of tutors known as SOS (Scottish Online Support) are also employed as mentors. This team have extensive experience of using online tools for supporting students and are recruited from different Faculties. They integrate regular hands-on workshops with an online forum where tutors can discuss their use of online media for supporting students.

Finally, the OU Library and Learning Resources Centre contributes to the professional development of tutors by delivering information literacy skills training and Web-based resources, including a wide range of electronic journals and books, and has led an innovative program in informal repositories for distance tutor communities, described below.

CASE STUDIES

Two case studies have been chosen to illustrate the existing use of online communities for tutors at the OU. Taken together, they show the range of purposes that such communities can serve, and the factors that influence participants when considering whether to make use of them. The final case study describes the potential for new tools to support such communities.

The first case study of existing online tutor communities is drawn from data collected from participants on multiple presentations of the Tutor Moderators course, which provides an experiential approach to the moderating of online forums. As well as providing training for staff, the course is a rich source of data on the existing uses of online communities at the OU, as perceived by course participants.

The second case study describes the factors that influence participation in a long running forum, sponsored by the OU in Scotland for discussion on the use of online media for supporting students.

Recently, the library has taken the lead on a joint information systems committee (JISC) funded project, PROWE (Personal Repositories Wiki Environment), in partnership with the Institute of Educational Technology and the University of Leicester Beyond Distance Research Alliance. This project investigates the potential of new online collaborative tools including Wikis and blogs (Hewling, 2006) for sharing ideas and information within a community of tutors. The final case study describes this project.

A Study of Existing Online Tutor Communities

Online forums are used in various ways for keeping tutors in touch with each other, and they can serve as a platform for CoPs, which may have a lifetime of several years. A study of existing staff forums at the Open University (UK) was recently undertaken in order to describe the range of purposes to which they were put.

The data is taken from a desk study of the transcripts from five presentations of the Tutor Moderator course, which ran in the first 6 months of 2006: in which 100 tutors took part. In the first week of the course, participants are asked to explore the forums on their desktop and to describe which they have visited, and what purposes the forums appear to have. They are then asked to download and comment on the relevance of a practitioner's framework for forums (Macdonald, 2006), which describes the relationship between forum purpose, expectations of participation, and the consequences for moderator roles.

By repeated reading of the transcripts of 74 responses, it was possible to identify a number of common trends in the descriptions of forums visited, and perceptions of forum purpose. The aim was to derive as full a picture as possible of the variations in perspectives of respondents, based on the principles of constant comparison.

Participants described a range of purposes for forums, the most common being that equating to the "staff room." Such online staff rooms are particularly relevant at the Open University (UK), where courses are supported by several tutors who otherwise rarely meet face-to-face. Participants described two types: those that were course related and catering for a fixed group of identifiable staff associated with a particular course; and those that were interdisciplinary (and generally plenary) forums, which catered to a shifting population of tutors from all Faculties. Table 5.1 summarizes these two types in terms of who used them and what purposes they served.

Much of the use of course related forums was for course related discussion, largely associated with current assignment marking; examples included requests for clarification and discussion of the interpretation of assignment wording or of marking schemes, or perhaps unexpected answers from students. At the same time, they served as a channel of communication with the course team or administrator, who used them for highlighting errors in the text, supplying further teaching resources, stop press notices and responses to queries from tutors. Much of this function was critically time dependent, because of the need to complete the marking of assignments.

> they are active and a reply to an urgent question usually takes only a few hours.... We recently were questioning our own understanding of a particular [assignment] question. I guess it takes a brave tutor to say—I don't get this—but once someone did it was huge relief and more added their concerns. (Tutor 10, Jan. 6)

> I find them very useful, particularly in relation to [assignment] questions that students may have misinterpreted and how we deal with answers that don't link up with the tutor guidance for marking. (Tutor 27, March 06)

The course related forums were also used for sharing resources with fellow tutors, for example model answers or checklists for the content of essays, or other teaching materials and tips for tutorials. The facility to be

Table 5.1.   Categories of Online Staff Room

Category	Group Members	Purpose
Course related	Fixed group: Identifiable tutors and their line managers on same course	Course related discussion: Assignment marking Communications from course team Sharing resources Peer support
Interdisciplinary	Plenary group: Shifting population of tutors, all faculties	Generic good practice: Question and answer Peer support/social

able to work collectively was much appreciated by some tutors who might not necessarily be expert in all aspects of the course.

> One of the very experienced tutors has posted his tutorial handouts on his own Web site and I discovered that fact from the [forum]. The materials he has produced are outstanding and have saved many of his fellow tutors hours of work. (Tutor 5, Jan. 06)

> I regularly go into the tutors' [forum] to get a soft copy of model answers for the assignments. I've been known to answer queries from fellow tutors and post checklists for the content of essays ... saves time that then can be devoted to discussing essay writing technique in the spirit of formative assessment. (Tutor 52, April 06)

Finally, they were valuable as a source of peer support, as a way of reducing isolation, keeping in touch with the course and the students' interpretation of it, and generally in making the job less lonely that it might otherwise be.

> a great way to get in touch with other [tutors], to keep in touch with the course team about things that we need advice about, or for us to give our own views and feedback. It's also a great way to share a smile and a joke occasionally ... many of us work in far flung places ... so it's good to feel part of a body of people from time to time. (Tutor 68, June 06)

Interdisciplinary forums were less frequently referred to, and most respondents who did had visited a generic staff forum, which is available to all 8,000 of the university's tutors. Not surprisingly, many found this particular forum off-putting as it suffered from too many messages and an ill-defined purpose. The forum was in use for a discussion of generic good practice in tutoring, for some questions and answers and for a wide range of social issues.

> there seems to be an intense discussion about politics and education provision. A debate is good, but in some opinions are quite forceful and may put someone off joining the [forum]. I would feel uncomfortable sending a message to this [forum]. (Tutor 65, June 6)

Such comments really underline the place of a CoP in the working life of tutors: if its purpose is central to the role it will probably be welcomed, and the community will be sustainable, not only providing factual information on demand, but also a sense of belonging and peer support, for those who contribute and also for those who read. This is very much in line with Wenger's (1998) ideas on CoPs, which are predicated around issues that matter to participants. However, any community with a more generic focus is likely to be further down a tutor's priority list than course related discussion. Indeed Preece (2000) suggests that broadly based communities may experience more interpersonal confrontation because participants have different expectations. In such cases, the size of the message base is critical and so is the clarity of purpose when deciding whether or not to read or contribute.

Sharing Experiences of Online Tutoring: The SOS Forum

With the potential of cross-faculty exchanges and the importance of a well-defined purpose firmly in mind, this section describes a successful innovation in providing space for the development of a long running interdisciplinary CoP. Over the last 3 years at the Open University in Scotland a forum for 200 tutors from all faculties has been organized and run to discuss approaches to supporting students using online media. The forum contains a central area for discussion or queries, in addition to a variety of resources. As part of a recent evaluation of the forum, the following is a brief report on a study that set out to identify the factors influencing forum use.

A brief qualitative e-mail questionnaire was sent out to all those participants who had read messages (but not necessarily posted) during September-November 2005 ($n = 79$), to establish tutors' perceptions of forum use. 41 questionnaire responses were received: these were analyzed by iterative reading of the transcripts, during which common themes emerged.

When asked what they felt was most useful about the forum, respondents cited the support of the community and timeliness as key benefits:

Knowing the [forum] is there and I will get a quick response if I run into a computer issue. (T23)

Ideas from others about how to make best use of computer for teaching. (T12)

At the same time, a key issue was the availability of their own time and perceptions of the relative importance of this forum. While many users clearly valued the forum enough to check new messages every day, others checked it when they had completed tasks that were central to their role, particularly contact with their students.

Usually check it when I'm checking my FirstClass e-mails anyway. (T37)

Only do this occasionally if I have time. (T7)

I do it automatically as I go round a variety of "secondary importance" forums. (T41)

The volume of traffic on the forum was seen as critical in determining patterns of readership. While some users already skimmed many messages to locate those of most interest, others who were presently reading all messages felt that they would have to be more selective should traffic levels increase.

As there's not much traffic I read it all, but I pass quickly over topics not of immediate interest. (T3)

All the messages at the moment, but if it got busier I would only read selected topics. (T15)

There was clearly a balance to be struck between the value of the forum in terms of relevant information and support, and the time available for participation. This reinforces comments made earlier on the need for a specific and well-defined purpose for such online communities, and their perceived value with respect to the core role of tutors. In addition, such largely generic provision relies on serendipitous encounter for participation, in other words it is unlikely that staff will log on specifically to participate in such communities, and so it important that it is readily accessible in relation to other tools and forums used for teaching and learning, otherwise it will not be used.

Preece (2000) comments that while communities with a clearly stated goal or purpose will attract people with similar goals, lurking will not prove worthwhile unless there is a critical mass of people willing to generate interesting content. Clearly, a balance must be struck between a community that is attractive because the discussion is relevant and current, and one which is overwhelming because it has too many participants.

Investigating New Tools—PROWE

The chapter so far has focused on tools already in use to support online tutor communities. It has shown how tutors may use them to develop community interaction surrounding topical issues, requests for help, information exchange and sharing. Issues which encourage success have also been discussed, for example, relevance, usability, and accessibility and those which discourage use, such as lack of a clearly defined purpose. What has not yet been addressed is the issue of whether the right tool was being used in the first place to meet these particular needs, or whether a new tool—or perhaps a combination of tools—might be more effective in extending the ways in which tutors can work together. The final study in this chapter describes a project that has been trialing the use of new communications technologies to support tutor communities virtually. Recent research into new communications tools like Wikis and blogs (see www.prowe.ac.uk) suggests that such tools offer enormous potential for extending interaction beyond asynchronous discussions, to include the creation of different online workspaces in which collaborative projects can be developed. These same tools can also offer file storage space allowing the development of personalized, individual, or group repositories from which access to multiple versions of cocreated materials can be offered to colleagues and possibly even to students. There is scope for adding other media to these repositories too. All of these features would seem to make such environments ideal for supporting a geograph-ically dispersed network of part-time staff whose continuing professional development needs are hard to meet because of their lack of proximity or shared space. The PROWE project, funded by JISC as a joint project with University of Leicester set out to test this premise.

Mapping Potential User Needs

The first task of the project was to map the potential users of any new environment, understand their relationship with technology, and their perceptions of online community. Volunteers were sought from among serving tutors by means of placing a news item on the front page of the TutorHome Web site which is the portal used by all tutors to access their online activities and resources. Participants for two focus groups were then chosen randomly from within the large group of volunteers who responded. Later a questionnaire e-survey was developed using the core focus group questions and sent to those volunteers who had not attended focus groups. A wide diversity of participants was represented in the focus groups. The volunteer group had an average length of service of 7 years, but this masked a range of experience from over 20 years to just a few months. They ranged from technologically innovative individuals to self-confessed "technophobes."

Somewhat surprisingly all but one of the volunteer tutors had broad-band access to the Internet at home. This was true even for those tutors who reported using the Internet for e-mail and basic level online discus-sion groups only. Some tutors had experience of using Wikis and other online tools; a few had personal blogs and one had a Web site of resources that he used to provide his students with access to online resource materi-als. Most tutors reported storing their teaching resources, tutorial notes and handouts on their home PCs, some used key or stick storage devices. Only two tutors had any previous experience of mobile learning devices such as Palms or PDAs.

Participants all expressed the wish for more interaction with other tutors and for more sharing of knowledge and resources. Many reported a lack of time for collaborative activity. One particular issue of concern was whether or not authors would be able to retain ownership of original materials while also offering them up for others to develop in new directions. Some were concerned about how they would continue to access the materials they would be sharing and expressed the view that they would wish to store them on their own personal computers. There was optimism about the possibility of developing a shared repository. However, ease of access and integration with other tutor activity and software would be critical. Simply put, using any new environment would need to become an effortless and integral part of the work of being a tutor and to better serve existing needs, or real needs that are not yet being met. Regarding the content that might be developed in shared space, this would relate to common issues potentially of concern to tutors whether course related or across disciplines.

Most respondents thought that there was potential in the new tools to support their continuing professional development needs. The diversity of opinions collected suggested commonalities would be difficult to find but interest in new communications tools was widespread. Many observations about potential uses complemented ideas expressed about virtual communities already in place at the university.

Mapping Potential Tools

Having developed a profile of potential user needs and wishes, the PROWE project looked next at the tools available to meet those needs. Software solutions already exist for most of the activities that tutors would wish to undertake. However, not all are available in any one particular Wiki or Wiki-type environment, or, where they are grouped together there are other issues to be considered—such as security, authentication, or storage capacity. Most Wikis are completely open, accessible to anyone, and thus are liable to interference or spam attack unless security is imposed, defeating the openness that such environments can facilitate. This vulnerability also makes them unsuitable for stable long-term repository use. Furthermore, Wiki principles, which allow any user to edit entries, make it difficult to store multiple fixed and noneditable versions of documents: a feature that would be required in order to ensure that contributors did not lose control of their original contributions.

Consideration of several dozen possible software programs of varying degrees of complexity and from both open source and commercial developers led to the choice of the open source product elgg (www.elgg.net) for testing because it offered the following features within a single online environment:

1. Repository potential, individually and for groups, and supporting multiple file and data formats

2. A collaborative structure where subcommunities can be created by any individual user or users

3. Allows the access permissions for all postings and files to be determined by authors on an item-by-item basis—options include private owner only access, as well as degrees of public access and therefore users remain in control of how accessible their work is to others

4. It supports storage of multiple versions of resources and does not compromise or delete original material in the course of version development

5. It supports personal and group, or community, reflection (and is thus a cornerstone of CPD)

6. It has community building resources, for example, a calendar and potential for a community Wiki in addition to blog and file space.

Since it was open source, it was unsupported but it was also potentially much more flexible. The biggest disadvantage was that it required frequent updating and was still very much under development. This was acceptable for PROWE purposes as this was a research endeavor but might not have been so if the project had wanted to invest in a more permanent, longer term solution.

Challenges and Barriers to Use

It has been a major challenge to develop an environment that can offer enough security with respect to access and the integrity of inputs to inspire the trust and confidence of its users. It needed to be flexible enough to encourage widespread uptake in order to ensure that it endured as a stable, secure, and supportive environment. Another challenge for the project was to link the development of repository deposited resources to individuals and not just to the institution in which they were presently teaching. This issue was not resolved but would be critical for any future development of such a system, either at the OU or elsewhere, because in order to ensure sustainability users need to continue to contribute materials. Providing long-term storage and recognition and thus supporting continued professional development over a career that may span multiple institutional affiliations without the need to keep moving resources, is one way of doing this.

Barriers to use of the PROWE environment at the OU were chiefly individual rather than technical or institutional. Expectations varied as to how the environment and its resources would be used. The biggest constraint was the effect of individuals' personal resource management strategies. Highly personal and individual, many practices had arisen in response to experience rather than deliberate strategy. Some influential experiences for participants related to past misadventures, for example a tutor who having lost data many years ago persisted in printing out anything with reuse potential and stored it in a cardboard folder. Other tutors reported that the only place they felt materials were safe was on their personal PC or laptop hard drive—even though these were not necessarily backed up to a level that would actually ensure no loss of the material in the case of any system crash—perception of security was paramount and individual.

There was little willingness to simply experiment with the new tool and see what might be achieved. Mainly this was to do with a perception by users that without specific guidance for using new online resources they "might do something wrong" or "not know what to do," reflecting the cultural expectation within the university that any new tool that is provided for tutor use has already been extensively pretested and will be accompanied by detailed instructions for use.

Looking Forward

Informal repositories such as those that can be developed in Wiki-based environments encourage the formation of communities at the same time as users are sharing and developing resources together. They add a new dimension to our experiences of online CoPs. These tools have potential to support tutor professional development over time, provided users are willing to experiment and invest time and energy in participation. They may be more attractive to time pressed tutors than many formal solutions to resource development because they can offer a lighter touch approach to information sharing and content development—the digital equivalent of sharing a book with a friend rather than trying to hunt down an obscure title via interlibrary loan. Experience with informal repositories may also serve as an introduction to the use of formal repositories such as those now being introduced institutionally and nationally for preservation of research outcomes and learning objects; and to a culture of sharing and reuse. If common technical platforms or software protocols (like the friend of a friend "FOAF" file) can be developed this new knowledge and peer support need not be confined to use in the institution where they originated either, but can move with individuals across institutions as their careers evolve. In sum, the challenges to ensuring sustainable communities using such tools are less technical than social and institutional.

CONCLUSIONS

There is much potential in making provision for the development of online communities for distance tutors. They can fulfil a valuable function in what is otherwise a professionally isolated existence. This chapter has reported on their widespread use at the Open University (UK), both as a central part of course related professional development, and for discussion of wider pedagogical issues such as the use of online media for supporting students. While online forums provide a tried and tested platform to support online discussion within a CoP, new Wiki environments also offer the potential for extending the use of communities to the development and sharing of resources.

Such communities provide a space for tutors with a common interest to develop shared practice in a safe environment. While some members of the group can be active in posting, others benefit from reading of their experience, so the community allows for differing levels of participation, as Wenger (1998) suggests. At the same time, this chapter has illustrated how the purpose of the community and its relationship to the core duties of staff has a major impact on group dynamics and decisions to join or leave the community. The enthusiasm for course related forums reflects the participants' interest in a community centred on issues that matter to them, and this interest probably ensures their sustainability. However, a community with a focus on more generic teaching issues is likely to be more marginal in its appeal, although it may certainly be of interest for the institution wishing to encourage continuous professional development among its tutors. In this case, the plenary group allows for active input by a few enthusiasts, and benefit for many more occasional visitors who read the postings. Such a community probably does not constitute Wenger's (1998) strict definition of a CoP, but it is nevertheless of demonstrable value. In such cases, the usability of the community in terms of where it is situated in relation to core duties is of particular relevance to maximize participation and serendipitous engagement.

Turning to Eraut's (2000) model of nonformal learning this chapter has illustrated how such communities can provide a space for sharing knowledge beyond traditional professional development events. They can contribute to "reactive learning," as members of the community respond with "help on demand" to queries from their peers. This has particular relevance and value for new tutors who are unfamiliar with the demands of the job, but is also helpful for those with more experience. Such communities can also contribute to "implicit learning," as tutors learn the language and culture of working for the institution, or the expectations of a particular faculty.

RECOMMENDATIONS FOR GOOD PRACTICE

The following recommendations for developing online CoPs for distance tutors are intended to provide useful guidance:

- It is worthwhile making provision for staff online communities with a remit for course related discussion, especially if their purpose is close to the core role of the distance tutor. Such communities may be used for sharing resources, interpretation of course materials, marking moderation, and for peer support. They can be sustainable even for small groups, because of their perceived relevance to the job.

- Communities of a more generic nature can also be of value but probably need to be based on larger plenary groups to ensure sustainability and maintain interest. They need to have a well-defined purpose that is of direct relevance to the user group. Consideration could also be given to providing benevolent moderation, in order to provide a welcoming presence, and to ensure that the group adheres to its purpose.

- Both types of community can be particularly appreciated by new tutors or those on new courses as they learn the culture of the institution or faculty, and meet new colleagues. In fact, the communities work well with different levels of engagement, some participants benefiting from reading messages, rather than posting them.

- In terms of usability, such a community should be accessible from the same desktop point as e-mail or any core tools and resources, so that staff regularly "pass" it while on their way to other duties. We see no advantage in placing staff development communities in a separate area to core duties: unless it is part of an accredited course in which staff are required to participate. By the same token, it is important that any discussion is just "one click away"—most staff have little time for complicated procedures, and easily lose interest. The software must be easy to contribute to, and must facilitate interaction. It must also be easy to retrieve and edit materials.

- Finally, the introduction of new platforms for online communities really needs to be innovative in terms of making "old" or recognizable aims easier to achieve, rather than taking users to places they have not yet decided that they want to go. Tools need to inspire confidence in potential users by offering secure access and integrity, and to provide the option for community participants to retain control of their original contributions. They should be sufficiently flexible to offer a variety of options for use, which might include access for students, and provide space for new participants in the community to learn use of these spaces in a nonthreatening way.

REFERENCES

Barab, S., MacKinster, J. G., & Scheckler, R. (2003). Designing system dualities: Characterizing a Web-supported professional development community. *The Information Society, 19*, 237-256.

Bowskill, N., Foster, J., Lally, V., & McConnell, D. (2000). Networked professional development: Issues and strategies in current practice. *The International Journal for Academic Development, 5*(2), 93-106.

Eraut, M. (2002). Non formal learning, implicit learning and tacit knowledge in professional work. In F. Coffield (Ed.), *The necessity of informal learning*. Bristol, England: The Policy Press.

Hewling, A. (2006, April). *PROWE (Personal Repositories: Online Wiki Environment)—a first look*. Paper presented at Networked Learning 2006, Lancaster University, England. Retrieved from, http://www.networkedlearningconference.org.uk/abstracts/pdfs/05Hewling.pdf

Leach, J. (2002). The curriculum knowledge of teachers: an analytic review of large scale national electronic conference environments. *The Curriculum Journal, 13*(1), 87-120.

Macdonald, J. (2006). *Blended learning and online tutoring: a good practice guide*. London: Gower.

Macdonald, J., & Hills, L. (2005). Combining reflective logs with electronic networks for professional development among distance education tutors. *Distance Education, 26*(3), 325-339.

Preece, J. (2000) *Online Communities: Supporting Sociability, Designing Usability*. New York: Wiley.

Sherer, P. D., Shea, T. P., & Kristensen, E. (2003). Online communities of practice: a catalyst for faculty development. *Innovative Higher Education, 27*(3), 183-194.

Wenger, E. (1998). *Communities of practice: Learning, meaning and identity*. Cambridge, MA: Cambridge University Press.

CHAPTER 6

SUPPORTING A DISPERSED COMMUNITY

CoP Development in the Caribbean

Sabine Little

The chapter outlines how the use of technology has helped to provide a framework for and support a community of practice (CoP) in the Caribbean, bringing together practicing teachers and educationalists from several islands, particularly Trinidad and Tobago and St. Lucia. The community is drawn from practitioners originally enrolled on a master's in educational studies at the University of Sheffield, and the program works closely with local institutions to help develop a CoP that allows practitioners to build on local resources and expertise and to draw up local research, rather than being continually reliant on first-world countries for literature and input. The initial facilitation of a CoP adopted an inquiry-based learning (IBL) approach that asked students to work collaboratively on a research project for which they identified research question and methodology, and conducted the actual research, with the aim of establishing working relationships that would outlive the students' involvement with the course.

Communities of Practice: Creating Learning Environments for Educators,
Volume 2, pp. 107–126
Copyright © 2008 by Information Age Publishing
All rights of reproduction in any form reserved.

INTRODUCTION

Does an emerging CoP gain from facilitation and from engaging with the concept of communities of practice (CoPs)? In what ways can technology be used to help a new CoP to establish itself and to cross geographical boundaries? This chapter illustrates how a group of practitioner-learners from the Caribbean used a collaborative inquiry task as part of their MEd studies to ask themselves whether they were, in fact, a CoP. As the term was unknown to most of the learners, this question led to detailed reading around the topic, followed by detailed discussions among the group. For me, the author, who facilitated these discussions, it was fascinating to see how the CoP itself developed in line with the practitioners' growing understanding of the concept and of themselves as members of a community. This chapter seeks to give a background to the context within which the development took place, including the problematization of facilitating online collaboration in a context that has a discouragingly low infrastructure, in an environment where access to technology is frequently limited to one or two computers per institution, and Internet connections are unstable and slow. Following on from the background, the chapter will turn to the CoP itself—using direct quotes taken from students' contributions online, it will seek to illustrate the "added value" of conscious engagement with the concept of an emerging CoP and its facilitation, including a sense of empowerment and excitement for the members involved. The conclusion will draw the main findings together and synthesise them into concrete ideas for practitioners seeking to engage a community of geographically distributed learners with the concepts behind CoPs.

BACKGROUND

Wenger (1998) describes meaning, practice, community, and identity to be the components of a social theory of learning. He stipulates three dimensions of practice that form part of a community, namely "mutual engagement" ("people are engaged in actions whose meanings they negotiate with one another," p. 72), "shared repertoire" (joint negotiated meaning on "routines, words, tools, ways of doing things, stories, gestures, symbols, genres, or concepts," p. 83) and "joint enterprise" (p. 73, see below). If measured against these three dimensions, it could be argued that many, if not all, collaborative learning groups fall into that category. The "joint enterprise" Wenger mentions here becomes a superimposed or mutually negotiated (learning) goal (pp. 78-79), with group members sharing their experiences and knowledge, engaging with each other in order to identify or construct knowledge. Wenger has been criticized for having too idealist a concept of community—see, for example, Fox (2002, 2005), who argues for the term "actor-networks," which includes the consideration for forces—positive and negative—into the collaborative process, and furthermore argues that that nonhuman elements are part of a network in the same way as human participants are. Cousin and Deepwell (2005) have explored the links between CoPs and networked learning environments, and have concluded that both share important aspects of a social theory of learning, relying on "hospitable and peer supportive learner environments' and 'communitarian values" (p. 57). Cousin and Deepwell's article is particularly useful in the extent to which it engages with the fact that networked learning environments are often constructed, rather than having evolved over time, as a CoP might. The authors argue that an externally managed group under teacher control is unlikely to be high on "internal means by which it can congeal into a community of practice" (p. 60), that is, to develop a "shared repertoire" or "joint enterprise." McLoughlin (1999) has published on cultural implication of technology use for online community development within the context of Aboriginal education. In this, she gave examples of differing practices in various countries regarding attitudes towards use of e-mail and chat, confidence in engaging in collaborative tasks, aspects of social networks and issues surrounding learner control. Her approach is particularly relevant aspect to this chapter, where the facilitator and the members in the community were from two different cultures. McLoughlin strongly proposes a constantly negotiated process of communication around shared meanings, supported by outlets for the sharing of experiences and problems, and a strong emphasis on collaboration, all of which were supported in this study.

Today, a learner community need no longer be identified by a joint geographical location, and several authors have identified differences in participants' social behavior, in that they are more willing to share personal feelings and opinions, but also experience less of a connection with (and thus moral obligation towards) their peers (Palloff & Pratt, 1999; Turkle, 1997). Brown (2001) describes a "three-stage phenomenon" in online community building, consisting of "making friends online," "conferring the community," (feeling kinship and satisfaction after long, threaded discussions), and "camaraderie," after long-term involvement in and association with the group on a personal level. Brown's concept of camaraderie seems related to Wenger's concept of "shared repertoire"; however, it can not be assumed that Wenger's model of CoPs effortlessly translates into an online environment. When it is taken into account that communication takes place through a technological medium, it is far more likely that collaboration will need to be facilitated, on a flexible scale, handing over more and more responsibility to the group. Gläsmann (2006) discusses a concept of "peer cognizance," which is of relevance as a first step towards CoP development and will be further outlined below.

The "Local" Context

The context for the CoP that provides the basis for this chapter consists of a group of 70 practicing educationalists from the Caribbean islands of Trinidad and Tobago and St. Lucia, enrolled on an MEd in educational studies provided by the University of Sheffield. The university's involvement in the Caribbean dates back to the late 1980s, when a group of teachers approached the school of education to request a tailored course in special needs education (Armstrong, 2001). From this original involvement grew a Caribbean program that entails the MEd, an action research certificate, an EdD program and a remote location PhD. The modules offered on these courses continue to be developed and adapted based on the students' needs, and the university supports the development of local educational research by hosting a number of conferences, allowing students to present their work, and attended by students and local educationalists alike. The aim of the program as a whole is the support of a local community of practice, allowing students to communicate with each other, share best practice, and engage in peer review and peer support, as well as providing local educationalists with the skills and knowledge to add to the educational research base in the Caribbean. The link between a community of learners and a work-related CoP has been discussed by Stacey, Smith, and Barty (2004), and finding ways in which the CoP could translate and continue across to the students' world of work was a constant deliberation of the course design.

In 2004, the program sought to integrate WebCT as a virtual learning environment (VLE), continuing to work closely with the students to identify ways in which technology could be used to support their learning experience. A survey conducted with all students on the MEd program at the time received a response rate of 86% (68 responses). Asked what they were hoping to get out of an increased use of technology, the main response was "access to online journals" (75% of responses). As this service was already available to students, the survey served to identify a miscommunication, which was subsequently addressed through a tailored training session. All other responses; however, were related to the increase of communication, namely "opportunity to stay in closer contact with university tutors" (54%), "forming a discussion unit with other students and sharing thoughts and work" (50%), and "opportunity to stay in closer contact with local tutors" (44%).

Based on this survey, the use of WebCT as a VLE was piloted with students enrolled on the optional "ICT and Education" module, on the basis that these students were considered to possess both the technological skills and the local knowledge to help make the VLE accessible to all students for the following year. As the module was optional, it led to the pilot being conducted with 21 students—15 in St. Lucia and 6 in Trinidad and Tobago. The design of the pilot was in the form of free discussions to which both groups of students (i.e., in Trinidad and Tobago, and in St. Lucia) had access. These free discussions had been requested by students, who wanted an opportunity to share thoughts relating to their work and practice both within their own cohort and across islands. In reality, however, there was little uptake, and only two students (one from each island) developed a brief inter-island rapport that lasted three full exchanges (i.e., six messages).

The evaluation of the VLE (completed in face-to-face focus groups) showed that students had little awareness of the concept of a CoP, although their concept of "community" was very strong. Students felt that they needed additional support in their discussions, and saw the VLE as an opportunity for the group to engage with some of the more generic aspects of educational research and the place their community held within it, as well as the concept of collaboration and CoP.

Based on this feedback, it was decided to roll out the VLE during the following year's educational research module (taught to the following cohort), which was compulsory and included a collaborative research element, thus inviting the problematization of the terminology and detailed engagement with the concept of CoP. The main body of the chapter outlines how the VLE was designed to try to encourage students to consciously reflect on their role within a collaborative research community and, following on from this, a CoP.

DESIGNING FOR A COMMUNITY

In order to support the emergence of collaborative educational research in the Caribbean, the module already required students to work in groups of three to five students in order to identify a research question, conduct the research, and write it up. The assignment completed for the module consists of a research report and a reflection on the research process, including the collaborative aspect. In designing the VLE, it was intended to illustrate to students that the collaborative part of the module was more than a research exercise, and that each group was only part of a larger CoP, consisting of all participating students as well as colleagues in the respective places of work, regardless of the geographical location. To achieve this goal, it seemed necessary to drive the students' thoughts to a point where they felt comfortable engaging with the concept of a CoP. Part of the issue is a reported reliance upon visiting lecturers for guidance, based on a perceived higher quality of education received there. Identifying the value of experience located within the student community was therefore part of the design, and students were encouraged to see themselves as inquiring practitioners with the right to hold and defend a position on any issue discussed. The module was taught in a face-to-face 1 week block in January, where the VLE was introduced. Following a generic welcome and meet-and-greet discussion, four structured discussions were scheduled roughly 3 to 4 weeks apart, giving students the space to build on these discussions through the development of their own topics. The four discussion topics chosen were positionality/validity, community of practice, research methodology, and reflection and evaluation. Each topic was further used to develop a stepped approach towards information literacy (IL), that is, encouraging the students to take on more and more responsibility for identifying the resources they would need to support their argument. In parallel to the full cohort discussions, each collaborative research group had a private discussion area they could use to plan and discuss their specific research project. Whenever student comments are used below, these were drawn from the full cohort discussions, and pseudonyms have been used throughout. The design of the environment has been summarised in Figure 6.1.

Visually, the design was kept deliberately "low-tech" in order to avoid long download times, while trying to instil in students a sense of ownership through the use of some local photographs (see Figure 6.2).

In the following section, each discussion topic will be outlined briefly, including some of the contributions students made to the discussions, before their comments on CoP development are highlighted further.

Discussion Topic: Positionality/Validity

Students had been given readings and had been encouraged to think of themselves within the context of their own research and practice. They were then asked to share their positionality with the group as a whole, and to consider how this positionality might affect their collaboration with others. Discussion quickly centered on issues the students perceived to arise out of different backgrounds among the group; however, many groups quickly discovered synergies and common ground, as well as a common goal. Although they did not use Wenger's (1998) terminology, students were, in effect, coming to realize that they were part of a CoP. Anette, one of the students, remarks:

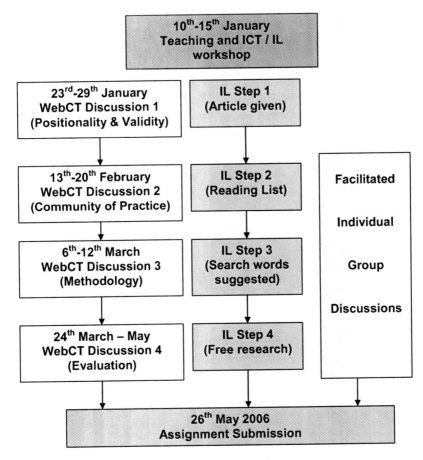

Figure 6.1.   Design of collaborative online environment.

I believe that every parent must help children to exercise their right to education and that they have the responsibility to provide a nurturing environment for these children in order for them to be successful ... this means that parents and schools must work collaboratively.

The schools under investigation are located in rural areas. Group members are on staff at either one of the schools or the other. This gives each person an equal opportunity to do insider research. It also allows for a fair amount of collaboration since data collection has to be done at both schools. Tasks have been set to individual members who have so far been very effective and efficient in carrying them out. (Anette)

At the time this discussion took place, students were still finalizing their exact research topics, and the discussion on positionality required

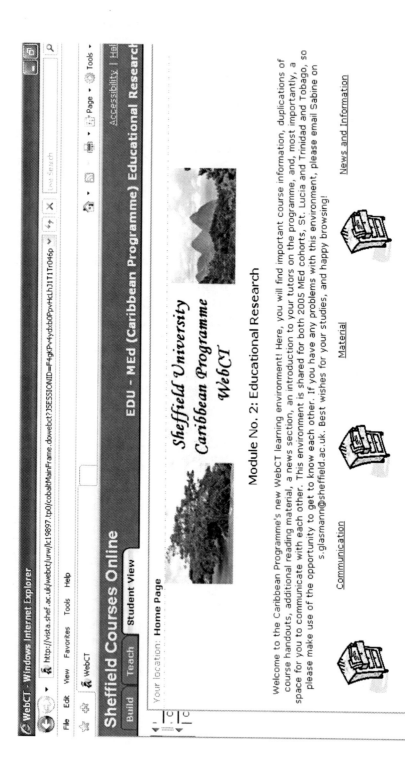

Figure 6.2. Screenshot of main page of the VLE.

them to consider their standing within the group, as well as what the group wanted to achieve as a whole. Effectively, students were beginning to identify a shared language, within which shared meanings were situated. This meant that, by the time students engaged in the second facilitated discussion, they were more used to engaging in mutual discussion surrounding their collaboration, finding it easier to recognize the concept of CoP within their own group.

Discussion Topic: Community of Practice

Students were given Wenger's (1998) definition of a CoP, as well as further articles (Ashwin, 2003; Renshaw, 2003; and Stahl, 2000). They were then asked to engage with these readings from the point of view of their own collaboration. One student remarks,

> Identifying the strengths of individuals and building on them has worked well for my group. By the end of the first meeting, we had chosen a leader and decided on our modus operandi. The group has since worked very well to the extent that we are almost inseparable. Whether we qualify as a community of practice is debatable, however, the argument forwarded by Lesser and Scorch (2001) [sic] that authority in a community of practice emerge through interaction and that communities develop their processes seem applicable to our situation.
> The present working relationship is supported by Lave and Wenger (1991, p. 98) who note that members of a community of practice are involved in a set of relationships over time. (Margaret)

I would argue that Margaret's comment is remarkable insofar that it is probably rare for a CoP to engage in such detail with the question whether they are, in fact, a CoP. Historically, the students involved in the study showed little willingness to criticize established literature (or indeed anything published!). One complaint brought forward consistently by tutors was that students by and large held the printed word as gospel, including sources found on the Internet. Yet, in engaging with the concept of CoP, Candice, another student points out:

> In my group I believe our success would largely depend on how well each of us are able to mutually engage each other to arrive at the shared repertoire of ideas, commitments, and vision.
> My only concern is that while the theory behind a "community of practice" does have its merit the time frame to achieve these goals would vary for each group to become a team and so for us in doing this module time is of the essence. Hence, my question, "Does this theory present some limitations by being too idealistic?" (Candice)

A deliberate strategy not to provide any literature antagonistic to Wenger had been used with the aim that students could familiarize themselves with the practicalities of the concept within their own context. It appears that situating the concept within their own environment finally gave students the freedom to criticize an established author, simply because his theory and their reality did not match, and this student was quick to identify the point already raised by writers in the field (see e.g., Fox, 2002, 2005).

Seeing themselves as a CoP provided a sense of empowerment, leading to the following discussion post, which was left in response to Candice's post above. Here, Anette gives some reason as to why she believes the student cohort does in fact constitute a CoP:

> Finally, we are all practitioners. Whatever we find out theoretically can be shared with other practitioners so that the gap between theory and practice can be bridged (Carr, 1995). Furthermore, we have a responsibility to communicate our findings directly to those involved (Robson, 2002) so that we can better our education system. (Anette)

In personal communication, it quickly becomes clear that students perceive both a strong desire and a strong responsibility to improve education in their respective countries. Being asked to engage with the concept of CoP initially on a smaller scale (i.e., within the course cohort) allowed students to explore the idea in relatively safe surroundings and facilitated by the collaborative structures in place for their learning experience. The online discussions allowed students furthermore to expand their community into the entire cohort of students, which logistically and geographically allowed for a representation of staff (i.e., students) from many schools on the island. Rather than being overwhelmed by the size of the education system, the facilitated environment allowed for a gradual increase in engagement and understanding, and supported those students interested in maintaining their CoP beyond the lifecycle of the module.

Thus, each student was encouraged to see themselves as part of a community of costudents and a community of staff employed by one particular school. Jointly, this meant that students explored the idea of a CoP of education practitioners on one Caribbean island; however, the combination of two islands (Trinidad and Tobago and St. Lucia) furthermore allowed them to engage in discussions that involved boundary-crossing Caribbean issues. This development of an awareness of CoPs on various levels was complex, and involved a coherent understanding of the various levels of collaboration and communication that others brought to the community. In fact, the way most students began to engage with the concept of CoP was through the concept of "peer cognizance":

a conscious recognition or awareness of others, an understanding of what we ourselves and those around us can know or understand, an observance and notice of others' behaviors and needs, and the acknowledgement of responsibility for those around us. As such, "peer cognisance" ties the individual to the social, combining individual and social needs to a mutually beneficial relationship. (Gläsmann, 2006, p. 229)

Once students had developed a sense of peer cognizance, it seems they felt ready to evolve into a CoP, although they themselves were now becoming critical of the term and when it could actually be applied, as further examples below will show.

Discussion Topic: Methodology

The discussion on methodology was intended to help students understand their choice of method for their research project; however, it simultaneously asked them to engage with the idea of the impact their research might have, and how their choice of methods reflected on ethical considerations. Furthermore, the discussion sought to invite students to read about research methods in greater detail, once more seeking to engage them to review their own collaborative research critically. In identifying the difficulties of research, the community aspect did not go unmentioned, as Virginia's long message below illustrates:

> When we stressed over the ethical review forms that we were required to fill out, it turned out that the considerations emphasized on those very forms, were the ones which assisted us in structuring our questionnaire. It took our group at least four grueling hours to complete the questionnaire. (Virginia)

Virginia uses the discussion board to share with the entire cohort her small group's approach to research, an approach that was echoed by other participants. It is clear how small group face-to-face discussions are involved in drawing together the research process:

> We have completed a pilot survey of the questionnaire, the results of which have been analyzed. These results led us into another round of deliberation where adaptations to the questionnaire were concerned based on the responses from the respondents.
> The ethical review forms, once thought to be time-consuming turned out to be a vital part of our research process. I am looking forward to working further with my group as we delve deeper into our study as we will require the strengths of each member. Our study involves a cross-sectional approach, that is, a sample chosen across three educational levels, early childhood, primary, and secondary. (Virginia)

It is interesting in the post above is both Virginia's description of her smaller group and the way in which members rely on each other to come to terms with the research process, and her awareness of the larger community, who might not be aware of the terminology (e.g., "cross-sectional approach"), and her immediate willingness to widen the scope for discussion by providing an explanation that will draw others in. Virginia also describes her CoP and how it changes as the group carries out the research:

> Our community of practice appears to be growing as we share our experiences and thoughts on the methods chosen, literature which can inform any aspect of our study and words of strength which may evoke laughter when we begin to experience the stress of the educational research process. (Virginia)

The research is seen as a group effort that requires mutual input and "the strengths of each member" to succeed. There is a sense of easiness to the collaboration, despite the reference to frustrating experiences. A sense of peer cognisance, if maybe not quite a CoP, is developing. The strong narrative tradition of the Caribbean students is often represented in the postings, giving detailed accounts of collaborative efforts. Karen illustrated how individual beliefs had to be combined in an effort to settle on a method:

> At first, my group thought that selecting our research method was a fairly easy task. After all, we all knew about interviews, questionnaires observation use of documents. When it came to justifying our chosen method, we met a lot of ticklish corners. Some wanted a questionnaire; others interviews ... everyone came with their justifications and we settled on two, the interview and observation. The process was not as simple as we had initially thought! (Karen)

Students spent a long time discussing their methodology, challenging each other's opinions and attitudes, though largely in their own, private face-to-face environments. When such challenge took place online, it was conducted in a circumspect, professional yet positive manner, highlighting good points as well as those that were to be challenged. Those challenged in this way responded in kind, encouraging a level of professional communication students had not engaged in before, and helping them to develop a shared language.

Discussion Topic: Evaluation and Reflection

Again, this discussion was intended to serve a number of purposes. On the one hand, students were asked to engage with their collaboration on a reflective level, and this reflection formed a considerable part of their assignment. In the past, reflections had occasionally veered into pointing fingers and describing in great detail how individual members hampered the group, without analyzing reasons, responses, or alternatives. Although students would not be submitting their actual posts in the assignment, it was believed that making reflection the focus of a discussion week would allow students to think more creatively and constructively about their collaborative research experience. At the same time, the week's discussion was used to gain students' views on the online experience as a whole, in order to take their views into account when future modules were planned.

At this point, students had mainly settled into the routine of providing references for their thoughts, but also to use each other as a resource for reflection and learning. Comments for this discussion reached the same lengths as those on CoPs, and again, many of the posts referenced the sense of community the students felt. David, one of the students, summarized the experience as follows:

> This group "Collaborative" research assignment has been very rewarding for me as part of my group. Four persons with varied backgrounds, life experiences, professional experiences, positions, and with varied philosophy of life came (were placed) together to pursue a common goal. For me, I was working with those persons for the first time. Initially there was trepidation as the grounds were tested, impressions created and working relationships established. Very important was the mutual acceptance and respect established from the beginning. Now our group has blossomed into a closely knit learning entity. We have started the makings of a "community of practice" and we have all expressed the desire for this to continue long after this module and the course is completed. (David)

It seems students recognize that a CoP might begin via a constructed task, but that any prolonged link and activity bringing stability are likely to occur through the group finding their own purpose, definition, and goal. One student, Dana, made a very clear separation between group, team and CoP, and illustrated her group's development:

> I understood from the get go that we were only a group and not a team until according to (Levin, 2005) "You have developed methods of working together and relationships have been formed between you i.e. through collaboration, you have begun to 'bond' and develop team spirit.' A 'community of practice' was only established after this 'bond' was created, after several group meetings in which we got to know each others' weaknesses, strengths and even some personal information.... However, I have learned that doing research affords me the opportunity to (according to Sikes 2005) 'make the world a better place' by inquiring, reporting and making recommendations that would be beneficial to the education system." (Dana)

The sense of pride and ownership came to the forefront again, but it also seemed that in reflecting on their engagement with collaboration, students found it easier to make the leap from seeing themselves as students to seeing themselves as researchers, as illustrated by Peter's comment:

> We view ourselves as a "community of researchers"—sharing each other's strengths for the common goal—to improve on our professional practice.

It is clear that students, through their engagement with their reading and with each other arrived at a working understanding of the concept of CoP, and that they saw themselves at varying stages of CoP development. The collaborative research aspect of the module, however, was not new, and yet past cohorts had not made the link between what they were reading and their own involvement before. Asking students to consider their role as part of a CoP was part of the new introductions to the module, as were the timed, focused online discussions. The section below seeks to outline in what way the form the discussions took may have influenced the CoP development.

FACILITATION OF DISCUSSIONS

All discussions were supported by a facilitator who knew all students personally and face-to-face from study schools—which potentially sets this virtual CoP apart from others. In facilitating the discussions, however, the facilitator was faced with a problem. On the one hand, students were experienced practitioners who doubtless had their own opinions, strategies as learners, and views on collaboration; on the other hand, very few of the students had used online discussions before, and none of them WebCT. Paired with the geographical distance, how could the facilitator make sure students would participate, and see the value of the exercise beyond the difficulty of getting to grips with the technology?

Initially, the face-to-face session at the study school proved to be the answer. In a 3-hour session, all students learned to access the university library and to post a message on WebCT (and, in some cases, to open a Web browser, write a message in Word or send an e-mail). Slotting the four focused discussions into various weeks of the timetable served some technical considerations, too, namely to allow students without access to arrange this well in advance, and to ensure a suitable time span between discussions in case some students had problems, so they would not miss the discussions. All this was done to allow for as smooth an establishment of an online community as possible.

The facilitation itself consisted largely of encouraging students to explore the resources within the group and the entire cohort, rather than expecting answers. As such, the facilitator effectively sought to support (IBL) within the community. This method of bouncing questions and issues back was initially intended to support IBL, but had the added effect that students began to see and engage with each other as experts with different strengths and experiences, all of value to the joint enterprise they were engaged in. This form of teaching is not particularly well-known in the Caribbean, and Virginia explains her attitude as follows:

> What I appreciated most about this form of engagement is that we the students owned the discussions although we were facilitated by you. In this way, the issues and tasks which were brought into focus did not appear too cumbersome to undertake. It was a novel way for us to engage in discourse with fellow educationalists outside of the sometimes foreboding atmosphere of the classroom. (Virginia)

Another aspect that the facilitator had initially thought of as a barrier was her "unfamiliarity" with the context within which the student community lived and worked. While she had visited schools, and obviously had long communications with students and was privy to their writings, she could by no means be said to be an expert in Caribbean education. Asking for clarification when she did not understand a reference or comment meant that students had a chance to explore their own community in greater detail, through the process of having to explain it for an outsider. In this way, they were gently encouraged to see concepts and ideas within context, helping them to establish shared experiences and a shared language for their CoP.

FUTURE TRENDS

The message from this chapter is not so much a future trend, but a future journey—after spending an entire module asking students to work collaboratively and to consider the concept of a CoP, where do they want to go? One student cited above has already clarified that the journey needs to continue as far as she is concerned, that it needs to survive the framework of the module. In their feedback, nearly all students supported that:

> this forum should be encouraged and should be extended to other modules as well. (Peter)

The future of the students' CoP was addressed as early as half way through the module, during the discussion on methodology. Following a particularly enthusiastic posting, the facilitator commented:

> What will be interesting to see is how the collaboration will help you with your more individual work on your dissertations (and future assignments), and whether you might even be able to find a way to continue your community of practice once you revert back to individual assignments—calling on each other to bounce ideas off, share literature, etc.—what do you think will happen? (Sabine)

This direct question sparked the following response:

> After this research assignment, I do hope to continue being a part of a community of practice sharing views, literature, and the like, with my colleagues. I believe that the only [way] we gain some perspective on our thoughts is if we allow ourselves to explore those of others.
>
> Knowledge was designed to be shared, for if it is kept to onself [sic] there is no growth in understanding and the development of concepts is at-risk where its evolution is concerned.
>
> One of the most effective ways in which I personally learn and develop my thoughts is through discourse with others, including those who are not in the field of education. (Virginia)

Extending the community beyond the cohort also plays a role in Peter's contribution to the discussion: "past students should be encouraged to contribute to this forum since they have a wealth of knowledge and experiences which could prove beneficial to us." This suggestion, if implemented, would widen the circle of the participating community considerably, spanning not only further schools and other institutions in the education system, but also working across the cohorts of the MEd degree program, blurring the line between assessed parts of the course and CoP further. This CoP, if it continues beyond the life of the course, is young, and the immediate need is for it to become self-sufficient, rather than to rely on a Western (or any) tutor for input. In reality, however, it is felt that the engagement with the concept of CoP and the provision of a virtual platform has merely given shape and purpose to an already existing community, one that it is hoped will continue to thrive.

CONCLUSION AND RECOMMENDATIONS

As outlined above, the development of a CoP among practitioners in the Caribbean was not down to the facilitator—it was the students' effort that made the venture a success. Although officially a "tutor" and "facilitator," a more accurate description would maybe be that of a more experienced community member—not a community of Caribbean teachers, but a community of practitioners who are hoping to have a positive impact on the education system. Seen from this position, the facilitator learned as much from the students involved in the study as they learned from me, if not more. Attempting to summarise these experiences and turn them into quick-and-easy guidelines appears to belittle the effort the students exerted into making the environment their own, and the successes they experienced. Despite technological difficulties, all students commented positively on the experience the online discussions awarded them with, and the challenges they had to consider. Praise was attributed to group members and the entire cohort, as well as the facilitation process (see above).

Although the example for this CoP is located in the Caribbean, there seem to be opportunities to expand on the experience in a far wider context—the following paragraphs aim to illustrate how some of the lessons learned may be adapted.

- A willingness to engage with the idea of a CoP, if not necessarily the terminology, can have a considerable impact on CoP development.

One aspect inherent to this CoP was the fact that discussion surrounding CoP development was firmly embedded in the facilitation process. Allowing students to trace their own development against the literature meant that they had an immediate, practical example that made it easier for them to challenge literature.

- Online support is vital, but will probably largely focus on 'bouncing back' questions aimed at receiving a straightforward answer for complex problems—discussing these in the group helps to develop the CoP.

Not supplying answers allowed students to recognize that their own opinions were valuable, and that the development of their knowledge was not necessarily dependent on one member, which they perceived to be more knowledgeable. This development encourages an IBL approach, which is vital if a community is to become self-reliant and independent. Throughout discussions, there is an ongoing trend of students relying more and more on each other than on the tutor, culminating in the positive response during the evaluation discussion, where students acknowledged that they "owned" the discussion (Virginia, see above).

- A sense of "peer cognizance" can precede the development of a CoP.

During the discussion around the concept of CoPs and CoP development, students quickly recognised that the more aware they became of each other's strengths, needs and knowledge, the easier the collaborative process became. This seems to illustrate that the facilitation of "peer cognizance" can, in fact, assist with CoP development.

- If the facilitation occurs from a facilitator who is a stranger to the culture in which the CoP is developing, pointing out that "strangeness" can help practitioners to engage with their own context in more detail, thus developing a better understanding of the community they themselves are part of, and developing a shared language and shared experiences.

It is often said that one truly understands something if one is able to explain it to somebody else. Being a stranger to the environment allowed the facilitator to ask questions that were genuine, in that she was not expecting a "correct" answer and truly did not know all of the circumstances under which the collaborative research process took place. This allowed students to explain their environment, leading to discussions and reflections that would not have occurred had these circumstances been taken 'as read' and gone unquestioned. The approach is again linked to IBL, asking students to actively reflect on and question the status quo within which they operate. The "strangeness" also allowed the facilitator to take a reflective stance on the entire process, prompting the question on sustainability cited in the section on "Future Trends" above. Although the focus here is on cultural differences; however, on closer inspection, it is in fact true that the facilitator of an online environment is rarely aware of the full circumstances under which others participate, making the approach transferable across a wide range of environments.

- If access is a problem, an initial plan for communication can help those without access to arrange alternatives—once the advantages of regular access are understood (e.g., enhanced communication with colleagues, higher motivation), this plan could be abandoned.

Technical difficulties do not feature excessively in this chapter, despite the fact that they presented the largest organizational problem encountered. The clear outlines of when communication would take place allowed students to plan their access, minimizing problems. Furthermore, however, it also meant that there was a concentration of messages at certain times; making collaboration more fruitful, as going through the trouble of gaining access was usually rewarded with a high number of contributions to read.

The CoP described in this chapter is largely part of a prescribed degree program, and one that seems to include only a small percentage of the potential membership, for example, the teaching community. In reality, however, engagement with the discussions the students had went much further—the research undertaken impacted on other members of staff in schools, and, through detailed engagement with ethics, on parents and pupils. The topics of the research itself integrated further members into the community—an overview of teacher stress levels in one case, parental involvement in education in another. In facilitating a community of learning that actively engaged with the concept of CoP, the first steps have been taken in establishing the CoP itself. The next step to be taken is for the outside facilitation to cease, and for the CoP to carry on through its own momentum and belief in itself as a driving force and an agent of change in the Caribbean.

REFERENCES

Armstrong, D. (2001). Developing the potential for distance learning modalities for teacher education. In A. C. Armstrong (Ed.), *Rethinking teacher professionalism in the Caribbean context: Conference proceedings 8th to 9th January 2001*. Sheffield, England: School of Education.

Ashwin, P. (2003). Peer facilitation and how it contributes to a more social view of learning. *Research in post-compulsory education, 8*(1), 5-18.

Brown, R. (2001). The process of community-building in distance learning classes. *Journal of Asynchronous Learning Networks, 5*(2). Retrieved January 30, 2006, from http://www.sloan-c.org/publications/jaln/v5n2/v5n2_brown.asp

Carr, W. (1995). *For education: Towards critical educational inquiry.* Buckingham, England: Open University Press.

Cousin, G., & Deepwell, F. (2005). Designs for network learning: a community of practice approach. *Studies in Higher Education, 30*(1), 57-66.

Fox, S. (2002). Networks and communities: An actor-network critique of ideas on community and implications for networked learning. In S. Banks, P. Goodyear, V. Hodgson, & D. McConnell (Eds), *Networked learning conference proceedings* (pp. 110-118). Lancaster and Sheffield, England: University of Sheffield.

Fox, S. (2005). An actor-network critique of community in higher education: implications for networked learning. *Studies in Higher Education, 30*(1), 95-110.

Gläsmann, S. (2006). *The concept of peer cognisance: Exploring participants' experiences of collaboration in a networked learning project* Unpublished PhD thesis. England: University of Sheffield.

Lave, J., & Wenger, E. (2001). *Situated learning: Legitimate peripheral participation*. London: Cambridge University Press.

Lesser, E. L., & Storck, J. (2001). Communities of practice and organizational performance. *IBM Systems Journal, 40*(4). Retrieved December 7, 2006, from http://www.research.ibm.com/journal/sj/404/lesser.html

Levin, P. (2005). *Successful teamwork! For undergraduates and taught postgraduates working on group projects*. Maidenhead, England: Open University Press.

McLoughlin, C. (1999). Culturally responsive technology use: Developing an online community of learners. *British Journal of Educational Technology, 30*(3), 231-243.

Palloff, R. M., & Pratt, K. (1999). *Building learning communities in cyberspace: effective strategies for the online classroom* San Francisco: Jossey-Bass.

Renshaw, P. D. (2003). Community and Learning: Contradictions, dilemmas and prospects. *Discourse, 24*(3), 355-370.

Robson, C. (2002). *Real world research: A resource for social scientists and practitioner-researchers* (2nd ed.) Oxford, England: Blackwell.

Sikes, P. (2005). *Unit 2: Life history workshop. Course material MEd educational studies, module 2: Educational research, Caribbean programme*. Sheffield, England: University of Sheffield.

Stacey, E., Smith, P. J., & Barty, K. (2004). Adult Learners in the Workplace: Online learning and communities of practice. *Distance Education, 25*(1), 107-123.

Stahl, G. (2000). A model of collaborative knowledge-building. In B. Fishman & S. O'Connor-Divelbiss (Eds.), *Proceedings of the fourth international conference of the learning sciences* (pp. 70-77). Mahwah, NJ: Erlbaum.

Turkle, S. (1997). *Life on the screen: Identity in the age of the Internet* New York: Touchstone.

Wenger, E. (1998). *Communities of practice: Learning, meaning and identity*. London: Cambridge University Press.

CHAPTER 7

VIRTUAL COMMUNITIES OF PRACTICE

A Vehicle for Meaningful Professional Development

Kathy Hibbert

This chapter is about the ways in which structure and design of a virtual learning environment (VLE), combined with deliberate strategies used in the discussion components by teacher educators contributed to the evolution of a virtual community of practice (vCoP) which proved to be a vehicle for meaningful professional development. The vCoP in the study presented here emerged as a way for teacher participants to engage in dialogue about their practice that they reported to be both transforming and transformative. It helped them shift from the role in traditional forms of professional development that casts teachers as "knowledge receivers" to one in which they became "knowledge producers." Strategies for creating conditions that support and sustain a vCoP are discussed, along with participants' responses to engaging in a professional community of practice (CoP). Finally, suggestions for ways in which the vCoP model might be expanded more broadly to serve meaningful teacher professional development are provided.

Communities of Practice: Creating Learning Environments for Educators,
Volume 2, pp. 127–148

INTRODUCTION

Over the past 3 decades, the focus and the substance of professional development in education have undergone significant changes. Technological advancements have introduced both positive and negative developments at a time when the influential National Staff Development Council (NSDC, 2006) in the United States is calling for "All teachers in all schools [to] experience high-quality professional learning as a part of their daily work." Entrepreneurs have tapped into the growing recognition of professional development (PD), promising such ventures as PD on demand, delivered to your desktop. Publishers of educational resources seek to expand their markets to encompass the PD that surrounds the implementation of their materials—effectively controlling the information communicated to teachers, and ensuring a renewable customer base. At the same time, school districts struggle to respond to a steady stream of government mandates. In the hierarchical structure of educational institutions, such mandates too often result in "top-down" delivery models of "training." For reasons that include insufficient time and resources, school districts resort to the adoption of training models that prove to be efficient delivery systems, but inefficient and ineffective forms of meaningful PD.

The adoption of training models to satisfy teacher PD needs can create a destructive dichotomy. Despite initiatives that ask teachers to consider developing engaging teaching and learning environments in their classroom, a traditional transmission model remains firmly entrenched with respect to teachers' learning. Such deficit forms of teacher professional development ignore current research in the field, which suggests,

> the new approach to professional development is more constructivist than transmission-oriented - the recognition that both prospective and experienced teachers (like all learners) bring prior knowledge and experience to all new learning situations which are social and specific. In addition, it is now generally understood that teacher learning takes place over time rather than in isolated moments in time, and that active learning requires opportunities to link previous knowledge with prior understandings. (Cochran-Smyth & Lytle, 2001, pp. 45-46)

Teachers, like many professional practitioners, possess various types of knowledge about their work they are not always able to articulate, and which is too often not acknowledged in packaged training programs that ignore the diversity of learners. The need to develop a scholarship of teaching and learning to document and learn from teachers' knowledge has long been called for (Shulman, 1987). Unlike many professions, teachers are provided insufficient occasions to deliberate about or reflect upon their practice with informed colleagues. Opportunities to make their practical and often "tacit" knowledge explicit (and therefore subject to examination and revision) within a supportive community of educators can allow teachers to engage in issues in ways that improve their practice.

An online vCoP structure can provide such a space for teachers to identify, articulate and examine their theories-in-use (Schön, 1983). In a recent case study researching teachers' interactions in the online environment, the formation of a vCoP emerged to offer several important functions. Through a process of mapping and analysis, the study illustrates the ways in which a vCoP first emerged and then functioned as a powerful means to help teachers shift from individual concerns with personal or micro issues to broader complexities at a macrolevel. At the same time, teachers were able to focus in depth on issues of immediacy and relevance to their daily practice in a supportive community of professional colleagues. The collaboration, as described in this chapter, contributed to an understanding of how the two relate and interact, one upon the other. It is through interactions with peers in a professional context that an individual teacher's knowledge, attitudes and skills can be brought into focus, and a culture of mutual respect and deeper understanding of professional practice can occur.

BRINGING VIRTUAL LEARNING TOGETHER WITH THE CoP CONCEPT

Virtual learning has increasingly become the medium of choice for adult learners who are actively involved in work, community or family situations, but seeking to further their education. Much debate currently exists around the capacity of the virtual environment to support the kinds of complex interaction desired in a teaching/learning environment (Hewson & Hughes, 2001, Hibbert & Rich, 2006).

Those of us working in the field of virtual learning environments (VLEs) have a responsibility to our institutions, and more importantly to our students to ensure that appropriate conditions for meaningful and engaging learning are met. Recent research suggests that popular online delivery systems "are designed to support only knowledge acquisition [resulting in] ... student outcomes ... restricted to reproductive learning" (Jonassen, 2002, p. 76). However, the process of writing, teaching, and researching courses online revealed more complex forms of teaching and learning that led to the conceptualization of the VLE as a CoP. The vCoP concept included both a space and a means for teachers to come together as professionals and work collaboratively to make sense of the continually shifting landscape and expectations that have come to be hallmarks of education.

The term CoP originated with Lave and Wenger (1991). Wenger (1998) took the concept further and suggested "engagement in social practice is the fundamental process by which we learn and so become who we are." From this, he developed a CoP model that places learning in the context of our lives as we participate in social practices. Practice is defined as a source of community coherence: indigenous enterprise, regime of mutual accountability, and shared repertoire. Wenger's model posits that meaning is derived through the negotiation of two main components, participation, and reification. Further, he examines the potential for a CoP to impact on this negotiated meaning, suggesting a need to respect the informed contributions of all members.

TEACHER PROFESSIONAL DEVELOPMENT IN AN ERA OF EFFICIENCY

In the current era of efficiency (Stein, 2001), much of what has been called "professional development" by school districts and governing bodies has been reduced to the transmission of information; the current of knowledge operating primarily in a downward flow from "top" to "bottom" with teachers firmly fixed as "receivers" of knowledge. A CoP concept repositions teachers in ways that support collaborative exchanges of knowledge and experience, leading to the construction of new understandings. A well functioning CoP environment serves to diminish the barriers created by institutions in ways that foster the rich exchange of ideas in knowledge networks.

In addition, with the focus fixed on cultivating CoPs, participants experience a shift away from mundane technological and knowledge management issues that plague many VLEs, to a focus on developing the social learning processes that support meaningful engagement. As such, a CoP environment contributes to the creation of an "enunciative space":

> the opportunity to articulate what it meant to be a teacher; to tangle with social issues beyond the technicalities of teaching; and having some agency within which to question and challenge the wider structures surrounding teaching and learning; and in the process gaining some ownership of the determination of one's own pedagogical work. (Smyth, 2001, p. 159)

A professional CoP is a special type of community in which the members share basic knowledge, standards, and criteria in a way that acknowledges the role of context and experience. Such a collective aims to support informed dissent, and in the process, assist teachers in their own efforts to grow. In the following case study, the evolution, formation, and maturation of the community are traced.

THE NEED FOR A PROFESSIONAL COMMUNITY OF PRACTICE MODEL FOR TEACHERS

In Canada, as elsewhere in the developed world, both teachers' work and the production of verifiably literate students are under the microscope. The introduction of accountability measures such as teacher testing, standardized testing of students, and a secondary school graduation requirement to pass a literacy test, contributed to the intensification of the focus on teaching literacy.

In the market environment, teachers "no longer deliberate about the aims of education as part of their professional responsibility; instead they deliberate about the means to achieve externally imposed ends as part of their craft" (Pring, 1996, p. 110). The difference in the level of dialogue between the two is remarkable. To limit the dialogue to debates about method ignores the more fundamental issues surrounding literacy problems (Larson, 2001). If teachers are suffering a loss of confidence and feeling alienated from their profession, the need for a supportive CoP is palpable.

It was in this highly politicized climate that teachers agreed to participate in research that sought to understand how teachers came to complex understandings about their own literacy practices. To conduct the study, I joined an online course for teachers of reading for the full 4-month term as a participant observer. The 23 participants were provincially licensed teachers voluntarily taking the course for "additional qualification" credit. The course design included a requirement of ongoing discussion with teacher educators and co-participants in both focused discussion areas (i.e., "rooms" created around particular topics) and informal discussion areas (i.e., a "Bistro" created for socialization and relationship-building). Discussions were designed around readings, online course content, questions, and feedback offered by all participants.

Clandinin and Connelly (2000) see "teaching and teacher knowledge as expressions of embodied individual and social stories" (p. 4). What stories are we living? How do those stories shape our practice? How do we negotiate our stories when we come together as a community (a group bonded by shared or similar purposes, professional interests or fellowship) of teachers?

The Research Design

Cochran-Smith and Lytle (1993) have long argued that what is missing in too many educational studies "are the voices of teachers themselves, the questions that teachers ask, and the interpretive frames that teachers use to understand and improve their own classroom practices" (p. 7). Therefore, a case study methodology was selected for its ability to capture and document the personal learning of teacher participants, teacher educators and researcher in a form that may be of benefit to others considering a vCoP as a vehicle for meaningful professional development for teachers.

After receiving ethical approval from the host academic institution, participants in two online reading courses were invited to participate in the research study. The key question in this study asked, Does the participation in online courses foster participants' critical reflective practice, personal and especially professional growth, and if so, how? From this overarching question, emerged a subquestion: In what ways does online learning evolve into a professional CoP, thereby providing "enunciative space" where participants are free to live their stories of practice? Previous experience teaching the same course in a face-to-face setting and the virtual setting had indicated that the VLE was well-suited as a vehicle for participants to engage with each other around the social practice of teaching reading. The task, in part, seemed to be to discover why?

The participants who provided informed consent included 20 teachers, 2 teacher educators, and the researcher as participant observer. Of the 23 participants, 3 were male, and 20 were female. Experience in classroom teaching ranged from a minimum consisting of preservice practicum experiences, to a maximum of 22 years in teaching. The average was approximately 5 years. The particular grades taught by the participants ranged from junior kindergarten in the early years' division through to secondary school teachers, and included three teachers assigned to district responsibilities at a board or regional level. Six of the participants indicated that they had taken some form of online learning in the past. Only consenting participants' stories were included in this chapter, and all names used are pseudonyms.

Data sources for the study included documents; (the record of written "conversation" in all discussion areas, course content, student assignments, course-related e-mail exchanges), field notes; (emerging theories, ideas, and impressions logged in relation to documents collected), investigator's journal (a record of connections being made in relation to my own life, scholarly and leisure reading, past teaching experiences—a record of my own "inner dialogue" during the process).

I attended to the ways in which teachers negotiated meaning in their literacy practices in an online community and in doing so, shape and are shaped by the environment.

To analyze the data, a critical narrative methodology was selected for several reasons. First, it is a methodology conducive to "critical participatory studies with classroom teachers" (Moss, 2004, p. 367) that demands rigorous attention to trustworthiness both in the interactions with participants of a study, and the ensuing reports generated from their stories. Second, it requires a level of vigilant subjectivity on the part of the researcher that was necessary, given my blurred insider/outsider status. Third, the methodology offered a means to develop an intersubjective understanding of the participants' experiences and allowed for multiple ways of interpreting the data through various theoretical lenses, which it is hoped, serve to stimulate and engage readers in critical examinations and dialogue about their teaching practice.

FINDINGS

In the online discussion forum being studied, some of the complexities of teaching practices were made visible through a unique amalgam of two language processes known to support learning; talk and writing (Bruner, 1990; Emig, 1983; Vygotskii, 1962, 1967; Vygotsky, 1978). The written dialogue created in the online discussion (among all participants including the teacher educators) served to initiate the discussions but also to clarify, synthesize, and analyze the product of those discussions. Because of the written account each post accrues, discussions about practice are subject to scrutiny in ways similar to Schön's (1983) conceptualization of reflection-in-action as teachers examine theories-in-use. In this way, reflective practice can become both deliberate and deliberative. Discussions about practice allow gaps between theory and practice to be addressed, explored, and more clearly understood from various perspectives. Participants' narratives (and interpretations of those narratives), academic research, and course readings need to be subject to critique and reflective thinking.

Smylie and Conyers (1991) have argued that it is necessary to shift from "deficit-based to competency-based approaches in which teachers' knowledge, skills and experiences are considered assets" (p. 2). The conceptualization of the online learning environment in this study represented such a shift, creating the potential to go beyond developing competencies, and instead approach the development of a critical complex epistemology (Kincheloe, 2004). A critical complex epistemology:

involves teachers as knowledge producers, knowledge workers who pursue their own intellectual development. At the same time, such teachers work together in their communities of practice to sophisticate both the profession's and the public's appreciation of what it means to be an educated person. (Kincheloe, 2004, p. 51)

A vCoP satisfies Argyris and Schön's (1992) desire to slow down the field experience and make it accessible. Access to the process allows us to study it in new ways. For example, in this study, participants in the online classes were seen to begin with the type of cover story described by Connelly and Clandinin (1999) when initially presenting themselves and their understandings of the teaching of reading to their colleagues. In time, the formation of meaningful relationships and the development of community provided the trust necessary for "lived stories" to emerge. In the "lived stories," participants made statements that challenged the institutional stories; revealing their fears, mistakes and concerns with sanctioned practices. As "lived stories" came forth, the teacher participants engaged in ways that clearly demonstrated their need for such a forum. The following samples of dialogue are taken from the case study to illustrate this evolution. They are included here to delineate the pattern that emerged from the data.

Entering the Virtual Community of Practice

Although a seasoned teacher, Najat was very nervous about the "technology" of the online environment, and like many, began the course expressing her fear and uncertainty:

> I'm nervous. This is my first online course and my head is really spinning. I peeked into this site last evening and then spent a sleepless night wondering if I could pull this off! (Najat, Elementary School Teacher)

Najat's confession (and others like hers) created a "crack" in the mechanical isolation suggested by the medium. Compassion spilled into the discussion, with offers of reassurance and support from colleagues, and served to humanize the environment and begin the necessary process of relationship building. At this level, participants are often seeking commonalities.

Initial Posturing

What I found initially disturbing was the degree to which the institutional "cover" stories (or what I have come to refer to as "Boardspeak") had supplanted the participants' voices. In their early discussions and responses to questions, it was not uncommon for participants to identify their practice solely with particular commercial programs and products sanctioned by their district. Decisions made at a systems' level became the accepted (and generally unquestioned) way of doing things. A good example of this was illustrated through a productive discussion about the "leveling" of texts. Leveling texts was a simple concept of matching readers with "appropriate" texts that the publishing industry has spawned into a lucrative commercial enterprise consisting of predefined categories with associated "ready-to-use" texts. Participants in the course explained that many of their boards have linked initiatives in developmental reading assessment (DRA) with an expectation that all texts be leveled. Before long, this "leveling tool" virtually usurped complex information gathered and utilized by both readers and their teachers as they learn to choose appropriate texts, thereby reducing the decision to a numeric or alphabetic standard.

In critical narrative work, it is important to challenge institutional stories in an effort to uncover their origins, and position them next to evolving understandings informed by both practice and theory. In an attempt to disrupt the institutional stories being told about "leveling texts" in the class discussion, I shared the following anecdote

---

I feel a little like Dave Barry when I say, "I swear I am not making this up," and I have to share it with you. Late yesterday afternoon, I met my husband at a local shopping center to purchase a family gift. While chatting with the storeowner, her son and husband arrived en route to a sports activity.

Mom:	Hello "Johnny." Are you ready for the game?
Son:	I'm a little nervous, but yeah.
Mom:	Did you remember your math book and your AR? (accelerated reader)
Son:	Oh. I got the math, but I didn't bring the book (Dad and son proceeded to back of the store to fix a snack)
Mom:	(To me) Is it normal for students to test out at a level that is lower than the year before?
Me:	That depends. Are they using the same test? Are you referring to a particular publisher's level? Did he read over the summer?
Mom:	I don't know what they are using, but he's really upset that he's not in a higher level. He's very competitive. (Calls to son.) Johnny—did you read today?
Son:	Yeah

Me:	What do you like to read? Who is your favorite author?
Son:	Oh, I guess I would have to say Gary Paulsen. I like all the Brian stories. And guess what mom—the teacher moved me up a level today!
Mom:	Really!
Son:	Yeah! Now instead of being 4.2-5.9, I am 5.3-6.4!
Mom:	Is Harry Potter in that level?
Son:	Just the first one (in the series).
Me:	Are you looking forward to reading Harry Potter?
Son:	Oh, I've read them all already. I'm just not in the level where I can read them in school.

I went on to discuss the books with him, to discern whether there was a suspicion of comprehension weaknesses and so forth. He was more than able to discuss all the books, draw links to others he had read outside of school and so forth, but neither mother nor son seemed to see the irony in what I have quoted you.

In this phase of the vCoP it could be seen that attempts to introduce counter narratives or theories that may provoke different ways of thinking about issues, were typically met with silence or a reassertion of the institutional story, strengthened by references to the numerous "PD sessions" that they had attended in their district that supported their stated position. I have learned that this sometimes happens when, for example,

- The student is not ready to engage with issues raised
- The student disagrees but isn't comfortable with how to respond or handle conflict in the environment
- The student personalizes the critique, viewing it as a rejection of who they are/what they do
- The student has not read the postings
- The subsequent posts to the discussion interrupt and redirect the trajectory of the ongoing dialogue.

In the vCoP, the teacher educators and I ensured that the probing questions, counter narratives, and issues raised were done so in a nonthreatening, nonjudgmental way. We shared our own questions and struggled with what is often "taken-for-granted," modeling a version of "think-aloud" protocol in the online discussion area. Gradually, perhaps after time for introspection and reflection, participants reconsidered earlier positions in light of new information. For example, Jayne resumed the discussion concerning the commercial leveling of texts, and offered an explanation that pressure from parents and working in an era of accountability contributed to her willingness to uncritically abandon her professional knowledge:

> there is a such a push now to be accountable for your marks and I find that parents are questioning more and DO want to see written work to justify why their child is not at their grade level in reading. (Jayne, Elementary School Teacher)

Erin agreed, adding "generally parents want to see written test results" but Teri began to consider the issue more broadly:

> the amount of assessment we are doing ... is taking some of the joy and fun out of learning ... the ongoing joke is that by the time all the paperwork and assessments are completed, we barely have time to teach the kids! I think sometimes we teachers get so focused on the end goal ... completing the novel, marking the responses, calculating the marks, doing the report cards, that we lose sight of what's most important. (Teri, Elementary School Teacher)

The Process of Reification

Through mutual engagement, participation, and reification weave together. When participants engage in the joint enterprise of teaching, there is opportunity to create relations of mutual, professional accountability. Through sharing their stories, participants create resources for negotiating meaning. Wenger (1998) discusses the concept of reification as:

> A certain understanding is given form. This form then becomes a focus for the negotiation of meaning, as people use the law to argue a point, use the procedure to know what to do, or use the tool to perform an action.... Reification occupies much of our collective energy.... Reification shapes our experience. (p. 59)

Reification is closely tied to participation as meaning is negotiated by members of the vCoP. It is a process of "working out" meanings through collaboration. Wenger (1998) cautions that reification "as a constituent of meaning is always incomplete, ongoing, potentially enriching and potentially misleading" (p. 62).

Once the process of reification is underway, participants saw it as a useful way of laying out their current understandings in a way that meaning could be negotiated. For example, Ariana shares an "institutional story" that she struggled with:

I have also been involved in in-services where groups of teachers are given a piece of work and then using the.... Exemplars Document for [Language Arts] assess it. This worked well because some felt differently about the piece than others but had to justify it using the exemplars. I personally think the examples that [are] given in these documents are higher than I am seeing my students achieve. The level 4 examples are excellent but not what I am seeing and I have the top ones and twos this year—really good students. If I based my marks on these exemplars, I would rarely give out an A.

Does anyone else think that the exemplar examples are not all that realistic for the grade level you are teaching or is just me? (Ariana, Elementary School Teacher)

Up to this point, no one had discussed the purpose for the assessments or the leveling—the strengths or limitations, or the way it could be useful and/or misused. This shift was significant, as it marked the beginning of a space for deliberation about teacher agency and educational ideals, and how even within the limits of the institution, there is a place for teachers to act.

The Maturation of a Community of Practice

Thinking critically about the institutional story is only one component of meaningful professional development fostered in a vCoP. As various researchers have noted, it is also necessary to interrogate our own personal beliefs and practices. Stewart entered the teaching profession after practicing law for several years. He was surprised by the complexities inherent in teaching, and regularly sought assistance before proceeding with his responses. To support Stewart, I began to share some of my own early assumptions and experiences when I began teaching. Eventually, Stewart began to shed his "cover story":

I'm embarrassed to ask this question.... In fact I wrote it last week, but my wife read it before I posted it, she said "Don't post that!" but I'm still confused. What is a basal reader? (And core text?) I've done my reading, I've asked other teachers, looked up basal readers in literacy books ... [but] one teacher at my school swears that basal readers are no [longer] made. (Stewart, Elementary School Teacher)

Stewart's confession was met with overwhelming response—both in the form of providing the technical response to his question, but more importantly, in the acknowledgement and sharing of what each did not know or understand.

When such struggles emerged in the context of the vCoP, the ensuing dialogue proved to be both transforming and transformative. As Atkinson

(2001) has noted, enunciative spaces must support, value and encourage teachers, or teachers will be less likely to take the risks that lead to real learning. In the vCoP, once participants' stories were written and posted, they were subjected to scrutiny from the other participants. Posting their stories required developing a "willingness to expose one's viewpoint to the critical gaze of others" (Furlong, 2001, p. 27). Exposing oneself to such scrutiny was not easy. Along with submitting to the critical gaze of others, was a need to take on some forms of reflective [professional] practice (Cochran-Smith & Lytle, 1993). As the course progressed, the defensive stance privileging the mantra of institutional stories diminished, and a more reflective, tolerant and thoughtful tone emerged:

> I have read many different postings from all different divisions. It is quite obvious that all of us have one thing in common - dedication to both our profession and our students. Whether our programs vary slightly or are completely different, everyone has shown interest in learning, sharing and discussing the insides and outsides of what we are passionate about - teaching. I cannot tell you how beneficial this has been to me. (Ariana, Elementary School Teacher)

The maturity of the vCoP contributed to the discovery of discrepancies between initial "cover stories" presented in the early portion of the course and the "lived stories" that emerged as trust and CoP developed. As other researchers have noted, the dual roles of being both teacher and learner in a collaborative, professional environment, produced insights that helped those involved grow both individually and together as professionals (Evans & Policella, 2000). The online CoP offered participants the opportunity to engage in a unique professional discourse as both teacher and learner. Furlong (2001) explains that such discourse differs from normal conversation in the ways that "participants explicitly criticize the background consensus concerning belief systems, norms, values and ideologies taken for granted in everyday life" (p. 27).

Jacalyn considered her own complicity in her situation:

> I do believe that often our knowledge is undervalued and we give in to external pressures. I think part of the reason is that we hear so many contradicting ideas and we don't take the time to do our own research and develop our beliefs in how and why we teach a certain way. It is often easier to follow the trend that has been set before us. We tend not to speak strongly enough about what we feel is best for education. I agree with [the claim] "whether for good or ill teachers are not usually very political creatures. They focus on the intense and immediate needs of the students in their classrooms and on the concerns of the parents, and they have little time or energy left over to mount campaigns to inform a broader public." When I read this quote, what jumped out at me was "the concerns of the parents." I know of a few

teachers, (myself included) who have assigned things like weekly spelling, phonics sheets, homework, because that is what the parents wanted. (Jacalyn, Secondary School Teacher)

As the course progressed, the "shifting patterns of resolution" could be seen (Berlak & Berlak, 1981, p. 264). Clandinin and Connelly (2000) refer to Geertz's (1988, 1995) retrospective look at anthropology and draw on his metaphor of a parade to describe these shifting patterns: "We know what we know because of where we are positioned ... if we shift our position, our knowing shifts ... as the parade changes, our relative positions change" (Clandinin & Connelly, 2000, p. 17). Because participant interaction generated a record of all dialogue, the vCoP captured the shifts; the ways in which participants wrote about their situation, themselves as practitioners in various contexts, and of the teaching and learning decisions that were made in light of given conditions.

Becoming Knowledge Producers

As they told stories about their own learning experiences, those of their own children and those from their classrooms, participants developed a much deeper sense of why the teaching of reading is so important and how vital they can be to the process. The vCoP setting provided participants with an excellent venue in which to share stories from practice and receive feedback or informed critiques. Feedback, from teacher educators and coparticipants, was vital in the promotion of further reflection upon choices and decisions in a dialogue of alternative possibilities and varying perspectives. A professional, supportive CoP demands multiple perspectives. It is often precisely our differences that generate rich discussions and critical analysis compelling us to think about our professional practice in new ways.

As participants told stories about struggles they have encountered (i.e., meeting the expectations of curriculum documents, administrators, parents, and the needs of students), both the telling of the story and the responses from other participants who have resolved similar issues, assisted their ability to generate new understandings and choose ways in which to more successfully proceed. As Wenger (1998) reminds us, indigenous enterprise is always negotiated by the professional community. Andrew, a veteran teacher of 15 years remarked:

It is easy to get into a routine, or narrow your focus in your teaching, and often you don't even realize you have done it. If find that I really need the opportunity to view other colleagues' lessons, discuss with my peers our rationale for doing the things we do and making the teaching choices we make, discuss areas of difficulty and seek my colleagues' opinions as I try to overcome these areas of difficulty. (Andrew, Elementary School Teacher)

As participants reflect on their practice and negotiate meaning for themselves, CoPs become both key to an organization's competence and to the evolution of professional competence (Wenger, 1998, p. 241). The ways in which participants in a CoP come to see themselves as competent has profound implications for the ways in which they engage in professional practice. Engaging in professional dialogue with other members of the teaching profession can lead to a shift both in identity (seeing themselves as professional) and ensuing behavior (acting in ways that are deemed professional).

The vCoP model offered participants an opportunity to engage in professional dialogue about their practice which is of critical importance in the twenty-first century where diversity, technological advances, and globalization (to name a few) have changed the context of who we teach, what we teach, and how we teach. In addition to experiential knowledge, teachers come to their practice with an implicit historical sense of what it means to be a learner. As Britzman (2003) observes, "Teaching is one of the few professions where newcomers [can] feel the force of their own history of learning as if it telegraphs relevancy to their work" (p. 1). Yet more than ever, teachers are asked to conceptualize and perform their work in ways that they never experienced themselves as learners (Darling-Hammond & McLaughlin, 1995). In some ways, the current context contributes to the feelings of fear and detachment that even seasoned teachers report experiencing in the present environment (Connell & Johnston-Kline, 1999). Adriana's comments illustrated her struggle about midway through the course:

> Me again ... I am still thinking about my response and I remembered something [I read earlier] ... "Until we are fully informed and professional, we will continue to use our new materials with our old mentality, to be victims of 'innovation without change'.... Instead of asking, what is the best way to teach reading?—Which focuses narrowly on methodology,—we should be asking, what needs to be done to teach children to learn to read?—Which includes the methodology, but also the critical, emotional, political, economic, and social influences that exist inside and outside of the classroom."
> My point exactly. Without the consideration of all of these factors, resources are just not [going] to ensure children are necessarily going to learn how to read. (Ariana, Elementary School Teacher)

Cochran-Smith and Lytle (1993) suggest that multiple forms of knowledge complement and inform each other. Academic knowledge placed beside experiential knowledge allows perspectives and knowledge to be interrogated in productive ways. Bringing theory and practice together in this way helps to ensure that teachers are connecting to broader understandings while solving their own practical issues. Teachers learn to value research and inquiry for the ways in which it can inform their understanding of their practice, while at the same time not become enslaved by it. In this type of collaboration, the aim is not to converge to one right answer, but rather to see if differences in relations of power and contextual realities can push participants to challenge the assumptions that guide his or her decisions and practices. In this approach, "difference acts as a template that helps the other (re)vision one's worldview" (Gitlin, Peck, Aposhian, Hadley, & Porter, 2002, p. 306). Thus, insider/outsider positioning can be used to inform, examine and reconsider knowledge. In the vCoP, participants learned to think more flexibly as they developed a repertoire of strategies, understanding more fully the complexities of their practice. Briana describes how this emerged for her:

> I have enjoyed and gotten more out of this course than any other course that I have taken before. I have read everyone's response to everything and was so impressed and learned so much from the professional dialogue that I experienced on line. I was sometimes driven to respond to postings because they triggered something in me, or because they made me look at things in a different light ... I can't begin to tell everyone how much their contributions have made me reflect on my own teaching, both good and bad. (Briana, Elementary School Teacher)

In a vCoP environment, participants deliberated about their practice as they participated in it. While deliberations about practice can provide a broader base of experience and circumstances, integrating theoretical and academic discourses provides an overarching framework and the tools needed to critique practice addressing larger sociopolitical and social justice issues. Thinking critically about one's own practice can be difficult intellectual, moral, and professional work. Since learning occurs in complex and diverse ways, it is a worthwhile process for professional teachers to acknowledge their conceptions of student learning, their beliefs and their current repertoire of strategies and processes for reasoning to action. Struggling through all of these issues within a community of their professional peers can be a valuable means to both personal and professional learning.

Cultivating CoPs in the Virtual Classroom

In the online CoP, participants and their teacher educators came together to participate in professional development. A sense of community cannot be mandated or forced, but conditions can and must be created to promote its development. These conditions were primarily cultivated in three distinct areas: the discussion area, the language used (questions, cues, prompts) and the type and timing of interaction with the teacher educators initially, and subsequently the group as a whole.

Palmer (1998) argues that teachers need to form professional communities in order to grow in their practice. He points to the irony that while teachers often can serve as the best resources for each other, the organizational structure of the school often inhibits such access. Lortie (1975), among others, has referred to teaching as a lonely profession, where "teachers learn to cope on their own" (p. 210). A vCoP can help counter such isolation in part through sustained and purposeful interaction. The course discussed in this study was designed to facilitate community building and interaction.

The structure alone however, is not sufficient to ensure success. This particular course, while not mandatory, was assigned a credit and was graded. The teacher educators and the participants contributed to and shaped the overall resulting environment as they brought themselves, their stories and whatever degree of willingness to challenge the "status quo" into the discussions. In particular, the online presence modeled by the teacher educators played a vital role in activating meaningful professional community and promoting the development of significant relationships. At the same time, there were instances where comments effectively limited or terminated discussion.

While it is important for an online CoP of this nature to subscribe to traditional course expectations such as providing clear outlines, grading rubrics, and course expectations, it is even more important to build discussion that is community oriented (i.e., that serves to promote fellowship) rather than simply task oriented. This entails creating an area for participants to share personal information and chat informally with their new colleagues. It is here that relationship building begins to occur, and it is the human relationships and interactions that foster growth as a type of interdependence develops.

It is also necessary to access individual and practical knowledge in ways that allow the participants' professional and course-related needs to be made visible and therefore able to be addressed. The type and structure of questions posed, the interactive design of the course and the way in which the teacher educators interacts surely come into play here. As Villaume (2000) has observed, in teaching, progress "is contingent upon a willingness to accept and participate in an ongoing search for discrepancies between beliefs and practices" (p. 21). Teacher educators in the course must first work hard to build trust and collegiality within the class at a personal level. When a trusting and supportive relationship has been established, they are able to engage in discussions that move beyond the local. This can involve developing large conceptual frameworks for example, in order to both synthesize and contextualize the mass amounts of information generated in course discussions. In so doing, teacher educators are able to model a type of metacognition for the students, while also situating the content in a way that illuminates and juxtaposes competing theories.

As participants both told and read stories online, they were challenged to confront ways in which they were complicit in reinscribing and perpetuating the characterization of teacher as disseminator. The vCoP offered participants multiple opportunities to serve various roles; teacher and learner to be sure, but also mentor, supportive friend, devil's advocate, challenger, and sympathizer to name a few. The process encouraged teacher-learners to explore nuances, while remaining grounded by evidence, experience, and context. It encouraged participants to value their own expertise while looking carefully at the implications of new learning. The struggle about practice evolved for many from isolated and internal to a more public form of struggle that invited colleagues to participate in the solution. Many participants reached new or clearer understandings, although not necessarily shared or common understandings. Rather, participants were more likely to develop a deeper understanding of other perspectives and new information to consider as they attempted to reconcile their own beliefs and practices within a broader context. According to Garrison, Anderson, and Archer (2003), it is this "ability to create critical communities of inquiry ... [that] distinguishes [the potential of] online learning from previous paradigms of distance education" (p. 113).

IMPLICATIONS AND RECOMMENDATIONS FOR CULTIVATING CoPs IN VIRTUAL SETTINGS

As this multifaceted case study has demonstrated, a well functioning professional CoP has the potential for bringing together several recognized areas emerging in the literature around meaningful and effective professional development

- The strength of participation in collaborative tasks
- The respect for teachers as intellectuals
- The need to develop and support teacher networks
- The benefits of school/university partnerships
- The call for a scholarship of teaching and learning

Teachers will tell you that they crave time for two things: to talk about their practice with interested and informed colleagues and uninterrupted, unmanaged time in their classrooms to get their work done. Too often, their time is micromanaged by bureaucratic mandates, with teachers cast in the role of technician, charged only with fulfilling an agenda set outside of their classrooms. While the value of district mandates is not disputed here, institutions need to recognize that teachers' intellectual curiosity must be nourished and stimulated in order to create the kind of energy and enthusiasm necessary to sustain an intellectually engaging environment in the classroom.

Expanding CoPs in Teacher Professional Development

The government mantra that has been heard for nearly a decade in many parts of Canada has been to "Do more with less." It is a mindset that has left many teachers feeling overwhelmed and burdened in ways that have contributed to record numbers of teachers leaving the profession. Others have viewed it as a challenge to seek new and creative solutions to manage the work that needs to be done, abandoning practices that are no longer justified. Technology can provide assistance with bringing teachers together in flexible, expansive ways that allow professional CoPs to flourish.

The vCoP in this study focused on teachers' experiences in two reading courses. As a multifaceted case study, the results are not intended to be generalized. Rather, the findings are shared as one approach of coming to understand the ways in which the conditions were established to allow the vCoP to emerge and be sustained. The understandings gleaned from this study have been applied to the development of more than 150 online courses taken by teachers provincially and from around the world. Subsequent courses for authors/designers and teacher educators were developed to maximize the potential for creating a vCoP in both the structure of the design, and the formation of the community in individual courses.

Technology can and should be exploited in ways that allow unstructured teacher networks to thrive and support not only a sharing of resources and expertise, but a meeting of the minds over issues that matter to teachers.

1. Begin with a focus on commonalities. In addition to building community, it serves as a foundation for trust to grow to a level necessary for participants to "tell" their stories from practice.

2. Provide space and acknowledgement that encourages participants to bring the significant issues from their practice, schools, and

districts to the group for feedback, multiple perspectives and problem solving strategies at a deeply intellectual and engaging level. Solving their own professional problems must be as important to the course credit as solving those issued by teacher educators.

3. Stimulate site-based problem solving opportunities that are connected to the participants' learning and professional development experiences at an academic level. Rather than providing surface level "canned" solutions, develop metacognitive approaches to problem-solving that can be applied and adapted in ways that stimulate critical, creative thinking, and knowledge generation in participants.

4. Exploit technology to reduce duplication of tasks, to enhance the learning environment, and to eliminate redundancy. For example, when school districts must all respond to government initiatives, the virtual community setting would be an ideal space to develop and coordinate resources that can then be used thoughtfully and intelligently by individual districts in ways that best meet their local needs. At the same time, participants engage in broader dialogues that counter tendencies for knowledge to become insular.

These four components can significantly reduce both the time and the efforts of individual teachers and school boards, while expanding their collective capacity for building a professional community of peers that serves as a meaningful vehicle for teacher professional development.

REFERENCES

Argyris, C., & Schön, D. A. (1974). Redesigning professional education. In *Theory in practice: Increasing professional effectiveness* (pp. 173-196). San Francisco: Jossey-Bass.

Argyris, C., & Schön, D. A. (1992). Redesigning professional education. In *Theory in practice: Increasing professional effectiveness* (pp. 173-196). San Francisco: Jossey-Bass.

Atkinson, L. (2001). Trusting your own judgment (or allowing yourself to eat the pudding). In G. Claxton (Ed.), *The intuitive practitioner: On the value of not always knowing what one is doing* (pp. 53-67). Buckingham, England: Open University Press.

Berlak, A., & Berlak, H. (1981). *Dilemmas of schooling: Teaching and social change.* London: Methuen.

Britzman, D. P. (2003). *Practice makes practice: A critical study of learning to teach.* New York: State of New York Press.

Bruner, J. S. (1990). *Acts of meaning.* Cambridge, MA: Harvard University Press.

Clandinin, D. J., & Connelly, M. (Eds.). (2000). *Narrative inquiry: Experience and story in qualitative research*. San Francisco: Jossey-Bass.

Cochran-Smith, M., & Lytle, S. L. (1993). *Inside/outside: Teacher resarch and knowledge*. New York: Teachers College Press.

Cochran-Smith M. & Lytle, S.L. (2001). Beyond certainty: Taking an inquiry stance on practice. In A. Lieberman & L. Miller (Eds.), *Teachers caught in the action: Professional development that matters* (pp. 45-61). New York: Teachers College Press.

Connelly, A., & Johnston-Kline, C. (1999). Frontlines. In A. R. Neilson (Ed.), *Daily meaning*. Mill Bay, British Columbia: Bendall Books.

Connelly, M., & Clandinin, D. J. (Eds.). (1999). *Shaping a professional identity: Stories of educational practice*. London, Ontario: Althouse Press.

Darling-Hammond, L., & McLaughlin, M. W. (1995). Policies that support professional development in an era of reform. *Phi Delta Kappan, 76*(8), 597-604.

Emig, J. (1983). Writing as a mode of learning. In J. Emig (Ed.), *The web of meaning: Essays on writing, teaching, learning and thinking* (pp. 122-132). Portsmouth, NH: Boynton/Cook.

Evans, J. F., & Policella, E. (2000). Changing and growing as teachers and learners: A shared journey. *Teacher Education Quarterly, 27*(3), 55-70.

Furlong, J. (2001). Intuition and the crisis in teacher professionalism. In T. Atkinson & G. Claxton (Eds.), *The intuitive practitioner: On the value of not always knowing what one is doing* (pp. 15-32). Buckingham, England: Open University Press.

Garrison, D. R., Anderson, T., & Archer, W. (2003). A theory of critical inquiry in online distance education. In W. G. Anderson (Ed.), *Handbook of Distance Education* (pp. 113-128). Mahwah, NJ: Erlbaum.

Geertz, C. (1988). *Works and lives: The anthropologist as author*. Palo Alto, CA: Stanford University Press.

Geertz, C. (1995). *After the fact: Two countries, four decades, one anthropologist*. Cambridge, MA: Harvard University Press.

Gitlin, A., Peck, M., Aposhian, N., Hadley, S., & Porter, A. (2002). Looking at insider knowledge: A relational approach to knowledge production and assessment. *Journal of Teacher Education, 53*(4), 303-315.

Hewson, L., & Hughes, C. (2001). Generic structures for online teaching and learning. In F. Lockwood & A. Gooley (Eds.), *Innovation in open & distance learning: Successful development of online and Web-based learning* (pp. 76-88). London: Kogan Page.

Hibbert, K., & Rich, S. (2006). Virtual communities of practice. In J. Weiss, J. Nolan, & P. Trifonas (Eds.), *The international handbook of virtual learning environments* (pp. 563-579). Dordrecht, the Netherlands: Kluwer.

Jonassen, D. H. (2002). Learning to solve problems online. In G. V. Glass (Ed.), *Distance education and distributed learning* (pp. 75-98). Greenwich, CT: Information Age.

Kincheloe, J. (2004). The knowledges of teacher education: Developing a critical complex epistemology. *Teacher Education Quarterly, 31*(1), 49-67.

Larson, J. (2001). *Literacy as snake oil: Beyond the quick fix*. New York: Peter Lang.

Lave, J., & Wenger, E. (1991). *Situated learning: Legitimate peripheral participation in communities of practice.* New York: Cambridge University Press.

Lortie, D. C. (1975). *Schoolteacher: A sociological study.* Chicago: University of Chicago Press.

Moss, G. (2004). Provisions of trustworthiness in critical narrative research: Bridging intersubjectivity and fidelity. *The Qualitative Report, 9*(2), 359-374.

National Staff Development Council. (2006). *Home page.* Retrieved July 7, 2006, from http://www.nsdc.org/

Palmer, P. (1998). The courage to teach: Exploring the inner landscape of a teacher's life. In A Lieberman & L. Miller (Eds.), *Teachers caught in the action practice* (pp. 10-146). San Francisco: Jossey-Bass.

Pring, R. (1996). Values and education policy. In M. J. Taylor (Ed.), *Values in education and education in values* (pp. 45-60). London: Falmer Press.

Schön, D. A. (1983). *The reflective practitioner: How professionals think in action.* New York: Basic Books.

Shulman, L. S. (1987). Knowledge and teaching: Foundations of the new reform. *Harvard Educational Review, 57*(1), 1-21.

Smylie, M. A., & Conyers, J. G. (1991). *Changing conceptions of teacher influence: The future of staff development.* Retrieved June 2002 from http://www.ed.gov/databases/ERIC_Digests/ed383695.html

Smyth, J. (2001). *Critical politics of teachers' work: An Australian perspective.* Oxford, England: Peter Lang.

Stein, J. G. (2001). *The cult of efficiency.* Toronto, Canada: House of Anansi Press.

Villaume, S. K. (2000). The necessity of uncertainty: A case study of language arts reform. *Journal of Teacher Education, 51*(1), 18-25.

Vygotskii, L. S. (Ed.). (1962). *Thought and language.* Cambridge: Massachusetts Institute of Technology.

Vygotskii, L. S. (Ed.). (1967). *Thought and language.* Cambridge: Massachusetts Institute of Technology.

Vygotsky, L. (1978). *Mind in society: The development of higher psychological processes.* Cambridge, MA: Harvard University Press.

Wenger, E. (1998). *Communities of practice: Learning, meaning, and identity.* Cambridge, MA: Harvard University Press.

CHAPTER 8

DISTRIBUTING TEACHING PRESENCE

Engaging Teachers of English to Young Learners in an International Virtual Community of Inquiry

Joan Kang Shin and Beverly Bickel

The rapidly expanding international field of teaching English to young learners (TEYL) needs trained and experienced TEYL teachers. Thus, professionals entering this emerging field are seeking new ways of acquiring knowledge and skills appropriate in their cultural and national contexts. Online courses can provide unique spaces for collaboration and learning for working teachers and can facilitate the creation of communities of inquiry locally, regionally, and internationally. The key to creating successful virtual communities of practice (vCoPs) of TEYL teachers is to build sustainable networks of professionals who disseminate their learning locally and continue to work and reflect together internationally. This chapter describes how participants from across 16 time zones joined an online distance teacher development course—offered in both 2004 and 2005 with funding by the U.S. State Department's Office of English Language Programs (OELP). Using Garrison, Anderson, and Archer's (2000) community of

Communities of Practice: Creating Learning Environments for Educators,
Volume 2, pp. 149–177

inquiry model to conceptualize the interaction among participants in the course, the instructor drew on culturally inclusive pedagogies to equip all participants as cofacilitators of the creation of new knowledge. Participants developed social and professional connections through open and critical discussion of teaching challenges in diverse educational and cultural contexts. Examples from the course illustrate how strategies to foster critical engagement and social connections promoted a shift in teaching presence from instructor to participants that set the basis for their subsequent teaching, training, and professional collaborations. The chapter concludes with recommendations for future research on vCoPs among English teachers.

Forging a learning community that values wholeness over division, disassociation, splitting, the democratic educator works to create closeness. (hooks,[1] 2003, p. 49)

INTRODUCTION

It is great that this course helped me to connect with other teachers around the world. I can learn from the different interesting ideas of teaching. We can exchange our culture, our ideas in a short time. The most important thing is that I have many friends within the same career as me. Although this course is finished, I'm sure we will still connect to each other. (Jira, Thailand, fall 2004 participant)

Jira was a participant in the first section of an online course titled "Teaching English to Young Learners" (TEYL) that has, through three different sections in two semesters, brought together over 60 participants from 29 different countries from North Africa, the Middle East, Central Asia, and Southeast Asia. The course was purposefully designed to connect English teaching professionals from around the world with the goal of creating a community of practice (CoP)—a community based on dialogue to sustain social relationships that support the sharing of ideas and the creation of new knowledge (Wenger, 1998). In order to form a CoP that could sustain itself beyond the scope of the 10-week online course, the instruction in the course would have to break the traditional model of teacher-centered instruction and instead locate the creation of new knowledge among the participants themselves. The central space for communication among the geographically dispersed participants was the course's asynchronous discussion board where thousands of messages were posted and exchanged. Through virtual course discussions, participants formed a community of inquiry (CoI)—an engaged and meaningful educational experience enacted at the intersection of social presence, teaching presence, and cognitive presence as conceptualized by

Garrison et al. (2000). The instruction employed inclusive pedagogies to encourage the social construction of knowledge among participants drawing on teaching experiences in their specific educational and cultural contexts. This chapter will further define communities of practice (CoPs) and describe the CoI framework, especially the notion of teaching presence, using examples from the course. It will show how the teaching presence of the instructor evolved to become a facilitating presence as participants took responsibility for leading the collaborative inquiry on the course discussion board, developing a sense of "closeness" in spite of challenging geographic and cultural distances. This CoI within the online course was an instrumental step in the initial formation of a vCoP beyond the course in which participants would be equipped to strengthen local professional development efforts and continue to communicate and collaborate internationally through conference presentations, publications, and online discussions about teaching English to young learners (YLs). Recommendations, issues, and future research questions conclude the chapter.

DESCRIPTION OF ONLINE TEACHING ENGLISH TO YOUNG LEARNERS (TEYL) COURSE

As English has become the language for global communication, diplomacy, commerce, media, travel, science, and technology, countries around the world are emphasizing the importance of English as a foreign language (EFL) instruction in their education systems (Crystal, 1997). Because English has become an international language, countries around the world have begun to require the study of English at young ages in order to prepare children for a world where English is a valued commodity (McCloskey, Orr, & Dolitsky, 2006). As the demand for primary EFL teachers rises, educational systems around the world need teachers trained in the new TEYL field. With limited opportunities to step away from work and family responsibilities to study abroad, many existing teachers are seeking new ways of acquiring knowledge and skills for TEYL. Thus, online distance teacher training programs are beginning to emerge in order to provide opportunities for EFL teachers around the world to have access to professional development networks while remaining actively engaged in their home communities. With innovations in Internet technology, Web-based applications can facilitate the creation of international CoPs, which rely on computer-mediated communication (CMC). With these capabilities in mind, the U.S. Department of State through its office of English language programs (OELP) proposed a new program in 2004 called the "E-Teacher Program" and, with the collaboration of five U.S. universities, launched five English teacher training courses initially focused on EFL teachers in Muslim-majority countries. One of these five courses was TEYL, and three different course sections from the first 2 years are the basis for the discussion in this chapter.

The primary goal of the noncredit, professional development course, which was designed like a graduate-level seminar, was to build a CoP among participants from up to 29 countries. They would be expected to work together to deepen their understanding of the theories and practices of teaching EFL to YLs, pose authentic teaching problems, and explore approaches and solutions appropriate for participants in their respective home countries. However, they would have to learn how to do all of this work using online course software, and many of them were wary of the online environment. Salif, a fall 2004 participant from Senegal, wrote,

> I was prejudiced about the online educational environment, labeling it "masquerade." That was before taking this course! Now I know it's as demanding and rewarding as the actual graduate classes. The online educational environment has however some advantages mainly when it comes to adult "students."

Like a graduate seminar, the course attempted to create a learning community that could delve deeply and critically into major issues surrounding TEYL in different countries. Because participants were spread out across 16 time zones, the only way for everyone to interact was asynchronously. Therefore, the site for building this online was in the Blackboard (Bb) course's asynchronous discussion board. A longer-term goal of the course was to develop ways to sustain the online community in order to support the continuing professional connections between participants and continue to support them as trainers and leaders in the local areas where they were expected to disseminate the teaching ideas and practices learned in the course.

The Course as Site of Research

Because the online TEYL course itself is the site of research for this chapter, it is necessary to understand the structure of the course, particularly as a source for data. The first implementation of this course took place September-December, 2004 and the second implementation was in September-December, 2005. See Table 8.1 for demographic information.

The 10 weeks of instruction introduced participants—experienced EFL teachers, teacher supervisors, and Ministry of Education officials from

**Table 8.1.   Participant Demographic Information
Fall 2004 and Fall 2005**

	1st Implementation Fall 2004	2nd Implementation Fall 2005 – Group A	2nd Implementation Fall 2005 – Group B
No. of participants	20	22	19
No. of countries	17	14	10
Countries	Bahrain, Bangladesh, Egypt, India, Indonesia, Jordan, Kazakhstan, Lebanon, Maldives, Qatar, Russia, Senegal, Thailand, Tunisia, Turkey, Turkmenistan, and Uzbekistan	Algeria, Jordan, Bahrain, Lebanon, Syria, Egypt, Israel/Palestine, Mali, Saudi Arabia, Senegal, Togo, Tunisia, Yemen	Afghanistan, Albania, Indonesia, Kazakhstan, Kyrgyzstan, Malaysia, Maldives, Russia, Tajikistan, Thailand
Years of teaching experience	< 10 30% 10–19 35% > 20 35%	< 10 74% 10–19 26% > 20 0%	< 10 68% 10–19 21% > 20 11%

various Muslim populated countries around the world—to the theory and practice of TEYL. Participants were encouraged through the assignments and discussion board activities to interact with the course content and with each other in order to reflect on their own experiences as professionals in the field and investigate the major problems and issues in TEYL. The centerpiece of the course, and the central location of this research, was the discussion board where the participants discussed their diverse teaching experiences in order to construct new knowledge of TEYL.

The learning experience consisted of weekly units during which participants interacted intensely with course content through various assignments as well as interaction with each other on the discussion board. Each week focused on a new topic related to TEYL methodology, such as basic principles of teaching YLs; teaching listening, speaking, reading and writing; storytelling; lesson planning; communicative language teaching; contextualized language instruction; and assessment. The topics reflect the main aspects of the field of TEYL and participants interacted with related readings and lectures presented through PowerPoint. Particularly noteworthy was the last weekly unit called "Beyond the Course" during which participants reflected on the past 9 weeks and plans for the future application of their learning. Participants were encouraged to continue professional development and plan for ways in which they could share what they learned in the course with other teaching professionals in their local areas and countries.

Each week, which began on Thursday and ended on Wednesday, participants followed a basic course structure as shown in Table 8.2.

Additional written assignments gave participants opportunities to understand each other's environments, find commonalities, and share ideas and resources. These assignments, some of which were completed by teams, became shared course resources. Assignments included:

- English education profile: National English education profile, policies and language requirements, school environments, materials, technologies.
- Student profile: Detailed description of students in participant's YL class
- Activities portfolio: Effective and motivating activities for all four language skills appropriate for a specific YL student profile.
- Annotated bibliography: Evaluate EFL textbooks and resources.
- Thematic unit plan: Culminating assignment that included four lessons linked by a theme appropriate for YLs.

It is on the discussion board, which had a different forum for each weekly topic, that the creation of a CoI was realized. As participants were informed from the beginning of the course, this was where the "real learning"—the social construction of new knowledge—would take place. As the chapter will show, certain elements of the course structure described above were examined as evidence in order to understand how an online teacher training course might support a professional international CoP.

Other sources of evidence from the course were the pre- and postcourse surveys and pre and postquestionnaires given to participants. The precourse survey helped the instructor to understand participants'

Table 8.2. Basic Course Structure for Online TEYL Course

Steps	Assignments for one unit	Weekly Unit
Step 1	Study readings and lecture for the week's unit	Assigned Thursday
Step 2	Reflect on the readings and lecture and write a 1–2 page journal based on a prompt given by the instructor	Due Monday
Step 3	Post main points from journal response on the discussion board	Due Monday
Step 4	Respond to at least two classmates' posts on the discussion board	Due Wednesday

demographic and professional backgrounds. The precourse questionnaire assessed what participants already knew about TEYL, what challenges they faced in the field, and what questions they wanted to have answered in the course. The postcourse questionnaire posed follow-ups to the questions from the precourse questionnaire in order to determine if participants received helpful answers to their questions and found solutions to the challenges they reported at the beginning of the course. In addition, an end of course evaluation survey used a Likert scale and open ended questions to elicit participants' thoughts on the course content, course instructor, and the online learning environment. Many of the participant quotes found throughout this chapter are from the end of course questionnaire.

The Course as a Community of Practice

> It was very interesting to participate in the online discussions on all the questions. Some of the course participants are very skillful teachers or they are even teachers' instructors in their countries themselves and they had a lot of ideas to share. (Polina, Russia, fall 2004 participant)

Online learning environments can provide unique spaces for collaboration and learning for working EFL professionals, especially across international borders. Lave and Wenger (1991) contend that learning occurs as a social process where a novice in the field can learn from more experienced members and all members of the community can acquire knowledge that is situated in real world experiences. Participants had a wide range of experience, from new teachers to teachers with up to 30 years of classroom experiences to teacher trainers at the university level. They could learn from each other and form dynamic collaborative relationships.

Wenger (1998) defines a "well-functioning" CoP as:

> a good context to explore radically new insights without becoming fools or stuck in some dead end. A history of mutual engagement around a joint enterprise is an ideal context for this kind of leading-edge learning, which requires a strong bond of communal competence along with a deep respect for the particularity of experience. When these conditions are in place, communities of practice are a privileged locus for the creation of knowledge. (p. 214)

This online course was purposely designed to create such a learning community that could lead to the creation of new knowledge and solutions for the difficulties teachers were discovering in the burgeoning field of TEYL. The challenge was to develop and sustain an international vCoP composed of teachers who spoke multiple languages, lived in 16 different time zones and had vastly different access to the Internet. Therefore, this course employed asynchronous CMC specifically focused on the discussion board to encourage interaction and build a learning community that could generate real life solutions to the often immediate issues facing participating teachers of English to YLs as soon as they stepped away from their computers. Although Lave and Wenger (1991) described CoPs in relation to "colocated" groups of participants, which means that participants are in the same geographic location, Lueg (2000) points out, CoPs that are geographically distributed, and communicating through CMC can still be considered a true CoP when "the members of the community are interacting with the real world and learning takes place in the real world, i.e., the overall situation is real, not virtual" (p. 3).

Therefore, we can call the online TEYL course a CoP that brought together English teaching professionals from around the world to a central virtual location in order to find real life solutions to the daily challenges facing them as active TEYL professionals. Indeed this vCoP was extremely valuable to the participants in this course because if they were to have taken this teaching methodology course face-to-face at the university in the United States, they would have had to leave their home countries. Study in the United States would actually make it impossible for them to apply the new methods and teaching activities often suggested by other course participants in their actual teaching contexts. Therefore, this vCoP was actually the perfect way to provide teachers with the opportunity to share the teaching practices relevant to their own country contexts, collaborate with a broader group of professionals to gain new ideas and insights into the field, and put those new ideas into practice for further reflection and refinement of the practices of teaching English to YLs.

COMMUNITY OF INQUIRY FRAMEWORK

According to Garrison et al. (2000), a graduate seminar, whether online or face-to-face, should ideally encourage the formation of a CoI, where participants deepen their understanding of course content and construct new knowledge through social interaction. As they explain, "a worthwhile educational experience is embedded within a CoI that is composed of teachers and students-the key participants in the educational process" (p. 84). The CoI model assumes that the central goal of higher education is engaged learning through social interaction among the students and

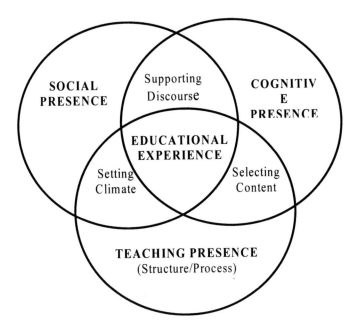

Source: Garrison et al., 2000.

Figure 8.1.   Community of inquiry.

teacher, whether online or face-to-face. As Figure 8.1 illustrates, a CoI creates a meaningful educational experience at the intersection of the three key elements: teaching presence, social presence, and cognitive presence.

Teaching presence describes various actions by the instructor, which include course and lesson design, facilitation of interaction among participants in the course, and provision of subject matter expertise. The teaching presence then sets the climate for social presence, which describes how participants bond with each other on a social and emotional level within a CoI. Finally, cognitive presence measures how much participants in a particular CoI construct meaning through social interaction with each other.

Teaching Presence

At the beginning of the course I expected that the instructor was the lecturer, but in fact [she was] not. The instructor is the advisor, facilitator and also the supervisor. (Jira, Thailand, fall 2004 participant)

Teaching presence is essential to quality interaction and learning in an online course. As Garrison (2006) noted, "Interaction and discourse plays a key role in higher-order learning but not without structure (design) and leadership (facilitation and direction)" (p. 6). As described by Anderson, Rourke, Garrison, and Archer (2001), teaching presence is comprised of three aspects: instructional design and organization, facilitating discourse, and direct instruction. See Table 8.3 for a list of indicators as determined by Anderson et al. (2001).

Most of the facilitation of discourse and direct instruction occurred on the public space of the asynchronous discussion board. Although various studies encourage the instructor of an online course to have a strong teaching presence that gives directives for the assignments and specifies expected behaviors on the discussion board to ensure that participants feel a strong sense of social presence or community (Finegold & Cooke, 2006; Meyer, 2003; Shea, Li, Swan, & Pickett, 2005), this chapter will show how instructors can establish a strong sense of teaching presence that also encourages participants to take responsibility for facilitating discussion and strengthening the social bonds within their own community

Table 8.3.   Teaching Presence Indicators

Teaching Presence	Indicators (Anderson et al., 2001)	Online TEYL Course
Instructional design and organization	Setting curriculum Designing methods Establishing time parameters Utilizing medium effectively Establishing netiquette	Introduced during course orientation In syllabus and course design of each 10 week unit
Facilitating discourse	Identifying areas of agreement/disagreement Seeking to reach consensus/understanding Encouraging, acknowledging, or reinforcing student contributions Setting climate for learning Drawing in participants, prompting discussion Assess the efficacy of the process	Ongoing process throughout the 10 week course On the asynchronous discussion board
Direct instruction	Present content/questions Focus the discussion on specific issues Summarize the discussion Confirm understanding through assessment and explanatory feedback Diagnose misconceptions Inject knowledge from diverse sources, e.g., textbook, articles, Internet, personal experiences (includes pointers to resources) Responding to technical concerns	Ongoing process throughout the 10 week course On the asynchronous discussion board

themselves. As the participant quote at the beginning of this section indicates, the instructor was not acting as a "sage on the stage" but behaved in a more facilitative manner.

Social Presence

It has helped to develop a feeling of camaraderie between teachers of different countries. Such an association if it continues will help in the enrichment and consolidation of so many concepts ... getting the ideas of a person sitting thousands of miles away and to know that they face problems similar to ours and look at the thing very much like us created a very positive feeling. (Jaya, India, fall 2004 participant)

In an online course, open space for communication not directly related to the course content is essential. Forging social bonds, a necessary part of the learning process, is incorporated in the CoI as social presence, which is an essential part of constructing meaning. Although it might be difficult to conceptualize how individuals at a distance who have never met each other could form interpersonal bonds through asynchronous interaction in online educational contexts, Rourke, Anderson, Garrison, and Archer (2001) found that CMC indeed does have the capacity to build such relationships. The authors developed a way to analyze these interactions by establishing categories and indicators for a thorough content analysis. As the above quote shows, participants did feel a sense of closeness and camaraderie through the geographic distance. According to Garrison et al. (2000), the original categories of social presence in their model of a CoI are emotional expression, open communication and group cohesion. Rourke et al. (2001) modified these categories for content analysis in the following way:

Emotional Expression > Affective Responses
Open Communication > Interactive Responses
Group Cohesion > Cohesive Responses

Affective responses refer to the display of emotional closeness, warmth, and openness among participants in the expressions used and personal information disclosed. Interactive responses are shown through the ways in which participants respond to each other. If there is a connection from one post to the next through a clear reference or through a direct reply or quote, then it is clear that there is interactivity among participants. Finally, cohesive responses refer to those behaviors that display a sense of community and commitment among group members. See Table 8.4 for

Table 8.4.   Social Presence Indicators

Social Presence	Indicators
Affective	Expression of emotions Use of humor Self-disclosure
Interactive	Continuing a thread Quoting from others' messages Referring explicitly to others' messages Asking questions Complimenting, expressing appreciation Expressing agreement
Cohesive	Vocatives Addresses or refers to the group using inclusive pronouns Phatics, salutations

the formal indicators for social presence established by Rourke et al. (2001) for use in content analysis.

Social presence in the CoI is much like Wenger's (1998) notion of mutual engagement where participants in a CoP engage meaningfully in shared activities through interactivity and the formation of social relationships. Each group of participants goes through its own negotiation of group identity and establishment of group cohesion that is specific to the identities and cultures within a particular group. It is through this social interactivity that participants can engage in critical inquiry of ideas, collective problem posing and creation of new knowledge. Critical inquiry that participants engage in through online discussions can be conceptualized through Garrison et al.'s (2001) notion of cognitive presence.

Cognitive Presence

It was so valuable and interesting to deal with and read about different ideas and experiences in teaching English language around the word, this matter gave me a deeper look about different cultures and points of view, encouraged me to adopt new methods and materials in my teaching process and opened my eyes to new aspects and solutions in TEYL. (Sabeen, Syria, fall 2005 participant)

Garrison et al.'s (2001) practical inquiry model operationalizes their notion of cognitive presence within asynchronous discussion. The model has four distinct phases that represent an "idealized sequence of the process of critical inquiry" (p. 4) that occurs on asynchronous discussion boards.

Phase 1: Triggering Event

- Participants pose questions or problems on the discussion board based on their personal experience.

Phase 2: Exploration

- Participants explore a particular issue or problem by questioning each other and sharing experiences and information. They shift back and forth between their own reflection and social interaction with the group.

Phase 3: Integration

- Participants begin to integrate the ideas shared in the exploration phase by connecting them to each other and proposing possible resolutions to the problems or issues. They continue to shift between reflection and social interaction, but now they begin to construct new knowledge or meaning through the interaction of ideas.

Phase 4: Resolution

- Participants find solutions to the problem posed and may possibly experiment or apply some of the proposed resolutions discussed in the integration phase. If participants cannot actually test the possible solutions in reality, they may still go through a process of thinking critically about the solutions and arrive at some consensus on the issue (Garrison et al., 2001).

Socially supported discourse on asynchronous discussion boards as the four phases on the practical inquiry model show can create a CoP which Wenger (1998) defines as mutual engagement in a joint enterprise, shared repertoire and the negotiation of meaning with the purpose of creating new knowledge. Notice in the participant quote above how the interaction with other participants and ideas encourage deeper thought leading to new methods and solutions to challenges in the field of TEYL. However, encouraging this type of discourse for an international group of participants who do not have an established relationship prior to being introduced to the online learning community is a complex process that requires establishing trust from the beginning of the course and encouraging social interaction among the participants. Thus social presence, the bonding of participants, is critical to cognitive presence, significant negotiation of meaning among them. The following section on the use of inclusive pedagogy and cultural pluralism in the online TEYL course illustrates how teaching presence can be distributed and social presence can be facilitated for the development of professional relationships among a culturally diverse international group of teachers.

CULTURALLY INCLUSIVE PEDAGOGY

When we say different teachers, we mean a panoply of experiences in various environments. What can be richer! Some confirmed my practices and ideas and others gave variants and parallel methods. (Hakim, Tunisia, fall 2004 participant)

When participants are placed firmly at the center of the learning process, the instructor's role becomes facilitative and the classroom becomes a more open and democratic space founded in "a deep respect for the particularity of experience" (Wenger, 1998, p. 214). As the quote above indicates, it is the richness of each participant's personal experience in his/her own country and context that built a strong foundation for learning. The online course instructor employed inclusive pedagogy as a central strategy to involve each participant holistically in the learning process (Adams, 1992; Banks, 1991; Darder, 1996; Giroux & McLaren, 1996; hooks, 1994; Tuitt, 2003). By foregrounding individual experience and the cu6ltural diversity, the instructor explicitly recognized participants as experts in their individual teaching and cultural contexts.

McLoughlin (2007) surveys research studies relevant to multicultural learning in online initiatives and discusses the importance of global inclusively in e-learning settings, where designers "must ensure cultural pluralism in instructional design, pedagogy, and all aspects of the educational experience" (p. 225). Accordingly, online educators are challenged to adopt appropriate learning theories, recognize cultural diversity among learners and in educational environments, and design learning environments based on culturally inclusive pedagogies.

Collaborative learning and dialogue are key to culturally inclusive pedagogy and, therefore, successful learning in international contexts. Faigley (1999) points out that "most learning is not 'self-taught,' not a solitary experience, and that people learn best learning with other people" (p. 137). Each classroom is respected as its own distinct pedagogical space where according to hooks (1994) "strategies must constantly be changed, reinvented and reconceptualized to address each new teaching experience" (pp. 10-11). Building a CoI online requires an open, comfortable space for sharing ideas and experiences where all participants are valued with their voices activated as an integral part of the learning process. Jaya, an fall 2004 participant from India, wrote, "It was indeed a great learning experience to share with groupmates' problems and ideas. Sharing was a very important part of both learning and socializing. The educational environment was healthy and invigorating."

The course took four approaches to implementing inclusive pedagogy online to create this "healthy and invigorating" context for the teachers' work together. This use of culturally inclusive pedagogy to guide teaching presence was instrumental in building social and cognitive presences and helped participants form a community that could sustain itself beyond the scope of the course.

1. Introductions to activate participants' voice and forge social bonds
2. Open and unstructured spaces for dialogue
3. Community building assignments to foreground diverse individual expertise and cultural contexts
4. Student moderation of the discussion board to promote learners autonomy

Introductions to Activate Participant Voice and Forge Social Bonds

Culturally inclusive pedagogy helps to activate student voice and forge social bonds. Therefore, the course began with participants introducing themselves personally, professionally, and culturally. The instructions for the first discussion forum "Introductions" follow.

> Please post a brief introduction of yourself to the class. Just click on INTRODUCTIONS.
> Feel free to share both personal and professional information about yourselves. Please be sure to use at least one of the following prompts below in your introduction.
> – Share an interesting fact about your country/culture that you think no one would know about.
> – Tell us one thing about yourself that makes you unique as a person or as a teacher.
> Post your introduction and then respond to others. Get to know each other by responding and asking each other questions. This is our chance to get to know each other before the course begins.

Then, the instructor modeled the kind of post expected for this introduction discussion forum by including acknowledgement of the struggles of adult language learners, sensitivity to the additional responsibilities of parent participants, and encouragement for participants to interact with each other.

> As the professor of this course, let me be the first to post a message with a brief introduction.
>
> One characteristic of the United States, where I come from, is its diversity and multiculturalism. I was born in Baltimore, Maryland near UMBC, and my ethnic background is Korean. Being Korean-American has made it possible for me to have exposure to more than one language and culture growing up.
>
> One of the largest influences on my teaching (outside the classroom) has been witnessing the struggles of my Korean parents to learn and perfect their usage of English in work and social situations. This has led me to greater understanding and appreciation of the challenges of language learning with adults. Another huge influence has been watching my young nephew grow up speaking three languages: English, Chinese, and Spanish. This has led me to marvel at the natural ways in which children acquire language. If you have children, you know what I'm talking about!
>
> Let's get to know one another. Tell the class about yourself and your country. You don't have to write about teaching children or teaching English. You can introduce yourself on any topic!

As it can be seen in this sample introduction by a participant in the 2004 implementation of the online TEYL course, the participants are establishing their relationships with each other through the introduction activity.

> Hi to all,
>
> Maybe I'm the last to get myself introduced, please accept my apology for this delay, trust me nothing could be done about it.
>
> Well, I'm Aamira, a 23-year-old English teacher from Lebanon, the most beautiful country in the Middle East area. Our country is well-known by its spectacular nature, the sea, the mountains, and its charming weather. Not only that, Lebanon is also famous by its archeological history. My nations and cultures have left us lots of tokens and traditions.
>
> I started teaching two years ago and believe me it was really hard for me to deal with those kids, especially that they were really giving me hard time at the very beginning. I was responsible for the special class that includes all native English speakers who came with their parents to settle in their homeland. So you imagine the alienation these kids experienced and the feeling of estrangement they were subjected to.... Well, it took me more than one month to get to know each student's problem and to help him/her to get over it. From this first year of teaching, I realized that the teacher is not only the one who explains a lesson to the class, and then tests them to check their comprehension and understanding, he's rather a friend who should love and care for his learners.

This year I'm teaching in two schools, one is an intermediate school from Grade 6 to Grade 9, the students there are weak but I'm trying to help them to the maximum, and they're really highly spirited and showing a great interest toward improving. I really feel satisfied till now with my first group of young learners. As for the second school, here lies the problem, can you imagine I'm teaching grades 10 and 11, they are almost my age and BOYS!!! at the very beginning they used to give me a real hard time.... But now thanks God it's working perfectly well, it's really magical!!

Enough talking about me now.... I just want to say it's a real pleasure to be participating in this online course and I'm looking forward toward getting to know all the participants in this course, and much thanks to all the professors.

My warmest regards,
Aamira

There were six responses to this message by the instructor and five other participants welcoming this person to the community. Here is a sample response that clearly shows the social presence being established:

Hi Aamira,

Nice to meet you another teacher from Lebanon.
I am Faida and I'm from Qatar. Don't worry, first years in teaching are always very hard.
I wish we have great time Aamira, full of ideas and communication.
I wish you all the best and all the luck in the world.

See you,
Faida

Through use of inclusive pedagogy in the introduction discussion forum, the instructor was able to create a space that encouraged participants to begin forming social bonds. As the examples above show, the participants are interacting with each other, building cohesion as a group, and expressing positive emotions related to getting to know each other in the course both personally and professionally, which are indicators of social presence. Therefore, use of culturally inclusive pedagogy is instrumental in establishing social presence.

Open and Unstructured Spaces for Dialogue

An online course that employs culturally inclusive pedagogies provides open spaces for unstructured communication not directly related to the course content. Participants need this space to socialize.

> Social communication is an essential component of educational activity. Just as a face-to-face school or campus provides places for students to congregate socially, an online educational environment should provide a space, such as a virtual café, for informal discourse.... The forging of social bonds has important socioaffective and cognitive benefits on the learning activities. The virtual café should be primarily a student space and not be directly tied to the curriculum. (Harasim, Hiltz, Teles, & Turoff, 1996, p. 137)

The course included two discussion forums where participants were free to ask each other questions or share information not necessarily related to the course curriculum—the "CyberCafe" and the "Q&A Forum." These open discussion forums evolved into places where participants shared information beyond the scope of the course including thoughts on recently attended conferences, planned presentations, recommendations of useful Web sites and books for TEYL, personal worries regarding the completion of the course due to the technical problems, and issues posed about the field of teaching English in different contexts. An example from the CyberCafe was the following post:

> Hello. I have a question to all the participants. Which version of English are you teaching: British or American? It is known that approximately 90% of people who speak English speak American English. In Russia they use the British version in schools. How about your countries?

This post was followed by six responses including the following:

> In Indonesia, the formal schools usually tend to British English. Private courses offer a variety of American, Australian, and others. Majority in communication, we do not really care which.
> What I usually do in my teachers training classes, I pointed the difference but let them choose whichever they like.
> I am working in the U.S. Embassy and one of our programs is English Language Fellow, where we bring ELT experts to works with institutions for a year. Most institutions are interested in joining the program, all request to get at least one native speaker. But when the expert happened to be African-American, they are kind of disappointed. In their mind, a native speaker should be American. But what is native American? That is difficult to say, right?
>
> Cheers from Indonesia,
> Aasera

These topics were not directly related to the course, but echo important discussions in the wider field of teaching English as a foreign language in participants' societies and professional networks.

In addition, when one participant still had not received the course packet of materials in the mail and wrote a desperate message to the Q&A forum; five participants responded with their stories of how they received their packet in the mail late as well, words of comfort, and suggestions for the participant to help her receive the packet. Indeed, having an open forum is a wonderful way for the participants to communicate with each other and lend their support to each other, thus helping to create stronger bonds. In addition, it is a space to bring up topics not in the course curriculum that are relevant and of interest to participants. As the examples above illustrate, creating a completely open space and unstructured space, which promotes cultural inclusively and learner autonomy, can assist in building social presence and encourage critical thought on self-determined topics. These actions in the open spaces support the formation of the vCoP within the online course.

Community Building Assignments to Foreground Diverse Individual Expertise and Cultural Contexts

Because culturally inclusive pedagogy situates the learner at the center of the learning process, the course assignments were designed to highlight diverse individual experience and cultural contexts. These assignments promoted their understanding of each other's contexts and encouraged the sharing of professional knowledge. As mentioned above, the instructor gave a set of community building assignments, which are listed below:

- English education profile: National English education profile, policies and language requirements, school environments, materials, technologies.
- Student profile: Detailed description of students in participant's YL class
- Activities portfolio: Effective and motivating activities for all four language skills appropriate for a specific YL student profile.
- Annotated bibliography: Evaluate EFL textbooks and resources.

The first two assignments, English education profile and student profile, were given in the first 2 weeks of instruction and required participants to write about their TEYL context in detail, from the national educational policies to the school policies and environment to their specific classroom situations, including descriptions of the YLs they are teaching. Upon completion of the assignment, the instructor posted all of the profiles on a Web page with links from each participant's name and country to the profile for everyone in the class to read. This helped the participants understand each other's teaching contexts and discover the similarities and differences in each other's teaching situations.

The activities portfolio and annotated bibliography were assignments given in the middle of the course. By this time, participants were able to post these assignments themselves in a public space similar to a Weblog. By sharing effective activities for TLs in all the four language skills and their favorite EFL textbooks, stories, and Web sites, all participants benefited from this collection of activities and resources. Including assignments like the ones described above were instrumental in building a sense of professional community among participants and set the stage for the kind of collaborative learning that genuinely appreciates the expertise of each participant and incorporates every participant's voice in the learning process. Therefore, these assignments were key steps toward developing the CoI in the online TEYL course.

Student Moderation of the Discussion Board to Promote Learners' Autonomy

Developing learner autonomy is a key element in culturally inclusive pedagogy. One of the markers of inclusively is to activate student voice and encourage student participation and collaboration. Although the teaching presence in an online course typically sets strict parameters for the interaction on the discussion board in order to increase the social and cognitive presences in a CoI, it is still necessary to encourage learner autonomy along side of these important parameters. In fact, two studies using Garrison et al.'s (2001) practical inquiry model framework to analyze the discussion board interactions described recommendations for effective strategies to moderate asynchronous online discussions to achieve higher levels of critical thinking (Celentin, 2007; Pawan, Paulus, Yalcin, & Chang, 2003), which included structuring the behavior of participants by setting strict requirements for participation on the asynchronous discussion board, such as deadlines for initial posts and responses and a suggested length for the messages posted to the discussion board, by modeling appropriate behavior on the discussion board, such as the length and quality of posts, and by being active participants in the discussion as well. However, Pawan et al. (2003) and Anderson et al. (2001) both encourage more learner-centred discussions by assigning students to be responsible for facilitating the discussions. As Pawan et al. explain, assigning specific discussion roles to establish teaching presence in a more learner-centred manner can "focus the discussion and give students authority and responsibility but students require training and modelling by instructors before they can assume the roles in an effective manner" (p. 136). Therefore, in the online TEYL course, the instructor used the "Starter-Wrapper" technique that was originally established by Hara, Bonk, and Angeli (2000). The goal of the Starter-Wrapper technique, which was used in the second implementation of the course, was to increase the levels of social and cognitive presence. See the description of the Starter-Wrapper roles in the instructions for the discussion board given to participants below:

Participants not only followed the instructor's modeling (Figure 8.2) in terms of the content of the starter and wrapper, but continued to differentiate the roles through their choice of font color, that is, the

---

Discussion Board

For the discussion board, post the main points of your journal for your classmates and instructor to read by Monday midnight EST. Please do **not** post your whole journal on the discussion board. Also, please type your posts into the text box. Do **not** attach your responses. You can attach extra handouts or pictures if you would like. Finally, post at least 2 responses on the discussion board by Wednesday midnight EST. You will be graded on the quality of your posts, so try to interact meaningfully in each post. *Here is where the real learning begins through interaction with each other!*

Discussion Board Seminar
For each unit, two participants will be responsible for managing the Discussion Board. These two people will respond to classmates' posts and ask questions that challenge, connect, and extend information posted to the discussion board. The two roles are:

(1) **Starter:** *This person will start the discussion by asking motivating questions and/or posing relevant problems related to the topics of the unit. S/he should post to the discussion board sometime before Monday. S/he will also keep the discussion going by getting participants to share ideas, explore the question(s), and think critically about the topics or problems posed.*

(2) **Wrapper:** *This person will encourage participants to find solutions and real-life applications to the problems posed by using motivating questions (like the starter). S/he will integrate the ideas shared by the group and then conclude the unit by summarizing all new ideas, solutions, and applications constructed through the discussion.*

NOTE: I will be the starter and wrapper for the first unit. My starter posts will be in green. My wrapper posts will be in purple. Please email me and let me know if there is a particular unit in which you would like to be a starter or wrapper. I will assign the schedule for the Discussion Board starters and wrappers by October 10th.

Figure 8.2.   Discussion Board.

starter messages were always posted in green and the wrapper posts in purple. Here are two examples of starter messages, the first one from the instructor.

Dear Sabeen,

Your ideas are expressed very well in your post!
　You wrote:
　"I think the most important factor is to create a second language environment similar to that of learners' native language, which is really a challenging factor but we can achieve it by adopting thoroughly co-operation between schools administrative, teachers and parents, and we need to allocate large budget for this purpose too."
　I have a question for you and everyone else:
　What are some specific things that each of the parties mentioned above (i.e., administration, teachers, parents) can do to create a "second language environment similar to that of learners' native language?" I guess I'm looking for some specific suggestions that we can take with us and try to promote in the future. Can anyone give me some suggestions?
　Thank you so much for considering this issue. It is so important, and I look forward to reading your ideas!

Prof. Shin

The instructor, as a model for facilitation, first gave positive feedback to reinforce the participant contribution and then focused the discussion on one part of the post by using a direct quote from it. In addition, the instructor showed how to further the discussion by posing a follow-up question for the group to move more deeply into the issue. The following is an example of a starter post by a student.

Dear Doaa,

You said "If you take it the other way" What do you mean by that? Is it by telling them with L1! Or rephrase it with another way? Please clarify. Also you add "the speaker was too fast for the student to understand." I hope this will never happen with YL classroom, because they need to listen to their teacher and follow all what s/he is saying. In this case s/he should talk slowly and clearly. Good luck with your classes I like your way of "wind up for the day" I think it fits with the elder students more than the younger.
　Here we come to Q2. While our unit this week is about listening, I have a question. If you have a song that belong to the lesson, or it is an introduction to the lesson, do you think that the students must know the song before they hear it at the class or they just hear it at the first time in the class with you?
　Do you have to use well known songs with your YL or try let them hear something new.

Best compliments,
Ahmed

In this example, the participant in the starter role used the same strategies as the instructor to further the discussion, thereby distributing the teaching presence on the discussion board.

ADAPTING THE COMMUNITY OF INQUIRY FRAMEWORK

At the beginning of the course, the CoI looked like Figure 8.3.

In the role of starter and wrapper, participants were engaged as facilitators responsible for the social construction of knowledge on the discussion board. As the participants became more responsible as discussion board moderators, the teaching presence of the instructor seemed to diminish. Garrison and Anderson (2003) describe this process, "As participants develop cognitively and socially, the more distributed teaching presence will become" (p. 72). This shift in teaching presence to the participants can be reconceptualized in this adaptation of Garrison et al.'s (2000) CoI model (see Figure 8.4).

The participants in the online TEYL course were all teachers or teacher trainers who were expected to disseminate what they learned in the course and become active in their local CoPs. Thus, the distributed teaching presence during the course would evolve further as participants transitioned out of the course. At that point, they became colleagues and leaders in multiple professional CoPs where there is no directive or even

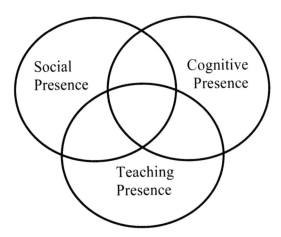

Figure 8.3.   Garrison et al.'s (2000) CoI model.

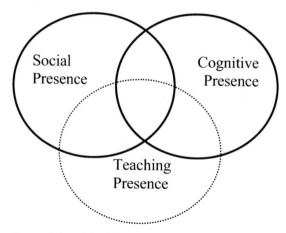

Figure 8.4.   Distributed role of teaching presence.

facilitative teaching presence. Yet, the social bonds developed during the course are essential to their continued work together on issues in TEYL. Therefore, the professional community that participants join after the course could be understood as the intersection between social and cognitive presences as represented in Figure 8.5.

VIRTUAL AND COLOCATED COPS BEYOND THE SCOPE OF THE COURSE

As a result of this course, each participant was expected to somehow disseminate their learning among other English teachers. In the final unit, called "Beyond this Course," participants wrote a journal entry about how they expected to apply their new knowledge in the future. The prompt

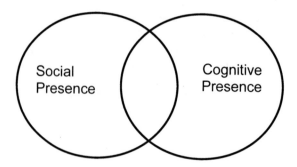

Figure 8.5.   Postcourse adaptation of CoI model.

was, "What is your role as a teacher, teacher trainer, or administrator in the field of TEYL? Describe what you can contribute to the teaching of English to YLs in your country." After writing the journal, participants shared their plans on the discussion board. Many of them planned to use what they learned in the online course to train other teachers in their schools and local areas. One enthusiastic fall 2004 participant from Senegal wrote, "Well, I'm going to be very busy from December 20, 2004 to January 23, 2005 trying to 'season' or spice some 'unseasoned teachers.' "

Another experienced teacher from Turkey described her dissemination plans:

> One of the big problems related to TEYL in Turkey is the lack of teachers specifically trained for this level. Using what I have gained in this course, I am planning to launch a series of workshops and/or in-service teacher training programmes in the primary schools in my area with a view to raising the teachers' awareness of the techniques, materials, etc. appropriate for YLs. (Rana, Turkey, fall 2004 participant)

In the months after the completion of the fall 2004 implementation of the course, some participants developed ongoing professional collaborations. Others became involved in colocated CoPs of EFL teachers in their geographic regions. Many used relationships and knowledge from the course to create or participate in local CoPs. Two teachers from the 2004 implementation who successfully created CoPs of teachers in India and Turkey (see volume 1 chapter 12 by Rana Yildirim from Turkey) joined the instructor in a colloquium at the 39th annual TESOL convention, the largest international conference for the field of teaching English to speakers of other languages (TESOL) in the United States, in Tampa, Florida in 2006. They described their experiences with their colocated CoPs as a product of the online TEYL course with the course instructor. Participants also began to publish articles for international publications, including six participants from Bahrain, Qatar, Turkey, India, Indonesia, and Tunisia who published their thematic unit plans from the online TEYL course in the 2007 issue of *English Teaching Forum* (Vol. 45, No. 2) which is in distribution worldwide. Furthermore, participants from Syria, Mali, Lebanon, Yemen, Saudi Arabia, Tajikistan, and other countries reported that they led workshops in their schools and regions and mentored new teachers based on what they learned from the online TEYL course.

Building on the best practices of the E-Teacher program, the U.S. Department of State's Office of English Language Programs (OELP) with the University of Oregon developed another online training program (Sept-Dec 2006) using the newly published OELP teacher training materials, *Shaping the Way We Teach English*. As a face-to-face follow-on, OELP then sponsored over 90 participants from countries in North

Africa, the Middle East, Central Asia, and Turkey (eight of whom had participated in the online TEYL courses) to meet together in January 2007 in Cairo, Egypt where they made presentations, attended training sessions, and collaborated with each other to evaluate the experience in their various online teacher training courses. They used the conference to create a plan of action for expanding the international CoP of EFL teaching professionals in its virtual and colocated forms. After the OELP sponsored conference, many of these same participants made presentations and led workshops at the 12th annual EFL skills conference at the American University in Cairo, where they provided over 40% of the conference presentations.

CONCLUSION

The goals of the online TEYL course were two fold:

1. To present a unique opportunity for international collaboration among TEYL professionals, identify common problems and concerns, and collectively seek culturally relevant instructional solutions to educational challenges in each country.
2. To empower and equip diverse participants to participate in an international TEYL community and to disseminate new knowledge locally and regionally as teacher leaders and trainers.

The instructor facilitated participants' learning about new TEYL teaching techniques while encouraging active social and cognitive presence by all participants. As strong teaching presence changed to facilitating and distributed presence, participants took more active and leadership roles in the class which prepared them to do the same later in their local CoP with other teachers. The use of culturally inclusive pedagogies was central to the facilitated international conversation about teaching and learning in diverse cultural contexts. Furthermore, the instructor's model of inclusive pedagogies helped prepare course participants to continue such practices in their own teaching and training. Adapting Garrison et al.'s (2000) CoI framework, it is clear that an online course for teaching professionals can shift from an instructional environment with a strong teaching presence into a student-led CoI with a distributed teaching presence that helps to forge social and professional bonds among course participants and support their performance as teacher leaders and trainers. If the instructor can successfully shift the teaching presence into a more facilitative presence by the participants themselves, then the bonds built among teaching professionals in the course will likely survive and possibly thrive beyond the scope of the instructional setting forming what we can now recognize as a vCoP.

There are challenging issues in developing any online CoP into a cohesive, collaborative whole that are particularly complicated when it is an international and vCoP—composed of individuals from 29 countries with real differences in life experiences and outlooks. The implementation of the culturally inclusive approaches that brought success to the online TEYL course discussed here will necessarily take their own forms in distinct learning spaces with unique participants who bring their knowledge and cultures, their classroom challenges, and their questions to any meaningful inquiry into teaching.

RECOMMENDATIONS FOR FUTURE RESEARCH

Online courses and online communities are increasingly part of our educational landscape. For teachers interested in global dialogues and inclusive pedagogies, learning how to maximize critical and engaged discussion online is fundamental. The CoI framework and its focus on its asynchronous discussion board described in this chapter calls for more research. While this chapter has primarily addressed questions of teaching presence, future projects could attempt to measure and describe the levels of social and cognitive presence in an online course utilizing the CoI framework, particularly for an international audience whose members have varying levels of proficiency in English (or other language used for international discussion). Other research may focus on the activities and sustainability of an international vCoP, for example, how it attempts to draw from and support various local CoPs and how barriers created by differences in technology and internet access might be addressed. Finally, it would be useful to examine carefully how a vCoP can connect local CoPs to each other in a sustained, internationally distributed network of English teaching professionals.

As this rich arena of research unfolds, what is certain to continue is the enthusiasm of teachers to participate in international dialogues about teaching and learning. As Polina, a participant from Russia during fall 2004, wrote,

> It was great! I have learnt so much about the teachers in different parts of the world. And what was the most surprising for me—we all have the same problems and the children are the same all over the world, and the schools are nearly the same and the teachers have the same aim—to teach better and better.

NOTES

1. bell hooks is a pseudonyum for Dr. Gloria Watson. Her explanation for the use of the lower case in her name is as follows. She explains that one of her great-grandmothers, a Native American, was named bell hooks and that her own use of the name is "about celebrating female legacies." When explaining the lower-case spelling that hooks prefers, she says it is "about ego: What's in a name? It is the substance in my books, not who is writing them, that is important."

REFERENCES

Adams, M. (1992). Cultural inclusion in the American college classroom. In N. V. N. Chism & L. L. B. Border (Eds.), *New directions for teaching and learning: Teaching for diversity* (pp. 5-17). San Francisco: Jossey-Bass.

Anderson, T., Rourke, L., Garrison, D. R., & Archer, W. (2001). Assessing teaching presence in a computer conferencing context. *JALN, 5*(2), 1-17.

Banks, J. (1991). Multicultural literacy and curriculum reform. *Education Horizons Quarterly, 69*, 135-140.

Celentin, P. (2007). Online education: analysis of interaction and knowledge building patterns among foreign language teachers. *Journal of Distance Education, 21*(3), 39-58.

Crystal, D. (1997). *English as a global language*. London: Cambridge University Press.

Darder, A. (1996). Creating the condition for cultural democracy in the classroom. In C. Turner, M. Garcia, A. Nora, & L. I. Rendon (Eds.), *Racial and ethnic diversity in higher education* (pp. 134-149). Needham Heights, MA: Simon & Schuster.

Faigley, L. (1999). Beyond imagination: The Internet and global digital literacy. In G. E. Hawisher & C. L. Selfe (Eds.), *Passions, pedagogies and 21st century technologies* (pp. 129-139). Logan: Utah State University Press.

Finegold, A., & Cooke, L. (2006). Exploring the attitudes, experiences and dynamics of interaction in online groups. *Internet and Higher Education, 9*(3), 201-215.

Garrison, D. R. (2006). *Online community of inquiry update: Social, cognitive, and teaching presence issues*. Unpublished manuscript. Retrieved October 8, 2007, from http://communitiesofinquiry.com/sub/papers.html

Garrison, D. R., & Anderson, T. (2003). *E-learning in the 21st century: A framework for research and practice*. London: Routledge Falmer.

Garrison, D. R., Anderson, T., & Archer, W. (2000). Critical inquiry in a text-based environment: computer conferencing in higher education. *The Internet and Higher Education, 2*(2-3), 87-105.

Garrison, D. R., Anderson, T., & Archer, W. (2001). Critical thinking, cognitive presence, and computer conferencing in distance education. *American Journal of Distance Education, 15*(1), 7-23.

Giroux, H., & McLaren, P. (1996). Teacher education and the politics of engagement: the case for democratic schooling. In P. Leistyna, A. Woodrum, & S. Sherblom (Eds.), *Breaking free: The transformative power of critical pedagogy* (pp. 301-332). Cambridge, MA: Harvard Educational Review.

Hara, N., Bonk, C. J., & Angeli, C. (2000). Content analysis of online discussion in an applied psychology course. *Instructional Science, 28*(2), 115-152.

Harasim, L., Hiltz, S. R., Teles, L., & Turoff, M. (1996). *Learning networks*. Cambridge, MA: MIT Press.

hooks, b. (1994). *Teaching to transgress: Education as the practice of freedom*. New York: Routledge.

hooks, b. (2003). Teaching *community: A pedagogy of hope*. New York: Routledge.

Lave, J., & Wenger, E. (1991). *Situated learning: Legitimate peripheral participation*. London: Cambridge University Press.

Lueg, C. (2000, September). *Where is the action in virtual communities of practice?* Paper presented at the Workshop Communication and Cooperation in Knowledge Communities, at the German Computer-Supported Cooperative Work Conference (D-CSCW), Munich, Germany. Retrieved March 6, 2007, from http://www-staff.it.uts.edu.au/~lueg/papers/commdcscw00.pdf

McCloskey, M. L., Orr, J., & Dolitsky, M. (2006). *Teaching English as a foreign language in primary school*. Alexandria, VA: TESOL.

McLoughlin, C. (2007). Adapting E-learning across cultural boundaries: A framework for quality learning, pedagogy, and interaction. In A. Edmundson (Ed.), *Globalized e-learning cultural challenges* (pp. 223-238). London: Information Science.

Meyer, K. (2003). Face-to-face versus threaded discussions: The role of time and higher-order thinking. *Journal of Asynchronous Learning Networks, 7*(3), 55-65.

Pawan, F., Paulus, T. M., Yalcin, S., & Chang, F. S. (2003). Online learning: patterns of engagement and interaction among in-service teachers. *Language Learning & Technology, 7*(3), 119-140.

Rourke, L., Anderson, T., Garrison, D. R., & Archer, W. (2001). Methodological issues in the content analysis of computer conference transcripts. *International Journal of Artificial Intelligence in Education, 12*(1), 8-22. Retrieved April 5, 2007, from http://aied.inf.ed.ac.uk/members01/archive/vol_12/rourke/full.html

Shea, P., Li, C. S., Swan, K., & Pickett, A. (2005). Developing learning community in online asynchronous college courses: The role of teaching presence. *Journal of Asynchronous Learning Networks, 9*(4), 59-82.

Tuitt, F. (2003). Afterword: Realizing a more inclusive pedagogy. In F. Tuitt & A. Howell (Eds.), *Race and higher education: Rethinking pedagogy in diverse college classrooms*. Cambridge, MA: Harvard Education Press.

Wenger, E. (1998). *Communities of practice: Learning, meaning, and identity*. London: Cambridge University Press.

CHAPTER 9

COMMUNITIES OF PRACTICE ACROSS LEARNING INSTITUTIONS

Thérèse Laferrière and Fernand Gervais

Internet-supported school-university partnerships for teacher education and professional development offer new possibilities for teacher learning. This chapter presents sociotechnical designs that stress the dynamics that come into play when people move from small-scale communities of practice (CoPs) or a local professional learning community to constellations of CoPs (virtual community). Three specific cases are presented, each one with its own level of internal coherence. Specifications regarding how design principles were applied are provided. These cases are all alternatives to conventional forms of teacher education and professional development. From day 1, two of the three cases were endorsed as innovative endeavors by the participating institutions. The third is a contrasting case. Network-enabled CoPs and the encompassing virtual community can benefit from the organizational processes in place within learning institutions when it comes to issues of sustainability and expansion. Moreover, the collaboration across learning institutions, as exemplified by the network-enabled CoPs, is also beneficial to these institutions in terms of bridging the divide between theory and practice.

Communities of Practice: Creating Learning Environments for Educators,
Volume 2, pp. 179–197
Copyright © 2008 by Information Age Publishing
All rights of reproduction in any form reserved.

INTRODUCTION

Over the last 10 years, researchers have shown a growing interest in the notion of CoPs, first described by Lave and Wenger (1991) and later expanded upon be Wenger (1998). Numerous books, research reports and scientific articles have further dissected and scrutinized it in ways Wenger himself could not have foreseen at the onset of his research with claim processors. Online communities and knowledge-based communities were certainly not at the forefront of his research endeavor. Obviously, his interest was elsewhere, namely in developing a sound conceptual framework about this notion. The concept itself covered a vast array of possibilities, from a group of friends involved in a hobby to a group of people sharing an occupation in a highly organized institution. Instead of defining what is or what is not, a CoP Wenger (1998) explored the nature of CoPs and described a set of features characterizing such a grouping. From this angle, every so-called CoP would more or less adhere to the features elaborated within the scope of his social theory of learning. It gave way to the emergence of parallel notions over the last few years, such as knowledge-based or learning communities. These are not necessarily congruent with the version proposed by Wenger (1998). In fact, most of them belong to a different epistemology as exemplified by Riel and Polin (2004). In order to avoid such a mishap a specific perspective will be kept in the background throughout this chapter. The idea will be promoted that the "small-scale local Community of Practice," where the significant part of our identity as an individual resides, still remains the core of the networked communities developed in various settings.

This chapter will focus on Internet-supported school-university partnerships for teacher education and professional development. It will demonstrate that, for virtual communities to be established on solid ground and to grow, both the support of the Web as a communication/collaboration space and anchorage in learning institutions across the professional development continuum is of great interest for designers of network-enabled CoPs. The three cases examined will show how this anchorage adopts different forms, each of them well adapted to the local CoP.

In the first section, the conceptual framework is presented, drawing on social perspectives on cognition (Rogoff, 1990) and a framework based on sociocultural theory (Engeström, 1987; Engeström & Middleton, 1996). The second section briefly describe three cases using the key concepts emphasized in the first section. The third section focuses on practical implications for the design of networked communities.

BACKGROUND

Basic Notions and Foundations

The notion of CoPs did not emerge out of a conceptual vacuum and the development of a social theory of learning was more than instrumental in this emergence. The conceptualization of learning as participation rather than acquisition finds its roots in the works of Lave and Wenger (1991), Bourdieu (1994) and neo-Vygotskians like Moll (1990) and Wertsch (1985). These researchers promoted a perspective centered on "praxis," an ancient notion revisited in our era and which comprised fundamental dimensions such as the sociohistorical one. Its focus on the idea that "we are what we do" took many turns, one of them leading to the emergence of fields like ergonomy and cognitive anthropology. This conceptualization was mostly ignored in academic circles and remained largely marginal in literature until the mid-90s. In fact, it gained momentum, from a popularity standpoint, when researchers from the "new Palo Alto school" at the Institute for Learning (IRL) and Palo Alto Research Center (PARC) championed notions like situated cognition (Brown, Collins, & Duguid, 1989), cognitive apprenticeship (Rogoff, 1990) and cultural cognition (Hutchins, 1995). The focus on social rather than individual dimensions of learning became quite appealing to many researchers, especially for those who did not come out of traditional schools in psychology, the perspective being put forward labeled as multidisciplinary. In fact, all the concepts related to the notion of CoPs (e.g., participation, engagement, reification, repertoire) fit very well with the desired trajectory of future teachers. Unfortunately, it does not seem to inspire those who are involved in the design of professional development processes. Teacher education has been systemized, structured, and conceptualized in such a way, inside and outside universities, that it is almost impossible to envision change or a reconceptualization such as the one proposed by CoPs without the presence and pressure of "new realities."

Schlager and Fusco (2004) were the first to connect the CoP notion, applied to teacher professional development, with virtual communities during the design of TAPPED_IN in the late 90s (Schlager & Schank, 1997). They suggested mutual engagement in a collective enterprise by the participating teachers that spans various stakeholder groups as the main characteristic of CoPs, but they also pointed to the importance of local professional CoPs. When members of a colocated CoP develop an online activity, they extend their interactions beyond physical meetings and to other CoPs. Institutionally based CoPs (e.g., a school-based CoP, a university-based CoP), which connect with self-improvement goals in mind, are part of the affordances provided by Internet-based activity centred on collaborative endeavors (Laferrière, Breuleux, & Erickson, 2004).

In this context, it is useful to make a distinction between horizontal and vertical networked-enabled CoPs. A horizontal network-enabled CoP is a community whose members share similar roles within or across their respective institutions. A vertical network-enabled CoP is a community whose members have different roles according to their levels of expertise regarding a specific approach or method, within or across their respective institutions. Sometimes, a CoP may be both horizontal and vertical as will be demonstrated through the scope of an activity theory framework.

University-School Partnerships for Teacher Learning: Subjects, Online Tools, and Artifacts

Sociotechnical designs that support, nurture, and harness the power of CoPs (Resta, in press; Schlager & Fusco, 2004) will be described through an activity theory framework (Engeström, 1987, see Figure 9.1). Agents as members of a same CoP used online tools and artifacts within their network-enabled community, defined here as a community whose members meet face-to-face at times and use the Internet to communicate and collaborate with one another. The main goal (or object-outcome) of the activity (ICT use for teacher learning purposes) in which they were engaged led to a transformed division of labor among participants. It was

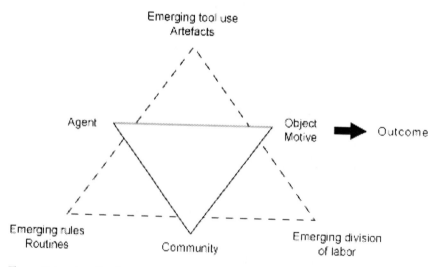

Figure 9.1.   Application of Engeström's (1987) activity theory framework.

exemplified through a specific set of rules and routines. Depending on the affordances of the technology in use, collaborative learning and/or knowledge building were supported. For instance, the database and embedded tools of Knowledge Forum, an advanced computer-supported collaborative learning (CSCL) environment, are designed to enable learners to engage in intentional learning and high-level processes of collaborative inquiry through written progressive discourse (Scardamalia & Bereiter, 1994). The database is an empty shell, and participants use a certain amount of tools to improve their ideas collectively. Other advanced CSCL environments have capabilities to support specific collaborative purposes. For example, Tapped In® offers numerous virtual rooms for distributed communities to communicate in a synchronous mode (Schlager & Schank, 1997).

The following sociocultural conceptualization synthesizes a 10-year experience in teacher education and teacher professional development in establishing or building on university-school partnerships with the support of the Internet and related tools. It illustrates the outcomes of a number of iterative cycles of reflection and actions. These cycles characterize networked teacher communities in the context of a number of Canadian schools and universities as well as a virtual community of support and communication in the use of ICT in teaching and learning, namely, TACT (Technology for Advanced Collaboration Among Teachers). Three sociotechnical designs featuring the contributions of three specific CoPs to the life of the TACT community are presented. In this design work, the set of principles described, emerged from earlier designs (TeleLearning-PDS)[1] anchored in university-school partnerships, which continue to serve our educational purposes.

Each CoP pursued its own specific activity, but became virtually part of a greater whole, namely TACT, a virtual community that produces knowledge on teaching and learning in networked classrooms (Laferrière & Nizet, 2006). A networked classroom, defined as a physical classroom environment with at least one computer connected to the Internet but

Table 9.1.   Design Principles

Ease of access	The classroom as a community of learners
Coconstitutionality	Diversity
Participatory design	Progressive distributed expertise
Multimodal social interaction	Collaborative reflective teaching
Local grounding	Collaborative knowledge building
Active collaborative learning	Interrelatedness

preferably more computers, is therefore considered the new workplace of the teacher.

CASES

The Contribution of the PROTIC Community

Learning to teach in a student-owned laptop classroom is the task-at-hand for this vertical network-enabled CoP, whose participants (school-based teachers, preservice teachers involved in student teaching, and university-based teacher educators) are participating from two different institutions, a university, and a school. Every term, six or seven pairs, each composed of a cooperative teacher and a student teacher, are created. They use online tools to engage school learners in project-based learning. Each member of the pair reflects on his or her experience in class in oral and written forms. Student teachers are asked to put forward elements directly related to their own professional growth. Therefore, they contribute to the development of TACT as a larger community. They are able to consult artifacts built over the last 10 years and stored in the TACT community Web site (http://www.tact.fse.ulaval.ca). Each term, a small-scale local CoP takes from (centrifugal effect) and gives back to (centripetal effect) the virtual community. At this point, observations are consistent with Wenger's (1998) perspective: the joint enterprise of the community (teaching in the networked classroom) has evolved and the shared repertoire has expanded through the two-way process of mutual engagement.

Through online discourse analysis, it has been possible to identify learning outcomes. They all point to the potential of this sociotechnical design to confront student teachers' traditional beliefs and help them forge their professional identities as beginning teachers in technology-rich classrooms. The analysis of conversations conducted during the 1999-2001 period revealed student teachers were able to develop a rationale for the use of laptop computers based on socioconstructivist principles. In addition, specific problems regarding their use in networked classrooms were addressed: classroom organization and management, planning, evaluation of cooperative/collaborative learning activities, and projects. During the 2001-2004 period, collaborative knowledge building became explicit. For example, the problem of student motivation and engagement was addressed collaboratively (Campos, Laferrière, & Lapointe, 2005). Moreover, student teachers' exchanges became more reflexive and less oriented towards practical problems (Allaire, 2006).

The 12 design principles alluded to previously are being transposed as follows in the PROTIC community's activity:

- Ease of access
  Except for a very few participants, access to Internet and a collaborative platform (Knowledge Forum) is possible from both school and home.

- Coconstitutionality
  The development of a sociotechnical infrastructure not only relies on electronic connectivity but on an increasing number of participants who value collaborative learning and knowledge.

- Participatory design
  The networking capacity is sustained and scaled through the Autumn and Winter Semester intake of student teachers, the renewed commitment of cooperative teachers who gave access to their classroom,[2] university supervisors who are also involved in collaborative research with cooperative teachers and graduate students through the university-school partnership agreement signed in 1994.

- Multimodal social interactions
  Participants meet onsite and online, cooperative teachers have access to the collaborative platform but student teachers are the ones engaged in online collaborative reflective practice. Since 1999, student teachers have clearly manifested a preference for collaborative rather than individual journal writing, problem setting and problem solving.

- Local grounding
  Whether planned or improvised, classroom events feed pairs' conversations (pre- and postaction). Primarily through the writings of student teachers, pairs contribute to the understanding of teaching and learning in the networked classroom through their colocated community, the PROTIC community, and the TACT community.

- Active collaborative learning
  In their colocated community and with the scaffolding of their university supervisor, student teachers engage in online collaborative learning.

- The classroom as a community of learners
  Pre- and in-service teachers are learning by doing as they design the networked classroom as a centre of inquiry where people,

resources and ideas are valued. The teachers and the school principal of the PROTIC program view themselves as a professional learning community, allowing legitimate peripheral participation (LPP) for one or two terms.

• Diversity
  Participants are different from term-to-term and so are the local events, circumstances, problems, and artifacts.

• Progressive distributed expertise
  Virtual collaborative spaces provide opportunities to share resources and expertise to solve complex and ill-structured problems.

• Collaborative reflective teaching
  Preservice teachers engage in collaborative reflective practice, which is a discursive process leading to the sharing and negotiation of meanings with others in a dialogical manner, on classroom organization and management of a student owned laptop (or networked) classroom and project-based learning in such a context. Moreover, conversation and actions are meant to complement each other for the coconstruction of knowledge: practice leads to negotiation of meaning, and clarification of meaning suggests relevant actions.

• Collaborative knowledge building
  When meaning is negotiated across the members of the co-located community, ways of understanding necessarily evolve. Knowledge resources are shared with other members of the PROTIC community and higher levels of understanding emerge.

• Interrelatedness
  Resources, events, agents, artifacts, and authors interconnect in ways that add continuity and integration to student teachers' experience as they learn to teach in networked classrooms. They add as well to the experience of practitioners' working in networked classrooms.

The PROTIC community, whose joint enterprise is teaching in a networked classroom, is an exemplar of participation nurtured and sustained through a university-school partnership. The sustainability of such a partnership is obviously a factor related to the viability of this CoP and, reciprocally, this CoP is providing focus and substance to the participants involved in the partnership. As agents situated in different institutions, participants have specific goals to achieve and roles to adopt (schoolteachers, preservice teachers, university-based teacher educators). In the PROTIC community, they share a common goal: understand better the use of laptops (tools) in networked classrooms when attempting to create powerful learning environments (object-outcomes) for school learners or student teachers. A reflective practitioner model (Schön, 1987) has been valued using networked laptops to clarify pedagogical intents and expected learning results. With respect to effective use of laptops, meaning negotiation has been promoted: negotiating the purpose and rationale of going online for interactions inside the classroom; sorting out online tools providing better learning affordances (Google, Inspiration, Knowledge Forum, and others). The classroom-based learning community was established a few years ago as a networked learning environment characterized by democratic processes, visible student engagement, role flexibility, meaningful learning tasks and projects, and various forms of evaluation. In order to understand how pedagogical intents and results converge—the definition given to effective use of student-owned laptop computers (or productivity)—some student teachers joined their cooperative teachers and a university researcher to conduct three iterations of a collaborative research that led to the writing and rewriting of an electronic book describing the practice of integrating ICTs in student-owned laptop classrooms (Partenariat PROTIC-FCAR-TACT, 2001).

As it evolved, the PROTIC community has inspired similar initiatives in primary and secondary education. Laval University's graduating teachers are displaying leadership in such initiatives and in other networked learning environments. When they do so, they are more likely to remain "virtually" connected afterwards to the TACT community. Moreover, the PROTIC university-school partnership has been extended to a junior college (CEGEP de Ste-Foy) which developed its own laptop program (PASCAL). A collaborative evaluation research project (Laferrière, Deschênes, & Gaudreault-Perron, 2007) is documenting the learning performance of the PROTIC graduates registered to this college.

The Contribution of the Remote Networked School Community

Learning to work in a networked school is the task-at-hand for this horizontal/vertical network-enabled CoP whose members come from various schools associated with 13 different school districts, each having small remote schools on its territory. Participants are professionals working in a networked classroom or school. During the first phase of the RNSI (Remote Networked School Initiative),[3] participants from three local sites interacted onsite and online with school-based participants or practitioners interested in the activity of remote networked schools (RNS). In phase two (2004-2006), 10 more school districts joined the RNSI.

Participants have been using online tools to support communication and collaboration among school learners. In each RNS, possibilities of networking between teachers and learners are being explored. Experts from the school district, school principals, and three participating universities collaborate in this venture. Their contribution is reflected in school learners' written discourse using Knowledge Forum, and can be accessed by other interested teachers and students of the same school district. Statistical data is made available online by the university-based research team. As they all use the same database on Knowledge Forum, each school's colocated CoP takes from (centrifugal effect) and gives back (centripetal effect) to their school district CoP. Given school-based teachers' participation, mutual engagement, and sense of being part of the same joint enterprise (teaching in a networked school), some school district CoPs have more vitality than others do. Onsite teacher meetings are prevalent but traces of their online planning through videoconferencing and exchange through e-mail and chat are accessible. School principals' leadership and support also make a difference, and two distinct small-scaled CoPs for school principals have been set up, one for primary and one for secondary school principals. They meet onsite and online (conference calls, videoconferencing) on a regular basis and support is being provided. Face-to-face knowledge transfer sessions allow representatives of all school districts to share accomplishments and interrogations. These moments are critical for the shared repertory of the larger RNS CoP to expand. Once again, the three main characteristics Wenger (1998) attributed to CoPs are displayed.

This sociotechnical design is aimed toward innovative teaching practice in small RNS. Through onsite and online communications, teachers have been either reinforced or confronted in their teaching beliefs and are forging their professional identity as RNS teachers. This process has been documented (Allaire et al. 2006; Laferrière, Breuleux, & Inchauspé, 2004) quite extensively. During the 2004-2006 period, the frequency of online meetings grew: teachers planned lessons together, teams of teachers met occasionally, a teacher or a school principal discussed matters with a faculty advisor. A particular impact of this initiative was not only to strengthen the local professional learning community or CoP but also to create constellations of CoPs along the way.

Another impact was the emergence of collaborative knowledge building among school learners (Allaire et al., 2006).

The 12 design principles mentioned above are reflected as follows in the RNS community's activity:

- Ease of access
  Over the years, broadband access to the Internet allowed for the use of a multipoint videoconferencing system (iVisit) and a sophisticated collaborative platform (Knowledge Forum).

- Coconstitutionality
  The premise for the development of a sociotechnical infrastructure is broadband access and people with a networking capacity and who value the activity of small rural schools and their individual contributions to the evolution of small towns.

- Participatory design
  The networking capacity is sustained and scaled from year-to-year by school administrators who establish partnerships with other schools. At first, three sites were involved. In the second phase, 13 school districts were involved and, in phase three, 23 school districts are likely to participate. Researchers from three Canadian universities (Laval University, McGill University, and University of Quebec at Chicoutimi) participate in the design and preservice students from two universities have their field placement in the RNS.

- Multimodal social interactions
  At the onset of a school-to-school partnership, participants meet face to face and, later, mostly online. Teachers have onsite and online (just-in-time) support available through their local school district or the university-based team. Over 50% of the activity on the videoconferencing system involves teachers communicating with each other or with experts.

- Local grounding
  Each site is considered critically important to the implementation of the RNS initiative. The principal and teachers in each participating school form among themselves a professional learning community. A particular impact of the initiative is that it strengthens the local professional learning community.

- Active collaborative learning
Teachers from the RNS experience together, and with teachers from larger schools, how to conduct online activities and projects for their students. Onsite and online facilitation is provided.

- The classroom as a community of learners
It is not unusual to find school learners from one grade involved in individual tasks while their teacher is working with students from the other grades. As they use online tools with their students RNS teachers are encouraged to see their classroom as a distributed community of learners.

- Diversity
Colocated teachers vary from year-to-year in small rural schools, as the turnover is high. Whether they stay in the same school or go to another school within the district, the local context (access to computers, collegial support, school principal leadership) is likely to differ and influence one way or another, the conduct of student online activities and projects.

- Progressive distributed expertise
From any school in the district, the text-based virtual collaborative space is accessible to teachers. Plans and resources can be shared and district-based facilitators play a supportive role.

- Collaborative reflective teaching
Teacher planning of learning activities and projects involving students from more than one classroom (preaction) and the debriefing afterwards (postaction) lead to the identification of successful practices. At times, a university-based teacher educator participates in the discussion.

- Collaborative knowledge building
The design of the RNS in small rural villages is a work in progress. Online communication and collaboration patterns are being uncovered and student learning results monitored (e.g., reading comprehension tests). The colocated community ways of understanding how their RNS may function are considered knowledge objects of value to members of the RNS community at large.

- Interrelatedness
  Resources, events, agents, artifacts, and authors interconnect in ways that add continuity and integration to teachers' actions in a remote networked school.

This CoP, whose joint enterprise is working in a networked school, is an exemplar of participation valued and sustained through school-school and university-school partnerships. As mentioned earlier its viability may depend on contextual factors such as the political will of policymakers and social local leaders, but it is also a matter of participation in the design of the RNS. Agents situated in different institutions (schools, school district headquarters, universities, CEFRIO) have distinct specific goals to meet and roles to play in the RNS community if a common goal can be achieved, that of enhancing the quality of education in small rural areas. Agents' use of broadband and social software (tools) transforms the classroom (community) into a networked classroom (object-outcome). Teacher collaboration is considered critical to the development of an alternative to online courses for small remote schools that want to make use of the Internet for securing their existence and that of the small villages of which they are an important part.

The Contribution of the ISPJ Community

This third case is a contrast to what has been highlighted in this chapter, that is, the interplay between small-scale local CoPs and virtual communities. The ISPJ (socioprofessional integration of kids) community draws participants from an online network of Vocational education teachers initiated by two national organizations devoted to new means of knowledge transfer.

At the onset of the ISPJ network, a face-to-face meeting was organized, but the emergence of the ISPJ community has been facilitated strictly online. All CoP participants, except the facilitator and one school principal, have been working with students sharing similar characteristics (demotivated youngsters, dropout candidates) registered to the same program, one that is offered in most schools across the province.

The 43 participants use the same collaborative online platform the online network is using (Work2gether). Through electronic forums and file exchange, teachers share thoughts, meanings, and resources. An analysis of the electronic forums showed that at least 10% of the members were very active in the forums. Participants exchanged over 100 documents they had authored or coauthored as teachers, which reflected that there was a connection between their individual practices (Laferrière,

Martel, & Gervais, 2005). The facilitator was active helping the CoP to identify projects. Participants valued their CoP and some of them devoted quite a bit of energy to ensure its sustainability across learning institutions, including time devoted to a 1-day meeting, its planning and follow-up.

Sustainability is a challenge as the ISPJ Community has no specific task-at-hand and therefore no structuring elements like intake routines, deadlines and organizations/institutions to report to. There is only one teacher per school working in the program and local administrative support for participation in the CoP is often lacking. Therefore, the centrifugal-centripetal effects may only occur through one person acting alone at the local level.

The design principles observed in the first two cases have barely been observable in the ISPJ CoP: ease of access is often lacking at school; coconstitutionality is applied at the individual-participant level only; participatory design and diversity are welcome; multimodal social interactions and local grounding, with colleagues engaged in the same specific practice, are almost nonexistent at the local school; there are early instances of active collaborative learning and collaborative reflective practice; the classroom as a community of learners, progressive distributed expertise, and collaborative knowledge building are almost absent. Yet, one would be inclined to think the participants are without any doubts part of a CoP that shares many if not all features with the earlier version brought forward by Wenger (1998). Why so? The obvious reason seems to reside in the fact this CoP existed without any real infrastructure or organizational process supporting it. Its vitality was somewhat natural: participation was self-imposed, face-to-face was almost impossible, resources, material, and formal training for the activity were virtually nonexistent and a clear sense of identity seemed to coexist with a strong feeling of being isolated. Oddly enough, these are features shared by the small scale CoPs referred to at the beginning of this chapter. With the exception of the presence of a facilitator, one might be able to find in the ISPJ experience the explicit conditions for the implementation of a "natural" CoP.

LESSONS LEARNED

The following proximal insights into the pros and cons of designing CoPs across learning institutions can now be exposed:

- Small-scale CoPs based in learning institutions are supported by well-established organizational processes that may or may not facilitate the application of the twelve design principles. On the one hand, the organizational local culture matters and, on the other hand, the democratically oriented culture of the virtual community is also of importance. The tension between both is thought to be most valuable for teacher education and professional development as it brings into consideration the concreteness of the local onsite/online activity and the thinking of a virtual community regarding network-enhanced teaching and learning.

- Small-scaled CoPs, be it a pair or a program- or a school-based professional learning community, engaged in both onsite and online activity, are intrinsic to the vitality of a virtual community. A small-scaled CoP that produces online artefacts provides evidence that helps strengthen its linkages with the virtual community.[4]

A particular dynamic comes into play when people move from small-scale CoPs or a local professional learning community to constellations of CoPs. Their new forms of interactions constitute an extension of their day-to-day experiences with their small-scale community. The situation of a Manhattan resident who travels extensively for work purposes can illustrate the phenomenon. Even though this individual gets involved in a whole range of new interactions, his professional world usually remains small; the people he relates to are not workers of the entire city of New York. Most of the time he identifies himself with coworkers in the same organization who are not that distanced from him. From this angle, the notion of this individual as a "planetary man" appears quite ludicrous or needs to be apprehended from another perspective. It should remind us never to lose track of "the small world" of the planetary man or rather of the link between the planet and the professional neighborhood of this individual. In short, there is a world of tension between what goes on in the small-scale community or local community and the virtual world. The planetary man is simultaneously pushed to the outside and pulled to the inside in such a way only coherence between the worlds can allow for emancipation. Therefore, it is useless to ask ourselves if such and such a virtual community has reached the status of a "real" CoP. It is much more appropriate to examine the connections between the local community and the one(s) being active in a virtual fashion.

FUTURE TRENDS AND CONCLUSIONS

Building on the above cases, each of them part of the major educational trend of network-enhanced learning environments we foresee the following developments:

- The consolidation of the networked classroom as the new workplace of the teacher: Whether it is a low or a highly networked classroom, the new workplace of the teacher will no more be restricted to what goes on within its four walls: outside participants may join in for specific learning activities and projects or educational online resources may be brought into the classroom.

- The rise of teacher knowledge management (KM): KM engenders new practices (Web sites, electronic portfolios, virtual tours of exemplary practices, student inquiry databases). A critical mass of classroom-based practices and their rationales that relate to one subdomain or pedagogical approach can be constituted. Issues of visibility and sustainability of exemplary practices are then reduced whereas ownership issues increase (e.g., the ownership of the databases of knowledge building communities). The creative commons model may apply or a network of learning institutions may promote coproprietary knowledge.

- The new balance between individual and distributed cognition: According to the perspective put forward in this chapter, cognition can never be seen as individual or as something that occurs essentially inside the head of an individual. In the three cases exposed, artifacts are not the product of nor do they belong to individuals and interactions are not geared towards individual performance. Interactions are more than a connection between individuals; they are the content, the nervous system of the whole group. Therefore, "I learn as much as I am willing to participate, and others learn in the same fashion through an arena conducive to negotiation."

- The merging of informal and formal learning: This networked workplace is congruent with principles brought forward by sociocultural perspectives for understanding cognition and conducive with the informal learning that takes place in CoPs (Lave & Wenger, 1991). It is also aligned with a conceptualization of professional development as participation in a school professional learning community (Dufour & Eaker, 1998; Fullan, 1993) or the design of network-based professional CoPs (Barab, Kling, & Gray, 2004).

- Farther reaches of collaborative research: More research is needed on the design elements of collaborative platforms. We need to learn more about the elements that are related to the cultures of the institutions involved in order to determine the extent to which they are properly structuring, regulating or scaffolding the interactions of teachers and students. Research is needed on the organizational issues related to designing network-enabled CoPs to determine the essential conditions that must be in place onsite and online. To these ends, researchers are encouraged to apply what they know about face-to-face interaction in their analysis of online interaction. It is also important for them to recognize and study what is uniquely feasible with new technology (group cognition, collaborative knowledge building) and the different ecologies and affordances of networked communities and tools that are diverging further and further from past face-to-face learning environments.

It should be pointed out that the implementation of alternative sociotechnical designs of teacher education and professional development was made possible through a favorable context: first of all a high level of coherence across learning institutions, secondly, the involvement of volunteer teachers and teacher educators sharing similar goals and thirdly, a strong support from local administrative units. The synergy between small-scale local CoPs, engaged in innovative teaching and virtual communities that instrument and capitalize on the local activity of participating members has been highlighted throughout this chapter. These sociotechnical designs do not contradict Schlager and Fusco's (2004) suggestion of aligning a community of practice with the professional development activity structure of a specific organization (e.g., a school district) but they point out an alternative design path.

NOTES

1. Funding for this virtual community was provided by the TeleLearning Network of Centres of Excellence (Canada, 1995-2002).
2. Each new cohort of volunteer students signs in as part of partial requirements to doing student teaching in the PROTIC program, a student-owned laptop program at École les Compagnons-de-Cartier (Quebec City, QC, Canada) emphasizing the use of ICT for teaching and learning, one that extends to all high school years and to one-third (375) of the school population (1,100 students).
3. The Remote Networked School Initiative, which is supported by the Quebec Government and began in the autumn of 2002, is in its third phase (2006-2008). The initiative is meant to be a solution for quality education in remote rural areas and the survival/growth of small villages. The other partner is CEFRIO, a liaison and transfer unit whose mission is to support Québec organizations with information technologies for efficient, productive and innovative purposes.
4. See the Web site of the TACT Community (www.tact.fse.ulaval.ca)

REFERENCES

Allaire, S. (2006). *Les affordances socionumériques d'un environnement d'apprentissage hybride en soutien à des stagiaires en enseignement secondaire: De l'analyse réflexive à la coélaboration de connaissances.* Unpublished doctoral dissertation, Université Laval, Québec, Québec, Canada.

Allaire, S., Beaudoin, J., Breuleux, A., Hamel, C., Inchauspé, P., Laferrière, T., et al. (2006). *L'école éloignée en réseau: Rapport final (Phase 2).* Québec, Canada: CEFRIO.

Barab, S., Kling, R., & Gray, J. H. (Eds.). (2004). *Designing for virtual communities in the service of learning.* Cambridge, England: Press Syndicate of the University of Cambridge.

Bourdieu, P. (1994). *Raisons pratiques: Sur la théorie de l'action.* Paris: Éditions du Seuil.

Brown, J. S., Collins, A., et Duguid, P. (1989). Situated cognition and the culture of learning. *Educational Researcher, 18*(1), 32-42.

Campos, M., Laferrière, T., & Lapointe, J. (2005). Analysing arguments in networked conversations: The context of student teachers. *Canadian Journal of Higher Education, 35*(4), 55-84.

Dufour, R., & Eaker, R. (1998). *Professional learning communities at work: Best practices for enhancing student achievement.* Alexandria, VA: ASCD.

Engeström, Y. (1987). *Learning by expanding: An activity-theoretical approach to developmental research.* Helsinki, Finland: Orienta-Konsultit.

Engeström, Y., & Middleton, D. (Eds). (1996). *Cognition and communication at work.* New York: Cambridge University Press.

Fullan, M. (1993). *Change forces.* London: Falmer Press.

Hutchins, E. (1995). *Cognition in the wild.* Cambridge, MA: MIT Press.

Laferrière, T., & Nizet, I. (2006). Conditions de fonctionnement des communautés dans des espaces numériques. In A. Daele & B. Charlier (Eds.), *Comprendre les communautés virtuelles d'enseignants: Pratiques et recherches* (pp. 167-186). Paris: Maison L'Harmattan.

Laferrière, T., Breuleux, A., & Erickson, G. (2004). Telecollaborative communities of practice in education within and beyond Canada. In A. Brown & N. Davis (Eds.), *World Yearbook of Education 2004: Digital technologies, communities and Education* (pp. 264-276). London: RoutledgeFalmer.

Laferrière, T., Breuleux, A., & Inchauspé, P. (2004). *L'école éloignée en réseau. Rapport de recherche,* CEFRIO, Québec. Retrieved October, 22, 2007, from http://www.cefrio.qc.ca/rapports
École_éloignée_en_réseau_Rapport_final_2004.pdf

Laferrière, T., Deschênes, M., & Gaudreault-Perron, J. (2007). *Rapport sur la réussite au Cégep de Sainte-Foy des diplômés du programme PROTIC offert par l'école Les Compagnons-de-Cartier de la commission scolaire Des Découvreurs.* Québec, Canada: Université Laval, Productions TACT.

Laferrière, T., Martel, V., & Gervais, F. (2005). *Une communauté de pratique en réseau (CoPeR) dans le domaine de l'insertion socioprofessionnelle des jeunes (ISPJ): Nouvelles voies de transfert de connaissances et perspectives futures.* Québec, Canada: CEFRIO & CTREQ.

Lave, J., & Wenger, E. (1991). *Situated learning*. London: Cambridge University Press.

Moll, L. C. (Ed.). (1990). *Vygotsky and education: Instructional implications and applications of sociohistorical psychology*. New York: Cambridge University Press.

Partenariat PROTIC-FCAR-TACT. (2001). *Gestion d'une classe, communauté d'apprentissage* [Online]. Retrieved October 22, 2007, from http://www.tact.fse.ulaval.ca/fr/html/fcar/gestion.pdf

Resta, P. (in press). *Teacher development in an e-learning age: A policy and planning guide*. Paris: UNESCO.

Riel, M., & Polin, L. (2004). Online learning communities: Common ground and critical differences in designing technical environments. In S. A. Barab, R. Kling, & J. H. Gray (Eds.), *Designing for virtual communities in the service of learning* (pp. 16-50). London: Cambridge University Press.

Rogoff, B. (1990) *Apprenticeship in thinking: Cognitive development in social context*. New York: Oxford University Press.

Scardamalia, M., & Bereiter, C. (1994). Computer support for knowledge-building communities. *The Journal of the Learning Sciences, 3*(3), 265-283. Retrieved October 22, 2007, from http://carbon.cudenver.edu/~bwilson/building.html

Schlager, M., & Fusco, J. (2004). Teacher professional development, Communities of Practice: Are we putting the cart before the horse? In S. A. Barab, R. Kling, & J. H. Gray (Eds.), *Designing for virtual communities in the service of learning* (pp. 120-153). London: Cambridge University Press.

Schlager, M., & Schank, P. (1997). Tapped In: A new on-line teacher community concept for the next generation of Internet technology. In R. Hall, N. Miyake & N. Enyedy (Eds.), *Proceedings of the Second International Conference on Computer Support for Collaborative Learning* (pp. 231-240). Hillsdale, NJ: Erlbaum.

Schön, D. A. (1987). *Educating the reflective practitioner*. San Francisco: Jossey-Bass.

Wenger, E. (1998). *Communities of practice: Learning, meaning and identity*. London: Cambridge University Press.

Wertsch, J. (1985). *Vygotsky and the social formation of the mind*. Cambridge, MA: Harvard University Press.

CHAPTER 10

TEACHER-LIBRARIAN COMMUNITIES

Changing Practices in Changing Schools

Eric M. Meyers, Lisa P. Nathan, and Matthew L. Saxton

Isolated teaching professionals run the risk of marginalization when schools undergo reform unless they have support for redefining and aligning their practice. The concept of communities of practice (CoPs) is demonstrated here to be a useful and powerful means for designing and supporting new roles and identities among education specialists. This chapter describes how a CoP developed when six isolated teacher-librarians joined university researchers in a project studying high schools undergoing reform. The description focuses on the specific activities that were utilized to encourage and support learning within the CoP. These attempts met with varying levels of success as the teacher-librarians began to reshape their professional identity and redefine their professional practice. The chapter explores the lessons learned in relation to the emergent and designed properties of a CoP striving to assist isolated practitioners working in educational contexts undergoing extensive change.

Communities of Practice: Creating Learning Environments for Educators,
Volume 2, pp. 199–221

INTRODUCTION

Teacher-librarians (TLs)—education professionals tasked with managing the school library and educating its patrons—work at the intersection of teaching and librarianship, attempting to balance the values, roles, and responsibilities of both. Adding to this tension, the context in which TLs operate is rapidly changing due to new educational philosophies and practices, as well as the explosion of information made available via the Web (Lonsdale, 2003). A growing body of research indicates that information and communication technologies (ICTs) and information literacy education have become a focus of their work, as well as a source of identity confusion, for TLs around the world (Moore, 2005).[1]

The ability to adapt well to reform initiatives is an essential skill for education professionals. Modern teachers work in an environment that will inevitably undergo periods of organizational and pedagogical transformation. A majority of these reform efforts focus solely on classroom teachers, marginalizing or eliminating "specialists" along with programs that are not perceived as making direct contributions to student achievement. The focus is almost exclusively on supporting changes to core content instruction. Throughout the reform process, educators who do not fit into the mould of a traditional classroom teacher are left on their own to modify their roles and practices to meet the changing needs of their school. Art teachers, reading specialists, counselors, and TLs are examples of the types of professionals who are often physically isolated from colleagues who share similar job descriptions.

This chapter describes a research project that centred on a group of geographically dispersed TLs whose schools were in the midst of structural and pedagogical reform. Initially the goals of the project included:

1. Developing an understanding of the issues faced by TLs during the reform process
2. Assisting the TLs in aligning their practice with the information needs of a changing school
3. Identifying best practices for supporting positive adaptation during this process

Early in the project, the research team utilized the CoP concept as a lens for analyzing the data and developing an understanding of the TL's professional world. The analysis suggested that in order for the project to have a positive and lasting influence on the practice of the TLs, the intervention and support that the team provided had to be better aligned with the learning needs of the TLs. Over a 2-year period, a CoP was developed as the TLs and the research team worked together to conceptualize new roles for TLs working in a changing school environment. This collaboration has evolved from a traditional informant—researcher relationship to one that recognizes the experience and knowledge that each member of the CoP brings to the table. The focus of this chapter is to share the "lessons learned" by the research team as they attempted to design activities that would nurture and sustain a CoP, which in turn would enrich and empower the work of isolated specialists.

The chapter begins with a description of the background of the project, the two types of members and the research methods used for data collection. To introduce readers to the contexts in which TLs work a brief introduction to the issues of teacher-librarianship is followed by two library scenarios synthesized from the six research sites. The scenarios also serve as an introduction to the application of Etienne Wenger's (1998) account of using the concept of CoP as both a lens for understanding and as a framework for design. After mapping the future direction of our research, we conclude by providing a summary of the lessons learned from this experience to serve as a guide for practitioners developing their own CoP.

BACKGROUND

The Small High School Libraries Project

In this project, funded by the Institute for Museum and Library Studies, six TLs are working with a team of researchers from the University of Washington (United States) to enrich our understanding of the TL's work environment and to engage in redefining their practice and program priorities while their schools are undergoing an extensive reform effort. The six schools are experiencing both structural and pedagogical changes, which in turn are influencing the governance and activities of each school's library program.

Through this particular reform initiative, comprehensive high schools of 800-2000 students are being subdivided into autonomous academies or "small schools" of 400 students or less. This subdivision carries with it serious implications for the libraries of those schools. Small schools purportedly provide an improved learning environment that results in increased academic achievement, lowered dropout rates, and improved parent, teacher, and student satisfaction with schooling. The teaching and learning approaches championed by small schools include: teachers personalizing instruction to facilitate student inquiry and to meet the needs of individual students; flexible curriculum focused on independent research; standards-based learning with intensive support to help students meet standards; and student demonstration of learning through projects, exhibitions, and performance-based assessments. Teaching and learning in a small school requires that the library and teacher-librarian provide a rich infrastructure of information skills instruction and services, reading and literacy advocacy, information and technology services, and resources management.

Fieldwork for the research project began in winter 2004-05 to continue until June 2007. The high schools are located across the greater metropolitan region of Seattle, Washington, and the surrounding rural area. The TLs range in experience from 11-22 years and share similar professional training and experience. The research team is made up of five individuals including faculty, doctoral students, and a former school library administrator. Four members of the research team have worked professionally as TLs.

The research team gathered data from the six school library programs and sought to understand how the changes brought about by reform influenced the contribution of the library and the TL to teaching and learning. Data collection consisted of regular observations of activities within the libraries and numerous interviews with TLs, classroom teachers, and administrators. The six TLs were also invited as a group to meet with the researchers to focus on the specific problems each one faced in their different contexts, as well as the challenges facing TLs more broadly (Meyers, Nathan, & Saxton, 2006).

The Challenges of Teacher-Librarianship

The literature of school librarianship abounds with roles for TLs to fill. Information literacy instructor, information provider, instructional consultant, reading advocate, and chief information officer are some of the roles that appear in the professional literature (e.g., American Association of School Librarians & Association of Educational Communications and Technology, 1998; Eisenberg, 2002; Haycock, 1999; Morris, 2004; Simpson, 1996). Conversations, interviews and observations over the past two years with the six TLs have indicated that they are well aware of the various job descriptions that arise from the literature. At the same time, they realize that it is impossible for one person to meet all of these expectations. They have been left on their own to decide which roles they are going to choose and how they are defined through practice.

Typically, TLs work as the sole professional librarian in their school. They are physically isolated from other TLs who may also be grappling to identify and define the roles that they are going to fulfil. In addition, a TL's contributions to teaching and learning are rarely made explicit to teachers, administrators, and other key decision makers at the school and district level. With little to no support for reflecting on their practice, the tendency of TLs is to focus their efforts on responding to immediate job pressures. This "putting out fires" mode leads to a fragmented or nonexistent set of long-term goals for themselves as professionals and the programs they create and maintain. Combined, all these factors create strong barriers to professional learning and career development.

During initial data collection, it was found that the issues mentioned above are intensified for TLs when schools undergo structural and pedagogical reform. Most reform efforts focus on classroom teachers, marginalizing, or eliminating "specialists" and programs that do not articulate their direct contributions to student achievement (Hartzell, 2001). New priorities and models of governance put a heavy strain on existing budgets. This can leave funding for the library in limbo from year to year, as priorities shift at different stages in the reform process. Models of professional development that target pedagogical reform, such as critical friends groups and curriculum coaching, rarely include the TL and focus almost exclusively on core content instruction. TLs are marginalized if they are unable to perceive and express how they contribute to the changing school environment and do not take advantage of the opportunity to redefine their practice and assert their relevance.

Despite the obstacles listed above, the evolving educational environment can be regarded as an opportunity for TLs to shape and cultivate a more effective information infrastructure within their schools. With planning and initiative, they can strategically guide the influx of resources and information technologies and shape their practice to fit the changing information needs of students and teachers. Successful reforms that involve authentic learning, critical thinking, or integrated lesson planning are information intensive and require increased use of information resources and tools. However, to take advantage of these prospects, TLs need to negotiate and define a new identity for themselves within their high schools. As we seek to understand the problems facing the TLs in the project, we are working to assist them in redefining their practice and program priorities. To this end, the CoP framework was employed as a lens to analyze their existing work and role identities, as well as a tool for designing learning opportunities.

UNDERSTANDING THE WORK OF TEACHER-LIBRARIANS

Portraits of Practice

To help with the initial data analysis, the theoretical CoP work of Wenger (1998) was used as a lens to examine the perceptions and activities of TLs (for another example of using the CoP concept in this manner, see Valerie Anderson, chapter 17 [PMH1] of this volume). According to Wenger, these communities evolve from actors engaging in the "sustained pursuit of a shared enterprise" in a social context (p.45). For example, classroom teachers, counsellors, TLs, principals and other members of a high school community come together around the shared practice of educating children in a given school setting. Their membership in this community of educators allows them to develop an identity around these activities as well as negotiate the shared meaning of those activities. To ground the discussion of the professional practice of TLs, there are two composite vignettes drawn from the project's data set. These vignettes are used to reveal some of the issues surrounding the TL's membership in both the classroom teacher and TL communities.

Vignette 1: Riverview High School

Joan Dixon gives a resigned sigh as she pushes through the turnstile into the cavernous library of Riverview High School. She calculates that at least three pleas for tech help have dropped into her e-mail in the 45 minutes she spent fixing Mr. Wood's projector. Joan has to shimmy between three books carts crammed with material waiting to be reshelved and two virus laden computer workstations in order to reach her computer. Just as she manages to reach the keyboard, Mr. Johnson strides through the turnstile. He demands to know if the library is free during fourth period. His 10th grade history class needs access to online and print materials for a project on Japanese internment camps. Joan is flabbergasted. How can Mr. Johnson expect her to pull together the needed print and online resources in the next 15 minutes? Her exasperation is apparent as she bangs open the library scheduling calendar. Although she is frustrated, Joan does not actually give voice to her thoughts. She is afraid to ask Mr. Johnson to avoid "dropping in" at the last minute because she does not want to upset him. Earlier in the year, he confided that he is overwhelmed by having to teach three entirely new classes this semester. All of the classroom teachers are grumbling about the recent department restructuring. This is not the time for Joan to make a fuss about scheduling library time. It is probably a good way to make enemies. Budget time is coming up and the pool of money from the reform grant has dried up. Her budget, even her job may be on the cutting block. She is never sure how the principal feels about her and keeping some teachers on her side can only help. Mr. Johnson notices the calendar slam and glances around the large, empty library. He wonders why Ms. Dixon resents classes actually coming in to use the materials. Is she afraid the keyboards will get dirty or the books will have to be reshelved? After Mr. Johnson leaves, Joan's gaze returns to her computer screen and yes, there are calls for help. There is also a reminder about the state-wide teacher-librarian conference next month. Glancing over at the three book carts and the "dead" workstations Joan decides to skip the conference. How can she leave the school without her services for 2 days? How many things would go wrong while she was gone? Even worse, what if nothing went wrong and the staff decided that they didn't really need her?

Vignette 2: Mountainview High School

When Kym Turner, the teacher-librarian at Mountainview High School arrives at 7:00 A.M., a small crowd of students is already waiting for the doors to open. Kym is decidedly not a morning person. She feels bleary eyed at this early hour but she is all too aware that the library serves as the school's only computer lab. Students have come to depend on the library doors opening early. Although it means missing the district wide teacher-librarian gathering this morning, she wants to let the students have time to finish homework assignments before the school day officially starts. By 7:30 A.M., two teachers have dropped by to ask for Kym's help developing new instructional units. All of Mountainview's teachers are struggling with the new block scheduling which just started in the spring. Classes are lasting 45 minutes longer and everyone has to adjust their teaching style. Although Kym was not asked to join one of the classroom teachers' Critical Friends groups, she has a good understanding of the challenges they are facing. She truly enjoys helping them design new units and pull together various resources. The teachers that she helps are so appreciative. The principal seems to know she is helping too. At least he mentioned it during their last catch-up chat in the hallway. She was tempted to ask him, once again, for an aide to help her with ordering, processing, shelving, and checking out books. These traditional library tasks take away from the other roles she wants to fill; information literacy instructor, reading advocate, instructional coach. However, how can she ask again, when she knows the budget is tight again this year?

Emerging Issues in the Librarian and Teacher Communities

In these vignettes, teacher-librarian TL is seen struggling with identity at the intersection of two different groups: librarians and classroom teachers. Their job title even suggests this sense of dual responsibility and split personality. Ideally, these two communities of practice are complimentary, as the multiple roles of the TL require engagement in both communities for success. In the following discussion, Wenger's (1998) concepts of mutual engagement, shared repertoire, and joint enterprise are drawn on to develop an understanding of how these two communities shape the daily practice of TLs, and to identify areas where support is needed.

Mutual Engagement

The TL community consists of all the other school TLs in their district or region, including persons with whom they might collaborate, collectively plan, engage in advocacy, or meet at the annual conference to exchange ideas. They have a shared literature and a common language, as well as tools and philosophical principles that guide the activities in which they engage. However, given the distance and physical isolation of their daily work, they have little or no opportunity for sustained discourse around the work they perform.

While structures for sharing practice exist in some school districts, the workload of TLs puts them in a double-bind: if they leave the building to meet with other TLs, their libraries will go unattended. As illustrated in both of our vignettes, many choose nonparticipation in these professional meetings as a compromise in favor of the school and their dedication to students' needs. In schools where the teachers had more control over the TLs working conditions (e.g., budget authority, job security, scheduling), these professional compromises were even more salient. It became clear that opportunities were needed for sustained and meaningful professional dialog that did not undermine the TLs position in the school or their personal sense of responsibility.

Shared Repertoire

The classroom teachers who were interviewed, with whom TLs work daily, did not have an understanding of the work and responsibilities of TLs, nor did they see the need to include the TL in conversations on the process of teaching. This oversight extends to the nongovernmental organizations that support reform at the school and district level. Part of the reform process includes providing educators with additional collaboration time with colleagues, as well as support structures for meeting, and protocols for elevating the teaching discourse. The TLs in the study, despite their status as teachers, were not granted such opportunities. One of the TLs remarked about this slight, "I've been forgotten about."

As a consequence of lacking a shared reform experience with other professionals, TLs were found to be adrift in the reform process. They lacked structures for thinking about how they might improve their own practice, as well as goals and creative visions. They often fell back on traditional library tasks and roles without concern for how others in the school were interpreting their work. Some of the TLs were in outright denial that their schools were really changing, while others voiced feelings of being powerless to influence the course of reform despite a clear stake in process.

Joint Enterprise

Libraries have been a traditional part of secondary schools in many Western countries, and it is often taken for granted that they provide an important service in teaching and learning (Lowrie & Nagakura, 1991). TLs believe, or have been conditioned to think, they "make a difference." However, not all stakeholders in the learning process share this view. The ease-of-use and ubiquity of the Internet has made some of the classroom teachers interviewed question the roles librarians play. One of them stated, "I can find information on the web as well as [the TL] can." TLs were not viewed by all stakeholders as contributors to the joint enterprise of teaching.

In the interviews with classroom teachers and administrators, they showed they were quite aware of the inputs to the library (personnel, budget, technology, physical space) but less aware of the outputs (student learning, contributions of the TL to curriculum and information services). Tensions emerged in some schools over access to library resources, while in others there were debates over the governance of the facility itself. Where reform efforts caused school leaders to look more closely at budgets and staffing, the contributions of the library were questioned. TLs, caught in the middle of these debates, did not know how to communicate their mission and contribution to key players in the school, the ones who were making decisions about the future of the library and its staff. TLs were found to be lacking support for working strategically, to showcase their contributions and to demonstrate how their work aligned with the overall educational mission of the school.

Identity from Multimembership

This struggle to resolve participation in multiple communities is referred to as the "nexus of multimembership" (Wenger, 1998 p. 158). The challenge in analyzing the TLs work in these two different communities was that neither community was providing the support necessary to assist the TLs in adapting to a changing educational environment. While the TLs worked daily with classroom teachers, the TLs expressed a different set of needs that arose from a style of work different from that of their teaching colleagues. Largely ignored by the organizations promoting reform, TLs stood as outsiders, marginalized in the reform process. The TL community, which does not traditionally provide training and professional development, is hampered by its distributed nature. Little time is available to meet with other professionals, and school district support structures are either modest in scope or nonexistent. Where such structures were in place, the TLs often overlooked them and focused on the immediate concerns of the day. "Fighting fires" often takes precedence over more strategic work, which requires vision, reflection, and the inspiration of like-minded professionals who share the same practice. The TL's membership in both communities was insufficient to sustain the necessary professional learning.

COMMUNITY OF PRACTICE DESIGN

Supporting Learning

After using the CoP concept as a lens for identifying and understanding the issues facing the six TLs, a strategy was needed to addressing these issues. Conversations with the TLs during data collection indicated that by providing structure and support might be possible to form a CoP to assist them in successfully adapting to their changing environment. The community would be made up of the six TLs and the five members of the research team. This idea shifted the nature of the study from observational to participatory. Wenger's work (1998), in particular his discussion of designing a "learning architecture" to support a CoP provided a useful foundation. The CoP design framework was utilized to conceptualize a series of activities and tools to nurture a CoP. Through working together, it was hoped to address the issues identified through the original CoP analysis and develop new models of practice for the TLs in their changing school environments.

The following is not an exhaustive account of the issues that were identified or the range of interactions that have occurred among members of the CoP. Instead, there are illustrative examples, attempts that have worked well and those that have had disappointing results. The lessons learned from these efforts will provide insight to others who attempt to nurture a CoP among isolated professionals. In the following sections Wenger's terms of engagement, imagination, and alignment frame the discussion. Engagement is the "active involvement in mutual processes of negotiation of meaning." Imagination is seeing "connections through time and space by extrapolating from our own experience." Alignment is "coordinating our energy and activities in order to fit within broader structures and contribute to a broader enterprise" (Wenger, 1998, pp. 173-174). The three design themes align with the three emergent qualities of a CoP discussed in section titled "Emerging Issues in the

Librarian and Teacher Communities" (joint enterprise, mutual engagement, and shared repertoire—see Table 10.1).

Facilities of Engagement

According to Wenger (1998), supporting engagement includes providing tools and space, both physical and virtual, for sustained interaction. This focus on supporting direct interaction dovetailed with one of the main issues identified during the preliminary data analysis. The six TLs did not have sustained interaction with fellow practitioners working in a reform context. Thus, providing a structure for communication between the participants became a strong focus of the project. The structure has taken two forms: (1) the TLs are provided with support to meet face-to-

**Table 10.1. Using the CoP Framework to
Address Issues in Practice Directly**

Lens		Design		
Theme	*Issues Identified*	*Theme*	*Facilities*	
Mutual engagement	Lack opportunity for sustained, practice focused communication with other TLs	Engagement	Physical (1) Arranging group meetings: (space, sustenance, substitute reimbursement) (2) Sharing activities/social opportunities	Virtual E-mail / LIST-SERV Private Web site
Shared repertoire	(1) Do not have an established discourse for understanding the reform process and possibilities therein (2) Lack knowledge of other librarians' interpretations of roles and responsibilities	Imagination	(1) Interviews structured to encourage reflection (2) Inspirational talks from field experts (3) Critical practice activity "What would happen if you were gone?"	
Joint enterprise	(1) Little communication/feedback with administrators and classroom teachers (2) No established mechanisms for evaluation or accountability	Alignment	(1) Setting up advisory boards/timelines (2) Developing and sharing 10 week reports (3) Tools for surveys and other feedback facilities	

face on a regular basis; (2) virtual tools have been set up to enable sharing in the times between face-to-face meetings.

Physical Community Support

Early in the project, the research team wanted to talk with all of the TLs about the project and the TLs wanted to learn about what was going on at the other school libraries. In order to support this communication, a group meeting was scheduled. Even though a centrally located meeting space was found, some of the TLs still had to travel a far distance to attend. Because of this time commitment, it was decided to make the gathering a day long affair with structured activities as well as time for informal sharing in order to make the substantial travel time and expense worthwhile. This decision added a new challenge because the TLs had to leave their libraries for an entire day, something many of them were reluctant to do (see section title "Joint Enterprise"). However, some of these challenges were addressed by providing funds for TL substitutes, travel reimbursement, refreshments, and lunch for the participants. Interest in the project combined with the monetary support proved to be enough of an enticement to bring everyone together. For the first gathering over 2 hours were set aside for each TL and each member of the research team to introduce themselves and share their professional background. During these introductions, it became apparent that there was a vast array of expertise sitting around the table. Animated conversations carried over to the lunch break as researchers and practitioners alike realized the potential of sharing ideas with each other.

After the initial gathering, the researchers made individual visits to each of the school libraries. At some point during these visits each of the TL's expressed gratitude for having the opportunity to attend the meeting and a desire to participate in future ones. Even a TL who had initially been hesitant to attend because she was not sure if she would "get anything out of it" was eager to make plans for the next meeting. This eagerness to increase participation has influenced the planning for subsequent gatherings as the TLs take a more active role in developing activities for the meetings, thus increasing their engagement in the CoP.

Virtual Community Support

Unfortunately, the attempts to foster sharing through interactive virtual tools have not met with the same level of success. A private LISTSERV and a password-protected Web site were created to encourage information sharing and provide information storage for community members. Researchers sent questions to the LISTSERV to attempt to spark lengthier conversation. Many of these requests asked TLs to analyze material that the researchers had formulated based on observations and interviews, but were not directly tied to the TL's daily activities. Below is an example of such a query:

> Hello! To summarize the stage we're at in the research project, we've now completed a number of site visits at each school, and also interviewed each of you and your principals. We've noticed that you are all at different stages in moving from a comprehensive high school to a small learning communities environment. We would like you to review a model that we've created based on what we've seen at your schools and the conversations we've had together. This model, which we loosely refer to as "The Conversion Matrix" identifies distinct phases of the conversion process and the roles of the school librarian in that process. We would like you to please review the model and the descriptions, and then share your opinions as to how well this model resonates with your personal experiences. The model is available online at http://inactive_url/matrix.html. Please share your thoughts by posting to the list.

Unsurprisingly, this request for feedback elicited no responses. In contrast, a TL who posted the following request for assistance received much higher attention.

> I am gathering information about creating a course for my library TAs. Right now, I have student assistants that are just getting pass-fail grades. But for next year, I would like to set up a regular letter-grade semester class, with curriculum, assignments, assessments, etc. Do any of you do this? If so, can you give me information, perhaps by attachment via e-mail? I have material from [high school] and [high school]. I also recently visited [high school] to see how it works there. I'd appreciate any suggestions.

Within a few hours, she received four responses from her peers ranging from a simple acknowledgement of the question to lengthy responses including attachments and sample policies. The virtual community generated the most response on items that were initiated by the TLs themselves and pertained to daily activities and challenges. Attempts to direct the conversation to more theoretical or abstract topics met with no response from the members. This supports the finding of Dubé, Bourhis, and Jacob (2005) that the relevance of virtual communities of practice (vCoPs) to daily work practices is strong indicator of their use and effectiveness.

Over the first 2 years of the project, the TLs have only initiated queries on the LISTSERV a handful of times. Researchers who have attempted to establish "blended" (face-to-face and virtual) learning communities have noted that not all groups will use the virtual space equally, and some learning communities prefer face-to-face interactions despite the affordances of the virtual space (Motteram, 2006). It may also be the case that the unequal power relationship that exists between researchers and their subjects is especially strong in this medium. For example, the research team has inadvertently stepped into the role of interviewer rather than fellow discussant by attempting to seed discussions. Previous research has suggested that language, including the way members of the group address each other, can play an important role in the structure and participation of communities (Tusting, 2006).

The second virtual community support tool is a password-protected Web site that was created to serve as a repository for ideas, lesson plans, favorite articles, and so forth. There have been a number of "hits" on the Web site from TLs looking and occasionally downloading documents that the research team has provided. However, the TLs are not contributing documents to the site. It is important to note that the research team set up the Web site and only the researchers had administrative access to the site. Therefore, to contribute content to the site a TL would have to send the information to the research team and request that it be uploaded. Again, the research team may have set up a power dynamic that the TLs found restrictive. There was no hesitancy in sharing ideas, lesson plans, or articles across the table during face-to-face meetings. However, this sharing could happen without a research team member's assistance. To encourage more interactive sharing via the Web site, perhaps a site should be created that provides the same access privileges to all of the CoP members. Whatever the reason, the Web site has not been a successful mode for supporting two-way interaction for the community.

Facilities of Imagination

Although fostering engagement through interaction is crucial to the development of a CoP, the research team was also striving to conceive of new practice models for the TLs. Their school environments were changing and the team needed to conceptualize new identities and roles for them in this shifting, complex environment. To encourage learning that takes complex contexts (such as schools undergoing reform) into account, Wenger (1998) suggests that facilities are needed which inspire imagination. He recommends activities and tools that encourage both reflexive and explorative thinking. Structured interviews, motivating speakers, and "What if" scenarios have been found to be helpful in encouraging both types of thinking. However, there have also been periods of "push back" when various members of the CoP have felt that the activities were going too far and no longer dealing with the reality that they experience in their schools.

Structured Interviews

Throughout the project, interviews with individual TLs have proven to be experiences that the TLs enjoy. Wenger (1998) describes the experience well by stating that interviews are an activity which participants "seemed to enjoy immensely ... taking these conversations as opportunities to explore opinions and engage in a process of reflection" (p. 48). An example of the type of structured interview, which proved to be invaluable for encouraging reflection, was termed the support circle interview. A circle diagram based on Hartzell's (1994) power/dependency mapping was combined with an interview protocol based in the perceived social network inventory, drawing on the concept of "reciprocality of support" (Oritt, Paul, & Behrman, 1985). At the start of this interview, the TLs were given a sheet of paper with a small circle in the center of the page. In a large ring around the center circle were 15 empty circles. The interview protocol asked the TLs to imagine that the middle circle represented themselves in their role as TL. The titles of people who helped them in their job and the titles of those who the librarian helped were to go in the outer circles. The next step was for the TL to add unidirectional or bidirectional arrows to indicate which way(s) the support flowed. These interviews were highly engaging for the TLs. They also found it intriguing to look at the diagrams they created a year later to see if their perceptions of support had changed (see Figure 10.1). The diagrams were helpful when the TLs were imagining possibilities for future practice. They provided a springboard for discussions around who they would like to see on the diagram in the future (e.g., 10th grade biology students or certain administrators). This type of structured interview provided opportunities for both reflection and exploration.

Motivational Speakers

Further opportunities for imaginative thinking have been provided by speakers who have motivated and challenged the community at the beginning of some of the day long gatherings. Often controversial, these speakers have pushed the community to consider the variety of roles TLs could create and fill as reforms, accountability, and new technologies drastically change the secondary school environment. Researchers and TLs have often engaged in animated discourse during morning coffee breaks, after a speaker leaves. There have also been times when a member of the group feels that the speaker has in some way, gone too far and lost credibility. This happened when one speaker suggested that the TLs need to take a more managerial role in their schools. Although the speaker went on to describe many of the tasks that the TLs already do, because of their dislike for the managerial label the TLs refused to acknowledge that those tasks were an important part of their future practice. However, the

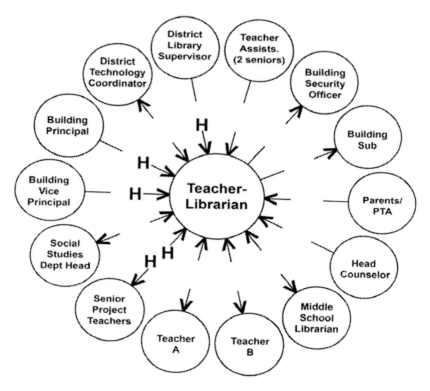

Figure 10.1.   Sample support circle document.

imaginative and creative work the CoP undertakes is not always easy or complimentary, and it was found that ideas become stronger as the members work through the various opinions and suggestions that the speakers have laid out before the group.

"What if?" Scenarios

One last activity bears mention under the imagination heading. One of the motivational speakers asked the TLs to rate their school on a scale of 1-10 in a number of areas that the school library discourse claims TLs have influence: Reading/language arts, technology skills, information literacy, and instructional resources and systems. The speaker asked the TLs to ask themselves, "What if the library program was discontinued? What would be the rating of your school in those same four areas?" This activity was a bit of a wake-up call for all involved. One of the most experienced TLs believed that her leaving the school would have little influence on the school's rating. This pronouncement led to an engaging conversation of why that might be the case and whether or not it was even a problem.

Facilities of Alignment

Although the activities that encouraged imagination proved to be engaging learning opportunities for all members of the CoP, they also needed to take part in activities that would help them focus on issues of contribution and accountability. How can the TLs better align their practice with the needs of their changing schools? Two inconsistencies emerged in the conversations with the TLs and other school stakeholders: (1) the role of the TL was interpreted differently by members of the school community; and (2) no clear mode of feedback existed between the TLs and classroom teachers or TLs and school administrators. This translated to a lack of clarity among all the stakeholders regarding the role of the librarian and to whom she was accountable. How did the TLs know what services were needed for their school? How did they know if they were doing a good job? How did classroom teachers and administrators know what the TLs were doing and whether or not they were doing a good job?

Determining how to align their practice with the information and learning needs of their changing school was a major challenge for each of the TLs. Two methods for encouraging feedback and accountability were suggested and developed during our CoP gatherings. Both were originally suggested by a visiting speaker, but the methods were developed over time through discussion and sharing among the members of the CoP.

Advisory Boards

The first idea to emerge was setting up a library advisory board. An advisory board would consist of a few key members of the teaching faculty who would meet with the TL on a regular basis to help the TL understand the needs of the school and to help the TL set short and long-term goals. However, this would not be a one-way line of communication. Through these meetings, the TL could lay out her time and budget constraints and ask the advisory board to help make tough choices concerning services and resources. This type of communication would provide the TLs with direct input from the teaching faculty and at the same time would enable the faculty to have a clearer understanding of the constraints inherent in the TL's practice. Discussion of the practicalities of setting up an advisory board provided an opportunity for the TLs to develop a list of potential advisory board members and to create a timeline for setting up the board.

The research team has continued to encourage this idea through individual discussions with the TLs during visits to their individual schools and by providing funding for two additional planning days during which the TLs will have the opportunity to continue planning and begin recruiting members to their advisory boards.

Ten-Week Reports

The second idea was quite simple in concept, but has proved difficult to bring into practice. A recommendation was made to have the TLs create a one-page report summarizing their activities every 10 weeks, which would be sent to the school principal. The goal of the report would be improve the TL's accountability and communication with the school principal and to encourage strategic planning. Group discussion around the idea was highly positive.

An outline was provided with some sample text, but a number of the TLs asked for a concrete model of how to write this type of report. One of the TLs mentioned that she was in the process of writing one herself. She was asked if it could be posted on the secure Web site when it was complete. Three weeks later the letter had not arrived. When asked about the letter, the TL expressed being reluctant to share because she did not think the letter was "good enough." Despite efforts to establish trust within the group, she was still reluctant to share her work. Currently, only two of the six TLs have actually written and submitted a 10-week report to their principal.

In summary, Wenger's (1998) concepts have proved to be effective in providing a framework for developing strategies to address the needs of TLs. Efforts to facilitate engagement and imagination among the group were largely successful, as time and opportunity appear to have been the main obstacles to overcome. Efforts at facilitating alignment have probably been less effective since this involves changes in attitude and behavior, as well as redefining relationships. As the project moves into its third year, it remains to be seen whether the CoP can enable all the participants to communicate and document their contributions in the reformed school environment.

FUTURE DIRECTIONS

The small high school libraries project is ongoing. The CoP has grown and evolved in different ways since its emergence. The interactions between the TLs and the research team have shifted from a strict researcher-informant duality to one of engaged participation in a learning community. The researchers have increased their expectations of the

TLs involvement, and the TLs have correspondingly stepped forward to take a greater role in negotiating the nature of their participation. This change has been most salient at the day long research conversations. At the first meeting, TLs assumed a largely passive role, providing feedback and information at the researchers' behest. They now contribute directly to the agenda and discussion, and in future meetings they are expected to exhibit stronger involvement, initiative and leadership. The TLs are moving from a peripheral mode of participation to a more central, guiding position in the community. The researchers are changing their stance as well, seeing the TLs as experts in their context with important insights to share with the team and with each other.

Throughout the coming years the learning that has occurred in the CoP will be documented to assist other practitioners facing similar reform challenges. The development of a small school libraries toolkit has already begun with the assistance of the cooperating TLs. This toolkit will include the products of the collaboration as well as the process of forming the CoP. The toolkit will be disseminated through a symposium gathering which will draw in library and education professionals, as well as reform organizations and school administrators, from around the state of Washington. Through this gathering, it is hoped to plant the seeds of other learning communities focused on improving the practice of TLs.

The research team will continue to grapple with questions related to the design of CoPs and the facilities necessary to encourage them. The CoP emerged and developed in the process of a research project, which included funding, staff, and support of a multiyear grant. In the absence of such resources, would practitioners be able to replicate and sustain the kind of learning group that was created? If yes, what means and tools would be necessary to foster engagement and active learning opportunities? Furthermore, what is the impact of different cultural and institutional norms on CoPs and vCoPs? Such communities cannot be mandated; rather, they emerge in response to needs or problems that arise in practice.

In the business world, companies have been actively cultivating CoPs as a corporate strategy, as a means of enhancing performance or gaining a competitive edge (Wenger, McDermott, & Snyder, 2002). As is often the case, the education field is one or two steps behind business innovations. The CoP concept is one that educational organizations will seek to leverage in the future to provide professional training and to support new models of practice. The success of CoPs in school contexts will depend on patient, careful cultivation, balanced with the need for accountability. Evaluating the effectiveness of CoPs—measuring their impact in terms of changing practice against the resources and time necessary to facilitate them—will be an important next step in the study of these structures for learning and professional development.

CONCLUSION

Coping with changing teaching and learning environments has often been thought of in individual terms—whether or not a person "gets with the program." Such a perspective places the onus for success on the individual practitioner without necessarily providing structures that support new ways of thinking and working, alone and with others. New workplaces and work practices demand community approaches rather than individual responses.

Based on the experience of working with TLs, several lessons and recommendations have been identified for those who wish to create and participate in their own CoPs:

Engagement

- Pay attention to the power dynamic within the group. Control over the resources (money, tools, incentives) and activities (agenda, mode and frequency of meeting) of the group strongly influenced the ways in which members participated.
- Flexibility and reflection are keys to developing effective, sustainable activities. The research team realized that they needed to change directions based on the needs of the group, rather than sticking with activities that they had worked hard to put in place, but turned out to be ineffective.

Imagination

- Support multiple levels of reflection. We found that following up an individual reflection activity with a similar group reflection activity was a powerful tool for encouraging new ideas and attitudes about practice.
- Draw on visions outside your group. By inviting outsiders to help our participants reflect and envision, we were able to broaden and elevate the conversation.

Alignment

- Building trust is essential to constructive discourse. Although trust was quickly established with the participant TLs quickly as individuals, gaining group trust was more challenging.
- Putting ideas into practice is hard work. There was a lot of enthusiasm in the group for the alignment activities developed together in our meetings; however, they did not always translate into changed practice.

All secondary teachers endure some form of professional isolation, as they spend much of their day exclusively in the presence of youth. Classroom teachers, however, enjoy the close proximity of colleagues with whom they engage in the problems of teaching, as well as the attention of reform advocates since they occupy school faculty in the greatest numbers. It has become clear that isolated practitioners can "fall through the cracks" in a reform effort, just as mainstream education can marginalize students with special needs. The work with TLs, a group of teachers with unique roles and responsibilities, which is described in this chapter, offers lessons for other isolated educators and teaching specialists. Art teachers, counsellors, reading specialists and others within the school suffer from being the "only one" of their type on staff. Their unique needs and professional obligations often create situations similar to those of TLs. Supporting practitioner communities by offering them opportunities to reflect and expand upon their work may help reduce isolation, improve their practice, and provide a framework for ongoing professional learning. This support can help the specialists tackle tough issues with the insight and expertise that develops from an engaged group of fellow practitioners.

Critical to successful use of the CoP to facilitate learning is its use as an interpretive lens to understand practice better. By first performing a thorough examination of the existing practice, it was possible to design features of a new community to "fill the gaps" in their existing support network. The learning then became targeted to needs, rather than ad hoc, and provided a greater sense of purpose and meaning. Combining observation with improving practice took on a dialogic relationship, the two activities influencing and strengthening each other. The facilities of engagement, imagination, and alignment served to strengthen both the professional bonds offered by the research project, as well as the TLs work in the school context. In this manner, CoPs can serve to reduce the effects of professional isolation, and engage practitioners to meet the challenges of a changing work environment.

NOTES

1. Those interested in the worldwide challenges facing Teacher-librarianship may wish to visit the International Association for School Librarianship (IASL) online (http://www.iasl-slo.org/)

REFERENCES

American Association of School Librarians and Association of Educational Communications and Technology. (1998). *Information power: Partnerships for learning*. Chicago: American Library Association.

Dubé, L., Bourhis, A., & Jacob, R. (2005). The impact of structuring characteristics on the launching of virtual communities of practice. *Journal of Organizational Change Management, 18*(2),145-167.

Eisenberg, M. (2002). This man wants to change your job. *School Library Journal, 48*(9), 46-50

Hartzell, G. (1994). *Building influence for the school librarian*. Worthington, OH: Linworth.

Hartzell, G. (2001). The implications of selected school reform approaches for school library media services. *School Library Media Research, 4*. Retrieved Retrieved June 14, 2005, from http://www.ala.org/ala/aasl /aaslpubsandjournals/slmrb/slmrcontents/volume42001/hartzell.htm

Haycock, K. (1999). *Foundations of effective school library media programs*. Englewood, CO: Libraries Unlimited.

Lonsdale, M. (2003). The impact of school libraries on student achievement: A review of research. *Australian Council for Educational Research*. Retrieved Retrieved August, 2 2005, from http://www.acer.edu.au/research/documents /schoollibraries.pdf

Lowrie, J. E., & Nagakura, M. (1991). *School libraries: International developments*. Metuchen, NJ: Scarecrow Press.

Meyers, E. M., Nathan, L. P., & Saxton, M. L. (2006). Barriers to information seeking in school libraries: Conflicts in perceptions and practice. *Information Research, 12*(2), paper 295. Retrieved January 17, 2007, from http:// InformationR.net/ir/12-2/paper295.html

Moore, P. (2005). An analysis of information literacy education worldwide. *School Libraries Worldwide, 11*(2), 1-23.

Morris, B. (2004). *Administering the School Library Media Center*. (4th ed., revised and expanded). Westport, CT: Libraries Unlimited.

Motteram, G. (2006). "Blended" education and the transformation of teachers: a long-term case study in postgraduate UK Higher Education. *British Journal of Educational Technology, 37*(1), 17-30.

Oritt, E. J., Paul, S. C., & Behrman, J. A. (1985). Perceived social network inventory. *Journal, 13*, 565-581.

Simpson, C. (1996). The school librarian's role in the electronic age. *ERIC Digest*. Syracuse, NY: ERIC Clearinghouse on Information and Technology.

Tusting, K. (2006). Language and power in communities of practice. In D. Barton & K. Tusting (Eds.), *Beyond communities of practice*. New York: Cambridge University Press.

Wenger, E. (1998). *Communities of practice: Learning, meaning and identity*. New York: Cambridge University Press.

Wenger, E., McDermott, R., & Snyder, W. (2002). *Cultivating communities of practice*. Boston: Harvard Business School Press.

CHAPTER 11

COMMUNITIES OF PRACTICE AT THE MATH FORUM

Supporting Teachers as Professionals

Wesley Shumar and Johann Sarmiento

Traditionally schools frame learning and the practice of teaching as the activities that go on within classrooms. In this arrangement, teachers usually are highly constrained in terms of their teaching activities and are increasingly seen as solely responsible for the learning of their students. In reality, the practice of education is invariably situated at the intersection of multiple communities of practice (CoPs). These include teachers' local and professional communities, the scientific communities related to the content areas of instruction (e.g., mathematicians, historians, etc.) and those associated with youth, parents, administrators, learning scientists, and policymakers, among others. Traditional forms of teacher professional development attempt to teach skills and provide opportunities to interact with other professionals, but this model is seen as weak and often very unsuccessful. In contrast, opportunities for teachers to expand the communities they belong to, enhance their own professional development and transform their own identities as teachers are better positioned to affect teaching and learning. The Math Forum is an interactive digital library that, since its inception in 1995, has focused on providing such opportunities for individuals to talk

Communities of Practice: Creating Learning Environments for Educators,
Volume 2, pp. 223–239

with others about math and work with others on math. As such, the Math Forum has become one of the premier sites on the Internet for math education. This chapter focuses on the ways that Math Forum has supported multiple overlapping CoPs among teachers and the ways that teachers have used the Math Forum to expand their sense of membership and interaction with diverse CoPs. Recommendations for CoP practitioners are outlined as well as further questions for research.

INTRODUCTION

This chapter looks at the CoPs that have developed around the Math Forum (http://mathforum.org/) an online mathematics education Web site at Drexel University for K-16 teachers, students, parents, and others interested in mathematics. The Math Forum is one of the premier education Web sites that balances a deep and rich collection of math resources for teachers and students with dynamic forms of interaction. The interactive services at the Math Forum range from asynchronous forms of interaction such as the Problem Of The Week (PoW), Ask Dr. Math and online discussions such as Teacher-to-Teacher (T2T), to synchronous services such as the new developing virtual math teams (VMT) chat environment. Further, many of the resources in the Math Forum collection are produced by reshaping interactions in the various interactive services. So for example questions and answers in Ask Dr. Math which were originally a student asking a volunteer math doctor a question about math become part of the Ask Dr. Math library which then allows other students to access the same question more quickly.

In this way, the Math Forum has developed a unique balance of what Wenger (1998) refers to as the balance between reification and participation. Wenger argues that the old bureaucracy is one that is too reified, stifling creative human activities by making individuals follow inflexible sets of procedures and does not encourage participants to live up to their full potential. Newer corporations and other organizations are much clearer about the balance needed between having structure (e.g., in the form of rules and procedures) but also supporting the creative input of individuals in the organization. For Wenger this balance is critical for the successful development of contemporary organizations and this chapter will show that the balance has contributed to the success of the Math Forum.

An open and interesting question is the status of the Math Forum as a CoP: is it one CoP or is it a collection of CoPs? On the one hand, there is a central staff of about 15 employees who make up the Math Forum; that group includes former teachers, software developers, and educational technologists. Most of the staff work in one physical location but several telecommute at least part of the time. This group, which has its own work culture (Renninger & Shumar, 2004), forms the core of the Math Forum CoP. At the same time, several of the services mentioned above have developed their own communities. For instance the Online Mentoring Project (OMP) and the Virtual Math Teams (VMT) Project, two projects discussed in this chapter, have their own CoPs that partly intersect with the core staff but are independent as well. In this way, the Math Forum is rather like a traditional community with overlapping groups and overlapping boundaries (Cohen, 1985).

While the Math Forum has many different groups who participate on the site, this chapter will focus on teacher communities that have developed at the Math Forum and the ways that the Math Forum supports teaching and teacher professional development (TPD). The chapter will begin with a review of some of the TPD literature that shows some of the major problems with TPD. Such critique underscores an interesting problem—the lack of development of true CoPs in schools. The chapter will then move to a discussion of the history of the Math Forum, how the culture of practice that developed shaped the organization, the resources that are published online and the ways that the participants engage with them. The chapter will then move to a discussion of some current efforts at the Math Forum to expand the forms of interaction available to participants, the Math Forum's new online TPD program and the VMT project that help teachers support students problem-solving activities. The chapter concludes with a discussion of the potential for online sites as facilitators in the development of true CoPs among teachers.

TEACHER PROFESSIONAL DEVELOPMENT

It is a truism among teachers and academics that TPD, for the most part, is not very effective. Teachers often describe a strategy of resistance when it comes to TPD. For instance, some teachers might select the easiest workshops available rather than trying to find one that is relevant to their teaching practices or challenges so that they are able to spend time in the workshop grading papers and getting other work done as a way of making the TPD time personally useful. In harsh contrast with this attitude, many professionals and school leaders working in TPD would like workshops and other professional activities available to teachers to have a real impact on teacher learning and support change in teachers' views and practices.

Most TPD consists of a few disjoint classes and has had varying levels of success at community building. The analysis of local and national TPD programs presented by Schlager and Fusco (2004) points out that traditional TPD, either online or face-to-face, has had little impact because it does not really change the practices that teachers engage in. They argue further that such professional development is fragmented and misaligned with the needs of teachers and schools. So, there is a bit of a dialectical interplay between the reification of most TPD and the ways that teachers resist or simply fail to engage with the TPD. The effect is that teacher practice is not changed.

One-shot workshops are still the dominant form of TPD whether online or offline. Schlager and Fusco (2004) observe that TPD needs to be sustained and to fit with school culture, in addition to being aligned with practice. They suggest that CoPs are critical for knowledge building and that knowledge building practices in all arenas are collaborative social processes that allow individuals flexibility of thought as well as different forms of support. Similar points are made by Renninger and Shumar (2002) regarding Math Forum support for teacher learning.

Schlager and Fusco's (2004) critique of TPD is nothing new or surprising. Several scholars have pointed to the same issues they point to and in fact, they draw on several of those scholars to make their critique (Little, 1993; McLaughlin & Talbert, 2001; Smylie, Allensworth, Greenberg, Harris, & Luppescu, 2001). What is interesting in their analysis is that they point out that while there is a lot of discussion about CoPs in education, there are in fact very few examples of actual CoPs within schools. As stated before, Wenger (1998) has pointed out that CoPs tend to flourish when there is a balance between reification and participation or interaction, and the lack of such balance can be one of the factors contributing to the difficulties faced by schools promoting the development of CoPs. Wenger's call for synergy between reification and participation in organizations fostering CoPs points to the fact that the very forms of reification, (whether they be the status hierarchy in the institution, rules and procedures, or the forms that people have to fill out to conduct daily activities) shape the ways members of an organization work together, and thus have the power to help people work together in more lateral—less hierarchical —groups. The late twentieth/early twenty-first century has seen the evolution of much of capitalism away from traditional top down companies toward these laterally organized companies where workers are semi-autonomous experts. They work in CoPs and tend to define the processes as well as the products of their work. Schools, on the other hand, have not been a part of this revolution in management. Ironically, they are still very much structured like the 19th century factory. Administrators tend to see teachers as somewhat incompetent and recalcitrant. Teachers often see administrators as out of touch and not valuing their professional skills. The one aspect where the school is not like the factory is that a teacher does have fair degree of autonomy within her own classes. In order to minimize the collective disciplining of administration, they close their doors and work as individually as they can. Between the isolation of teachers and the top-down management practices of administrators, CoPs struggle to develop within schools and yet, as a recent Rand Report (Shapiro, 2003) points out, teachers need to have ongoing and effective professional development in order to teach effectively. The value of CoPs in which teachers can be actively engaged in order to develop their practice appears evident and yet elusive.

As we have seen, it is difficult for teachers to engage in a CoP in many school settings. Therefore, the opportunities to build knowledge collaboratively are often not as open to teachers as they are in other professions where actual daily practices are more visible among peers and where organizational structures support self-directed learning more actively. On the other hand, online learning environments like the Math Forum open up the possibilities for the personal crafting of community by teachers, and hence foster new opportunities for CoPs to develop among teachers and other agents interested in teaching and learning. In fact, the Math Forum first became involved in TPD somewhat by accident through its experience working with teachers and students. Because for the Math Forum the goal was to create a community of practitioners who engage in doing math together, the way professional development has been approached since the beginning has been quite different. The next section will summarize the history of the Math Forum and the development of the Math Forum as a culture and a community. This is followed by a discussion about a number of positive Math Forum projects where effective CoPs are being developed.

MATH FORUM HISTORY

The Math Forum history has been documented in some detail elsewhere (Renninger & Shumar, 2002). This chapter touches on a couple of important elements of that history to illustrate the ways CoPs have developed at the Math Forum. The Math Forum has never placed technology as the only driving force contributing to the development of a community of engaged participants or as a panacea. Rather, as a community, the Math Forum's attitude toward technology has first been to think about ways it could be shaped to foster conversation and interaction around mathematics and second as a way to make resources accessible as in the case of problems, curricular materials, or ideas that could be shared with teachers, students, parents, and anyone interested in math.

The Math Forum began as a small group of staff members and a geometry discussion list on the Internet pre-Web. This discussion list fostered conversation around issues in geometry education and geometry problems. One of their first challenges, as far as enabling rich ways of participation, was to create ways to visualize problem solving on the Internet. As a result, they were central to the development of The Geometer's Sketchpad® a software tool still used by geometry teachers. As the Internet grew and the Web developed so did the Math Forum. They moved from being geometry focused to being an online resource for all of K-12 mathematics. As the community grew in numbers and interests the goal of increasing opportunities for people to problem solve and to talk about math continued to develop. With the development of the Web, the Math Forum began to do teacher workshops both face-to-face and online in order to assist practitioners with the successful integration of these new resources into their teaching practices. The work with teachers, in turn, helped to shape and expand the online community, and helped to build resources and volunteers working with the site.

Early workshops with the Math Forum were also critical opportunities to codevelop with teachers a vision of how the Math Forum community saw problem solving. To this day solving math problems is a central part of the Math Forum workshop. The Math Forum staff believes that thinking about math requires doing math and talking about what you are doing. During Math Forum workshops they also taught teachers to use the set of internet resources emerging from the engagement of other teachers engaged in the community. Interestingly, early research at the Math Forum showed that there was a correlation between teachers who were not strong with technology use and teachers who were not strong in math. The reverse was also true. These initial Math Forum workshops allowed teachers in one day to learn to author Web pages, and publish those Web pages to the Internet to begin to build their own math Web site. This was a very empowering experience for many teachers in such workshops since they developed a completely new way of thinking about themselves and what they were capable of doing as mathematicians, as teachers, and as members of an online community of practitioners.

These early Math Forum workshops had an impact that extended well beyond the expected outcomes, in some cases, addressing school-based problems in ways that surprised participating teachers. For example, in one workshop conducted at a remote school, the Math Forum staff discovered that the network supports necessary to have Internet access were not in place and proceeded to string up modems and wire a lab so that the workshop could be done. In another example, air conditioners were brought to a local school in Philadelphia when the Math Forum staff realized that the room provided for a workshop lacked these resources. In both of these cases, the teachers were very impressed with the Math Forum staff and were energized by their attitude toward problems. Schools are often very de-personalized bureaucratic institutions and so when one encounters problems there is often no one to turn to, leaving teachers feeling very disempowered as practitioners since their teaching practice relies heavily on school supports. In contrast, the Math Forum attitude toward problem solving is the same whether those problems are math problems or practical problems. By example, the Math Forum shows teachers that they can have agency even in bureaucratic situations and this is a very empowering position (Emirbayer & Mische, 1998).

The Math Forum culture that developed out of this history is one that focuses on problem solving and empowerment; it is one that is utopian in its sense of what people can do and it uses technology to share resources and improve communication between people. This culture, coupled with the power of the Internet has lead to new ways that teachers can think about their own identities as problem solvers and as mathematicians at the same time that they can reimagine the diverse CoPs that they are part of and the ways that they can contribute to them. The following sections of this chapter will explore some specific projects at the Math Forum and then make some summary observations about how CoPs have developed through these projects.

Problem of the Week: Problem Solving and Collaboration

The Problem Of The Week (PoW) is one of the oldest services on the Math Forum site along with the Ask Dr. Math service. The PoW is a regular nonroutine challenge problem that is posted on the Math Forum Web site for students and classrooms across the United States and the world to send their solutions and, in some cases, receive mentoring on their problem-solving work. The PoW began as a geometry PoW. As the service expanded the Geo PoW was one of many PoW offered. At the moment, there are four specific PoWs: math fundamentals, pre-algebra, algebra and geometry. The problems themselves are a product of the Math Forum culture and its focus on problem solving. The Math Forum staff meets weekly to write problems and do math together. They have been doing this for years.[1] When a problem has been vetted by the team, it is then posted on the Web site. See Figure 11.1 for an example of a math fundamentals problem.

Students have several days to solve the problem and then submit their answer with an explanation of the problem solving. Students are then mentored by a staff member or a volunteer. They are encouraged to think more about their answers and to revise and resubmit sometimes even if

Problem of the Week
Problems Library

<u>All Problems of the Week</u> || <u>Teacher Office</u>

<u>Print This Problem</u> | <u>Solution and Commentary</u>

1310: Baseball Trivia

As you may know, the Math Forum office is located in Swarthmore, Pennsylvania. Swarthmore is a short drive from Philadelphia, and many of us enjoy attending Phillies games at Veterans Stadium. The game of baseball provides many opportunities to use our math skills. This week's problem was presented as a trivia question at a recent game.

How many runs do the Phillies have to score before the scoring base runners have covered a mile?

Bonus: The seating capacity for Eagles football games at Veterans Stadium is 65,352. The average price of tickets is $42.83. If 85% of the seats are sold for the game, what is the ticket revenue?

<u>Submit your answer to "Baseball Trivia"</u>

If you are under 13, you must have permission from your parent or teacher to participate in this web project. You will be asked to provide the email address of your parent or teacher when you register. At any time, parents or teachers may request that we remove personal information by writing to removal@sdp or by contacting us via postal mail or telephone (800-756-7823 x20950).

[<u>Privacy Policy</u>] [<u>Terms of Use</u>]

Done

Figure 11.1.   Math fundamentals PoW problem from The Math Forum PoW library.

they have the right answer. A scoring rubric is used to comment on students mathematical problem solving and their communication skills; they also get a written mentored reply along with their score on the rubric. Nonroutine challenge problems are a nice example of illustrating the Math Forum philosophy. These are problems that require thought and students must talk about them. They are not problems that allow one to just plug in a formula and get an answer and so they encourage mathematical conversation and mathematical thinking.

Over the years, the Math Forum has developed a large library of past PoWs. These problems are a resource that teachers can use. There is also a large archive of student solutions to problems and mentored responses to student solutions. This archive has, in more recent times, become a resource that the Math Forum has begun to use to help teachers and pre-service teachers think more about teaching mathematics.

The PoW is not only a useful service that math students and teachers can benefit from, it is a diverse CoP itself. There are many volunteer mentors in the PoW system. Mentors begin to learn to mentor by apprenticing. They are given student answers to mentor but their reply to the student is in fact vetted by a staff member or a senior mentor. Once the apprentice mentor's reply is deemed good enough it is sent to the student. After a mentor has worked with the system for a while, and has consistently good replies that they have written for students, they are then given direct send and do not have to have their replies vetted any more. Maybe after a while they will mentor apprentice mentors too.

Two projects to grow out of the PoW environment are the OMP and the Leadership Development For Technology Integration Project (LDTIP). Each project uses the resources of the PoWs and the potential of the PoWs for training teachers to think about mathematics, student learning, and mentoring. An additional strength of these projects is that they use course modules and workshops the are imbedded with the larger Math Forum CoP so that they bring a dynamic and active CoP to teachers and preservice teachers who often do not have these communities or cultural traditions at their disposal.

The online mentoring project started as a 3-year NSF funded project. It continues today at a number of universities. Central to the OMP is the Online Mentoring Guide (OMG), a course module constructed in WebCT. In the OMG, preservice teachers first solve a PoW math problem and submit their answer. They then mentor each other as they begin to build a CoP among each other; they then discuss the idea of mentoring and what its key features are. After that discussion of mentoring, they look at the Math Forum's principles of mentoring and modify that document with their own thoughts on mentoring. This revised guideline serves as a template for their future thinking about mentoring. The rest of the OMG familiarizes preservice teachers with the PoW back office and how to mentor students. They then go to mentoring live students in the PoW environment. Like other volunteer mentors in the PoW system, their replies to students are vetted preferably by their instructor who has already become a senior mentor in the PoW system. Like most of the Math Forum activities, the layers of interaction around discussing math and pedagogy become very rich as different participants interact in the service.

The LDTIP project is also a project based in the PoW system but focuses on doing both face-to-face and online workshops with in-service teachers in Houston and Philadelphia. This project is in its first year and the goal is much like the goal of the OMP. The project will give teachers opportunities to practise math by solving PoW problems themselves and discussing those problems and solutions with each other. These opportunities to do math and to discuss it with peers is something that teachers very much need but often do not get the chance to do. The workshops will also focus on pedagogical issues as teachers use the PoW to diagnose how their students and other students solve problems and what some of the strengths and weaknesses are in the student problem solving. Again because of the flexibility of the online resources at the Math Forum this project promises to give teachers an opportunity to be part of a community of educators/learners themselves and improve their own practice through their participation in that group.

Virtual Math Teams: Reifying Community Participation From Multiple Perspectives

Being a mathematics educator implies interacting regularly and in diverse ways with overlapping and interdependent CoPs. These might include teachers' local and professional communities, the scientific communities related to the content areas of instruction, and those associated with youth, parents, administrators, learning scientists, and policymakers, among others. However, few opportunities exist for teachers to actively and effectively bring together such diverse communities and link the roles that they, as practitioners, play in such communities. One particular key example of this divergence is the usual distancing of the teacher as a practitioner of mathematics instruction from the students or practitioners of mathematics learning. As described before in this chapter the Math Forum provides a diverse array of opportunities for teachers to expand the communities in which they participate, enhance their own professional development, and transform their own identities as mathematicians and teachers. One key aspect of this process and our approach to it lies on the opportunities that teachers have to interact with the actual mathematical work of students. In this section, ways are discussed in which participation in a new, student-oriented online community for mathematics learning is envisioned to contribute to the professional development of teachers.

The strategy of having teachers work together to study student work is one of the most promising professional development approaches developed in recent years (Killion, 2002). The Math Forum has traditionally focused on providing similar opportunities for teachers to talk with others about math, work with others on math, and use the mathematical work of students and other members of the community as a learning resource for all. Usually, the type of student work used corresponds to online asynchronous conversations that students and mentors develop around the PoW offered by the Math Forum. As such, teachers have access to the students "workings" through the mathematical problems proposed by the Math Forum instead of just having access to their final work. Through these materials, teachers have a special window into the thinking and learning processes that students of mathematics develop and can use them to guide their own pedagogical reasoning. Through this experience teachers place themselves in the role of mentors as well as mathematicians and learners of mathematics as they themselves work through a problem that is new to them (unlike most of the problems used in regular classrooms), engage with the same mathematical work that learners do, and think about providing feedback to students. To expand this experience, the Math Forum has started to investigate new ways of providing teachers access to other snapshots of the students mathematical activity and offer expanded opportunities to engage with such resources. The VMT project is a step in such direction.

In the VMT project, small groups of students come together to work on problems similar to those used in the PoW service. Instead of working individually and asynchronously, in VMT students work together in small groups through a special online environment that provides them with an array of tools to conduct their collaborative problem-solving activity, sustain it over time, and interact with other interested individuals and groups (see Figure 11.2).

Initially, VMT has concentrated on designing an online environment and service so that secondary students can do collaborative math problem solving through the Internet effectively. This has been a rich and enlightening experience that in itself demonstrates the value of multiple perspectives and CoPs interacting together (Wessner, Shumar, Stahl, Sarmiento, Muhlpfordt, & Weimar, 2006).

Although the central focus of the VMT project is on understanding and supporting the student groups and their learning interactions, the participation of teachers has become crucial to its success and has also led to the exploration of the interdependence between student and teacher CoPs. At the moment, two central ways can be seen in which the intersection between the community of instructors and the community of learners enriches the forms of participation and learning available to the participants. The first is by reifying what mathematical activity actually is from the point of view of the learners, and the second is by promoting dialog on multiple perspectives to bridge the worlds of instruction and learning.

One central challenge that mathematics teachers face in their professional practice is anticipating, guiding, and monitoring the doings of learners as they develop new skills and expand their ways of participating with mathematics. Based on personal learning experiences, general professional knowledge, and other sources teachers construct instructional activities, which are then presented to students and produce the type of dynamic feedback necessary to change and adapt later activities. Specially, in whole class settings, the planning—implementation—adaptation cycle happens rapidly and teachers use

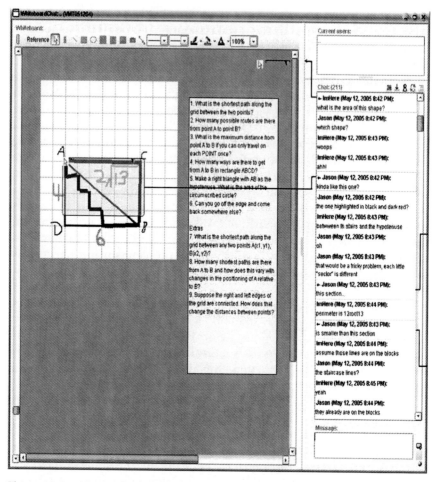

Figure 11.2.   VMT Collaboration Environment with graphical references from
The Chat Area to The Shared Whiteboard.

overall patterns of engagement (e.g., class participation) and outcomes
(e.g., homework or exams) as clues on how to guide next steps.
However, these opportunities to monitor learners' understandings and
the processes used to construct them can be greatly enhanced by having
richer access to the mathematical experiences of students. It is in this
sense that the CoP centred on instruction intersects with the CoP where
learning or being a student of mathematics is a central concern. For this
to occur, teachers need improved opportunities to access the
mathematical work of their students and to reify such work in ways that

are valuable to their CoP. An example of this experience can help us see this interaction more clearly.

It is the second time that this virtual team of secondary students meets online to work on figuring out the mathematics of a "grid-world," a world where one could only move along the lines of a rectangular grid. In their previous session, a few days ago, Drago and Estrick worked on exploring the grid-world and attempted to create a formula for the shortest distance between two points A and B in this world. This time, they are joined by two new team members, GdO who had worked on this problem with another team once before and MathWiz who is new to the task and to the team. A total of five teams are concurrently working on this math problem. Mentors review the teams' work in between sessions (by accessing the teams' chats, which are persistently recorded) and provide feedback to the teams while also alerting them to the findings and emerging questions that are being generated by all the teams. Since all of these interactions happen online and are recorded, they are all accessible to others. How could artifacts derived from these interactions serve as an effective resource for the professional development of math teachers?

On the one hand, these records of the students' collaborative work on the math task provide a rich picture rarely available to teachers. In these interactions, students exhibit their own methods for conducting mathematical problem solving, work through their possibly divergent mathematical concepts, and coconstruct new ways of making sense of mathematics on their own. Because of the collaborative aspect of these

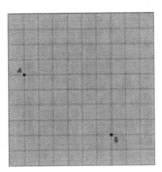

Your group has gotten together to figure
out the math of this place. For example,
what is a math question you might ask
that involves these two points?

Figure 11.3.   Grid-World Task.

interactions students engaged in the active work of expressing their ideas and trying to make others understand and engage with their own ideas as well. The excerpt in Figure 11.4 from one of the teams' online chats illustrates the richness of these materials.

As part of the VMT project and in our role of designers and researchers these kinds of materials provide us with a rich and highly authentic opportunity to explore subtle aspects of the values, principles, and routines of being a member of the community of learners of mathematics. These materials also inform, in contrast, aspects of the corresponding elements of being a teacher or a designer of instructional activities. Notice for example how issues such as personal interest (e.g. "there really isn't an answer to number 6 though ... that's why it's interesting"), problem diffi-

218 Moderator	So, now you can identify questions that interest you from, for example some of the ideas from that list of questions generated by all the teams, or you can create new questions. Then you can go on to answer the ones that you are most interested in.
219 gdo	ok
220 drago	do you know hwere the points are locatied?
221 mathwiz	i can't think of any, but numb er 6 looks interesting
222 drago	number 7
223 mathwiz	so which one should we do?
224 drago	I don't know, anything that interests us I guess
225 gdo	#6 is interesting to me
226 drago	problem is
227 drago	there really isn't an answer to number 6 though
228 weisbari	joins the room
229 mathwiz	yeha
230 gdo	that's why it's interesting
231 drago	it depends who is giving the problem
232 mathwiz	the grid probably extends for ever,
233 mathwiz	but if it's a curved space, it might meet
234 gdo	assuming if it doesn't.........
235 drago	that would make things too complicated
236 drago	I guess
237 gdo	y?
238 drago	but it could work maybe
239 mathwiz	what if we asssumed the grid is a universe...
240 mathwiz	i guess your right
241 gdo	ok
242 gdo	i understand
243 drago	well, first of all, the paper would crumple (if it were real) to form a sphere
244 mathwiz	why a sphere?
245 gdo	?

Figure 11.4.   Excerpt from VMT Chat.

culty (e.g., "that would make things too complicated"), authority (e.g., "it depends who is giving the problem"), and progressive exploration (e.g., "the grid probably extends for ever, but if it's a curved space, it might meet") are framed in this short excerpt. By providing access to these kinds of student experiences for teachers, and structuring their use, we hope to promote the reflective use and reification of pedagogical ideas that take into consideration the intersection between participation in the communities of teaching and learning.

Despite the apparent advantages of these records of students' mathematical work, a word of caution needs to be expressed. Such resources seem to "reify" the work of doing mathematics and learning but, as Wenger advises, "the power of reification—its succinctness, its portability, its potential physical presence, its focusing effect—is also its danger" (Wenger, 1998, p. 61). The challenge lies in designing active and effective opportunities for teachers to engage with such artifacts in ways that are relevant for their own professional practice. This is precisely the challenge of the interdependence between reification and participation that Wenger (1998) posed in his presentation of the theory of CoPs. One way of trying to address this challenge is to envision the Virtual Math Teams community as encompassing a diversity of roles and forms of participations each one defined by its own values, concerns, and central activities but all anchored on the actual lived experience of doing mathematics.

A MODEL FOR ONLINE TEACHER PROFESSIONAL DEVELOPMENT

This chapter has looked at a couple of the projects and services at the Math Forum. There are several unique features to the Math Forum culture and community that stand out (Renninger & Shumar, 2002). Central to all Math Forum activities is creating opportunities for people to talk about math and to do problem-solving together. Thus work of the Math Forum, by its nature, necessitates a community of participants and it is collaborative in nature. Further the Math Forum community has naturally evolved into a well-balanced CoP. Leaders on the site are teachers or others interested in mathematics who have come to the site to have good conversations about mathematics and math pedagogy. They themselves are often individuals who apprenticed on the site at an earlier stage. These individuals are very invested in helping others meet their goals for math education and so form a very supportive group of colleagues who nurture interest and support individuals, taking new risks to stretch their ability to problem solve and to work with students (Renninger, 2000).

The Math Forum, as was shown in the above projects, has been leveraging the potential of this online community to reach new audiences of teachers and to meet, more systematically, the needs of those teachers. Using the power of the Internet to transform space and time the Math Forum has created new opportunities for TPD and student learning by brining the Math Forum culture and community to individuals anytime, anywhere.

The future challenge for the Math Forum as they scale up these professional development opportunities will be to maintain the dynamic culture and the CoP and not to become too formula driven in their effort to create online workshops, modules, and courses. If they are able to do this, they may have the ability to have a real impact on the teaching of mathematics.

Current efforts at the Math Forum involve attempts to create groups where TPD can take place within the context of the Math Forum site. In this way, the Math Forum is attempting to build on the insights of Schlager and Fusco (2004). By combining face-to-face workshops with continuous online support, as well as cultivating leaders from among teachers involved in different workshops, the Math Forum is attempting to use the power of their online CoPs to make TPD more useful for teachers and the real needs they have. The effort is also aimed at creating a sustained community where teachers feel the support and interest of others and that support and interest is long lasting.

Doing this is no easy task. There are many pressures in schools that work against teachers' efforts to engage in sustained work with each other on curricular and pedagogical issues. It will remain to be seen if the Math Forum community can be a presence in teachers' lives in a regular enough way to transform the kind work they do.

NOTES

1.   The weekly meeting to write and do math is called Math Monday because it began as a regular Monday meeting. Now Math Monday moves to different days according to the schedule, but it happens every week and is still called Math Monday.

REFERENCES

Cohen, A. P. (1985). *The symbolic construction of community.* Chichester, London, New York: E. Horwood and Tavistock.

Emirbayer M., & Mische, A. (1998). What is agency? *American Journal of Sociology, 103*(4), 962-1023.

Killion, J. (2002). What works in the high school: *Results-Based Staff Development. National Staff Development Council, Oxford, OH.* Retrieved on February 20, 2007 from http://www.nsdc.org/connect/projects/hswhatworks.pdf

Little, J. W. (1993). Teachers' professional development in a climate of education reform. *Educational Evaluation and Policy Analysis, 15*(2), 129-151.

McLaughlin, M., & Talbert, J. (2001). Professional communities and the work of high school teaching. Chicago: University of Chicago Press. Retrieved March 3, 2007, from http://www.rand.org/publications/RGSD/RGSD174/RGSD174.pdf

Renninger, K. A. (2000). Individual interest and its implications for understanding intrinsic motivation. In C. Sansone & J. M. Harackiewicz (Eds.), *Intrinsic motivation: Controversies and new directions* (pp. 373-404). San Diego, CA: Academic Press.

Renninger, K. A., & Shumar, W. (2002). Community building with and for teachers: The Math Forum as a resource for teacher professional development. In K. A. Renninger & W. Shumar (Eds.), *Building virtual communities: Learning and change in cyberspace* (pp. 60-95). New York: Cambridge University Press.

Renninger, K. A., & Shumar, W. (2004). The centrality of culture and community to participant learning at and with the Math Forum. In S. Barab, J. Grey, & R. Kling (Eds.), *Designing for virtual communities in the service of learning* (pp. 181-209). New York: Cambridge University Press.

Schlager, M. S., & Fusco, J. (2004). Teacher professional development, technology, and communities of practice: Are we putting the cart before the horse? In S. A. Barab, R. Kling, & J. H. Gray (Eds.), *Designing for virtual communities in the service of learning* (pp. 120-153). London: Cambridge University Press.

Shapiro, J. K. (2003). *Exploring teachers' informal learning for policy on professional development.* Santa Monica, CA: RAND. Retrieved March 3, 2007, from http://www.rand.org/publications/RGSD/RGSD174/RGSD174.pdf

Smylie, M. A., Allensworth, E., Greenberg, R. C., Harris, R., & Luppescu, S. (2001). Teacher professional development in Chicago: Supporting effective practice. Retrieved September 15th 2005, from http://www.consortium-chicago.org/publications/pdfs/p0d01.pdf

Wenger, E. (1998). *Communities of practice: Learning, meaning, and identity.* London: Cambridge University Press.

Wessner, M., Shumar, W., Stahl, G., Sarmiento, J., Muhlpfordt, M., & Weimar, S. (2006). Designing an online service for a math community. In S. Barab, K. Hay, & D. Hickey (Eds.), *Proceedings of the International Congress of the Learning Sciences* (pp. 818-824). Mahwah, NJ: Erlbaum.

CHAPTER 12

HEADS TOGETHER

A Professional Online Community of Practice for Scottish Headteachers

Kevin Thompson and Michael Hartley

This chapter explains the strategies and practical techniques used to initiate and grow Heads Together—an online community of headteachers within primary, secondary, nursery, and special educational needs sectors in Scotland. It reflects on the impact of training and describes a number of tools such as the hotseat, which allowed headteachers unprecedented access to public leaders and other tools promoting professional debate and conversation. Great use was made of self-portrait profiles and photographs of the members to engender a community spirit. Three international online conferences were introduced allowing Heads Together from different countries to share ideas and experiences. One of these is examined in detail showing perceived benefits by headteachers. The vital role of the facilitators in nurturing the Heads Together community and encouraging participation among its members is discussed throughout. Finally, this chapter shows how the community gained genuine acceptance by many as a professional tool rather than as an optional distraction and how a spirit of peer support and networking has grown and flourished. Our role in this was relatively short— 2 years—but a working,

Communities of Practice: Creating Learning Environments for Educators,
Volume 2, pp. 241–265
Copyright © 2008 by Information Age Publishing

vibrant community was handed over to Learning and Teaching Scotland (L&TS) at the end of that time.

INTRODUCTION

Heads Together was born from the success of a similar project which Ultralab, a learning technology research center at Anglia Ruskin University, ran in England for the Department for Education and the Environment, called Talking Heads. This was a pilot project, which placed around 1,200 new headteachers into a closed online community. It was based upon Think.com software, written by data base company Oracle in the United States, and given freely to students as a millennium celebration. Although its features were aimed at young people, they could also be used for private communities for groups of professionals.

Following the success of Talking Heads, the Scottish Executive Education Department (SEED) requested a similar pilot in Scotland. Subsequently Heads Together was set up as a joint venture between Ultralab and L&TS (who subsequently went on to run the community) as a 12-month pilot in 2002.

The community was facilitated (initially by two facilitators) on a full time basis and members communicated without having to be online at the same time (asynchronously). Messages were left and responded to as and when people logged in.

There are over 2,000 headteachers in Scotland spread over 32 local authorities and while they meet infrequently in small networking groups this project gave the opportunity for larger scale collaboration.

The Original Aims

The original aims of the project as stated by SEED were to:

1. Support the development of existing Scottish headteachers' management skills
2. Support Scottish headteachers in their day to day role by providing them with a mechanism for mutual support, the potential solution of problems and the sharing and creation of new ideas
3. Reduce the isolation of headteachers in small or remote schools
4. Raise the information and communication technology (ICT) skills of participating headteachers

5. Make participating headteachers aware of the potential role of ICT for management and administration, learning, and teaching

The growth of online learning environments/communities in recent years has been impressive and learners worldwide in higher education, public schooling, business and government are "demanding educational opportunities in an 'anytime and anywhere' format" (Schrum, 2002). However, group interactions online are rarely spontaneous, as they need to be cared for and nurtured: facilitated. Facilitation is essential if online communities are to succeed, although, as Kim (2000) points out, "you can lead someone to a community but you can't make them actively participate" (p. 2).

Rheingold (1993) defined virtual community as

> social aggregations that emerge from the Net when enough people carry on those public discussions long enough, with sufficient human feelings, to form webs of personal relationships in cyberspace. A virtual community is a group of people who may or may not meet one another face to face, and who exchange words and ideas through the mediation of computer bulletin boards and networks. (p. 5)

The idea of "social aggregations" in cyberspace was highlighted by Cothrel and Williams (1999). They interviewed people who worked together online, but their initial definition of community as, "a group of people who use computer networks as their primary means of interaction" did not find agreement among their respondents. The users' were more inclined to describe themselves as participants in "communities of practice" (CoPs) or "communities of interest." Furthermore, those people who were associated with "community" had a sense of what is called "commonality: common interests, purpose or objectives." Cothrel and Williams' research suggested, "the social element was critical to distinguishing a community from a mere group of individuals" (p. 3).

According to Wenger (1998), we all belong to CoPs because they are an integral part of our daily lives and, contrary to Rheingold's definition, Wenger insists that a CoP is "not just an aggregate of people defined by some characteristics" (p. 6). He takes Cothrel and Williams (1999) findings further by maintaining that there are three components which associate "community" and "practice" and form the source of a community's coherence: mutual engagement, joint enterprise and shared repertoire.

Furthermore, for a learning community to be successful, it must, as Kim (2000, p. 4) maintains, have three basic community design principles:

- "long-lasting communities almost always start off small, simple and focused, and then grow organically over time-adding breadth, depth, and complexity in response to the changing needs of the members, and the changing conditions of the environment."
- "community building is a constant balancing act between the efforts of management ... to plan, organize, and run the space, and the ideas, suggestions, and needs of your members."
- "Empower your members over time."

These, were key aims within the Heads Together Project.

The chapter discusses previous lessons learned from experience with the Talking Heads project (Chapman, Powell, & Ramondt 2002) and examines the key features of the Heads Together project and the various strategies used to encourage and maintain participation. The second section reflects on the induction of the headteachers and the development and structure of the online community. In the third and fourth sections the design of the community is discussed, in particular the software tools used to engage members, strategies to increase participation and the introduction of further initiatives to encourage community development. Statistics relating to increasing participation over the 2-year period of the pilot are discussed briefly in the fifth and sixth sections, highlighting the potential for developing similar CoPs, while emphasizing the facilitator's role in developing and sustaining participation, mutual engagement, and motivation within a CoP.

HEADS TOGETHER COMMUNITY DEVELOPMENT

Member Induction Initiation

It was determined from the start of the project in 2002, by SEED, that each headteacher would be given a full day's training in the use of the Oracle Think.com software, including an explanation of the philosophy of online community. During this time, the headteacher's photograph was taken and posted in the community and they were encouraged to write a brief "About me" section within the community—both actions intended to increase interaction within the community. Headteachers were also asked to contribute anonymously as to what they hoped to gain from participation. Responses mention both support and a sharing of experience.

- "I hope to be part of a supportive community."

- "Mutual support in increasingly problematic times for school leaders."
- "Hopefully a supportive community willing to share ideas and provide possible solutions to the challenges that lie ahead" (Anonymous quotations from Heads Together community, 2002).

Headteachers also made frequent mention of the loneliness that the project aims hoped to address:

- "To lose the feeling of isolation that we all experience from time to time."
- "This is a very lonely job. The idea of mutual support is very exciting" (Anonymous quotations from Heads Together community, 2002).

Some wanted to increase their ICT level and make use of electronic communication at a professional level:

- "Increase computer skills and ability to make better use of ICT for management tasks."
- "I welcome the chance to communicate electronically without phone calls bouncing back and forth" (Anonymous quotations from Heads Together community, 2002).

Subsequent feedback gathered at the end of the training sessions showed that headteachers valued the day highly, with over 99% grading it as good or very good. This view was supported by comments such as:

- "I think this whole scheme is very exciting and has enormous potential as a means of support, particularly for isolated rural headteachers."
- "Worthwhile session and I hope a worthwhile and fulfilling tool - looking forward to getting started" (Comments from online feedback given to Ultralab at training sessions, 2002).

Community Structure

Based on experience gained with Talking Heads, it was decided to keep the community structure within Heads Together as lean as possible, thereby simplifying navigation and reducing the number of places, which headteachers would need to visit. In the English pilot (Talking Heads) around 12 different subcommunities existed, which members had to actively choose to join. It was felt by the headteachers involved, that this was a barrier to participation due to other demands on their time within the school day (Chapman, Powell, & Ramondt, 2002). Consequently, in Heads Together all the members had access to all the subcommunities, resulting in participation across the different sectors, that is, nursery, primary, secondary, and special needs.

ONLINE COMMUNITY DESIGN

The initial software for the project was identical to that used by the Talking Heads pilot, namely, Think.com. The design specification of Think.com created by Ultralab and developed by Oracle provided a tool that enabled the online environment (in Heads Together) to mirror, and build on, face-to-face discussions. In order to emulate real life as much as possible, several user-friendly tools enabling mutual engagement and collaboration were included within the software. Below the overall design of the online community is discussed as well as some of the tools it comprises. These tools had to be readily usable by participants, the intention being that they would eventually create their own community activities.

Overview of the Heads Together Community

The Heads Together community was subdivided into different pages to simplify navigation, and allow the individual sectors to address issues specific to their area within education. Using the conversation tool, this portal hosted the Welcome conversations that asked heads to leave information about themselves and their school. Verbal feedback showed that these were interesting and useful to heads and eventually contained information (school size, staffing, etc.) on almost all head teacher

Table 12.1.   Additional Pages

Direct publishing page	For publishing issues headteachers wished to rise with their peers
Staff room	For the lighter side of life and where several heads provided their favorite holiday destinations and jokes
Technical page	Hints and tips on better use of the software
Useful links	URLs outside Think.com that were of interest to other heads

Table 12.2.   Development of the Direct Publishing Page

McCrone	The staffing and salaries restructure (headed by McCrone) was of great interest and much controversy in Scottish schools
SEN	Special educational needs—some schools specialise in this form of education, others have departments within the mainstream
Secondary	A discussion area for matters of most interest to secondary schools
Primary	A popular area as most of the community members were primary headteachers
Nursery	The project was open to heads from ALL sectors including nursery
Management	Pages specific to school management issues
Cybrary	An innovative idea to share policies and other related documents (see below)
Feedback page	For comments and criticisms of the site

members. Later in the project, this information was transferred to a searchable database.

As the direct publishing page grew, it became more difficult to navigate and members were asked for suggestions about restructuring. Feedback from the headteachers both during training days and online, identified areas, which they saw as essential to the development of the community. The pages listed in Table 12.2 above were subsequently added.

Participation across and between the different sectors very soon became the norm, with primary headteachers advising on secondary issues and vice versa, thereby adding a whole new dimension to the concept of the community.

This was an interesting development in that the sharing of experience, management, and leadership skills led to discussion of common issues within their respective schools and the wider educational system.

The Use of Community Software Tools to Increase Participation

The Toolbox

The Think.com software provided access to a number of tools, which headteachers could access to create and publish items of interest, issues for debate, or discussion within the online community. Most of the tools available were eventually used by various members, the exceptions being audio and video. Reasons for this included "a lack of confidence, lack of expertise in using such tools, time or simply the non-availability of suitable hardware/software within their school" (feedback from

Figure 12.1.   The toolbox.

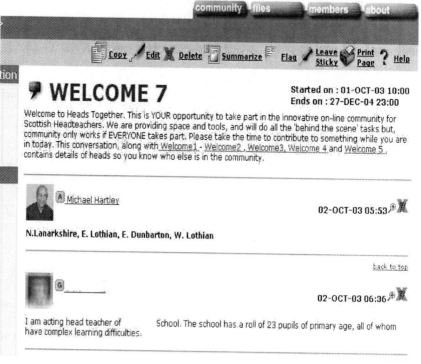

Figure 12.2.   The conversation tool.

headteachers at training Days). The tools most used, were the conversation, debate, brainstorm, hotseat, and file items. The primary use of the file tool was for uploading policies, which were published, within the cybrary (the online policy bank) (see Figure 12.1).

The Conversation Tool

This was a linear tool allowing a question or stem at the top and then a simple set of responses in time/date order. All responses and the question were attributed to their contributor. It was used far more than any other tool within the software (see Figure 12.2).

The Debate Tool

This tool allowed a series of options or viewpoints to be given as responses—ranging from a simple "yes/no/don't know" to something far more complex. It required more thought in setting up, and was subsequently used less. However, it proved useful in gathering opinions on matters of national importance. Once again, all responses and the question were attributed to their contributor although these details have been removed here (see Figure 12.3).

The Brainstorm Tool

This was a unique tool in that it allowed any contributor to remain anonymous, although the initial setter of the question was named (subsequently this too was removed—see Figure 12.4). This tool was used for very sensitive discussion where people's thoughts and ideas were

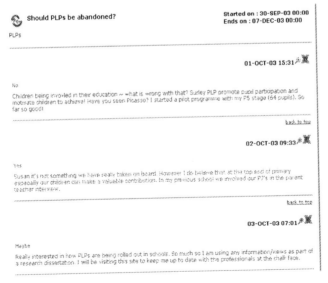

Figure 12.3.   The debate tool.

What do you need from a community 2

Started on : 15-JAN-03 00:00
Ends on : 22-JAN-04 00:00

The first of these is now full so please add ideas here. Previous one may be found <u>here</u>

"Many Heads make light work"..."Two Heads are better than one" ...."It helps to talk".

"This will provide the shoulders for heads to rely on."

Just four quotes from Heads already in the community.

What are your hopes, aspirations, ideas etc for what Heads Together Community can do for you...

.....and also what you can do for others since community is a two way process.

Click on an icon below to contribute an Idea

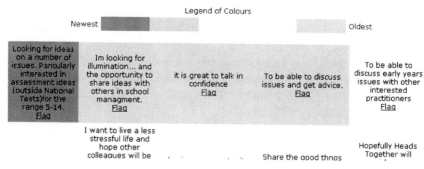

Figure 12.4. The brainstorm tool.

<u>back to top</u>

13-OCT-03 13:15

Q? Jenny As a very small rural school we have had to adapt circle time mainly because we all know one another so well.Have you considered the small rural setting and made any adaptions to your programme to accommodate the special circumstances of a small close knit community.

<u>back to top</u>

18-OCT-03 06:18

Dear Kate Truly, I know alot about the problems of working with small schools. I first freelanced my ideas for circle-time for Wiltshire LEA in the very early 80's. They have many small rural schools – some one-teacher and many two-teacher schools...in fact the Small Schools association funded my first bursary as part of an action research project. What I learnt during that time is that there are both tremendous potentials and pitfalls!!

Figure 12.5.   The hotseat.

important but not their identity. It allowed headteachers to be critical at times when they were nervous about their name being made public.

The Hotseat

This tool was similar to the conversation tool but more structured. It allowed a thread of answers or feedback to be grouped together and to promote structured dialogue. Its biggest use was when Guests came into the community to fill the hotseat role (see Figure 12.5).

The Cybrary

The cybrary (Figure 12.6) did not form part of the Think.com toolbox. As detailed later, it was an innovative idea to share policies and other related documents, which combined with the file tool, developed into a major resource area within the community. Below the hotseat, cybrary, and brainstorm tools are discussed in more detail.

1. CURRICULUM	
Art & Design - Barassie Primary School	
Balanced Curriculum - Lowport P.S.	
Communication & Language - Linburn School	Music Policy - Barshare P.S.
Drama Policy - Dalmellington P.S.	Music Policy - Cargenbridge P.S.
Drama Policy - Saltoun P.S.	Prayer - St Andrew's Academy
Drugs Education Policy - Aberlemno P.S.	Physical Restraint draft policy - Firth P.S.
English Language Policy - Achnasheen P.S.	Reading Policy - Stanley P.S.
Handwriting Policy - Bells Brae P.S.	Religious & Moral Education - Bargarran P.S.
Health Policy - Sandness P.S.	Religious & Moral Education - Blackness P.S.
Homework Policy - Stirling H.S.	Religious & Moral Education - Bonhill P.S.
ICT Policy - Eday Primary School	Religious & Moral Education - Dunblane P.S.
ICT Policy - Foligarry School	Religious and Moral Education - Longhaugh P.S
ICT Policy - Forthill P.S.	Religious & Moral Education - Strath of Appin P.S
ICT Policy - Greenwood Academy	R.E. Policy - Todholm P.S.
ICT Policy - Kirkland Park P.S.	Science Policy - Toward H.S.
ICT Policy - Mid Calder P.S.	Science Policy - Tighnabruaich P.S.
ICT Policy - Pairc School	Sex Education - Longridge P.S.
Language policy - Glenburn Primary	Social Subjects - Carnish P.S.
Learning Policy - Greenwood Academy	Spelling Policy St.Palladius P.S.
Learning Support - Lochmaddy P.S.	Support for Learning- Kirklandneuk P.S.
Learning Support-Sandwickhill P.S.	Support for Learning-Laxdale School
Library Policy - Golspie H.S.	Support for Learning - Lawthorn P.S.
Maths Policy S1/2 - Rack P.S.	Support for Learning - North Roe
Maths Policy-Bayble P.S.	Support for Learning-Sgoil nan Loch
Maths Policy - Cragston School	Support for Learning-Stornaway P.S.
Maths Policy - Doumby Community School	Support for Learning - St. Angela's P.S.
Maths Policy-Glencairn P.S.	Support for Learning policy - St Clement's P.S.
Maths Policy- Leverhulme P.S.	Talk Policy - St Kessog's P.S.
Maths Policy - Northmuir P.S	Writing Policy - Kincaidston Community School
Maths Policy-Shelibost P.S.	
2. ATTAINMENT / CHILDREN'S DEVELOPMENT & PROGRESS	3. LEARNING & TEACHING / DEVELOPMENT & LEARNING THROUGH PLAY

Figure 12.6.   The cybrary.

Hotseats

The hotseat concept featured from the start of the pilot and was a key strategy within the Heads Together community. It was designed to allow headteachers access to an expert or invited guest for a short period—usually 3 weeks. The invited guest submitted a starter paper on a topic of current educational interest, providing headteachers with the opportunity to question online and asynchronously, aspects of the paper with the hotseat guest.

Over the 2-year period of the pilot Heads Together project, 15 guests sat in the virtual hotseat. The ability to discuss key issues with highly regarded educational figures was an important and very successful strategy for encouraging participation.

In order to ensure that the community was continuously refreshed, it was aimed to host a new hotseat once a month. This was not always achieved due to a variety of reasons, some administrative some political. Timing of hotseats was very important. Experience demonstrated that certain times were better than others, for example, before and after school holidays tended to be periods of reduced activity. Additionally a number of headteachers were "lurkers," who simply read what was written but did not contribute. This group exists in any online community and is not a bad thing, since they too are learning from what others say.

Some of the topics covered in the Hotseat were important issues in Scottish education and included:

- E-charter for children
- Standards in schools
- Education and accountability
- Challenge for all of us—school inspectorate
- Promoted postrestructuring
- Future face of the teaching profession—general teaching council
- Leadership is all
- Releasing excellence through building self-esteem
- Combating bullying
- Scottish qualifications authority

Guests included international education figures and representatives of the general teaching council Scotland and Her Majesty's (HM) Chief Inspector of Schools.

Analysis of the hotseats revealed that a core group of a dozen heads returned and asked questions in two or more hotseats while other questioners varied from event to event. This demonstrated that some heads were beginning to feel more comfortable in using this medium on a regular basis. Although the number of questions appeared small (sometimes only two or three), it should be born in mind that all members of Heads Together had access to the answers, irrespective of the questioner and realistically, only so many questions can be asked on a particular topic.

The hotseat was one of the key attractions of Heads Together. It provided busy headteachers with a unique opportunity to communicate one-to-one with many interesting and leading figures in the world of education.

The Cybrary

Another major success story of the Heads Together community was the cybrary.

Headteachers were asked to bring a policy document with them to their training day and were taken through the process of uploading this into the community—the objective being to share these with other schools.

The numbers of policies grew very quickly, and some retrieval system needed to be found. Following discussion among members, the policies were categorized based on the "How Good is Our School?" headings—a set of quality indicators developed by HM Inspectors of Education, namely:

- Curriculum
- Attainment/children's development and progress
- Learning and teaching/development and learning through play
- Support for pupils/children and families
- Ethos
- Resources
- Management, leadership, and quality assurance

Some adjustments to these headings (italics) were made to include the corresponding category used by nursery colleagues.

Members' responses varied when they were asked to bring a school policy for uploading during their training day. On average, more than 50% of attendees agreed, despite some feeling less than confident that their policy was "good enough" for public consumption, resulting in over 1,000 policies from across the whole of Scotland made available for sharing! There were soon very many comments of thanks and praise on both the concept and the policies themselves from community members. This was said to be an "incredible resource" and many subsequently questioned why they had not shared these earlier through some other mechanism.

- "Thank you for your 'Learning and Teaching' policy. We will use this as a very positive and well thought out basis for our own smaller school where I AM the 'Senior Management Team.' "
- "Great idea the policy swapping. Too many exceptionally overworked HTs are working in isolation attempting to develop guidelines for staff, pupils and parents thinking that it has not been done before—most things have been! The sooner the Heads Together network spreads across the whole country the better."
- "Very interested in ICT policy. This will certainly help us in our next development plan. I will now attempt to add some of our policies as a payback! Thanks again."
- "Policy swapping is an excellent idea. I have downloaded language policies to help a working group I'm on. I will publish this when completed. Thank you to all who have published their language policies. It helps us greatly" (Quotations from headteachers on feedback page of Heads Together).

Some headteachers used the policies directly, while others used them as a staff development exercise giving out four or five different policies on one topic.

Since the software was not designed with such regular and organized uploads in mind, the whole process became labour intensive; with the facilitators having to reformat pages using Web page software on a daily basis, nevertheless, feedback indicated it was well worthwhile.

By April 2004, the hit count on the cybrary stood at 10,908; the most visited page of the whole community, after the default front page. "Hits" are a crude measurement, counting only the number of times a page has been visited—not by whom or when, but without any other statistics available were the best indicator possible. A number of policies recorded several hundred visits, which along with the many positive comments demonstrated that headteachers showed this feature to be an invaluable resource.

Some technical issues arose from time to time, for example, not all documents contributed were in Word format. Advice for the future would be to try to ensure all uploads were in a common format.

Brainstorm—Anonymity on Demand—the "Agony Aunt" Feature

Headteachers wanted to discuss some sensitive issues without being identified and although confidentiality was stressed throughout the project, there was still concern expressed that "others" may be watching. Agony Aunt was set up as a page on its own to address this. The brainstorm tool was chosen since it provided total anonymity. Finally, by using the facilitator as the question "master" no headteachers names were identifiable.

Over a 3 month period there were six separate issues raised. Interestingly, some questions appeared uncontroversial and could easily have been asked elsewhere, while others chose this forum in which to engage colleagues' opinions on more difficult areas.

Probably the most sensitive issue raised by headteachers was to discuss their employers. Comments received were somewhat hard-hitting, a sign of increasing confidence in the community forum. Many of the issues raised had quality responses and apparently, heads were learning from the experience of others—the whole essence of professional online community.

From a facilitation viewpoint, this was a time consuming activity in that it needed checking daily and when new questions were raised they had to be copied into a new brainstorm to maintain anonymity.

FURTHER EFFORTS TO INCREASE PARTICIPATION

Activity within the community fluctuated depending on what was happening at any one time both internally (e.g., hotseats, etc.) and externally (e.g., holidays, etc.). There was, nevertheless, a gradual increase in participation as membership numbers grew as a result of more headteachers being trained. Ongoing changes to the structure of the community ease of navigation and an apparent growing confidence among headteachers in using the tools, further contributed to the increase in participation.

In 2003, SEED engaged George Street Research (2003) to conduct an independent review on Heads Together. In the published report one of the suggestions made by was, "a need to continue to enhance and build the Web site, ensuring inclusion of topical issues" (p. 3). They further commented that, "there is an assumption on the part of some headteachers that the Heads Together site remains static rather than continually evolving and growing" (p. 10).

Redesigning the Community Front Page

One strategy to address these comments was to redesign the community front page—keeping it short, dynamic with changes every few weeks, and encouraging more commitment from participating Heads themselves.

Two new items were introduced:

- A regular discussion based on topical articles in the *Scottish Times Education Supplement*—the main paper for Scottish Teachers
- The feature "What's Happening in Our School," led by headteachers talking about novel events in their own schools

What's Happening in Our School?

This was designed to try to increase the interest and traffic through the online community.

In many respects, it resembled the structure of the hotseat, which allowed headteachers access to an expert or invited guest for a short period. The main difference however, was that a headteacher was now asked to "host" or "guest in" a hotseat for a 2-week period, based on something innovative happening in their school. The intention was to attract greater interest in the site and meant that each host headteacher featured had to commit to coming in regularly over the 2-week period to respond to queries/comments. Topics and sector were varied but included:

- Brain gym
- Debono's thinking hats
- Gaelic medium education
- Partial immersion of foreign language in primary school
- Shared/cluster headship

Interest in this area continued with many schools being introduced to new practices and increasing numbers of heads coming forward to share ideas.

Synchronous Discussion—A Virtual "Cheese and Wine Evening"

As part of the research, the real-time aspects of the community were investigated, that is, would people respond to communicating at the same time? The software was not really designed with instant messaging (IM) features; however, on this first occasion, it was decided to use the hotseat tool for synchronous discussion. In choosing this particular tool, it was possible for a number of threaded discussions to take place.

Invitations to join the evening along with an explanation of its purpose were sent out, approximately 2 weeks in advance, to some 1,000 head-teachers who had already undergone training. It was hoped that this first "synchronous chat" event would give head-teachers a feeling of mutual support and allow community members to develop "a spirit of collaboration." The title was chosen in a humorous parallel to a real social event.

Headteachers Response

The reaction of headteachers to the event was very positive and not short on humor, for example:

- "What a brill idea. Time is so short at school, cheese and whine only allowed. Wine is much better!"
- "Edam good idea!!"
- "Do I have to wear virtual clothes or will my usual M&S effort do?"
- "I'm up for it—let me know what cheese to get!!"
- "Sounds interesting - I'll have my glass at the ready!!!"

In total, 12 headteachers participated with 62 questions asked and 92 responses. A number of headteachers accessed the event but did not actually participate (lurkers), as evidenced by over 500 hits on the page.

The event enabled headteachers to identify with each other and the problems they encountered within Heads Together.

The facilitators role in this instance was:

- To welcome head-teachers as soon as they started to participate online
- To host the conversation(s) when necessary
- To provide support to any headteacher having difficulty accessing the Cheese and Wine page or in making a contribution
- To thank headteachers for their participation as they left the event

Lessons Learned

Synchronous activity is, of necessity, facilitator intensive but in this instance proved worthwhile. Throughout the synchronous communication, several issues were raised which headteachers and facilitators agreed needed to be addressed within the community, for example excessive scrolling—a reminder that page design is important; family time versus work; guilt about using the community during school day; making time for using the community; access both to Internet and the hotseats; a need for local level support groups; keyboard shortcuts and ICT in management.

A final comment:

> More cheese and wine evenings, please. What a wonderful way to chat with headteachers informally. This could be the springboard for developing the habit of using Heads Together more. There is definitely an excellent supportive element here.

Photographic Competition

In order to further encourage participation, a photographic competition was held It was hoped heads would use the technology in their school, for example, a digital camera, and to use their Heads Together skills to upload entries to the community. A digital camera was offered as a prize to the best entry with certificates going to all the other entrants.

Headteachers were invited to submit a photograph along with some text reflecting their school ethos. The competition ran over 2 months and attracted 13 entries from nursery, primary, secondary, and special educational needs sectors. The displayed entries received 194 hits indicating that although relatively few took part, others were interested to see what they had achieved.

In practice, some headteachers managed to upload work themselves; however, the majority e-mailed them to the facilitator to do this for them.

International Conference on Inclusion

This was a collaborative venture between Heads Together and Pen-i-Ben, the Welsh equivalent. The hotseat program was well established in the framework of Heads Together and it was shown that having a high profile player sitting in the hotseat would be an ideal opportunity to generate interest not only among community members, but extend an invitation to contacts in other countries. A leading national figure in inclusive education in Scotland was suggested as the hotseat guest for this occasion. Existing links between members and others provided the opportunity to contact and invite headteachers from five countries to participate in the Conference thus delegates from Scotland, Wales, England, New Zealand, and Greece all took part. It was decided to run the conference in a closed community and membership would have to be sought by those who had expressed interest. Certain elements were seen as key to the success of the conference:

- The conference had to be advertised to ALL the online groups within Heads Together
- Those who wished to participate in the conference were required to register in order that interest could be gauged
- Conference information was prepared outlining the timetable and duration
- The conference papers would only be available by logging on and signing into the conference

Organization

The online conference was planned to run for 10 days with a lead in period when conference papers would be available and a period after the guest speakers ceased to answer questions when the conference would still be open for papers and contributions to be read.

All members were e-mailed an invitation as it was envisaged that this might generate some interest among heads that had not yet taken part and would demonstrate the type of activity that participants could expect online. In addition, contact was made with headteachers in Wales and England, along with educators in New Zealand and a headteacher in Greece.

Eighty-two people registered an interest in attending the conference and were duly admitted to the community when the arrangements were completed. The conference ran for 10 days with 20 delegates asking detailed questions and receiving equally detailed answers. The 356 hits during the conference and 447 hits after the conference closed to contributions indicated that more users read the content than asked questions. Essential to the conference format was the ease of online navigation, especially for those not familiar with the community. The solution was a conference map, making the conference format driven thus ensuring that there was a clear focal point for all the activities. Subsequent feedback from members showed that this was a success.

Lessons Learned From Utilizing the Hotseat Tool

- The delivering of high profile guests in a conference format straight to busy headteachers' desktops created a great deal of interest.
- High profile people are willing to give of their time and energy.
- Conference papers do not need to be weighty. A body of related knowledge can be assembled from the conference contributions.

- Conference members want advice and straightforward answers.
- Conference members are willing to share their experience and resources.
- The community hotseat format is useful to collate thoughts on given ideas.
- The format is sufficiently successful to warrant further exploration as a means of increasing participation and communication.
- The very nature of the asynchronous online conference environment can overcome national boundaries and international time zones, and establish clear channels of communication between participants.
- There is the potential to explore the creation of a programme of online conferences, for headteachers—two in an academic year would be sufficient.

The online community structure and navigation worked well and there was little evidence of attendees having difficulties in finding their contributory items.

Recommendations

- A face-to-face event at which community members could plan a programme of work which they could then continue online (suggested by headteacher members)
- This strategy could be used as a way of launching a CoP—stemming from the expression of interest in those who applied to attend
- The online conference format could be extended to increase the international dimension. Other nations' school leaders would benefit from the debate
- Another seminar could be run using these techniques in order to further develop the model
- Conference guests need to be highly prominent in their field to engender sufficient interest and momentum to the activity
- Advertising and marketing must be given a higher profile role for future event(s) to be successful

HEADS TOGETHER PARTICIPATION STATISTICS

The software was not written with easy access to user statistics in mind since its primary intended users were children. However, page hits was available and allowed a crude indicator of interest. These were skewed by facilitators working and by training days. Considering the above proviso, a summary of Heads Together statistics follows.

Total Members and Visits

Out of a pool of approximately 1,300 members, the total visits to Heads Together for each month during December 2003 and the first quarter of 2004 was as follows (see Figure 12.7).

It should be noted that the above visits do not specify the actual number of members logging in as one person could log in several times in a day. The statistics were further influenced by the fact that 23 separate training days for headteachers took place over the 4-month period and as part of the training session, they would log in and log off several times in the course of their day.

What emerges from the data is the steady rise in the number of hits each month on the Heads Together community. Discounting those hits, which would have resulted from participation during training days, including facilitators' activity while working online, the pattern was one of increasing growth.

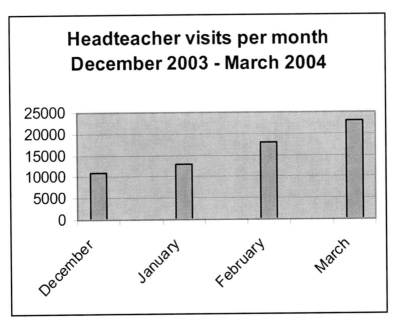

Figure 12.7. Headteacher visits per month Dec. 2003–March 2004.

Figure 12.8 shows the number of hits on the respective pages within the Heads Together community during the month of March 2004. The front page served, primarily, as a navigation center to the community pages, the hotseat subcommunity, the "What's Happening in Our School Hotseat" and "Current Educational News." The second bar—the cybrary was clearly the most popular page visited after the mandatory front page.

The Weekly Pattern of Hits

Analysis of data collected first thing Monday and last thing Friday during February and March 2004 provided some indication of community activity over weekends and weekdays (Figure 12.9).

Taking into consideration the reliability of this data, the statistics provided an indication as to patterns of use. Allowing for the incidence of training days impacting on the number of hits recorded, the data provided a base line measurement with regards to logging on and visits to Heads Together. The results show a difference between week and weekend activity as headteachers became more confident using the community as part of their working day. The period from February 23rd to March 12th saw a fluctuation in the number of hits; this was most likely due to this period coinciding with schools' half-term holidays (see Figure 12.9 above).

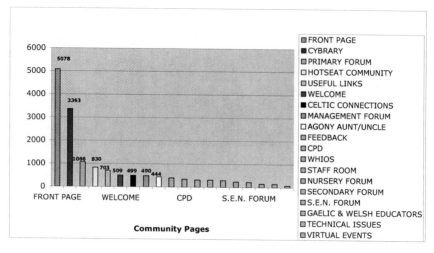

Figure 12.8.   Hits by page   –March 2004.

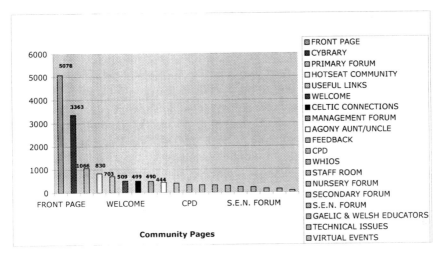

Figure 12.9.   Heads Together front page hits by week/weekend Feb.–March 2004.

FUTURE TRENDS

L&TS have since produced two generations of their own customized software for online communities and have expanded Heads Together to encompass college sector principals. This is based on the software discussed above but includes additional features such as IM. It would be interesting to research how software changes have affected the community.

The experience with Heads Together prompted the development and facilitation of Celtic Connections, a pilot CoP that allowed Welsh language headteachers and Gaelic headteachers/educators in Scotland to share experience and good practice concerning bilingual education. The benefit of such CoPs for bilingual educational communities, nationally and internationally, is an area that it would be useful to develop in the future with Welsh colleagues.

It can also be concluded from the success with international conferences that there are many commonalities in teaching throughout the world. An integrated CoP, comprising members from many different countries, would be an excellent extension to this project.

It is also possible that these techniques could be transferred to many other professions and that with adequate funding there is the potential to have a community of practice for lawyers, doctors, and even politicians.

Conclusions

At the time of handing over the Heads Together project to L&TS, a vibrant online community of headteachers had been established throughout Scotland. The original aims of the project as stated by SEED (1.1) were mostly all met by the end of the project period.

Headteachers commented frequently within the community on how their management skills increased through collaboration (Aim 1). There is also frequent mention of mutual support, sharing of issues and reduction of isolation (Aims 2 & 3). Feedback from training days and subsequent increased community use is evidence of increased ICT skills (Aim 4) and the project itself is one excellent example of using ICT to aid management and administration by mechanisms such as the cybrary (Aim 5).

Over the project period, many discussions took place and efforts were made to focus on features, which, based on experience in Scotland and in England, would help to sustain similar communities in the future. There appears to be an interest and a great potential for many other communities in Scottish education encompassing class teachers, middle managers, and other educationists. At the time of handing over the project to L&TS, there were over 1,500 head teacher members in the Heads Together community. A large majority of these had been provided with training as mentioned.

In the authors' experience, online community can be a very fragile flower and changes to the look and feel of the software or to the community focus, must be handled with great care in order that community members do not feel alienated. It is after all, their community.

However, in general terms any online CoP requires a variety of ingredients to make it successful.

- It needs to be vibrant as the members provide the content of the community; therefore, no participation leads to no content.
- It must be relevant and offer access to features or people that would not otherwise be available. If useful resources can be provided, as in the cybrary, and if the community changes regularly, members are more likely to return.
- Keep the number of areas small as increasing these leads to dilution of contributions.
- Give "quick wins" where possible, that is, if visitors leave with something valuable then they will return.

What is clear is that participation, mutual engagement and motivation cannot be developed and sustained successfully within a CoP without effective facilitation.

REFERENCES

Chapman, C, Powell, S, Ramondt, L. (Eds.). (2002). *Talking Heads short report.* Retrieved September 25, 2006, from http://intra.ultralab.net/~leonie/cothsreport02/index.html

Cothrel, J., & Williams, R. (1999). *How some folks have tried to describe community, Nancy White. cited in Full Circle Associates* (Resources). Retrieved April 2005 from, http://www.fullcirc.com/community

George Street Research. (2003). *Evaluation of Heads Together pilot project.* Retrieved October 18, 2007 from www.Scotland.gov.uk/library5/education/headsfinal.pdf [quote Page 10] page 3.

Kim A. J. (2000) *Community building on the Web: Secret strategies for successful online communities.* Berkeley, CA: Peachpit Press.

Kim A. J. (2001). *Exclusive interview with Kim A. J. author of community building on the Web: Secret strategies for successful online communities. February 27, 2001.* Retrieved October 18, 2007, from http://www.elearningpost.com/articles/archives/exclusive_interview_with_amy_jo_kim/

Rheingold, H. (1993). *The virtual community: Homesteading on the electronic frontier.* Retrieved September 25, 2006, from http://www.rheingold.com/vc/book

Schrum, L. (2002). Dimensions and strategies for online success: Voices from experienced educators. *Journal of Asynchronous Learning Networks, 6*(1), 57). Retreieved October 18, 2007, from http://www.sloan-c.org/publications/jaln/v6n1/v6n1_schrum.asp

Wenger, E (1998). *Communities of practice: Learning, meaning and identity.* London: Cambridge University Press.

CHAPTER 13

GRADUATE PROFESSIONAL EDUCATION FROM A COMMUNITY OF PRACTICE PERSPECTIVE

The Role of Social and Technical Networking

Linda G. Polin

This chapter describes the value and means of revisioning graduate professional education as an activity that occurs at the intersection of three topics: practice, pedagogy, and digital culture. The chapter considers social computing applications as a mechanism to support a shift in the context of graduate professional education from schooling for transfer to situated engagement. The community of practice model of learning supports this shift in roles and activities for students and faculty by increasing peer-to-peer engagement and opportunities to engage with experts and expert practice beyond what is locally available. Recognizing that practitioner-students often are not involved in vital, active, engaged, professional communities outside their workplace, and that many faculty members in teaching universities are, likewise, not centrally involved in a larger research community, the chapter offers a view of social and technical networking tools that create participation structures to bridge these communities. The chapter

Communities of Practice: Creating Learning Environments for Educators,
Volume 2, pp. 267–285
Copyright © 2008 by Information Age Publishing
All rights of reproduction in any form reserved.

illustrates these ideas by reference to two graduate blended programs (combining online and face-to-face settings).

INTRODUCTION

This chapter describes academic life at the intersection of three related topics: community of practice (CoP), a pedagogical model; digital culture, as embodied in the current and future student population; and postsecondary education, in particular graduate professional education. The aim is to illustrate ways in which social computing applications enable the use of a CoP model in graduate professional education. The illustrations are drawn from two hybrid, or blended, degree programs (a mix of face-to-face and online interactions) at the graduate school of education and psychology at Pepperdine University. These fully accredited programs have each been in operation for more than a decade. One is the MA degree in educational technology, begun in 1998; the other is the EdD degree in educational technology leadership, begun in 1995.

The Changing Face of Graduate Professional Education

The most recent study of graduate education in the United States, conducted by the National Center of Educational Statistics (NCES), is now nearly a decade old. Trends first seen in those data are now part of the reality of graduate professional education (NCES, 1996). Ten years ago, it was clear that students in master's and doctoral programs in professions other than law and medicine are increasingly older, working adults, in midcareer. These are students with professional identities anchored in their local practice. In the field of education, these include teachers, principals, curriculum supervisors, librarians, technology coordinators, special education instructors, counselors, museum staff, and corporate trainers. They come to graduate education seeking professional development beyond what is available to them on their own at their local workplace.

Ironically, in the field of education site-based isolation is keenly felt. Most practicing teachers, administrators, or managers are not involved in vital, active, engaged, professional communities. They do not attend conferences outside their locale. They do not subscribe to and read professional journals in their field. For many, even access to colleagues at the workplace can be quite limited by incompatible schedules that allow rare, brief opportunities to engage on matters of substance. Yet historically, these same full-time workers will not find any greater opportunity to connect to the professional practice when they come to the university as part-time students or commuter students. These students will not be working on campus with faculty as part of an externally funded project. They will not be available to engage with peers and near-peers in the campus coffee house, to occupy teaching assistant or research assistant positions, to accompany faculty to project meetings, to hear guest speakers and consultants on campus.

Like the students they teach or the colleagues they train, these educators arrive at the university classroom to acquire knowledge in one formal context in order to transfer it to another practical context at a later time. This traditional model of instruction in higher education has been, and largely remains, a model of learning as the acquisition of knowledge, transmitted from the faculty expert to the student novice, with the aid of text and, sometimes, audiovisual media.

NEW IDEAS ABOUT LEARNING

Over the past 2 decades, learning theory itself has evolved as researchers have sought to understand the failure of cognitive transfer to deliver on its promise (Brown, Collins, & Duguid, 1989; Resnick, 1991). From studies of learning in informal settings (González et al., 2005) learning on-the-job (Hutchins & Klausen, 1998), in practitioner communities (Suchman & Trigg, 1996), and in everyday life (Rogoff, Murtaugh, & de la Rocha, 1984), researchers from anthropology, sociology, sociolinguistics, psychology, and communication, have identified of social engagement around shared work as a powerful mechanism for supporting learning. This research work has combined with Russian psychology to form a family of social learning theories (Cole & Engstrom, 1993; Lave & Wenger, 1991; Vygotsky, 1978). These are known variously as situated learning, cognitive apprenticeship, distributed cognition, activity theory, sociocultural historical theory, and communities of practice (CoPs). The first three focus on the scaffolding power of situativity, of experiencing learning in the context of its use. Available artifacts, peers and near-peers contribute to and shape the learning process (Lave, Murtaugh, & de la Rocha, 1984). Activity theory, sociocultural historical theory, and the CoPs model move beyond the emphasis on context to consideration of social and historical influences as critical mediators of the learning process. For these social learning models, learning is viewed as a kind of enculturation of the individual into a system of practice. The additional benefit from these broader views of context is derived from the recognition that most imped-iments and challenges to learning tend to arise from the sociopolitical and cultural-historical roots of practice and practitioners. Though there are clear differences among variations of social learning theories, they share a powerful central premise: that learning is most readily accom-plished through engagement with more knowledgeable other people and with objects in authentic practical settings.

One model in particular is appealing for its attention to both the indi-vidual learner and the larger context in which the learning takes place. That is, it offers an explanation of how the practice evolves, as well as how individuals develop and change within that practice. This CoP model describes learning as the transformation or development of the individ-ual, as evident in his or her changing identity and practice. First proposed by Lave and Wenger (1991) as an analytic model for understanding how people learn in context, it has since become widely popular as a theory of learning. There are many interpretations and extensions of the original notion. These are extensively discussed elsewhere (Riel & Polin, 2004).

Two key notions are community and practice. In a CoP, the community can be defined as a group of people:

> whose identities are defined in large part by the roles they play and relation-ships they share in that group activity. The community derives its cohesion from the joint construction of a culture of daily life built upon behavioral norms, routines, and rules, and from a sense of shared purpose. Community activity also precipitates shared artifacts and ideas that support group activ-ity and individual sense-making. A community can be multigenerational; that is, it can exist over time in the comings and goings of individuals. In short, a community differs from a mere collection of people by the strength and depth of the culture it is able to establish and which in turn supports group activity and cohesion. (Riel & Polin, 2004, p. 18)

As used in the CoP model, practice refers, not to repetitive behaviors intended to increase memory, but to a body of practical knowledge used to accomplish work, that is, a domain or field of expertise.

Within a cultural framework, the CoP model describes ways in which the sociocultural structures of a community mediate the development of the individual, from an initial novice state of limited participation to a fully developed identity of deeper participation. In addition to describing the development of the individual, the CoP model describes how practice communities also evolve or advance the practice itself, by continually accruing new members, tools, and experiences that inform and influence practice, and the body of knowledge upon which it relies.

RELOCATING GRADUATE EDUCATION IN
A PROFESSIONAL PRACTICE COMMUNITY

In this chapter, the central design application of the CoP model is in the reconceptualization or revitalization of the practice of graduate programs in the field of education. The enterprise must recognize the larger profession of education as the central practice, to include research and development activities, as well as classroom teaching. In research universities, this is less of an issue, because these activities and identities are visible and available for full-time graduate students. For universities less centrally involved in research, with part-time students or commuting students, this requires a shift in practice. Graduate students must then be seen as coming to university to deepen their participation in the profession of education, not of schooling, and the design of their experience there must reflect that definition of the practice.

Historically, graduate students have come to the university as a continuation of their participation in the practice of schooling. They come as students. This is a practice though, at which they are already quite adept, as demonstrated by their participation at the highest level, that is, graduate school. They bring to campus a set of long-held notions of what it means to be a student, a set of expectations about what will happen in their classrooms, what their role will be, and what sort of participation structures will be there for them to engage. They behave as students, and traditionally, faculty members behave as teachers. This constrains graduate education within a practice of schooling.

If they were studying engineering, medicine or law, the discontinuity between their graduate school experience and their practical identity might be more evident, though in those professions, graduate education typically makes use of field experiences and real world cases as curricular material. However, since education students are educators in real life, the familiarity of roles, relationships and activities in traditional graduate education classrooms obscures the problem. Just as they find in their own settings, here at graduate school the practice relies upon an acquisition and transfer view of learning as the collection and storage of knowledge outside the context of its intended use.

The Special Problem of Education as a Practice

The practice of education is a varied one, ranging from the schooling of young children, to the professional development of working adults, to the science of research and theory development. Historically, though, this has not been a well-integrated community. There continues to be a perceived division of labor in which the university is the source of theory and basic knowledge, and the field is the location of practice and practitioners (Simon, 1992). With their own lived experience denied and marginalized in the face of formal theory, teachers, and other "real world" educators who come to graduate classes are often faced with the choice of rejecting their own experiential knowledge or rejecting what they hear in class.

Ironically, this tension between worlds and identities represents the potential power of graduate education to be a transformative experience for the student. To do so, graduate professional education must open up its discourse to include the language of local, albeit limited, practice. Conversely, when welcomed in to the larger professional culture, students must be willing to problematize or question their own practical beliefs. When graduate education is reconceptualized as supporting engagement in a CoP, the discourse is recontextualized from a classroom transmission and transfer discourse to a discourse of collegial collaboration and negotiation around authentic work. Here, a social learning model can thrive as members of the same professional community, with differing expertise, engage in real world work.

Getting to Community of Practice

There are many cultural historical barriers that make it difficult to shift from a transmission conception of university learning to a socially constructed one. To begin with, students come to the university; the university does not come to them. The very locations in which groups meet to learn, structure particular participation opportunities and identities in the room. Rooms are designed to place the instructor at the front, behind a buffering piece of furniture. Learners sit in undifferentiated rows, rarely in the same place twice. More critically, there is no enduring presence between class sessions; no place for shared or exchanged materials and artifacts to remain located in the room, and little opportunity for engagement outside the time parameters of the class.

University instructors' classroom activity is generally not representative of their expert practical activity; they do not talk in ways and about subjects they would with colleagues. They are behaving as teachers, working to convey a curriculum, talking about practice, not from within it. Education faculty members know their identity includes an active connection with professional organizations and with the peer reviewed journals and conferences those organizations sponsor. They know it means connecting with peers on projects and engaging in intellectual discussion of new and emerging ideas in the field. If instructors carried this identity into their classrooms, it would surely affect the nature of their engagement with the students they find there.

In our own graduate programs, we have reconceptualized our class-room teaching identities to more fully integrate with our professional identities in our field. That is, we take our role in the courses we teach as helping students experience, as much as possible in their novice condition, what it means to be, to know, in our field. Thus, the reason to study a particular curriculum is because in this domain, the professional community relies on this knowledge in this field, and to practice in the profession is to know and make use of these ideas. So too, we faculty members and our students must not only know about and talk about but know from use and talk from within real practice (Lave & Wenger, 1991).

Historically, this is more readily accomplished on campus with full-time graduate students. On campus, opportunities exist for graduate students to engage with faculty and outside experts through teaching and research assistantships, through attendance at guest lectures, and brown bag lunch discussions, and simply from hanging about in the hallways and coffee house frequented by faculty, postdocs, and fellows. In American graduate education, however, this tradition is at risk as an increasing proportion of graduate students are unable or unwilling to give up full-time work to pursue their advanced degrees.

This trend is exacerbated, potentially, when graduate education moves online to accommodate students' need for flexibility. Such a move might seem to create an even broader divide between students and faculty, field and university. However, in online programs, few if any, preexisting traditional university structures exist. This grants us the freedom to construct structures that support different ways of participating and different roles to occupy (Polin, 2003). As will be seen later in this chapter, Web-based applications for supporting a CoP model of formal education are there for us to embrace. In some ways, it is easier to make this conversion through emergent networking technology than with traditional course tools in a traditional course setting on campus. The rest of this chapter will examine how the CoP model and new tools of the Web support a reconceptualization and redesign of graduate education in our two hybrid programs that combine online and face-to-face formats.

TECHNOLOGY AND COMMUNITIES OF PRACTICE

If we look to the tools that are available to help us in this new role, we find the very same tool sets with which a growing digital culture is equipping our current and future students: tools that support networking, collaboration, coconstruction, and community access. It is perhaps a wonderful coincidence that learning theory and Web technology have entered an era in which social engagement and community connections are leading concepts.

In 1992-93, the Internet evolved the application we all now know as the World Wide Web. In 2010-11, children born with the Web will be heading to college. Already there is plenty of evidence to suggest that this generation experiences interaction and handles information differently from prior generations (Gee, 2003; Ito, Okabe, & Matsuda 2005; Prensky, 2001; Tapscott, 1998). While they are not yet in our graduate college classes, their influence is already being felt as they appropriate and repurpose the Web to support their reliance on social networking. Although the Web was and is clearly about networking, connecting, linking, it has been primarily about doing so for information transfer and commerce. Since the rise of peer-to-peer applications, most notably first for music file swapping, Web-based social networking applications have increased to the point where, in 2004, O'Reilly Media coined the phrase Web 2.0 to reference a new generation of Web functionality.

Applications that have emerged as Web 2.0 tools focus on collaboration and sharing, coproduction and social networking. Among the most widely used applications are those listed here, but many more come into being every day. It is a difficult list to keep up to date. Indeed, we have a found a critical role in our own local community is that of the academic "geek," the faculty member and his or her IT (information technology) support muse, both of whom thrive on exploration and experimentation on the cutting edge of peer-to-peer applications. As of this writing, the application functions listed here are employed in various ways in our programs.

- Wikis for collaborative, mediated, content production (writing and other representations) and organization by a practice community.
- Blogs and phone blogs for shared journaling, with commentary by readers
- Social bookmarking and tagging for storing and sharing collections of web sites, many include a reputation management feature that allows people to rate items in a thumbs up or thumbs down fashion
- Social networking sites for connecting peers with similar interests or needs
- Voice communication software for real-time small group voice interaction; often with the capability for file sharing on the fly
- Visualization tools for graphic display of networks or concepts or both,
- File sharing sites, often with reputation management features that allow users to upload, view, and rate homemade productions

- Virtual worlds for real-time, multiuser interactions in persistent yet modifiable settings that exist even after any particular user logs off

The affordances of ground-up social and technical networking tools support a shift in graduate education toward a CoP model. Moving to a hybrid of face-to-face and online learning, we can use these and other web-based community-oriented applications to support interaction and access to knowledge networks; and put peer-to-peer, or peer-to-near-peer, or novice-to-expert connections within reach. These tools also explicitly represent notions of continual modification of content through participation, a crucial counterpoint to typical student perceptions of university knowledge as static, dated, and isolated.

CONVERGENCE: SOCIAL COMPUTING, SOCIAL LEARNING AND GRADUATE EDUCATION

On the threshold of this socially and technically networking world, in 1995, we created a new doctoral program as a hybrid program combining face-to-face and online engagement. We understood and sought to employ a social learning model in the design, but had no idea how radically our teaching and our conceptions of course content would change as we immersed a formal learning program into a networked world.

With limited university resources, we looked to the growing pool of shareware and freeware tools. These applications are built by small groups or individuals, and donated or very modestly priced. They are notable in this context for two reasons. First, these are almost always need-driven developments, built from the users' point of view. Second, products that fill a strong need develop a community of programmer-users who continue to donate time and energy to maintain, debug, and extend the application. Almost all the compelling and successful Web 2.0 applications come from this heritage. These tools, widgets, and applets, are all about making it easier for people to interact, to communicate, to work together, to share material, to cocreate.

It is no surprise that when we looked to the Web as a place for teaching and learning, we found ourselves choosing these applications over more traditionally oriented commercial products, such as course management systems (CMSs). CMS packages were designed to be sold to large schooling enterprises, and as such, they were built to reify the existing practices of schooling: lecturing, turning in papers, testing, and grading. These are the functions at which these packages excelled. We knew we wished to move in a new direction, not to simply port an existing program onto the Internet. We knew we hoped to create new participation structures for faculty and students. We knew that software packages that merely echoed traditional classroom practices were not going to work for us. Thus, we needed to turn to different technologies to accomplish the supporting structures of a CoP for our students.

A Closer Look at Virtual Worlds

Initially we were one of the few online programs that made any use, let alone extensive use, of virtual worlds as chat environments in our classes. For us, these places came the closest to providing the "campus coffee house atmosphere" we desired for our students, that is, a casual, informal location for real-time conversation. Several applications offer voice over Internet (VoIP) chat or written text chat as part of their larger course management system. We have found these programs reify the existing power and authority structure of the university, giving control to the instructor who can "pass the microphone" or otherwise call on students who "raise their hand" or queue up in a line for a turn to speak. Instead, we use a Web application called Tapped In®, a self-contained, browser-based, real-time, multiuser, virtual chat world designed and maintained by SRI (Schlager, Fusco, & Schank, 2002). Tapped In® was developed with the CoP model in mind, initially to support teacher engagement around science and mathematics education.

> As an online crossroads, Tapped In® has been quite successful in achieving its original goals of bringing together and forging new relationships among education practitioners, providers, and researchers from around the world on a daily basis. Thousands of different people log in each month to engage in activities that include course and workshop sessions, group meetings, and public discussion spanning a wide range of K-12 topics. (Schlager, Fusco, & Schank, 2002, p. 121)

As of this writing, we have also begun using a graphical version of a virtual world, Second Life. We have an island in this virtual world, which serves many functions: collaborative space for graphical project work, class meeting space, and even clubhouse for our student chapters of national organizations. This puts important professional links in tangible proximity. The ACM student clubhouse, the MA degree students' course projects and the doctoral program's classes occupy adjacent physical spaces, and hopefully, suggest adjacent conceptual spaces as well.

This virtual world chat environment differs from the traditional bricks-and-mortar classroom in other important and productive ways. First, of course, it does not contain the usual signs, tools, and symbols that structure power and authority. There is no "front" to the room that is held by the instructor. Anyone can speak at any time, without raising his or her hand to seek permission. Furthermore, the nature of chat as a "real-time" experience constrains the length of each person's written utterance to a sentence or two (for chat is truly written speech and not prose). This means it is difficult and clearly inappropriate for one person to take over the conversation with long displays of text. This confounds the tendency to rely upon lecture. Chat is best used for quick exchanges and emergent topics, some of which will be pulled into the foreground of discussion by participants as they take up the topics, whilst others will be pushed to the background. Any topic that arises can still be taken up should the instructor or student choose to carry it over into the asynchronous discussion area.

Our virtual world chat environments have been used to support guest speakers, and even guest classes. Guests are able to join us across time and space, at little cost. We have had faculty members from other universities visit, with and without their students, during our class time; we have engaged with authors and researchers about their work. Our guests do not come to lecture or make formal presentations to the class. They come to engage in dialogue. Typically, students will have had a research report or article to read before hand, and the conversation will unfold around that document. Perhaps because they have a live author/researcher to engage with, students tend to ask questions about the process rather than the content of what they have read. Why did the researcher make use of this instrument? Why do they think the study came out the way it did? These sorts of engagements are more powerful than typical guest speaker appearances because the constraints of the technology push the engagement into dialogue, and the visitors and students are talking from within an experience of the practice, not about it.

However, the very features that liberate the dialogue can also result in chaos. With a class of 20 students all talking at once, the result can be a mélange of topics, rapidly scrolling by in the text window. However, because we value these open expression of the chat environment, we have learned to manage the liabilities of the chat system. In our case, classes are partitioned into two sections, for purposes of the chat sessions. Each session is scheduled at a different time of day, depending on the time zone spread in the class.

Second, online chat classes tend to be very intense. Everyone is very focused. Talk in the chat room is, after all, written speech and is unconstrained by hand raising or passing the virtual microphone. Over the years of using chat environments with students in our master's and doctoral program, we have determined that the best duration for an online chat session is about an hour. At the end of an hour or so, students and their instructor are worn out. After an hour, the conversation tends to wander.

Third, we typically do not attempt to recreate the same class session in the morning and evening groups. We have found that it is much more useful to discuss related but separate topics, thus requiring students in one group to read the transcripts of the other.

The Expanding and Enduring Classroom

By moving instruction online, we are able to jettison many of the overt power structures and constraints of the university classroom, perhaps the most important of these is the time constraint of the course schedule. The lights never go off on the Internet. Students and instructors are never kicked out of the room to make way for the next class. In short, online class never ends, and like a normal collegial relationship, can extend in the wee hours of the night or the interstitial spaces in the workday. A powerful tool for supporting these extended relationships and engagements is the asynchronous, threaded discussion.

While chat is a wonderful tool for chat, the rapid fire and short bursts of "talk" do not suit deeper discussion and thoughtful debate. For that, we rely upon asynchronous threaded discussions, also known as Web boards, forums, or group discussion spaces. Initially we employed an NNTP news server application of the sort that had historically been used on the Internet to support CoPs in such domains as wine tasting, feline diabetes, model train collection, home renovations, and skiing. When university concerns about security forced us into a commercial course management system, we balked at this instructor-centric reenactment of a knowledge transmission culture. However, we have found some ways bend the rules to suit our model. This includes, for instance, changing the status of all enrolled students in a class to "teaching assistants," thus giving them the power to modify content and menus, to initiate discussion forums, and create group folders.

Threaded discussions do not in and of themselves transform didactic instruction into negotiated collaborations connecting practice experiences with expertise in theory. For that, we rely upon two pedagogical strategies. First, we make an explicit request for students to put words to their practical experiences and connect them with words from text and classroom conversation. Second, we do not ask students comprehension questions designed to see if they have done the readings. Instead, we ask them to coconstruct and extend meaning.

A favorite instructional ploy requires students to select sections from course text, a quote that they like, resonate to, endorse or otherwise find compelling. They are asked to post that material, with page numbers, and then explain why they selected it. Likewise, they are asked to find a section of text they dislike, firmly disagree with, find confusing or otherwise irritating, and to post it, with page numbers, and an explanation. Students do this during the reading process, not after, to engage with the construction of meaning in the text, not just accept it on face value.

As they become adept at coconstructing meaning with peers, students are asked to anchor a selection of text with an example from the workplace, for an even more explicit effort to connect theory and practice. The example can raise questions when it does not conform to interpretations of the theory or models raised in the course, or it can serve as a case. Students are encouraged to use the formal language of theory to discuss their cases, thus also providing a space for trying out new language in a familiar context.

While our CMS does not include a reputation management system, which lets readers evaluate postings, we have borrowed and modified a clever strategy first heard from Dr. Sarah Haavind (personal communication, June 12, 2002). Periodically throughout their first semester, students are asked to find a posting made by a peer that helped them understand something or that otherwise moved the learning forward in the class. They must cite the selection and provide a justification for their choice. Then, they must find a posting they themselves have made, which they feel meets the same criteria. Again, they must cite and justify. This sort of activity directs students to see and to seek value in peer-to-peer conversation, as well as in text and teacher. It also opens up a discussion on what it means to engage in meaningful discussion on academic topics.

Access to Expertise and Generations

As the Web has evolved new technologies supporting community connections, we have embraced them. Most recently, podcasting has found its way into our online toolkit. Podcasting refers to the distribution of digital files in MP3 format, suitable for playback on an iPod or other MP3 player. The "casting" part of podcasting refers to the distribution mechanism, a push technology called RSS 2. Listeners can subscribe to a podcast stream, which means new podcasts will be sent to them automatically.

Podcasting is not interactive. It is a broadcast medium, and when visual or written materials are also embedded, it makes a self-contained package of information, easily delivered and reviewed. Podcasting, when used to deliver lectures, does not offer any transformation of old style learning, of learning as transmission, a point lost on many faculty members. In a recent story in the *Los Angeles Times*, podcasting was severely criticized as the tool of student slackers (Silverstein, 2006). Professors found that podcasting lectures resulted in increased absenteeism in large lecture courses at universities. One instructor whose podcast lectures resulted in declining attendance responded by cutting back on her online offerings to force students to show up to get the material. At least one professor in the news article understood the absurdity and irony, and

> is working to enliven his lectures with material and interaction that students can't get on the audio or video "coursecasts"; he wants to move to a Socratic teaching method and foster more discussion, while using technology to relay more of the basic information. (p. 1)

The same story reports results of a UCLA survey of 142 schools taken in 2005, in which 43% of the respondents indicated that frequently they were bored and 58% had fallen asleep in class (Silverstein, 2006).

Web technologies such as podcasting and consumer appliances such as iPods are revealing the inherent weaknesses of old transmission style pedagogies. Why should a student show up in person just to listen to material that can be heard at a more convenient time and place? Frankly, why should the professor show up just to read her lecture? Does this mean there is no role for the podcast blast? No. It means the technology itself is not going to get you there.

My first homemade podcast was not to convey content, but to calm down a class of students that had worked itself up to near frenzy level about a large project coming due. I did not want to take up class time with one of those discussions in which students try to negotiate the assignment, but I did not want to let the innuendo and misconceptions slowly boil behind the scenes, between class sessions. Instead, I created a podcast offering a low-key, somewhat humorous explanation of project expectations. It did the job, and it did not take a lot of technical knowledge to accomplish.

My second podcast actually was focused on academics more than logistics: but not to convey a lecture. I wanted to offer students greater intellectual context for a very difficult text. Again, if I had taken class time, I would have felt compelled to limit my remarks due to time constraints. Via podcast, I was able to offer a bit of a history about the author, his academic lineage, his current work, and the role the book plays in a landscape of writing on the subject. I explained why I had selected the text and what my intentions were for them as readers. In this way I hoped to be able to not only help the students make meaning more easily, but also to connect them with a sense of the community of researchers pursuing this line of work. Later that semester we met with the author and one of his doctoral students through a video conference. They were both in England and my students were gathered for one of their occasional 5-day face-to-face sessions in Los Angeles. Interestingly, the most powerful part was the chance for the doctoral student to interact with another student nearing the completion of her dissertation process. She described her study, and thereby how she chose to use the theoretical model in a real world investigation.

The third podcast was not made by me. We require our students in both the master's and the doctoral program to attend a national conference as part of a course. The doctoral students were attending the American Educational Research Association meeting. I handed out six iPods, with microphone attachments, to student pairs, and asked them to interview speakers they heard and found interesting. They were responsible for determining their interview questions. Each night, they edited their podcast files and shared them through the RSS feed for the class. The MP3 file format of the audio recordings compresses the recording files and makes it fairly easy to distribute segments as long as 20 minutes.

The iPods in the third example functioned merely as a tool that enabled the students to negotiate access to researchers and other presenters at a national conference on education. The need to edit down the recordings required students to make choices about what was valuable to hear and what could be cut. The opportunity to share podcasts meant that everyone received more connection to the community as a group than they could have accomplished alone. The ability to archive these for future students meant that this participatory network would live and grow.

Reification and Participation: Blogs, Wikis, and LISTSERVS

A healthy CoP is a dynamic group. Even as expert practitioners ply their profession, the community and its practice are open to newcomers and journeymen, and to the new ideas and tools they bring in to the community by virtue of their comembership in other communities. For instance, I am the mother of a 12 year old, as well as being a researcher interested in digital culture. From my twelve year old, I learn a lot about handheld gaming and game devices. That knowledge is with me when I am being the researcher, and I am likely to introduce it into the practice community. Because my 12 year old is a girl, I also bring an awareness of gender issues in technology to my work.

In a healthy community, the practice, the knowledge base and the tool sets are all open to influence and change from the comemberships or concurrent identities that members bring to the community through new ideas, tools and artifacts. In this way, the practice can continue to evolve and not become brittle and cultish. However, where there is expertise and change, that change may be perceived as challenge. As community members participate and introduce changes into the practice, they are essentially challenging the acknowledged expertise. Lave and Wenger (1991) described this as a tension between reification (i.e., the freezing of knowledge in a concrete artifact) and participation (i.e., the variation of knowledge that arises in practice from the participation of diverse people). This tension can be a vitalizing mechanism for communities. After all, there must be some solid core of domain knowledge that is captured and stable enough to be shared, but there must also be a dynamism that allows that knowledge base to continue to update, develop, and innovate.

Students of all ages tend to find school a place of frozen knowledge manifested in a predetermined curriculum of competence. Educational practitioners in schools experience the stress of new ideas that challenge their role and core knowledge, their very practice. They are not comfortable with the notion of an evolving practice, and yet, that is exactly what the practice is in the research arm of the community, to continue to evolve the practice through developing knowledge. For university faculty members, expertise is not static. New knowledge is constantly produced in the field, as evident in the never-ending parade of research grants and peer-reviewed publication. Clearly the fields in which university faculty claim expertise are continually evolving.

It would be very powerful for novice graduate students to have access to that tension, to see the mechanism of knowledge emergence, to hear the controversy and contention, to understand this tension as healthy and productive, and to learn to participate in it. Faculty see this in their professional lives; some suffer through it personally, for example, trying to publish qualitative work in peer-reviewed journals when ethnography was still an oddity. How can graduate students gain access to these experiences?

Many communities within the broad landscape of education run LISTSERVS, that is, subscription e-mail. Much like the threaded discussions, LISTSERVS allow people to post and comment on postings via e-mail to a membership group. For instance, I am a member of LISTSERVS on information technology (ITforum), on communities of practice (com-prac), action research (PARnet) and a few others. In one of my courses, I require my doctoral students to join and lurk on the XMCA LISTSERV, which was created in support of the *Mind, Culture and Activity* journal. The core group on this LISTSERV is comprised of experts and near-experts in activity theory, and yet a lot of the discussion that passes through that list focuses on disagreements, refinements, new ideas or extensions of theory, research paradigms, tools, and settings for theory in practice. There have been semesters in which the postings in XMCA have served as a text for my course.

Often a LISTSERV community will decide to discuss a member's paper, or will select a paper from the current issue of a journal to discuss. Members will post questions and share resources. Sometimes discussion reveals the larger sociopolitical context of the topic from the point of view of the various countries in which members reside. They also announce postdoctoral openings, upcoming conferences, and related content from fields of inquiry in which they are also members. In short, this is a rich and vibrant nexus of practitioners, and it is very accessible to students through their mere participation in the LISTSERV group.

LISTSERVS are not the only venue where students can participate peripherally in the dance of participation/reification. The venerable institution of peer-reviewed publication is becoming a more open process thanks in large part to the lure of online community publication and dialogue through reputation management applications. In a recent *Wired* article, Rogers (2006) describes a growing phenomenon altering the traditional process of peer review of academic publication. After describing the process, the time fame, and the errors in the current system, he describes several rigorous, peer-review processes in the scientific community that happen to be mediated on the Web by virtue of Web 2.0 applications such as Wikis, which allow commentary on posted articles. He concludes:

> An up-and-coming researcher can get more attention from the right experts by publishing something earthshaking on arXiv than by pushing it through the usual channels. Crazy ideas will get batted around in moderated forums, which is pretty much what the Internet is for. Eventually, printed journal articles will be quaint artifacts. Scientific papers will be living documents with data published on Web pages—commented on, linked to, and mirrored by labs doing the same work 6,000 miles away. Every research effort will have thousands of reviewers working in real time. Today's undergrads have never thought about the world any differently—they've never functioned without IM and Wikipedia and arXiv, and they're going to demand different kinds of review for different kinds of papers. (pp. 30-32)

While his enthusiasm might be forgiven for being a bit excessive, he does make the point that new technologies are challenging the practices of venerable old communities in academe. Most importantly, they are opening up access to the community of practice in ways from which our novice graduate students can greatly benefit.

FUTURE TRENDS

Current graduate students are not the group most au fait with Web 2.0. Often they are not particularly fluent with the Web at all. Recent data from the Pew Foundation's continuing study of the Internet and American life makes it clear that as of 2006 the actively peer-to-peer digital group is the 18-26 years olds (Lenhart, Madden, & Hitlin, 2005). However, it also indicates that the Web-born, the preteens, those heading to college in 2010-11, may well be the tipping point. These groups bring a sentiment, a culture, of production, and coproduction, of networking and collaboration. As faculty rethink programs and their own roles in those programs as brokers to a broader practice community, the upcoming students will be there to take advantage of the opportunities, ready with peer-review sensibilities from reputation management experiences; ready with publication and commentary as community norms; ready with the understanding of social capital through networking. It should be a very exciting time for us all and we must be ready to engage with them in these ways, or lose them to alternative educational enterprises that do understand learning as a social, situated, heterogeneous, collaborative, cultural experience, such as corporate universities and for-profit, private, start-up institutions (Meister, 1988; Schank, 2005).

SUMMARY

This chapter has offered a perspective on graduate professional education as an activity arising in a community of professional practice. It has suggested the role of technical networks and tools in supporting social networks, and anchored those ideas with illustrations from current practices in two graduate programs offered as hybrids of online and face-to-face settings. However, these practices and the tools that support them will continue to evolve. The CoP model as a design touchstone helps us make reasoned choices that can be both strategic and innovative.

REFERENCES

Brown, J. S., Collins, A., & Duguid, P. (1989). Situated cognition and the culture of learning. *Educational Researcher, 18*(1), 32-42.

Cole, M., & Engestrom, Y. (1993). A cultural-historical approach to distributed cognition. In G. Salomon (Ed.), *Distributed cognitions: Psychological and educational considerations.* (pp. 1-46). London: Cambridge University Press.

Gee, J. (2003). *What video games have to teach us about learning and literacy.* New York: Palgrave MacMillan.

González, N., Moll, L. C., Tenery, M., Rivera, A., Rendon, P., Gonzales, R., et al. (2005). Funds of knowledge for teaching in Latino households. In N. Gonzales, L. C. Moll, & C. Amanti (Eds.), *Funds of knowledge: Theorizing practices in households, communities, and classrooms* (pp. 89-111). Mahwah, NJ: LEA.

Hutchins, E., & Klausen, T. (1998). Distributed cognition in an airline cockpit. In Y. Engestrom & D. Middleton (Eds.), *Cognition and communication at work* (pp. 15-34). London: Cambridge University Press

Ito, M., Okabe, D., & Matsuda, M. (2005). *Personal, portable, pedestrian: Mobile phones in Japanese life*. Cambridge, MA: MIT Press.

Lave, J., & Wenger, E. (1991). *Situated learning: Legitimate peripheral participation*. New York: Cambridge University Press.

Lave, J., Murtaugh, M., & de la Rocha, O. (1984). The dialectic of arithmetic in grocery shopping. In B. Rogoff & J. Lave (Eds.), *Everyday cognition: Its development in social context* (pp. 67-94). Cambridge, MA: Harvard University Press.

Lenhart, A., Madden, M., & Hitlin, P. (2005). *Teens and technology: Youth are leading the transition to a fully wired and mobile nation*. Washington, DC: Pew Foundation, Internet and American Life.

Meister, J. (1988). *Corporate universities: Lessons in building a world-class work force*. New York: McGraw Hill.

National Center of Educational Statistics. (1996). *Graduate and first-professional students. National postsecondary student aid study*. Washington DC: U.S. Department of Education, Office of Educational Research and Improvement.

Polin, L. (2003). Learning in dialogue with a practicing community. In T. Duffy & J. Kirkley (Eds.), *Learner centered theory and practice in distance education* (p. 18). Mawah, NJ: LEA.

Prensky, M. (2001). *Digital game-based learning*. New York: McGraw-Hill.

Resnick, L. (1991). Shared cognition: Thinking as social practice. In L. Resnick, J. Levine, & S. Teasley (Eds.), *Perspectives on socially shared cognition* (pp. 1-22). Washington, DC: American Psychological Association.

Riel, M., & Polin, L. (2004). Online learning communities: Common ground and critical differences in designing technical environments. In S. Barab, R. Kling, & J. H. Gray (Eds.), *Designing for virtual communiites in the service of learning*. London: Cambridge University Press.

Rogers, A. (2006). Get Wiki with it: Peer review—the unsung hero and convenient villain of science—gets a makeover. *Wired, 14*(9), 30, 32.

Rogoff, B., Murtaugh, M., & de la Rocha, O. (1984). The dialectic of arithmetic in grocery shopping. In B. Rogoff & J. Lave (Eds.), *Everyday cognition: Its development in social context* (pp. 67-94). Boston: Harvard University Press.

Schank, R. (2005). *Lessons in learning, e-learning, and training*. Alexandria, VA: Pfeiffer.

Schlager, M., Fusco, J., & Schank, P. (2002). Evolution of an online community of education professions. In K. A. Renninger & W. Shumar (Eds.), *Building virtual communities: Learning and Change In Cyberspace* (pp. 129-158). London: Cambridge University Press.

Silverstein, S. (2006, January 17). The iPod took my seat. *Los Angeles Times*, p. 1.

Simon, R. (1992). *Teaching against the grain*. Westport, CN: Bergin & Garvey.

Suchman, L., & Trigg, R. (1996). Artificial intelligence as craftwork. In S. Chaiklin & J. Lave (Eds.), *Understanding practice: Perspectives on activity and context* (pp. 144-178). New York: Cambridge University Press.

Tapscott, D. (1998). *Growing up digital: The rise of the net generation*. San Francisco: McGraw-Hill.

Vygotsky, L. S. (1978). *Mind in society: The development of higher psychological processes*. Cambridge, MA: Harvard University Press

CHAPTER 14

LEARNING COMMUNITIES ARE NOT MUSHROOMS—OR— HOW TO CULTIVATE LEARNING COMMUNITIES IN HIGHER EDUCATION

Mélanie Bos-Ciussi, Gillian Rosner, and Marc Augier

This chapter looks at advances of information and communication technologies and their effect on learning processes. The study is based on a large sample of students in a business school and the chapter provides a definition of online communities, especially in an educational environment. The chapter also addresses the issue of the difference between networks and communities, and provides guidance to teachers or professionals who need to create such environments. The main message of this chapter is that social bonds are essential for a community to emerge. This implies a total break with the traditional role of teacher as "dispenser of knowledge." One can extrapolate that the role of teacher might move towards that of coach dealing with complex environments and/or problems that require group solutions. The teacher, through course design, must also prepare a fertile environment where learning communities can grow ... in other words,

Communities of Practice: Creating Learning Environments for Educators,
Volume 2, pp. 287–308
Copyright © 2008 by Information Age Publishing
All rights of reproduction in any form reserved.

learning communities will not just "mushroom" in the absence of favorable conditions.

INTRODUCTION

McLuhan's (1964) approach to new technologies stands out as prophetic: after the initial shock triggered by new technologies, "the real revolution" is in the "prolonged phase of 'adjustment' of all personal and social life to the new model of perception set up by the new technology" (p. 118). Forty years on, advances in information and communication technologies (ICT) have fundamentally heightened social interest in knowledge sharing and social networking on Internet. Although some believe that technology disconnects us from our "natural selves," enthusiasm for online social networking would indicate that the contrary is true. The figures produced by Nielsen NetRatings in May 2006 show that online networking is growing ever faster and attracting more and more Internet surfers: 45% of American Web surfers—68,8 million individuals—are members of an online network. The biggest of these is MySpace with 38,359.000 members (8,210.000 in April 2005), followed by blogs and MSN groups. The education sector has its own success story: Facebook, created by Harvard students in 2004, is now (as of 2006) the most popular online social network in English for high school and university students with over 6 million active members all over the world.

This virtual "retribalization" (McLuhan, 1964) raises questions in an educational environment as nowadays most teachers and professionals use the Internet to communicate, teach, and learn. What do these people exchange? Do they exchange best practices, tips, common interests, tacit, or explicit knowledge? Can the online socialization "success stories" mentioned above bring anything to the educational perspective? How do we proceed from "social networking" to "social learning" (Lave & Wenger, 1991; Vygostki, 1986) in an educational context?

The focus of this chapter is on knowledge sharing in an educational environment. It looks at how tools such as forums and chats may lead to the emergence of a virtual community of learners. The purpose of the next two sections is to provide professionals and educators with insights into the challenges of setting up online learning communities from a pragmatic point of view. The first section seeks to clarify the background of the study: the challenges of network technologies in a higher education institution (HEI). Media-based social bonds in online learning environments are also defined to clarify the different social structures that emerge in such environments, these range from networks to online learning communities.

The second section presents three case studies in which the following questions are explored: first, how do learning communities emerge and second, which factors lead to this emergence? Finally, future trends, which concern pedagogy and the teacher's role, are proposed.

BACKGROUND

Challenges in Higher Education

As the possibilities for interaction of both teacher and student increase thanks to online tools (e.g., forums, chats, e-mails, Wiki, blogs) research points to a need for teachers to master more sophisticated pedagogical techniques (Lafferière, Bracewell, & Breuleux, 2001) in order to encourage learners to collaborate, debate, and share knowledge through learning activities. In other words, teachers must be able to make the most of network technologies for active and situated learning (Henri & Pudelko, 2006; Lave & Wenger, 1991). However, teachers or professionals face various challenges when setting up facilities for social learning on the Internet.

First, they have to manage new communication tools (synchronous and asynchronous) with various modes of distance collaboration. Recent studies show that most of learners' interactions on forums are linear information exchanges. Sociocognitive interactions (i.e.. discussions and debates, knowledge sharing about content related topics) and socioaffective interactions (small talk, jokes, expressions of feelings etc.) are observed in forums but only in a minority of instances (Audran & Daele, 2007; Ciussi & Simonian, 2004; Lafferrière & Nizet, 2006). So how can teachers make use of online communication tools to increase student participation and sociocognitive interaction online; how can they encourage the emergence of a genuine learning community?

The second challenge faced by professionals teaching online is the creation of various online activities. This implies creating scenarios and storyboards using collaboration strategies that combine strict rules and resources with enough "teacher distance" for the student to learn both on his or her own and within a group. So what is the right balance between teachers' formal learning activities (imposed by the "teacher") and students' self-involvement and participation (deriving from self-motivation)?

This chapter will try to answer some of these questions and focus on the complexity involved in the emergence of a learning community within a pedagogical setting that is largely online and at a distance. In the next subsection, we look at what is generally included under the heading of "online communities" and explain what is meant here by a learning community, in the specific context of higher education (HE).

From online Networks to Virtual Communities of Learning

New technologies find social outlets through various forms of cyber-communication, among which we find online networks or communities. These latter two terms are often used interchangeably when they appear on the Internet since both have in common a feeling of "belonging," and both are maintained through the social bonds between their members.

Dynamic Structures and Strength of Ties

Indeed, online social structures are characterized by the type of social bonds between their members. According to Granovetter (1973) who largely studied social structures dynamics, the strength of bonds or ties varies, and may be weak or strong:

- Weak ties involve little emotional content and infrequent relationships. This type of tie forms "local bridges," where messages are diffused to a wide range of people such as those found in Internet distribution lists. Weak ties therefore tend towards simple information exchange or linear transmission of content. This type of exchange exists in most online networks, for example, a "technical" forum structured as frequently asked questions.

- Strong ties involve stronger emotions and more frequent relationships. These ties could encourage the emergence of online communities as socioaffective topics might be discussed and community consciousness may arise, as well as sociocognitive debates and "affects regulation" (Bruner, 1997, p. 69).

It should be added that in practice, it is not always so easy to draw hard and fast lines between the types of social link in play. This means that the borders between these types of social structures are not always clear-cut. Communities and networks can merge into one another, disappear, and reemerge according to circumstances. Thus, a network of practice (NoP) may transmute into a community of practice (CoP). This transmutation may be for only a few members of the network, and may only last for a limited time.

Bearing these thoughts in mind, let us define what is meant in this chapter by network, communities of practice (CoPs) and learning communities.

Online networks allow the transmission of material or information by means of "relational resources" (Lemieux, 1999) whereas online communities involve the emergence of a microculture (Audran & Daele, 2007), whose members share "a common set of cultural values and practices" (Zarifian, 1996). These practices aim, for the most part, to recreate an informal meeting place in space-time where community relations may be revived or created (Foucault, Metzger, & Pignorel, 2003; Foucault, Metzger, Pignorel, & Vaylet, 2002). Communities should thus emerge from the participants' activities as these arise from strong social links.

Online communities are themselves subdivided into categories according to Henri and Pudelko (2006). Two of these will be referred to: professional communities (CoPs) and learning communities.

CoPs are made up of "groups of individuals who have a common history and who interact strongly, share knowledge and encounter problems within the same organization" (Wenger, 1998, p. 11), whereas "learning communities" (Henri & Pudelko, 2006; Lafferière Bracewell, & Breuleux, 2001) are so called in a educational environment.

Learning communities are made up of students as opposed to CoPs, which are made up of colleagues or professionals. A learning community is not everlasting, but has a lifespan corresponding to a course, a project or an academic year. The community is the fruit of the teacher's wish to encourage learning by doing. This may be through collaborative projects or any pedagogical approach that encourages students' active participation through self-expression, that is, through negotiating meaning with fellow students (debates, sociocognitive conflicts). This situation (instigation by the teacher) is the basis of the paradox of learning communities.

The Paradox of Learning Communities

As Henri and Pudelko (2006) and Brown and Campione (1995) have mentioned, a learning community cannot be considered as just another community because it arises from certain well-defined pedagogical objectives set out in official school programs. The learning community is an artificial construct created by the teacher with a didactic goal. It is this artificiality that makes the learning community paradoxical: a community ought to arise by itself (Wenger, 1998) as it emerges from the participants' activities. However, in the case of a learning community, it is artificial right from the start. It is created by the teacher, thus perceived by students as an obligation. This paradox brings us back to the question of balance raised in the introduction: how far, in education, can we eradicate the distinction between obligation (teachers create the community artificially) and necessity (the community emerges from students' needs).

How should we deal with this paradox in order to enable a community of learners to emerge? In other words, how can we boost a network of students to become an authentic (nonartificial) community?

A community will only emerge if members participate and share strong links in a way that is visible to all (for example in forums or a shared repertoire). How then should the teacher consider nonvisible members (i.e., members who may not write in the forum, but may well observe or even communicate with other mediated tools like phone, chat, MSN, etc.)? Indeed, it is precisely these "invisible" exchanges that encourage the social relations necessary for the emergence of a community as a "microculture" (Audran & Daele, 2007).

This brings up the question of evaluation. How do we evaluate the contribution of someone who is "only" an observer? We can "force" him/her to speak, just as in the classroom we can pick on him/her to answer. This artificiality may destroy the very sense of community that we are trying to evoke, as the whole situation becomes teacher-dominated once more. It would be interesting to analyze in the following case studies the percentage of interactions that are, for example, "under the control" of the teacher and which formal and informal tools are used by the participants.

ONLINE COMMUNITIES: SOME CASE STUDIES

The first case study will focus on how different communities emerge within a virtual learning environment (VLE), specifically the Webintec VLE, using Dokeos[1] technology. It is a good illustration of the fluidity between online communities. Case studies two and three concern the emergence of potential learning communities in Ceram Business School on the same VLE as in the first case study.

Case Study 1: Webintec at CERAM: A VLE With an Attitude

The selection, installation, and customization of a VLE often constitute a very difficult journey. Software companies usually provide solutions designed for firms. This is a paradoxical situation: learning systems are not built for learning institutions (i.e., schools) but for companies, where the problem is different. This can be easily summarized:

- A university with 10,000 students will have 10,000 learners registered in its VLE, a small IT team to handle it, and the professors who manage the courses are (mainly) not IT specialists.

- A company with 10,000 employees may have fewer than 1,000 learners registered in its VLE, and a strong IT department to handle it as part of the company information system (IS). The tutors are specialized in addressing learners' technical problems. Few mentors will address content questions that tutors cannot answer.

When a learning institution, such as a business school starts to implement a VLE, it usually goes through the normal steps: it seeks existing solutions, contacts their providers, then realizes that no solution is really what it wants and that it is all much more expensive than expected. In this process a benchmark could have occurred. Such an analysis would have demonstrated that big institutions with an IT department in place were able to set up and use an existing VLE. Smaller institutions may be struggling with tools that are too big for their needs or they may be developing their own tool. Both solutions are very expensive: in one case, you have to buy something with too many functions that you will never use, in the second case, you have to bear the whole cost of developing the tool.

This is where the community paradigm comes in: it is too difficult for only one institution to develop the tool. In addition, the tool cannot be maintained if this depends only on one or two "geeks" in one university. However, since the community of schools is looking for such a tool, could not our school community put together resources to develop the perfect tool, or at least the tool we need?

The traditional answer to this has been partnership. A few schools join together and create another entity, and this entity is in charge of the tool's development. This solution is difficult to put in place because it introduces a lot of administrative tasks and because it is very rigid: how are new partners to be included, what happens when an old partner resigns from the team? How are costs distributed? Should they be in proportion to the size of the institution or according to the motivation and need for the project? How are communications between professors and the development team regulated? In fact, the partnership reproduces many of the difficulties experienced with a traditional software company and adds some of its own for good measure. There is another solution, easier to put in place without the overhead introduced by a formal partnership. The idea is to share the development of the tool between institutions with the freedom for those of stepping in or out of the project. This solution is called free software.

Free Software

The Free Software Foundation (FSF—http://www.fsf.org/) was established in 1985 by Richard Stallman, former researcher at the Massachusetts Institute of Technology (MIT). It is dedicated to promoting computer users' rights to use, study, copy, modify, and redistribute computer programs. The FSF promotes the development and use of free software. Free software is a matter of liberty, not price. To understand the concept, you should think of free as in free speech, not as in free beer. Free software is a matter of the users' freedom to run, copy, distribute, study, change, and improve the software. The interesting point about free software is that its existence relies on "developer communities." People sharing the same needs or the same values work together. Most of them may never meet physically because they may be in any town in any country and they are only linked via the Internet. What makes them meet in the cyberspace is the software project they share, usually for their personal or institutional needs.

What makes this model very successful to develop software tools has been described by Eric Raymond (1998) in "The Cathedral and the Bazaar." He compares the "quiet, reverent cathedral-building" used in the traditional approach to the "great babbling bazaar of differing agendas and approaches" used in free software projects in general and Linux in particular. The main difference is may be having users very close to developers, users being themselves developers most of the time. "More users find more bugs because adding more users adds more different ways of stressing the program. This effect is amplified when the users are codevelopers" (p. 21).

Free software development started for system tools (e.g., operating systems, Web servers, mail servers) it is now widely used as well for application software (e.g., office suites, Web browsers, mail clients), and also educational or learning software.

From Philosophy to Hacking

A few years before CERAM was trying to implement a proprietary VLE, a professor of philosophy in Belgium was going through the same journey, with the same troubles. He had very simple requests and questions, but the only answers he could get from the technical staff of the VLE he was using at that time were too technical or beyond his scope: a university with 20,000 students. He started to use small free software tools that were closer to his needs: for example, forums, document sharing on the Web. He then realized that he could put these tools together (because they were open source) and build a package that would provide all the functions in one. He realized he was gradually turning a small development for his personal needs into a tool that several of his colleagues might also be interested in using in their classes. At this point, several real problems needed solving before going any further: who would maintain this software? Who would ensure future developments and sustainability? The answer was free software development project we know now as Dokeos.

The idea behind it is the same behind each free software project: "Every good work of software starts by scratching a developer's personal itch (Raymond, 1998, p. 23).

Several other professors at different institutions had the same personal itch; by joining together inside the same development community, it was possible to build a tool that is now used in more than 1,000 institutions and in 34 different languages. These numbers can show how clever it was to open the source code of the Dokeos VLE instead of making it a closed solution. Such figures would have been very difficult to obtain in a traditional manner without employing a huge team of programmers. However, the software was not only free. The decision had also been taken at the outset to make it user friendly, and this further contributed to its success. The tool thus has clean interfaces instead of screens bloated with useless functions, simple tools that do not require the user to be a computer scientist. This simplicity was the result of the paradigm shift that started in the way the VLE was developed.

Dokeos proposes the same kind of community organization for the way content is created, and the way it is used. The community of developers thus proposes a tool to a community of teachers. In a standard tool, there is a hierarchy of administrators, content creators, tutors, and so forth. In Dokeos there is no such thing, there are only three levels: administrator, professor, and student. The administrator as usual, can do everything but his or her task is mainly devoted to maintenance. All course creation and content development is delegated to the professors. In Dokeos, professors can choose to create as many courses as they wish using the tools of their choice. All of this can be done without recourse to the administrator. Thus, course development can proceed quickly because each teacher is able to be master of his own online domain. To make this possible, the tools have to be kept very simple: most Dokeos tools can be used with no documentation because they use the most popular icons and labels found on any standard graphic user interface. However, this is not all. At their own level, students also have the same capabilities. They can even enroll into courses that are open to the whole online world (if the professor has chosen this level of "openness"). However, the professor remains in charge of setting the level of confidentiality, and decides who can view or enrol into his courses.

This set up results in a VLE that involves three groups of people that would potentially create three communities. These communities could work independently, or alongside each other but our experience shows that they have a lot of interaction. This is represented in Figure 14.1.

In fact, many developers are also professors. They build the tool according to what they want to do in their job. Several students can be professors in some courses, and this inevitably impacts on the way the

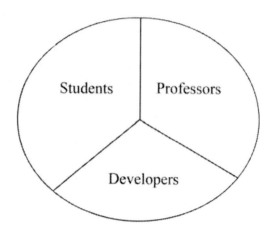

Figure 14.1.   The three communities of the VLE.

other students and professors use the tool. An example of this could be a student instigated frequently asked questions (FAQ) dealing with course content. As we shall see later, this is the type of exchange that could potentially develop into a learning community.

We will now analyze the dynamic of the interactions which take place in distance learning situations which are initiated by the teacher, thus within the student community. We choose to present two case studies based on two online courses that were carried out at Ceram Business School over the past 2 years through the Webintec portal.

Case Study 2: A Participative English Course

It is perhaps not surprising that much has been contributed to this debate and to pedagogical practice by the world of English for foreign language (EFL), for it was here that the communicative approach took root (Widdowson, 1978). In some ways, EFL has an advantage, for in the world of language learning, "mere" practice in communicating is how a lot of learning takes place. This is of course less true for most other academic subjects. However, in Ceram Business School, online tools have been the catalyst for a renewed pedagogical approach across the board.

This case study describes a course that took place in 2003. Eighty students took part in this 2-week online component of what was also a weekly face-to-face class. The students were all second year students of the business school, most of whom have a reasonable level of English language competence. The aim of the face-to-face class (1.5 hours per week) was to encourage discussion and debate, and this was continued/initiated through the online component. This consisted of a forum where the teacher posted a controversial statement each week. The students were asked to contribute a personal reaction to the statement. They were told that their contributions would count as part of their "participation" grade for the course (it was also made clear that the evaluation was of their willingness to participate rather than the linguistic quality of the contribution or viewpoint expressed). Students were not specifically asked to react to each other's contributions; however, it is interesting to note that this did in fact occur spontaneously, with relatively heated discussion and debate.

The forum generated a large number of messages (224) within a short time (2 weeks). The participation rate was high (75%) and the forum was consulted regularly (1,325 messages read). The teacher intervened very little on message content or about the exchanges in general (9% of messages). The course content was the subject of interaction (88%) rather than technical questions (6%) or questions about evaluation (4%). To carry out this analysis Audran and Simonian's (2003) exchange typology was used as well as Lafferière and Nizet's (2006) dynamic model of participation[2]. It can thus be seen that by far the majority of interactions were sociocognitive exchanges concerning the actual course content: discussions were often "altruistic" in nature, in other words, students got involved with each other, exchanged contrasting opinions or questioned each others' points of view and even attempted to change others' viewpoints (Lafferière & Nizet, 2006, p. 167). Thirteen percent of contributions can be classified as socioaffective. They are of two types: "self expression" (a personal version of another contribution, expression of personal satisfaction/dissatisfaction), and directed towards others (suggestions or solutions). The links between these students are therefore fairly strong, whether they are sociocognitive or affective, because they go beyond a simple linear exchange of information. We can therefore suppose that in this case, the ingredients necessary for the emergence of a community exist, even though formulation of principles following a consensus of opinion between students—that is, truly collaborative work—is in the minority (6% of exchanges).

The question then arises as to what conditions made this environment a fertile one for the emergence of a community? Was it the fact that the students already knew each other in class? Was it the actual subject under discussion? Was it the user-friendliness of the tool? It is highly likely that students participated initially because it was a compulsory requirement for the course. However, their subsequent discussions arose from the interest of the "controversial statement," Subsequent teacher intervention in these exchanges was very limited (9% of messages), suggesting that successful online interactions with potential for a community to form emerged above all from the students themselves (91%).

Case Study 3: Internship Follow-Up 100% Online

This 6-month online activity resulted from the wish to accompany 375 students in an out of school move towards professional experience (from January to June 6). Students have monthly online "meetings" with personal tutors (35 professors from the school, each being responsible for about 15 interns). At the same time, CERAM put two online courses at students' disposal. These dealt with important areas of competence for those embarking on professional life: Project management and managerial competence (communication, dealing with conflict, negotiation, and teamwork). Each of these courses represents over 40 hours of self-directed learning (lessons and simulations of professional situations) and was to be completed during the 6-month internship. Communication tools included a chat and a forum on every chapter of the course and for the online coaching. A Wiki was set up 2 months later in response to student demand (in order to share experience with others) and two blogs were set up by tutors on their own initiative. It is important to note that all students participating are part of the same student cohort, so they do have a feeling of identity with the group as a whole. It would be interesting to know if the group identity evolves over the period of distance learning.

Evaluation techniques are the following:

- Analysis of quantitative data from the server.
- Analysis of corpus of texts from forums and chats. A qualitative conversational analysis was carried out regarding Audran and Simonian's typology (2003) and Audran and Daele's (2006) "3 sociodiscursive phases of construction of on line communities."
- Finally, an online self-evaluation questionnaire answered by 352 students gave an insight into how the community experienced this period online (did they use other tools, if so for which topics, for formal or informal discussions).

The first observation (Figure 14.2) is that the number of messages posted in each "formal" tool (i.e., tools set up by the teacher) varies from 234 (forum) to 355 (chat) and two (Wiki) (all activities included). None of the blogs initiated by tutors generated comments. Students' hardly used the Wiki. This is because a Wiki is public. However, three blogs were created by students during their internship.

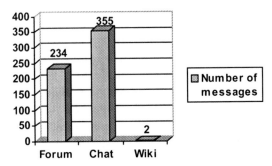

Figure 14.2.   Total corpus: 591 messages spit into three tools.

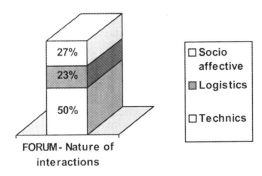

Figure 14.3.   Content analysis of forums (sense units: one message can contain various sense units).

The second observation (Figure 14.3 above) is that forums generated messages based predominantly on technical questions (total: 50% messages) and instructions (logistics and evaluation: 23%) that is, linear exchanges, therefore weak ties. It can be seen that 55% of these interactions come from students and 45% from tutors because the exchange is limited to FAQs. The activities are mostly constructed along the lines of the expert vis-à-vis the novice (linear exchanges). We also notice that "socioaffective" exchanges represent a small proportion of the total (27%). This nevertheless indicates linking or connecting (Lafferière & Nizet, 2006) between the learners, that is, stronger ties than simple information exchanges. All of these are initiated by students. In the case under study, this type of exchange gave rise above all to expressions of frustration (self orientated) but also to encouragement, and/or mutual support between students who are "community orientated."

Indeed, in Table 14.1, we can observe group awareness: ("as to everyone else," "just wanted to let u know how I feel," "have you seen how we have to watch out" ... "may Jimi Hendrix be with us."

Eric has finished the course, but still participates because he wants to share his thoughts and remotivate Aude and the others. This thread could be part of Audran and Daele's most advanced phase of construction of a community identity, the "alter consciousness" (Audran & Daele, 2007, p. 4). This is indicated by the use of "us" instead of "I" or "you." For Lafferière and Nizet (2006), these socioaffective exchanges constitute the affective basis necessary for the coconstruction of knowledge—the prerequisite for a true community of learners.

The third observation (Figure 14.4) is that chat messages were mainly based on course content and sociability, depending on who initiated the chat.

If the teacher is the initiator, the chat is content related (60%); however, if students are the initiators, the chat is used mostly for socializing (80%, example of invitation to meet face to face).

A fourth observation (Table 14.2) concerns the number of messages analyzed by teachers. Do the forum and chats reflect all exchanges

Table 14.1.   Thread of Discussion—
Shared Frustration and Encouragement

Mathieu

Nothing to add to the general problem—the same sh*** happens to me as to everyone else I suppose ... but I just wanted to let you know how I feel about all these anomalies.

Aude

Hey, have you seen how we have to watch out for the (limited) connection time on Webintec? Because I tell you, don't mess around with that stuff—the machine is heartless!!!

Eric

Hey, poor old Aude—no luck eh?!! You're going to have to start all over again. Well I managed to finish everything two weeks ago, and I've recorded my results so I'm not going to touch a thing now! I'm just sitting here waiting for judgement day. Good luck and may Jimi Hendrix be with us!

David

It's really not fair. These computers are the pits. Maybe we should to go back to the abacus—at least they were reliable.

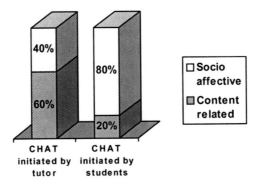

Figure 14.4.   Content analysis of chat.

Table 14.2.   Percentage of Informal Discussions

Data From Student's Self-Evaluation	Forum	E-mail	Course Chat	MSN/ Yahoo	Phone	Total
Interactions with tutor	20%	57%	7%	10%	6%	100%
Interactions with students	8%	6%	5%	39%	42%	100%

between students? Are they tangible proof of an online community identity? Thanks to the online questionnaire, a better idea was obtained of how the student actually lived the experience as a member of the community. This therefore extended the "teacher" viewpoint, which was based on what could be observed from student use of teacher instigated "formal" tools (cf. paradox in the first section).

It can be seen that most of the students' exchanges were informal (telephone (42%) and MSN (39%)). % Twenty percent of communications with tutors happened on the forum, but were mostly via e-mail (58%). Why do students often use other tools instead of the ones planned by the teacher? Does this imply that the current platform tools are not user friendly? Does it mean that students lose contact with the school when they are away? On the other hand, does it mean that students do not want to share everything with the institution or the school? To find out, those three specific questions were asked in the final questionnaire.

In response to the first question, students do not think that new communication tools would do better (30% say no, 40% hesitate). For the second, 74% of students kept the same social links as before with their peers, 5% increased it, and only 21% lost track with colleagues. It therefore seems that most students did not lose contact even at distance. The third question indicates that they did not use Wikis or blogs for a simple reason: Students make (as do we) a strong distinction between "public" and "private." They will not share very informal information on a network made for "work." People will usually do what is easiest: here, the easiest thing is to use chat or phone, or to see each other (20% met face to face).

In the online questionnaire (open questions), some evidence was found that students do not want to share their experiences with everybody: JBI is a student who did his work placement in Madagascar. He lived in the same conditions as the locals, that is, in a ghetto. Each month he would send his monthly "life story" in a humorous and lucid document. One student wrote, "So the idea is basically OK, but in fact, no one could care less about the life of JBI." Another student went so far as to send out a parody of JBI's monthly newsletter.... On the other hand, we have a student who says the opposite "It's a pleasure to read contributions like JBI's newsletter"

There are two different student profiles which are independent of the learning situation created by the teacher: some students have a social and "community profile" (57% of our sample), whereas others have an "individualistic" profile (47% of our sample). The community profile means that they kept contact, had the feeling of belonging to the same student cohort and thought that mutual support is important; 40% of them worked together on the two online courses, and suffered more from physical absence (43%) than individualistic profiles, admitting to missing friends.

To conclude, can it be said, in this case study, that a learning community emerged? Most formal interactions from forums were weak links and based on self-centred information sharing. At the most, we may think that, for active participants (average of 9% on forums and chat), a community consciousness may have arisen as threads of discussion did take place. These were often based on mutual support in order to get over technical problems encountered frequently by 127 students (25%). However, a large quantity of informal interaction took place among students. This is may be why, from the student's point of view, they have the feeling of belonging to a community even when they are far away from each other (57%).

Finally, can it be claimed that, just because it is difficult to spot the community identity, (as identified by strong ties and sociocognitive debates in forum), learners did not constitute a learning community? If we consider Wenger's (1998) social learning theories, is simply participating in such common activities not a factor of learning in itself (47% said that they learned more from doing a course online than from the actual course content). From spontaneous learning, they write:

> I learned that just knowing how to do something isn't enough: you also need actual practice in real life.

I learnt to schedule priorities, manage deadlines in my own time, learned about e-learning: how to ask a question on a forum, write a frustration in a message in a constructive way, manage conflict and negotiate in a soft way.

Thus, from this online experience students did appear to learn some of the transversal skills that a future manager requires.

RECOMMENDATIONS AND FUTURE TRENDS

The questions raised in the first section of this chapter and the results from the case studies allow us to represent social activities of virtual campus learning communities as shown in Figure 14.5.

According to the literature, the community identity should arise from stronger socioaffective links, thus a microculture (Audran & Daele, 2007; Zarifian, 1996). The identity of the community is shown (see Figure 14.5) as existing within "a virtual frontier," inside which the microculture develops through socioaffective links. In this figure, communities may emerge as a continuum of networks. In reality, it varies according to participants, periods, topics of discussions and so forth.

It is important to highlight the specific features of communities in the educational environment (Figure 14.6). For online interaction between students to take place (i.e., for a community to emerge), the teacher must stay in the background. In distant situations, the teacher can no longer communicate content directly through personal charisma (unlike the classroom situation for example). They must instead create content that will encourage students to interact. A teacher must set up (and be prepared to implement) strict rules in order to encourage exchanges to emerge (environment (a) in the Figure 14.6).

Without this strict framework, the interaction will not happen. Thus, the course is deliberately bounded by rules, obligations and the evaluation of participants. However, all these measures contribute to an

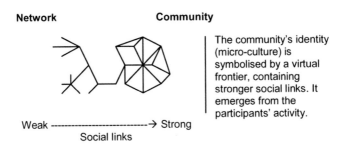

Figure 14.5.   Emergence of online communities.

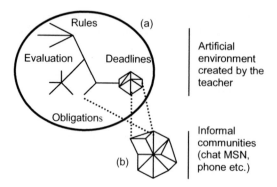

Figure 14.6.   Emergence of online learning communities.

"artificial learning environment." This is why, as seen in case study 3, students socialize on chat, telephone and face to face meetings—outside the course structure (environment (b) in Figure 14.6); these socioaffective interactions are mostly informal. However, they also constitute an often essential point of contact in order for meaningful (i.e., student centered) sociocognitive debates to take place.

What encourages spontaneous or semispontaneous communities to emerge within the educational context? How can we boost participation and sociocognitive or affective debates on the course content, within the course structure? What elements should be incorporated into the course design to maximize transfer from informal socialization (b) to discussions based on course content (a)? Here are some key issues.

Boosting Participation

It was found from case studies 2 and 3 that this transfer can be maximized, or "boosted," through use of controversial statements, problems and/or unpredictable complex situations involving all participants. This is to be expected, as it reproduces what occurs in face-to-face everyday situations: Strangers do not normally communicate spontaneously unless an external event gives them reason to do so. Kimble and Hildreth (2005) refer to "using face-to-face meetings to "turbo-boost" existing relationships" (p. 109).

Such external boosts provoke student based interaction and discussion from which the teacher is largely absent.

Which boosts work best? What types of activity promote interaction and learning? It is preferable to boost with content related issues rather than technical issues, which should be minimized as they caused frustration (i.e., the activity "doesn't work"). The booster should provoke conflict, debate, shared or negotiated meaning between students. These types of activity are more likely to provoke the emergence of a genuine online learning community.

Which group configuration works best? How can this be incorporated into the course design?

- Competition between subgroups encourages intragroup solidarity and act as a stimulus to interaction.
- Groups whose members have different knowledge and/or competencies. This encourages learning from each other and creates a need for information, which should result in interaction.
- Course design involving problems requiring group action: this promotes mutual support, which can be a vital component for the emergence of the community identity, as in case study 3.

Mutual Support

In mutual support networks, relationships are above all forged between colleagues. These relations are multidimensional. In other words, they include different types of interactions, with varying emotional loads, from discussion about the ongoing training course, information exchange, suggestions, help and advice. This type of support is perceived by younger students as the teacher's role. The transition to peer support has to be created through the course design. Ideally, course design using some of the elements suggested above might lead to peer support (for example, a student led FAQ—perfectly possible if a multilevel tool is used). If this is taken to its logical conclusion where learners are effectively learning from each other, the learning community could become a CoP. This is a good example of the social structure's fluidity and transitivity mentioned in the first section.

However, the above scenario must be recognized as an ideal. Most often, in an educational situation, a balance has to be struck between teacher set-up and student takeover. The classroom, even online, is an artificial construct. The community that arises purely from the learning activity will therefore always have its artificial side. All we can do is to set up the rules and aim for the closest approximation possible to spontaneous interaction. A good metaphor would be a football game: the rules of the game are set out by FIFA (teacher), however, this does not prevent a group of footballers (learners) from concentrating fully on their own interaction and play during a match (course).

CONCLUSION

In these case studies, we draw together information and communication as two complimentary vectors of online learning situations. In effect, we have seen that both weak and strong bonds exist between online learners. This implies that exchanges may be simply information based or tend towards a learning community. As we saw, socioaffective interactions, even outside the learning situation, can contribute to a fertile environment for a community to grow. A key ingredient of this environment is social cohesion, which allows for mutual support messages and/or discussion to take place. These types of interaction can lead to the emergence of a learning community in an educational context: exchanges are centred on course content. However, further research is needed to explore the effects of socioaffective interactions on the performance of sociocognitive tasks. To what extent should we favour socializing in an online course (socioaffective interactions), or should we only focus on the course content (sociocognitive interactions)? What should our attitude be towards informal learning and implicit knowledge in a learning community? Furthermore, we cannot ignore the question of evaluation. How should we evaluate informal learning and peer-to-peer mutual support if they arise (as in our third case study) and according to which criteria? Ultimately, how far does the teacher need to be in control?

Furthermore, even if all the conditions necessary for the emergence of online communities are satisfied, are they sufficient to guarantee that the community will indeed emerge?

In complex self-organized systems (such as a living organism), the whole is more than merely the sum of its parts. If a community can be considered as a complex self-organized system, does this mean that once the community has taken root, it has its own dynamic over and above the conditions that brought about its existence? Is it in some way autopoïetic (Varela, 1989), to use the biological term—in other words, does it become self-perpetuating—like a colony of mushrooms springing from fertile ground?

NOTES

1. Dokeos is a free software and the name of its sponsor company, it will be described in details later in this section (http://www.dokeos.com).

2.   The typology of Audran and Simonian (2003) is based on three types of interactions: content related, technical questions, and logistics. We added the socioaffective category for exchanges like small talk, jokes, mutual support, and so forth. The typology of Lafferière and Nizet (2006) classifies a grid with six types of interaction: self-other-community oriented exchanges on one axis and short-term resolution-problem solving-knowledge sharing on the other.

REFERENCES

Audran, J., & Daele, A. (2007). *Forums et liste de diffusion: Rapport à la communauté et "micro-culture."* Congress AREF, Strasbourg.

Audran, J., & Simonian, S. (2003). Profiler les apprenants à travers l'usage du forum. *Information Sciences for Decision Making, 10,* 21-32.

Brown, A., & Campione, J. (1995). Concevoir une communauté de jeunes, lèves. *Revue française de pédagogie, 11,* 11-33.

Bruner, J. (1997). *Car la culture donne forme à l'esprit.* Paris: Eshel

Ciussi, M., & Simonian, S. (2004). Lé change favoris, par l'organisation relationnelle de contenu. *International Journal of Information Sciences for Decision Marketing, 18.* Retrieved from http://isdm.univ-tln.fr/PDF/isdm18/57 -simonian-ciussi-augier.pdf

Foucault, B., Metzger, J.-L., & Pignorel, E. (2003). Les réseaux d'entraide entre apprenants dans la e-formation: à la recherche d'espaces d',changes et de communication. *Deuxième colloque de Guéret, 4,* 5.

Foucault, B., Metzger, J.-L., Pignorel E., & Vaylet, A. (2002). Les réseaux d'entraide entre apprenants dans la e-formation: nécessité et efficacité? *Education permanente,* 152-167.

Granovetter, M. (1973). The strength of weak ties. *American Journal of Sociology, 78*(6), 1360-1380.

Henri, F., & Pudelko, B. (2006). Le concept de communauté virtuelle dans une perspective d'apprentissage social. In *Comprendre les communautés virtuelles d'enseignants* (pp 105-126). L'harmattan: Charlier & Daele.

Kimble, C., & Hildreth, P. (2005). Dualities, distributed communities of practice and knowledge management. *Journal of Knowledge Management, 9*(4), 102-113.

Lafferrière, T., & Nizet, I. (2006) Conditions de fonctionnement des communautés dans les espaces numériques. In *Comprendre les communautés virtuelles d'enseignants.* L'harmattan: Charlier & Daele.

Lafferrière, T., Bracewell, R., & Breuleux, A. (2001). La contribution naissante des ressources et des outils en réseau à l'apprentissage et à l'enseignement dans les classes du primaire et du secondaire. *Rapport SchoolNet.* Retrieved from http://www.tact.fse.ulaval.ca/fr/html/revue/revue01.html

Lave, J., & Wenger, E. (1991) *Situated learning: Legitimate peripheral participation.* London: Cambridge University Press.

Lemieux, V. (1999). *Les réseaux d'acteurs sociaux.* Paris: PUF

McLuhan, M. (1964). *Understanding media: The extensions of man.* New York: McGraw-Hill

Raymond, E. (1998). The cathedral and the bazaar. *First Monday*, 3, 3. Retrieved from http://www.catb.org/~esr/writings/cathedral-bazaar/cathedral-bazaar/

Varela, F. (1989). *Autonomie et connaissance*. Paris: Seuil.

Vygostki, L. S. (1986). *Pensée et Langage*, Paris: La dispute.

Wenger, E. (1998). *Communities of practice*. London: Cambridge University Press.

Widdowson, H. (1978). *Teaching language as communication*. England: Oxford University Press.

Zarifian, P. (1996). *Travail et communication*. Paris: PUF.

CHAPTER 15

ENABLING DUALITY IN TEACHING AND LEARNING ENVIRONMENTAL DECISION MAKING

A Role For Communities of Practice?

Chris Blackmore

This chapter considers some of the domains, practices, and communities involved in environmental decision making and some related needs for both teaching and learning. Some challenges are identified for educators in the context of environmental decision making: their changing roles, distribution of learners, needs for social learning, the role of distance learning and use of the Internet. Contexts of education, social learning, and environmental decision making are first reviewed to see why structures such as communities of practice (CoPs) are needed. A case study is presented to help consider what can support teaching and learning environmental decision making. This case is about an Open University course produced by educators for and with other practitioners. Analysis of the case study and wider communities involved in environmental decision making focuses on three areas (1) what is meant by CoPs in these contexts, considering distinctions

Communities of Practice: Creating Learning Environments for Educators,
Volume 2, pp. 309–325
Copyright © 2008 by Information Age Publishing
All rights of reproduction in any form reserved.

among different groups and communities, their purposes, characteristics and relationships (2) design of supportive learning systems with online elements and (3) conceptualizing teaching and learning. The conclusion is that there is a need for teaching and learning to be viewed as an inseparable and complementary duality in which CoPs potentially have an important role.

INTRODUCTION

This chapter explores how the ideas and practice of CoPs can support both teaching and learning environmental decision making. Environmental decision making (EDM) considers environmental factors alongside economic, social, political and other factors. Nearly all decision making could have an environmental dimension but in practice, economic factors often dominate (Open University, 2006). Integrating environmental factors with these other factors is also characteristic of sustainable development, which contextualizes most EDM. Over the past couple of decades, issues of environment and sustainable development have come to the fore in many sectors, including education (Huckle & Sterling, 1996; WWF, 2000). This trend has developed as globalization and consumerism have rapidly gained momentum worldwide.

Communities of educators involved in environmental and sustainable development education go well beyond the formal sector. One such example is given by Smyth (2002) who noted in the build up to the United Nations (UN) World Summit on Sustainable Development that:

> The education community, for whose support the UN was calling, is a broad spectrum of people from all of the stakeholder groups, the formal sector of education at every level, many kinds of non-formal education and the local administrations on which they depend. (pp. 2-3)

Many communities and practices have been involved in the domains of such United Nations Summits and their ensuing activities. They could be conceptualized as "constellations of communities of practice" (after Wenger, 1998) but according to Smyth (2002), this education community had no recognized structure at that time. References to CoPs rather than just to communities in this context have been relatively recent. Many CoPs associated with EDM and sustainable development have emerged in recent years. There are also many groups who do not explicitly use the language of CoPs, but adopt similar principles in creating learning environments for practitioners involved in EDM. Both kinds of group include educators, in a broad sense. Most groups and their processes can also be seen, from different perspectives, as having different purposes. While recognizing that CoPs are highly diverse, one of the core questions to be addressed in this chapter is *what are the implications of conceptualizing a teaching and learning situation in the context of EDM as a Community of Practice (CoP) rather than as another structure?*

Four sections follow this introduction. the second section includes background on the nature of learning for EDM in order to understand why CoPs might support educators in this context. It includes examples of CoPs. The third section is a case study in open and distance learning that considers domains, communities, and practices associated with an Open University course on EDM. The fourth section analyses the case study, its contexts and the roles of CoPs. The fifth section contains conclusions.

Learning For Environmental Decision Making—Education and Social Learning

> Knowing enough, and acting wisely enough, across the full range of environmental and related health issues seems daunting. The interconnections between issues, the pace of technological change, our limited understanding and the "time to harm and then to heal" of ecological and biological systems that can be perturbed over decades by our technologies together present an unforgiving context. (Harremoës et al., 2002, pp. xv)

The case for both education and social learning for EDM is premised on our need both to know enough and to act wisely enough. Education and social learning overlap but have different focuses. Education usually has connotations of guidance of learning of individuals. It originated from the Latin *educere* from ex (out) *ducere* (lead) in the sense of rearing or bringing up. Those recognized as educators in the context of EDM include people from both formal and nonformal sectors. These individuals might be teachers and lecturers from schools and universities, education and project officers from nongovernmental and community-based organizations or others with specialist skills or knowledge.

The need for interaction among those involved in education in this area is well recognized. For instance, the United Nations decade for education for sustainable development began in 2005. It includes environmental aspects alongside social and economic and one of its four key objectives is "to facilitate networking, linkages, exchange and interaction among stakeholders in education for sustainable development" (UNESCO, 2005). At this international level, the purpose of linking multiple stakeholders in education for sustainable development is to learn our way together to improve quality of life and wellbeing for many. Sustainable development also requires (1) recognition of our interdependencies (2) maintenance of our life support systems and (3) avoiding depletion of our shared and increasingly contested natural resources.

Social learning can refer to both collective learning and individual learning that results from social interactions. In social learning that concentrates on collective learning the role of a facilitator is likely to be at least as much recognized as that of an educator. (The roles of an educator and a facilitator of social learning are not mutually exclusive but often lead to people with different purposes and skills.) The rationale for collective learning in EDM often lies in resource dilemmas where there are competing claims on the use of natural resources (Röling 2002; Röling & Woodhill, 2001) characterized by common pool resources, multiple stakeholders, interdependence, controversy, complexity, and uncertainty (SLIM, 2004). In some areas, such as water catchment management, the dynamics of activities suggests that not just collective action but concerted action is required (SLIM, 2004). (The term "concerted action" uses the metaphor of a concert to suggest actors working together, each with a role in a performance that takes place at a particular time.) In such circumstances, learning becomes part of a process of negotiation among stakeholders that leads to action. This negotiation often requires skilled facilitation.

Wenger (1998) elaborated a "social theory of learning" that defines learning as a social and historical process, as distinct from a "theory of social learning" that might infer a primary focus on collective rather than individual learning. Wenger (2004) focused on both individual and collective learning, on identity at individual level in CoPs and on large-scale learning systems. De Laat and Simons (2002) usefully plotted individual and collective levels of learning processes against learning outcomes and in so doing identified four kinds of learning: (1) individual learning (2) individual learning processes with collective outcomes (3) learning in social interaction and (4) collective learning. Learning EDM includes all these kinds of learning but given competing claims for natural resources, those that have collective outcomes, resulting from individual or collective learning, are particularly challenging and are often referred to as "social learning" in this context. In contrast, traditional education programs have focused on learning processes and outcomes of individuals, while still recognizing the social contexts of individuals and the significance of collective outcomes. Hence, the primary focuses of education and social learning tend to be different (Blackmore, 2005). Recognition of collective learning in some educational contexts appears to be increasing, with more assessment of group work.

CoPs in the domains of EDM that could be seen as contributing to learning include those for improving management of water resources (e.g., RCD-CoP, the Resource Center Development CoP of the International Reference Center for Community Water Supply); collaborating in environmental programs (e.g., the environmental CoP of the U.S Army

Corps of Engineers) and learning about conservation (e.g., the CoP created by the Learning Network of IUCN—the World Conservation Union). Learning is at the core of these CoPs and some teaching, in the sense of the facilitation and guidance of the learning of others. They seem to involve diverse practitioners that include educators, in a broad sense. However, few would describe these environmental CoPs as primarily the learning environments of educators. What are the relationships among environmental CoPs and educators CoPs? In order to address this question there is a need to stand back a little and consider whether only groups that describe themselves as CoPs count as CoPs or whether groups that have similar principles to CoPs should also be included. The case study in the next section explores this issue. It is about teaching and learning among distributed staff and students who have been supporting and doing EDM. The relevance of CoPs to this context is discussed in the fourth section. Another question later addressed, under the subheading "Teaching and Learning as a Duality" is whether it is useful to frame learning and teaching for EDM not only as education, which implies educators but also as social learning, which implies facilitators.

Why and how might CoPs support educators in the context of EDM? The rest of this chapter goes on to address this question; taking forward from this section the following: a need to recognize,

1. The breadth of the education community involved, including both formal and nonformal sectors

2. The multistakeholder and multiorganizational nature of EDM situations, which has led to a focus on social learning as much as education and the facilitator as much as the educator

3. The distributed nature of interdependent stakeholders (e.g., across water catchments) who might need to work both together and individually towards collective outcomes

4. The existing and potential roles of educators in supporting individual and collective learning and concerted action

5. The dynamics of teaching and learning

ENVIRONMENTAL DECISION MAKING AT THE UNITED KINGDOM'S OPEN UNIVERSITY: A CASE STUDY OF DOMAINS, COMMUNITIES, AND PRACTICES

Etienne Wenger (2007) on his Web site identifies three characteristics of a CoP: a shared domain of interest, a community that interact in joint activities in pursuing this interest and development of shared practice. The course discussed in this section can be thought of as a CoP, both because it has these three characteristics and is in line with the more detailed criteria of Wenger, McDermott, and Snyder (2002). It can also be thought of in other ways, which are discussed. In this case study the most obvious domain of interest is the course. The community of the course is mainly Open University students and staff. The practices of the course are learning and teaching EDM using a systems approach, also known as "systemic EDM." Other CoPs can be identified in the context of the course as many students have other roles outside the course as practitioners. Many students and staff can be thought of as boundary spanners between the course community and their other communities. Academic staff who can be identified as educators are not only developing their practice of teaching but they are, in the process, deepening their understanding of systemic EDM, partly through their interactions with students.

Who is Involved?

Well over a thousand students from the United Kingdom, other parts of Europe, Zimbabwe, and Uganda have completed the Open University's postgraduate course "T860 Environmental Decision Making: A Systems Approach" since it was first presented in 1997. A new course by the same name (T863) replaced T860 in 2006, which is attracting yet more students. (For the purpose of this chapter, T860/3 will be referred to as one course.) Thousands of other students have completed further courses in the postgraduate programs to which these courses belong (Blackmore & Morris, 2001). Open University course teams of academic and nonacademic staff have developed and presented T860/3. These teams include part-time associate lecturers who tutor the course. This case study considers some of the experiences of these students and staff from the perspectives of learning systems.

The Open University Context

The Open University (OU) is the United Kingdom's largest university with over 200,000 adults currently studying OU courses and materials. Currently this represents 22% of all UK part-time higher education (HE). Over 70% of OU students remain in full-time employment throughout their studies. The OU also claims to be the UK's leading e-university. There are over 16,000 electronic conferences with more than 2,000 student moderators (ePolitix.com, 2006). The OU has been a pioneer of open entry and supported open learning; usually distance learning

(Daniel, 1996; Whitsed, 2005). Most undergraduate courses have no entry requirements and students study at home in their own time. They receive a range of course materials which might be text, audio, video, and/or DVD-based, and have access to course-specific Web-based resources. Students have a tutor who they usually interact with online and by phone and are supported by a range of central services including online access to library facilities. Most courses have electronic conferences where students, tutors and course team interact. Traditionally FirstClass software has been used for this purpose and this case study comments on that experience. The OU will soon be using Moodle for its virtual learning environment ("Open University Applies Moodle," 2005).

Student's Processes and Context

A student of T860 would typically become aware of the course through the OU's Web site, their previous studies with the OU or other advertising material. They register for the 30-point, 6-month course to start in either May or November (180 points are usually required for an MSc). Shortly before the course begins, they receive text-based, audio, video, and computer-based material and details of how to gain access to e-mail and computer conferences. They are contacted by e-mail or phone by their tutor, an OU associate lecturer. Before the course starts, students usually begin their online interactions with introductions taking place among other students, tutors, and the course team. Assessment of the course is by three assignments, submitted, and returned online and a project in which they use the course concepts and conceptual framework to inquire into an EDM situation in which they are themselves a stakeholder. These situations range enormously. Some are work-based for instance regarding an environmental scheme or policy, or site-based, such as those regarding a conservation area or site for waste management. Others are home or community-based perhaps regarding transport or a new infrastructure development within a community or the challenge of EDM at household level. Some students can identify situations in which they have a large and active stakeholding, others are just beginning to engage with environmental issues in an active way and have more passive stakeholdings or more remote links. Hence, student interactions regarding their EDM through this course also vary.

The domains and practices of EDM are diverse and some T860 students, in a series of interviews, easily identified either communities or networks to which they belonged, associated with their work-based practices. These networks and communities were often described as distributed and multiorganizational, particularly where environmental policy in an organization was just starting out and those involved discussed their experiences and sought advice from others in similar roles but in different organizations. They included people facing similar challenges in their practices, for example, in areas such as managing landfill sites, river basin management, or environmental regulation and legislation. Individuals identified with say, a group of environmental regulators or health, safety and environmental managers with responsibilities similar to their own but in different geographical locations or in slightly different contexts. Being a part of these communities or networks was seen as important to the identity of the individuals concerned. There are professional membership organizations associated with these groupings (e.g., the UK's Institute of Environmental Management and Assessment), important because they provide professional recognition, events, good Web sites or magazines for professional updating. However, communities or networks were seen as more associated with the domain and its associated practices than with any one organization.

Some students did not identify with external groups in their EDM and their interactions mainly focused on the course or their overall programs of study. They chose a specific environmental decision-making situation that was fairly new to them and which they used as a basis for their project. However most students, whatever their stakeholding in EDM, were able to identify a range of elements in their learning systems that include people, courses, events, artifacts, online, and other resources (Blackmore, 2006). Alumni from this course in some cases go on to other OU courses and in some cases, they do not. The OU has active student and alumni associations to which some but not all students belong.

Staff's Processes and Context

The staff involved in T860/3 take some different roles. Some, usually academics based on the OU's main campus in Milton Keynes or its UK regional offices, design and develop the course in terms of content and pedagogy, developing and monitoring course assessment as part of staff development. Others are associate lecturers who tutor and assess the course and are often based in other universities or working in environmental practitioner roles. Others join the course team from within and outside the university, as critical readers. Other staff are concerned with editing, publishing, development of computer-based or Web-based material. Yet others are concerned with administration, scheduling, marketing, evaluation of students' experiences, and distribution of materials. Staff interact with each other in meetings and online during course development, through staff development activities, through the processes of assessment during presentation of the course and they interact with students either as tutors through assessing and advising on the course and/or through the course's electronic conferences.

Whither CoPs in This Case Study?

What does the above description of an open learning, distance taught course, its related communities, and its context offer to help understand how teaching and learning for EDM can be supported through CoPs and other structures? Environmental and educational communities are brought together through this course. The practices of systemic EDM are at its core and so too are the practices of teaching, learning, and course development. Three aspects of this case study will now be analyzed. The first concerns what is meant by CoPs and other structures in this context. The second concerns how learning systems with online or "virtual" elements can be designed to support EDM and the third how teaching and learning are, and can be, conceptualized and how CoPs fit into that process.

ANALYZING THE CASE STUDY AND ITS CONTEXT WITH CoPs IN MIND

CoPs and Other Structures

What relevance do CoPs have to this OU course and the situation described in the case study? Many staff at the OU have found meaningful the ideas of CoPs and learning communities in the context of their teaching and research and have reflected on the strengths and limitations of considering their groupings in these contexts as communities (e.g., Blackmore, 2004; Ison, 2000; McCormick, 2003; Thorpe, 2002, 2003).

Wenger et al. (2002, p. 42, Table 2-2) identified the following features of a CoP that distinguish it from other social structures such as departments, teams, networks, or communities of interest:

1. What purpose? To create, expand, and exchange knowledge and to develop individual capabilities
2. Who belongs? Self-selection based in expertise or passion for a topic
3. How clear are the boundaries? Fuzzy

4. What holds them together? Passion, commitment, and identification with the group and its expertise

5. How long do they last? Evolve and end organically

Wenger et al. (2002) also distinguished formal departments, operational teams, project teams, communities of interest, and informal networks using the same questions. They attribute other purposes to other social structures, for example, project teams have the purpose of accomplishing a specified task and informal networks receive and pass on information to know who is who. Wenger et al.'s focus on the purpose of these structures links well with other systems traditions. Soft systems methodology (Checkland & Scholes, 1999), in particular focuses on the activity of specifying a "root definition," which includes a clear statement of purpose in the form "a system to."

The structure and process of OU course development and presentation can be conceptualized in different ways. A project or course team with less fuzzy boundaries than a CoP is one way. However, while some aspects of start and end dates of course processes are predetermined, others are negotiable. All of Wenger et al.'s (2002) distinctions for a CoP could apply to the T860/3 course community. This course could be thought of as having the same purpose as a CoP, that is, *"to create, expand and exchange knowledge and to develop individual capabilities,"* or quite a different purpose, that is, it could be described as *"a system to encourage students to approach EDM critically and systemically and enable them to gain qualifications, while at the same time providing a means of livelihood for staff and environmental credibility for the university."*

In OU systems traditions (Blackmore & Ison, 2007; Systems Practice Managing Complexity, 2007), the boundary between elements and processes within a system and outside it, in its environment, is likely to change with its purpose and underlying worldview. A CoP focus, that is, on increasing knowledge and capabilities, might concentrate on facilitating individual and group learning processes, and providing other resources so that knowledge can be created and all involved can help to support each other. Whereas a focus on students' EDM and qualifications and staff livelihoods might focus more on outcomes than facilitating learning processes. There are aspects of both these scenarios associated with T860/3, which led to focus this chapter less on the question of whether it is a CoP, and more on question of how can thinking of it as a CoP help? One immediate response to this question in the light of what has been said so far is that a focus on developing and improving practice rather than just achieving outcomes can be encouraged by a CoP focus. The course community does already focus on both but in particular in online interactions it has been found useful to keep the principles of CoPs in mind, for example, regarding sharing repertoires of resources, regular interaction through joint activities, and valuing participation, events, and a diversity of roles in the community.

There is an identifiable community of students, staff, and others associated with T860, with the domain of systemic EDM and its associated practices. This community focuses more on learning about and teaching EDM than actually doing it. This community could not be thought of as a community of educators but it does include some of them. In understanding its relationships with other groups that could be thought of as CoPs, Wenger's (1998) notion of "constellations" of interconnected practices is a useful one. This notion acknowledges the relationships among some CoPs but also their differences. A T860/3 CoP could be thought of as part of a constellation of practices within the OU and in the wider world. Students and staff associated with T860/3 also identify with other OU domains and others have elsewhere explored the idea of OU course teams as constellations of CoPs (e.g., Thorpe, 2002).

Designing Learning Systems and CoPs With Online Elements to Support Environmental Decision Making

Teachers and learners around the world concerned with EDM in the context of sustainable development are characterized both by their increasing numbers and by the, often distributed, nature of people focused on particular issues. This has led to a huge growth in electronic communication and use of the Internet to support distance learning in this context. This kind of virtual world is often part of a larger picture with other face-to-face and media elements incorporated into individual's or group's learning systems. The way in which these elements are used and for what purposes, in particular in relation to environmental action, has changed in recent years. For instance, many environmental reports can now be easily accessed and free of charge, lobbying, and consultation take place online and blogs are used to exchange ideas and provide alerts of unfolding events. Online discussions are part of the T860/3 course, providing opportunities for sharing ideas and experiences. The course Web site also plays an increasing role for students in providing easy access to resources. Online elements have long been part of course design at the OU but the way in which they are used has evolved with increasing access to Web pages, online conferences and forums and e-mail.

Wenger et al. (2002) discussed the challenge of distributed communities and noted that factors such as distance, size, organizational affiliation and cultural differences can make building and sustaining communities significantly more difficult than in local communities. They stated, "Distributed communities ... need as much or more than local communities, a set of regular events to give the community a heartbeat ... purely online connections can feel timeless and out of sync with the often urgent rhythm of everyday work" (pp. 128-129). In the context of T860/T863, planned face-to-face meetings for the course team and assessment tasks for students could perhaps be thought of as giving the community a heartbeat. Spontaneous events also occur such as groups of students arranging to meet informally. These are sometimes enabled by online discussions.

Hildreth, Kimble, and Wright (2000) also commented on the place of "events" and noted how one group (the management team of IT support of a major international company) during the periods of communication on e-media felt that the momentum gradually slowed until a physical meeting picked it up again. Hildreth (2004) has discussed the ideas and practices of "virtual CoPs" who rarely or never meet. OU communities include many people who interact online and never meet. However, they do meet with people in other communities, bring their experiences of those interactions to their OU courses and build on their OU learning experiences with people in other communities. The question from this section to take forward regards the role of virtual elements in future. Already the Internet and online communication have become very significant in EDM. What will it evolve to in future and how can we design learning systems with a virtual element that will most support EDM?

Teaching and Learning as a Duality

Thinking of the elements and processes of T860/3 as a community of systemic environmental decision-making practice, focused through the conceptual framework of the course, seems to enable the practitioners involved to engage in a different kind of learning from that of a group of teachers and students primarily focused on completing a course and gaining qualifications. There is no suggestion here that the qualifications are not important (they are central to T860/3) but there seems to be a lot to be gained from valuing the different kinds of knowledge and knowing that students and staff can contribute to the practice of EDM (Blackmore, in press). Harremoës et al. (2002) suggest that "lay" and local knowledge as well as relevant specialist expertise need to be used to address environmental issues. In the context of taking a systems approach to EDM the "specialist" expertise is as likely to come from students as from teaching staff, whose expertise lies in the systems approach of the course and the examples covered by the course, not necessarily in the students' chosen environmental decision-making situations. Hence, both students and staff have much to learn from and with each other in relation to EDM. Although each individual has a staff or student role and responsibilities there is a dynamic duality between teaching and learning. The idea of dualities (complementary pairs) rather than dualisms (negating opposites) permeates systems and CoPs theories (Hildreth & Kimble, 2002; Kimble & Hildreth, 2005; Reyes, 1995; Wenger, 1998). That learning and teaching need to be a complementary pair is nothing new. However, what is the nature of this duality in the context of this case study and would working more as a CoP than a course team encourage it? Each individual, whether student or staff could be considered at different times to be involved in both activities to some degree, taking a role in facilitating or guiding the learning of others while achieving their own learning. The traditional roles of student as learner and academic as teacher are certainly evident in the T860/3 processes. However, the reverse can also be found.

As part of their assessment, students are asked to critique the course framework of ideas, including their own use of it, in the light of their project experience in their chosen environmental decision-making situations. These projects and critiques have certainly provided opportunities for learning by staff as well as a wider community of students, though constrained to some degree by the nature of the assessment processes. As the course continues to evolve, new ways in which these insights from students might inform others are being explored. In the FirstClass conferences, students and staff can both be seen guiding and learning. While the intended learning outcomes for the course seem to be achieved by many students, the full potential for both learning and learning about learning EDM seems yet to be realized through this OU course team approach. The course brings together a unique cross-section of educators and other practitioners involved in EDM but its focus is probably too short-term to enable a mature CoP to form. What alternative CoPs or other supportive structures might be encouraged to emerge for the longer term?

Standing back from the case study it is possible to consider a wider range of "environmental CoPs" in which learning is prominent (e.g., those mentioned near the end of the second section). Is the idea of a duality of teaching and learning still a meaningful one? An education mindset would often identify someone as guiding or leading the learning of another. An educator usually has a distinct role. A mindset of social learning, on the other hand, can focus on both individual learning in a social context or on collective learning where the role of facilitator is acknowledged, but not usually in the sense of traditional leadership. Perhaps a duality between learning and facilitation might be more appropriate here? Different members of a community engaged in social learning might be responsible for facilitating their learning processes at different times. The role of educators in relation to EDM has changed over the past decades. Facilitation and teaching overlap. But in environmental decision-making situations, which are often characterized by high degrees of uncertainty and complexity and some institutional barriers to learning (Harremoës et al., 2002), multilevel social learning is required (Blackmore, 2007; SLIM, 2004) and perhaps through CoPs educators can be enabled to challenge traditional more dualistic patterns of teaching and learning? Nascent CoPs in these contexts are already indicating that CoPs can provide a better basis for learning than more traditional models (LEARNing project, 2005).

CONCLUSIONS

The domains and practices of EDM present many challenges for teaching and learning. Recognition of the interconnectedness of individuals and groups' EDM for society at large and collectives at other levels has led to an increased focus on what de Laat and Simon (2002) distinguish as collective learning and individual learning processes with collective outcomes which others (e.g., SLIM, 2004) recognize as social learning. Educators have been joined by others who are concerned with promoting learning who would not perhaps describe themselves as involved in the task of education but more as facilitators of social learning. In these contexts, there are many distributed learners who identify with multiorganizational CoPs or networks including some associated with teaching and learning, such as the one focused on the Open University course "T860/3 Environmental decision making: a systems approach." This chapter was less concerned with whether this course situation could or should be described as a CoP and more with how it might help those involved if it were thought of in this way. While conceptualizing T860/3 as a course will undoubtedly remain important, particularly during course production, it appears that much could be gained by both students and staff by thinking of the course community in terms of CoPs. Online interactions and valuing of students' experience through project-based assessment have helped students and staff to recognize that teaching and learning can be an inseparable and complementary duality. In the wider world of environmental communities in which educators participate, CoPs could play an important part in strengthening this duality and in helping those involved to adapt to the changing roles of educators in EDM.

REFERENCES

Blackmore, C. (2004). From one-off events to learning systems and communities of practice. In A. Cristovão (Ed.), *Proceedings from Sixth European International Farming Systems Association Symposium* (pp. 449-458). Vila Real, Portugal: UTAD.

Blackmore, C. (2005). Learning to appreciate learning systems for environmental decision-making: A "work-in-progress" perspective. *Systems Research and Behavioural Science, 22,* 329-341.

Blackmore, C. (2006). Engaging with learning systems and communities of practice for environmental decision-making. In N. Gould (Ed.), *Multi-organisational partnerships, alliances and networks: Engagement. Proceedings of MOPAN 5, international conference* (pp. 37-40). Devon, England: Short Run Press.

Blackmore, C. (2007). What kinds of knowledge, knowing and learning are required for addressing resource dilemmas? A theoretical overview. *Environmental Science and Policy, 10*(6), 512–525.

Blackmore, C., & Morris, D. (2001). Systems and environmental decision-making: Postgraduate open learning with the Open University. *Systemic Practice and Action Research 14*(6). 681-685.

Blackmore, C. P., & Ison, R. L. (2007). Boundaries for thinking and action. In G. Mohan, A. R. Thomas, & M. Wuyts (Eds.), *Research skills for policy and development: How to find out fast* (pp. 47-71). London: Sage.

Checkland, P. B., & Scholes, J. (1999). *Soft systems methodology in action* (2nd ed.). Chichester, England: Wiley.

Daniel, J. S. (1996). *Mega-universities and knowledge Media: Technology strategies for higher education*. London: Kogan Page.

De Laat, M. F.e., & Simons, P. R. J. (2002). Collective learning: Theoretical perspectives and ways to support networked learning. *Vocational Training: European Journal, 27,* 13-24.

ePolitix.com. (2006). A division of "Dods" which is a political information, public affairs and policy communication specialist of the United Kingdom and the European Union. Retrieved January 30, 2007, from http://www.epolitix.com/EN/Forums/Open+University/727BF843-0F01-4425-B982-E1BEFF63E1E5.htm

Harremoës, P., Gee, D., MacGarvin, M., Stirling, A., Keys, J., Wynne, B., et al. (Eds). (2002). *The precautionary principle in the 20th Century: Late lessons from early warnings*. London: European Environment Agency, Earthscan.

Hildreth, P. (2004). *Going virtual: Distributed communities of practice*. London: Idea Group.

Hildreth, P., Kimble, C., & Wright P. (2000). Communities of practice in the distributed international environment. *Journal of Knowledge Management, 4*(1), 27-37.

Hildreth, P. M., & Kimble, C. (2002). The duality of knowledge. *Information Research, 8*(1), paper 142. Retrieved October 18, 2007 from http://informationr.net/ir/8-1/paper142.html

Huckle, J., & Sterling, S. (1996). *Education for sustainability*. London: Earthscan.

Ison, R. L. (2000) Supported open learning and the emergence of learning communities. The case of the Open University UK. In R. Miller (Ed.), *Creating learning communities. Models, resources, and new ways of thinking about teaching and learning* (pp. 90-96). Brandon VT: Solomon Press.

Kimble C., & Hildreth P. (2005). Dualities, distributed communities of practice and knowledge management. *Journal of Knowledge Management, 9*(4), 102-113.

LEARNing project. (2005). *Learning in European agricultural and rural networks: Institutions, networks and governance.* (European Union Fifth Framework project. Contract no. HPSE-CT-2002-60059). Retrieved January 30, 2007, from http://www.inra.fr/learning/

McCormick, R. (2003). *Theoretical perspectives of relevance to networked learning communities.* Unpublished report for the National College of School Leadership.

Open University. (2006). *T863 Environmental decision-making: A systems approach.* Course books. Milton Keynes, England: Author.

Open University applies Moodle on grand scale. (2005). *Distance Education Report, 9*(24), 3-6, 2.

Reyes, A. (1995). *A theoretical framework for the design of a social accounting system.* Unpublished doctoral dissertation, University of Humberside.

Röling, N. (2002) Beyond the aggregation of individual preferences: Moving from multiple to distributed cognition in resource dilemmas. In C Leeuwis & R. Pyburn (Eds.), *Wheelbarrows full of frogs: Social learning in rural resource management* (pp. 25-47). The Netherlands: Koninklijke Va Gorcum.

Röling, N., & Woodhill, J. (2001). From paradigms to practice: foundations, principles and elements for dialogue on water, food and environment. In *Background documents for dialogue on water, food and environment: National and basin dialogue design workshop.* Retrieved January 30, 2007, from http://www.iwmi.cgiar.org/dialogue/index.asp?nc=9188&id=1078&msid=115

SLIM. (2004). The role of learning processes in integrated catchment management and the sustainable use of water. *SLIM Policy Briefing No 6.* Retrieved January 30 2007, from http://slim.open.ac.uk/page.cfm?pageid=policybriefs

Smyth, J. (2002). Are educators ready for the next Earth summit? *Millennium Paper Series Issue 6. Stakeholder Forum for a Sustainable Future.* Retrieved January 30, 2007, from http://www.unedforum.org/publications/millennium/millpaper6.pdf

Systems Practice Managing Complexity. (2007). *BBC/Open University Web site OPEN2.NET.* Retrieved January 30, 2007, from http://www.open2.net/systems/

Thorpe, M. (2002, May). *Communities of practice.* Inaugural lecture presented at the Open University in Milton Keynes, England.

Thorpe, M. (2003). *Communities of practice and other frameworks for conceptualising, developing and evaluating NCSL's initiatives in linking staff and school communities.* Unpublished report for the National College of School Leadership.

UNESCO. (2005). *Decade of education for sustainable development Web site.* Retrieved January 30, 2007 from, http://portal.unesco.org/education/en/ev.php-URL_ID=27234&URL_DO=DO_TOPIC&URL_SECTION=201.html

Wenger, E. (1998). *Communities of practice: Learning, meaning and identity.* London: Cambridge University Press.

Wenger, E. (2004). *Learning for a small planet: a research agenda.* Retrieved January 30, 2007, http://www.ewenger.com/theory/index.htm

Wenger, E. (2007). *Web site.* Retrieved January 30, 2007, http://www.ewenger.com/theory/index.htm

Wenger, E., McDermott, R., & Snyder, W. M. (2002). *Cultivating communities of practice.* Boston: Harvard Business School Press.

Whitsed, N. (2005) Supporting e-learning-a view from the Open University: *Health Information & Libraries Journal, 22*(4), 301-304.

WWF and partners (2000) Professional practice for sustainable development book 2: Developing cross-professional learning opportunities and tools. Godalming, Surrey, England: WWF-UK.

CHAPTER 16

THE ADULT LITERACY EDUCATION WIKI AS A VIRTUAL COMMUNITY OF PRACTICE

Erik Jacobson

This chapter asks whether a large Wiki can be considered a community of practice (CoP) and whether or not this is a useful question to ask. The focus of the chapter is the Adult Literacy Education (ALE) Wiki, an ongoing creation of adult basic education teachers, administrators and researchers. The ALE Wiki has a core group of very active contributors, over 700 registered users, and more than 720 pages of content. The chapter includes a description of choices the organizers made when constructing the Wiki and how those choices create the potential for the ALE Wiki to create a small CoP at its center. The chapter uses the concept of CoPs as a heuristic to examine the multilayered participation structure of the Wiki. The conclusion is that while the ALE Wiki as a whole cannot be considered a CoP, the concept is a useful way to identify some of the strengths of the Wiki and to note the limitations of working with such a large group.

Communities of Practice: Creating Learning Environments for Educators,
Volume 2, pp. 327–345
Copyright © 2008 by Information Age Publishing
All rights of reproduction in any form reserved.

INTRODUCTION

The ALE Wiki is an ongoing creation of adult basic education teachers, administrators and researchers working mainly in North America. The ALE Wiki was started as a grassroots effort and is not sponsored by any civic institution or organization. Two main goals informed the creation of the Wiki. The first goal was to make current research and professional wisdom on the topic of adult literacy available to more people in the field. The second goal was to create a space where conversations started at conferences and workshops could continue. In this way, it is an attempt to help move beyond the limitations of one-shot workshops and panels. The main Wiki site (Adult Literacy Education Wiki, 2007) currently has more than 700 registered users and over 720 pages of content. The Wiki features archives of electronic discussion groups, annotated bibliographies, thematically organized citations of relevant research, and links to other Web sites. The ALE Wiki has its own electronic discussion list (for very active participants) and has a reciprocal relationship with more than a dozen other electronic discussion groups (many of them sponsored by the National Institute for Literacy in the United States). Information from and about the Wiki is disseminated on these lists and information from the lists is captured and utilized on the ALE Wiki. Because ALE Wiki participation is not strictly limited to the Wiki site itself, it is difficult to identify the exact boundaries of the ALE Wiki or to speak authoritatively about membership. As in other online settings that have multi-layered participant structures, it is possible to participate in a variety of ways. To understand how these different participation structures might impact the functioning of the Wiki, this chapter will look at the ALE Wiki using the communities of practice (CoPs) framework. Can the ALE Wiki be considered a CoP or is it simply a large online communal repository of information?

Although in recent times corporations and other institutions have been consciously trying to develop CoPs based on principles expressed by Wenger, McDermott, and Snyder (2002), the ALE Wiki organizers were not attempting to create a CoP based on any proposed models. For that reason it will best to consider the concept of CoPs in a heuristic sense (Lea, 2005, p. 181), as a model for learning rather than as a template for building a working group. In this sense, examining the ALE Wiki as a potential CoP may be more in keeping with an earlier generation of work on CoPs that looked for these learning structures in a variety of non-formal settings (Lave & Wenger, 1991) rather than from a best (business) practices perspective.

This chapter will review the history of the Wiki, consider some choices that were made that have helped the Wiki to grow, and will examine what the CoPs framework can tell us about a project like the ALE Wiki. It will draw on content from the Wiki itself (including comments posted by participants), communication between Wiki participants, and personal experience as one of the founders and organizers of the Wiki.

DEFINING COMMUNITY OF PRACTICE

The concept of CoP has stirred much interest, and there is no shortage of definitions. For the purposes of this chapter, CoPs will be understood as described by Wenger (n.d.) on his own Web page: "Communities of practice are groups of people who share a concern or a passion for something that they do and learn how to do it better as they interact regularly." In this case, because the community has developed in an online environment (through the creation of a Wiki and the use of e-mail) with limited opportunities for physical colocation, it is what has been called a virtual CoP. Although the use of computer mediated communication means that a virtual CoP will differ in some ways from a physical community, at their core both formulations of CoP share the same concepts. For all CoPs, it is the shared learning and interest of its members that keep it together. These groups are "defined by knowledge rather than task, and [they exist] because participation has value to its members" (Wenger, 1998a, p. 4). This sense of intentionally learning together, rather than simply completing a task, is what makes the CoP more than a team. Indeed, the knowledge that is gained should not be limited strictly to the task at hand, and one clear value of being in a CoP is that it helps members "learn about new developments in their field and build a sense of affiliation with others in similar circumstances" (Lesser & Fontaine, 2004, p. 15). As will be discussed below, the solidarity that a CoP provides is important for adult basic educators working in an underfunded and marginalized discipline.

Wenger (1998a) suggests that a CoP defines itself along three dimensions:

1. What it is about
    As understood and continually negotiated by members of the community

2. How it functions
    The formal and tacit agreements that bind members together

3. What capability it has produced
    The shared repertoire of communal resources, routines, artifacts, and so forth.

As noted above, the ALE Wiki was not started with a given model of virtual CoPs in mind. However, to be considered CoP ALE Wiki participants should be able to address the questions that Wenger (1998a) proposes. Do the members have a common understanding of the goals of the ALE Wiki? What kind of tacit and explicit protocols are used to provide structure and guidance for Wiki participants? Last, in addition to the Web site itself, are there other shared routines and sensibilities that have developed among users of the ALE Wiki? The answers to those questions will vary depending upon which one the multiple groups of ALE Wiki participants is being examined.

BACKGROUND: THE NEED FOR THE ALE WIKI

The impetus for starting a Wiki focused on adult literacy education was informed by two problems facing adult literacy practitioners: (1) A limited (and limiting) approach to disseminating research on adult literacy on the part of the federal government of the United States of America, and (2) limited opportunities for professional development for adult literacy practitioners in the United States.

Federal Dissemination of Adult Literacy Research

One of the highest profile means of disseminating research in the United States is the What Works Clearinghouse (United States Government, 2007). This Web site is maintained by the United States Department of Education and according to its own Web site: "The What Works Clearinghouse (WWC) collects, screens, and identifies studies of effectiveness of educational interventions (programs, products, practices, and policies)" (United States Government, 2007). At the time the ALE Wiki began (the autumn of 2004), the government had not posted any information about "what works" in adult literacy education, although it was promised to be "coming soon." One goal for creating the ALE Wiki was to fill that gap. Rather than waiting for the U.S. government to fulfill its promise, by working together and sharing information practitioners could start identifying effective interventions themselves. The coming soon tag remained on the site for over a year. It was finally removed, but not because any information about adult education has been uploaded—now there is not even the promise of adult education content in the clearinghouse. This makes the ALE Wiki more important than ever.

Of course, the WWC is not the only method of disseminating research about adult literacy. In 2002, the National Institute for Literacy released

Research-Based Principles for Adult Basic Education Reading Instruction (Kruidenier, 2002), based on the work of the Reading Research Working Group. Like the work of the National Reading Panel (a previous panel that focused on kindergarten to third grade), the Reading Research Working Group only considered research that was experimental in nature. One criticism of this approach was that by focusing solely on experimental studies (a total of 70) the report would have limited scope and would exclude a great deal of information that was based on nonexperimental data. In comparison, the ALE Wiki was conceived of as a resource that would be inclusive of all research methodologies and that would have a prominent space for practitioner wisdom that is based on practice.

Limited Professional Development Opportunities for Adult Literacy Practitioners

The National Board for Professional Teaching Standards (in the United States) suggests that effective teachers are members of learning communities (Senge, 1990) that provide participants with ongoing opportunities to collaborate on policy, curriculum, and staff development (Leonard & Leonard, 2003). This is not surprising since research on adult development and professional growth points to the need for teachers to be engaged in long-term, collaborative projects that focus on concrete issues. Indeed, a survey of adult literacy teachers working in the United States (Sabatini, Daniels, Ginsburg, Limeul, Russell, & Stites, 2000) found that 48% of those participating in collaborative teamwork rated it the most useful form of professional development, compared with 1% who found it the least useful. By contrast, only 31% of those participating in (typically one-shot) workshops found that format to be the most useful. However, opportunities for collaboration and participatory professional development are rare in the field of adult basic education.

One reason that collaborative professional development is limited in adult literacy instruction is that the field has traditionally been staffed by part-time workers who have few opportunities to interact with one another. In addition, programs have limited budgets for professional development activities. A survey of adult educators' working conditions conducted in the United States by the National Center for the Study of Adult Learning and Literacy (Smith, Hofer, & Gillespie, 2001) found that:

- 23% received no paid professional development time
- 32% received only one to 12-hours a year of paid professional development time
- 47% had not engaged in curriculum development projects

- 52% read adult literacy-related materials less than 20-hours a year
- 65% stated that there was no teachers' room in their program where they could meet informally with colleagues
- 65% did not participate in peer coaching
- 65% had not participated in a study circle

The results of the study suggest that new and inexperienced teachers are not provided with opportunities to join a group of people who, as Wenger (n.d.) suggests, "share a concern or a passion for something that they do and learn how to do it better as they interact regularly."

Many teachers still go to workshops and work on their own time because of their commitment to the field, but Smith, Hofer, and Gillespie (2001) reported that some teachers received little or no information about what was happening in adult education at the federal or state level. Many were surprised to hear that a field of "adult education" exists at all. These teachers had no access to journals that service the field or resources that can be found on the internet. One new teacher described her orientation this way:

> When I was interviewed, I was hired on the spot. I was brought upstairs to the room I would be teaching in and I was shown this big cabinet. They opened up the cabinet and they said, "Here are the materials." That's it. That was my orientation. (p. 2)

The ALE Wiki offers the possibility of collaboration, and creates a space for participatory professional development to occur. In other words, one goal of the ALE Wiki is to provide a virtual community for a field that sometimes struggles to maintain existing physical communities. In the absence of a local community of practitioners, the virtual community can help isolated practitioners connect with the larger world of adult literacy education. Another goal is to provide an online environment where practitioners can easily find relevant research and professional wisdom. A third goal is for researchers and practitioners to discuss possible topics for research based on the kinds of questions and problems practitioners struggle with. By knocking down the wall between academic researchers and the teachers and students their research is intended to help, insightful and productive dialogues can occur.

BUILDING THE ADULT LITERACY EDUCATION WIKI

The ALE Wiki began as an idea passed back and forth between two adult literacy practitioners. After several weeks of phone calls and exploratory work, the first version of the ALE Wiki went on line on November 27, 2004 with one of the founders, David Rosen, serving as the Wiki organizer. The front page of the Wiki announced the intention of the site:

Welcome to the Adult Literacy Education (ALE) Wiki!
Learn about adult literacy education here, including English language learning, numeracy, and adult basic and secondary education. Add knowledge from your professional wisdom teaching adult learners, from research, or from your experience as an adult learner.

The slogan that was adopted for the Wiki was "We're workers, not lurkers!" This reflected the intended participatory ethos of the space. This was going to be a communal project, and everybody needed to roll up their sleeves and work together.

In December of 2004 in Sacramento, California, the ALE Wiki had its first public unveiling at the Meeting of the Minds: The National Adult Education Practitioner-Researcher Symposium. During the symposium, the Wiki organizers announced the creation of the site, and invited all who were interested to a postsymposium Wiki meeting. A dozen people attended this meeting and were shown the ALE Wiki in its rudimentary form. The presenters demonstrated how the Wiki worked and solicited ideas for what kind of things could go in a Wiki focused on adult literacy instruction. At that point in time, nobody in the group knew that much about editing in WIKI, and the best way to organize the information was an open question. People left the room giving their commitment to work together, but without a template for what the Wiki should look like.

From that point, the ALE Wiki grew quickly. First of all, information from the Meeting of Minds symposium was collected and uploaded, links were found to research reports and important Web pages, teacher writings, annotated bibliographies, and archived discussions from other electronic discussion lists. Topic areas started to emerge as raw information was organized and participants identified their own areas of interest. There are now 30 topic areas, including topics such as learner persistence, technology, numeracy, and project-based learning.

Over the history of the Wiki, some important decisions have been made that help the Wiki to grow in ways that allow it to be a place where people can share their mutual passion and interest in learning how to do it better. Six key choices will be described below.

The Virtual Presence of the Wiki Organizer

The home page of the ALE Wiki has a message from David Rosen, who has taken on the role of the primary Wiki organizer. The Wiki organizer facilitates the discussion list for active users and has taken the lead in promoting the Wiki at various conferences across the country. ALE Wiki participants have noted that having an identifiable Wiki organizer virtually present as part of the Wiki creates a different feeling for the space—it signals that the site is staffed by fellow practitioners and that it is not merely a portal or a cold repository for information about adult literacy education.

The Creation of a Discussion List for Active Contributors

As soon as the Wiki was created, a related electronic discussion list was created for people who were really committed to building the site (some gave themselves the nickname "the Wikiteers"). Membership on this list is controlled by the Wiki organizer, but it is open to anybody who becomes a topic area leader or who is otherwise very involved in the ALE Wiki. None of the people who started the group were experienced with using Wiki software, and members learned together how to get the Wiki up and running. From the beginning, participants were in communication about the nature of the Wiki (e.g., "What kinds of things should we be including?"), the structure (e.g., "How do I divide the topic area up?"), and how to use the Wiki editing software ("How do I format a page?"). Participants were striving to be what Davenport (2004) refers to as double agents, comfortable both with the content of the domain and the infrastructure of the on-line space. Being a worker, rather than a lurker, means taking responsibility for figuring out how the tools work. Early on, there were often messages along the lines of "Hey, check it out, I just figured out how we create a table of contents!" Later, the active participants had suggestions about the Wiki that were increasingly sophisticated (e.g., "The home page needs to be reformatted to reduce the amount of scrolling required to read it.") The electronic discussion list has continued to be the place where participants who are heavily involved in ALE Wiki activities meet to ask questions and get feedback on what they are working on.

The Use of Topic Area Leaders

Once the Wiki started to have content, it was organized into topic areas. From an initial 12 topic areas the site has grown to include 30. Some areas have remained steady, other have disappeared or merged with other topics. To promote the development and maintenance of each topic, participants with specific areas of expertise volunteered to keep an eye on topics they were particularly interested it. Initially the topic areas leaders were drawn from the small group of people who started the Wiki, but as the Wiki grew topic area leaders often came from people who had not been part of the initial group. Finding leaders for new topic areas, or replacing topic area leaders who have had to reduce the amount of time they spend on the Wiki, requires ongoing outreach. Announcements are made on related lists about the need for the topic area leader, and the Wiki itself has a list of topic area leaders. For example, on the current list of topic area leaders it reads, "Adult Learners' Self-Study—How about you?" This is a direct invitation to users of the Wiki to take on the topic area, and in effect, join the core working-group of active participants. Those that take on the roll of topic area leader often find that it enhances their ability to teach and learn in other venues. As an example of this, Bill Muth, coleader of the ALE Wiki section on correctional education noted (personal communication, January 21, 2007), "I was able to use the ALE Wiki summary [of correctional education] as a training document with teachers from within the Federal Bureau of Prisons." This is a case of a Wiki participant taking full advantage of the communal resources that are always evolving, and discussing the use of those resources with other active Wiki participants.

The Creation of the "Who's Here" Page

Another aspect of the Wiki that is designed to support the participatory ethos is the Who's Here page. In this space, registered users can upload descriptions of themselves and currently there are 69 listings. Typical listings describe the part of the Wiki the participants work on most actively (including being a topic area leader) and highlight what involvement the person has in adult basic education. This creates a space that is marked by the virtual presence of a community of participants— Wiki users who are interested can learn something about the people who are doing the work on the Wiki or who are participating in the online discussions.

Members who post personal information on the Who's Here page also use the space to comment on how they conceptualize the ALE Wiki itself. One member (McNaughton, 2007) notes, "I value the wealth of shared information on this website and the whole philosophy underpinning this very interactive demonstration of a 'community of practice' at work. I'm pleased to be here." Another member and topic area leader (Fedele, 2007) notes that, "I believe endeavors such as this ALE Wiki capture the spirit of democratic participation and innovation." Some briefs in the Who's Here section use evocative metaphors to describe the Wiki. One veteran member of the ALE Wiki (Craig, 2007) notes that she is fascinated by the Wiki as "a kind of organism for thinking." Another member (Narumanchi-Jackson, 2007) explains, "I have never participated in an online community—I do not consider listserves in this category—but my husband started a wiki recently. His description of the organic and evolutionary nature of Wiki both disturbs and intrigues me." Many other participants describe their interest in exploring and experiencing "this thing" that is the Wiki.

Proactive Mentoring as Part of Outreach

Starting with the very first meeting, the organizers of the ALE Wiki have taken every opportunity to mentor people's participation proactively in the Wiki. The Wiki organizer has provided personal technical assistance (over the phone and via e-mail) to people who are interested in participating but who feel they need help getting comfortable with the technology. At national conferences and regional workshops, adult education practitioners are introduced to the idea of the Wiki, shown examples of resources that are already on line, provided with guidance in how Wiki editing works, and given opportunities to make contributions in real-time. These workshops move beyond simply giving an overview to scaffolding participation in the Wiki. Even after 2 years, the description of the ALE Wiki remains the same—ALE Wiki event organizers explain that, "We are not experts on Wikis or online environments, so please join us in this grand learning experiment." This approach has helped the Wiki expand into new populations and may help in preventing the ALE Wiki from becoming insular. Wenger (1998a) notes that, "it is therefore important to pay as much attention to the boundaries of communities of practice as to their core and to make sure there are enough activities at the boundaries to renew learning." ALE Wiki organizers believe that questions posed by newcomers help the community to continue to learn.

Promoting the Wiki

In addition to offering workshops on getting involved, many active ALE Wiki participants make a conscious effort to promote the Wiki in different forums for adult education practitioners. These people can be described as "community evangelists" (Stuckey & Smith, 2004) who spend their own time and resources to promote the value of the Wiki to the field. Frequent postings about new content and subject areas in the ALE Wiki are made to other electronic discussion lists. At times topic area leaders use these other lists to request information that they will use to build up a certain topic area. These associated discussion lists have benefited from the ALE Wiki's ability to organize information and make it accessible to participants (e.g., discussion list archives are organized by discussion threads). At the same time, the ALE Wiki has benefited from being connected to the discussion lists, receiving membership and support from list subscribers. Active promotion of the Wiki has raised its profile in the field.

The ALE Wiki is promoted internally by means of the discussion list for active participants and by a page titled "Special Events." This page tracks ALE Wiki related events (e.g., conference presentations, journal articles devoted to the topic, references to the ALE Wiki in other contexts) and reinforces the idea that the ALE Wiki is something more than a repository for information.

THE ALE WIKI AS A VIRTUAL COMMUNITY OF PRACTICE

Given the description of the structure of the ALE Wiki, we can now return to the initial question—can the ALE Wiki be considered a virtual CoP? To answer this question, two key elements of CoPs must be examined—the nature of community membership and the type of learning activities that occur.

Types of Community Members

Although a CoP is made up of people who share a similar passion and interest in learning together, participation in community activities is not uniform across all community members. In their description of a CoP, Wenger, McDermott, and Snyder (2002) describe the following three levels of community membership:

1. The core group (10-15% of the whole community)
    This group takes the lead on projects and shapes discussions
2. The active group (15-20% of the whole community)
    This group is active, doing work and participating in discussions
3. Peripheral actors (the remainder)
    This group participates but may not be a highly visible presence in the community. Peripheral actors may have private conversations about what is happening, but do not contribute to the main conversations.

In addition to these groups, there is also an outside community, looking on and joining when interested. Similar levels of participation also mark the ALE Wiki: the following groups are associated with the Wiki.

The Core Group (Less than 1% of all Registered Users)

This group is made up of all topic area leaders and discussion list members. They directly affect the shape of the Wiki by formatting topic areas and by soliciting new information from other discussion lists. They remain engaged in conversations about what the goals of the ALE Wiki should be, act as "community evangelists" and express a clear value in being a member of the Wiki.

The Active Group (Less than 1% of all Registered Users)

This group is made up all registered users who make frequent contributions to the Wiki (uploading information or editing previously uploaded text at least once a month). They are involved in adding content and editing the format, but may not directly communicate their thoughts about the Wiki to others. They are involved in an implicit conversation about the Wiki (based on the material record of their choices) rather than an explicit one.

The Peripheral Actors (Impossible to Estimate the Total)

This group is made up of registered users who do not make frequent contributions, regular readers that are not registered, and participants in other discussion lists that are associated with the ALE Wiki. All of these types of participants share knowledge of the existence of the Wiki (and so are not complete outsiders) and benefit from information that is distributed as part of the ALE Wiki's outreach efforts (e.g., announcements on discussion lists about new research findings that are housed at the ALE Wiki space). They may also make comments on those discussion lists that spur ALE Wiki members to adjust the content or structure of the ALE Wiki. In addition, these peripheral actors have the potential for becoming active members.

Looking at the levels of membership using terms from the CoPs framework helps highlight the differences between these groups and in that sense the concept of CoPs is a useful heuristic. The core group can evaluate its own effectiveness by looking at the measures Wenger proposed— the creation of shared goals, a means to maintain a functioning space, and what capabilities it has produced. This same evaluation would not be an appropriate way to categorize the productivity of the other 99% of Wiki participants who are more likely to think of the Wiki as an online resource rather than a community. However, other aspects of CoPs might be helpful to examine movement between these groups, and this topic will be taken up next.

Types of Learning

As part of its desire to "learn how to do it better," the core group solicits help on the ALE Wiki discussion list and other national lists. Often people ask for this help in a conversational tone and format. For example, a recent posting asked, "Does anybody have examples of teacher-created assessments they'd be willing to share?" In order to build and maintain the Wiki the core group has increased their knowledge of topics such as:

- The scope and shape of the field of adult literacy instruction
- Specific content about adult literacy issues
- Wiki technology and editing
- How to maintain an online community space against vandals
- How to connect this space to other spaces

Other learning activities are more elaborate in terms of participant structure. For example, the professional development topic leader is also a moderator of a national discussion list on the same topic, and she has used this overlap to help her to develop a matrix of professional development models. She began by posting a question to the list she moderates, asking for input about types of professional development. She then took that information and uploaded a draft matrix of types of professional development to the Wiki. The core group of the ALE Wiki was able to discuss the matrix, and then follow-up conversations took place on the national list. By taking this approach, the core group, the active group, and peripheral actors were all involved in the learning activity.

The ALE Wiki also has some sections that are dedicated to supporting the participation of interested newcomers. The "Directions" page contains information about editing (text formatting) and there is a frequently asked questions (FAQ) page that poses questions that walk readers from a basic understanding of the Wiki to information about adding new features to the Wiki. Below are questions taken directly from the FAQ section:

- (1.1) What is a Wiki?
- (1.2) What is the Adult Literacy Education Wiki?
- (1.3) What can I do here?
- (1.4) How do I add my own ideas, experience, resources, research?
- (1.5) What are the rules about copying material into the ALE Wiki?

- (1.7) What is the ALE Wiki netiquette?
- (1.14) What is an ALE Wiki area leader? What does this person do?
- (1.15) I want to add a new topic area. How do I do that?

There is also a glossary section in the Wiki that contains explanations of terms used in the Wiki, covering adult literacy education terminology (e.g., contextualized curriculum, portfolio assessment), computing technology (e.g., server, HTML) and Wiki-specific terms (e.g., broken link, threaded e-mail discussions). The directions, FAQ, and glossary combine with more hands-on mentoring to form a significant resource for participants who wish to become more involved. This structure has the potential of helping participants move toward the core of the group through the type of legitimate peripheral participation (LPP) that marks a CoP (Lave & Wenger, 1991). A new participant might hear about the ALE Wiki from a discussion list, surf over to review the current contents of the Wiki, send an e-mail to ALE Wiki organizers about a topic that is missing, receive an invitation to become a topic leader and get mentoring in setting up the page.

However, given the number of registered users (almost 700), there is a built-in limit to the number of these kinds of opportunities. While a large number of participants can always move from being peripheral actors to being active community members (by uploading content or editing entries), only a small number of people can move into the core group of participants. This is due to the fact that membership in the core group is typically grounded in being a topic area leader and there are only a small number of topic areas. For this reason, a distinction must be made between the generalized potential for LPP (Lave & Wenger, 1991) and the actual opportunities presented to any one member. It may be that structures like the ALE Wiki reach the limit when it comes to the scalability of LPP as a learning activity. If this is the case, the ALE Wiki will have to look at other models of facilitating the learning of peripheral actors.

FUTURE TRENDS

Using the concept of CoPs to analyze the ALE Wiki raises a number of questions about the future of the project. The three discussed below seem increasingly important as the ALE Wiki moves into its third year of existence.

The Tension of Continued Expansion

As noted above, over the years there has been a steady increase in the number of topic areas covered by the ALE Wiki. If there is added growth and the Wiki continues to use the same organizational structure, this will mean that there are increasing numbers of topic area leaders joining the core group. There is the possibility that the Wiki could be a victim of its own success, in that the core group of committed participants could become so large that it can no longer function efficiently. Wenger (1998b) notes that,

> Defining a joint enterprise is a process, not a static agreement. It produces relations of accountability that are not just fixed constraints or norms. These relations are manifested not as conformity but as the ability to negotiate actions as accountable to an enterprise. (p. 82)

With too large a core group it may be difficult to manage these relations of accountability and almost impossible to negotiate a working consensus on the goals of the Wiki itself. If the Wiki grows to a certain size, the core may not be able to sustain itself as a CoP.

At the same time, there is a danger in creating new guidelines for membership into the core group, as this action will create a hierarchical structure that runs counter to the Wiki's participatory ethos. In addition, reducing or limiting the number of potential topic areas may cause the Wiki and the community to stagnate. To continue to thrive, the Wiki needs to strike a balance between supporting growth and maintaining functionality. In other words, the ALE Wiki needs to find its own online model of sustainable development.

Struggling to Provide Definitive Answers

Recently there have been an increased number of requests to have a section in each area of the ALE Wiki that has answers to commonly asked questions (e.g., "What are some proven ways to help students with limited English proficiency increase their English literacy skills?"). Depending upon the nature of the question, providing short and authoritative answers may or may not be feasible. Many aspects of adult literacy education do not have a research base, and the professional wisdom may be limited. Even with a large group of experienced educators online, it may not be possible to provide the kinds of definitive answers people are looking for. This is not unique to the ALE Wiki. Bradshaw, Powell, and Terrell (2004, as cited in Rheingold, 2000) suggest that "online communities are perfectly suited to generating ideas and exploring positions, but less good at achieving consensus or making joint decisions" (p. 199). To date the ALE Wiki has provided information about what others have said about a given topic and members have not attempted to make the kinds of joint decisions necessary to provide definitive answers about instructional questions. As the size of the Wiki grows, and more informal users want to take advantage of the resources, the Wiki will have to negotiate the tension of being "credible, professional and relevant for busy practitioners, yet remaining informal and friendly" (Stuckey & Smith, 2004, p. 162).

At the same time, an increase in the number of pages devoted to questions and short answers may change the nature of ALE Wiki participation. If people start to come to the Wiki mainly for quick answers to focused questions, they may not engage in the kind of exploration the Wiki is built to provide. If there is an increase in the number of peripheral actors that have no interest in moving into the active or core group, the potential for LPP will wither. There is a danger that the relationship between the core group and the peripheral actors could change from potential fellow community members to authors and audience. This issue may be an inherent part of structures that combine a core working-group with more fluid or ambiguous participation structures.

A Limited Ability to Provide Mentoring

Although the ALE Wiki has done hands-on outreach and mentoring at conferences and workshops, it remains to be seen how effective it is in facilitating entry to adult educators who find themselves isolated from the field. The online resources noted above (directions, FAQ, and the glossary) are helpful, but using them may require a certain level of comfort with both the content area and the technology. Experienced teachers can find help with the technical aspects of the Wiki, and newer teachers with a technical background can find support about the education content, but new teachers with little technological background may struggle to participate. The Wiki organizer and the core group members provide mentoring on a voluntary basis, which limits the number of teachers that can receive direct support. Future mentoring must move beyond the core group to recruit mentors from members of the active group.

Furthermore, a concern remains about those teachers who do not even recognize that there is a field of adult education. These teachers might come across the Wiki while trying to find the answer to a question (e.g., what is meant by learner persistence?), but they may not stay to explore beyond that. If a user enters the Wiki through a topic area, rather than from the home page, how readily do they get a sense of the Wiki as a community that welcomes their participation?

CONCLUSION

Can the ALE Wiki be considered a virtual CoP, and what does it matter for participants if it can be? The answer to that question perhaps depends upon which aspect of the ALE Wiki is being considered. As noted above, the ALE Wiki has a complicated participant structure, with a core group of organizers, an active group that has a looser affiliation with the site and countless people who have a passing relationship with the site (as unregistered users, surfers, or members of associated discussion lists). Stuckey and Smith (2004) explain that when trying to identify whether or not a group of people is a CoP, "One's view of the matter depends significantly on one's role or place in a community. People near the core of a community experience the community features more readily, while people on the periphery may only see a loose network" (p. 151). In the case of the ALE Wiki, the core group of ALE Wiki organizers appears to benefit from having a shared passion and a unifying commitment to learning how to better support the functioning of the Wiki. They have managed to negotiate a common goal for the Wiki, to create functioning agreements that keep the group cohesive, and have facilitated the uploading of a tremendous amount of information about adult literacy education. These accomplishments would seem to qualify the core group as a CoP. The size of both the active group (registered participants who make frequent contributions) and the peripheral actors (unregistered users and others) make it difficult to assess how they might feel about whether or not they are in a CoP. It is more than likely the large group of unregistered users and other peripheral actors see the ALE Wiki as an online resource, rather than a community that they belong to.

The value of trying to determine if the ALE Wiki is a virtual CoP may be that it will help the core group of organizers to frame and address questions about the Wiki itself. For example, the concept of levels of membership can be used to make distinctions between types of actors. This is no small matter, since as Hildreth and Kimble (2004) point out, "while the pervasiveness of Internet technologies has enabled the creation of networked communities, they have also made it increasingly difficult for people to know the scope and range of their 'virtual' social networks" (p. xii). Rather than trying to draw a map of the network, ALE Wiki organizers can instead think about the levels of membership, how participation needs to be supported at each level, and how to support participants from moving one membership category to another. This includes creating opportunities for LPP and other forms of mentoring.

In this regard, using the concept of CoPs to analyze the ALE Wiki may be more productive than attempting to see the ALE Wiki as an affinity space, described by Gee (2005) as a space where people interact. Gee believes that focusing on the space, rather than membership in a community, allows people to avoid possibly contentious discussions about who is and who is not a member. This might be true, but membership signifiers and defined positions (e.g., Wikiteers, topic area leaders, registered users) "may well serve to be an attractant to community members looking for professionalism and quality and it certainly makes clear the pathways for moving into the centre of the community" (Stuckey & Smith, 2004, p. 60). With the current structure of the ALE Wiki, those defined positions are in place, but it remains to be seen if moving to the center of the community is something large numbers of Wiki participants want to do.

REFERENCES

Adult Literacy Education Wiki. (2007). *Main page.* Retrieved on January 21, 2007, from wiki.literacytent.org/index/php/Main_Page

Bradshaw, P., Powell, S., & Terrell, I. (2004). Building a community of practice: Technological and social implications for a distributed team. In P. Hildreth & C. Kimble (Eds.), *Knowledge networks: Innovation through communities of practice* (pp. 184-201). Hershey, PA: Idea Group.

Craig, M. (2007). *Who's Here profile.* Retrieved on January 21, 2007, from http://wiki.literacytent.org/index.php/Michele_Craig

Davenport, E. (2004). Double agents: Visible and invisible work in an online community of practice. In P. Hildreth & C. Kimble (Eds.), *Knowledge networks: Innovation through communities of practice* (pp. 256-266). Hershey, PA: Idea Group.

Fedele, M. (2007). *Who's Here profile.* Retrieved January 21, 2007, from http://wiki.literacytent.org/index.php/Mariann_Fedele

Gee, J. (2005). Semiotic social spaces and affinity spaces: From the Age of Mythology to today's schools. In D. Barton & K. Tusting (Eds.), *Beyond communities of practice* (pp. 214-232). London: Cambridge University Press.

Hildreth, P., & Kimble, C. (2004). Preface. In P. Hildreth & C. Kimble (Eds.), *Knowledge networks: Innovation through communities of practice* (pp. viii-xxi). Hershey, PA: Idea Group.

Kruidenier, J. (2002). *Research-based principles for adult basic education reading Instruction.* Washington, DC: The National Institute for Literacy.

Lave, J., & Wenger, E. (1991). *Situated learning.* London: Cambridge University Press.

Lea, M. (2005). "Communities of Practice" in higher education: Useful heuristic or educational model? In D. Barton & K. Tusting (Eds.), *Beyond communities of practice* (pp. 180-197). London: Cambridge University Press.

Leonard, L., & Leonard, P. (2003). The continuing trouble with collaboration: Teachers talk. *Current Issues in Education*, 6(15). Retrieved October 15, 2007, from http://cie.asu.edu/volume6/number15.

Lesser, E., & Fontaine, M. (2004). Overcoming knowledge barriers with communities of practice: Lessons learned through practical experience. In P. Hildreth & C. Kimble (Eds.), *Knowledge networks: Innovation through communities of practice* (pp. 14-23). Hershey, PA: Idea Group.

Narumanchi-Jackson, V. (2007). *Who's Here Profile.* Retrieved January 21, 2007, from http://wiki.literacytent.org/index.php /Varshna_Narumanchi-Jackson.

McNaughton, P. (2007). Who's Here profile. Retrieved January 21, 2007, from http://wiki.literacytent.org/index.php/Pauline_McNaughton

Rheingold, H. (2000). *The virtual community: Homesteading on the electronic frontier (revised edition).* Boston: MIT Press.

Sabatini, J., Daniels, M., Ginsburg, L, Limeul, K., Russell, M., & Stites, R. (2000). *Teacher perspectives on the adult education profession: National survey findings about an emerging profession.* Philadelphia: The National Center on Adult Literacy.

Senge, P. (1990). *The fifth discipline: The art and practice of the learning organization.* New York: Currency/Doubleday.

Smith, C., Hofer, J., & Gillespie, M. (2001). The working conditions of the adult literacy teachers: Preliminary findings from the NCSALL staff development study. *Focus on Basics, 4*(D), 1-7.

Stuckey, B., & Smith, J. (2004). Building sustainable communities of practice. In P. Hildreth & C. Kimble (Eds.), *Knowledge networks: Innovation through communities of practice* (pp. 150-164). Hershey, PA: Idea Group.

United States Government. (2007). *The What Works Clearinghouse.* Retrieved January 21, 2007, from http://www.whatworks.ed.gov

Wenger, E. (1998a). Communities of practice: Learning as a social system. *Systems Thinker.* Retrieved September 16, 2006, from http://www.co-i-l-com/coil/ knowledge-garden/cop/lss.shtml

Wenger, E. (1998b). *Communities of practice: Learning, meaning and identity.* London: Cambridge University Press.

Wenger, E. (n.d). *Communities of practice: A brief introduction.* Retrieved September 16, 2006 from, http://www.ewenger.com/theory /communities_of_practice_intro.htm.

Wenger, E., McDermott, R., & Snyder, W. (2002). *Cultivating communities of practice.* Cambridge, MA: Harvard Business School Press.

CHAPTER 17

IMPLICATIONS OF A VIRTUAL LEARNING COMMUNITY MODEL FOR DESIGNING DISTRIBUTED COMMUNITIES OF PRACTICE IN HIGHER EDUCATION

Richard A. Schwier and Ben K. Daniel

The metaphor of virtual learning communities can be used to inform the design of distributed communities of practice (CoPs) in higher education learning environments. In this chapter, constituent elements drawn from a model of virtual learning communities are presented. These elements are elaborated to provide advice to instructors, instructional designers, researchers, and community architects, including how to enhance trust, a sense of history, identity, mutuality, plurality, autonomy, participation, trajectory, technology, learning, reflection, intensity, social engagement and communication. The chapter concludes with a discussion of fundamental elements of virtual learning communities that have direct relevance to the design of distributed CoPs in higher education.

Communities of Practice: Creating Learning Environments for Educators,
Volume 2, pp. 347–365
Copyright © 2008 by Information Age Publishing

347

INTRODUCTION

The central premise of this chapter is that virtual learning communities (VLCs) are related to CoPs, particularly when CoPs are distributed. There is much to be learned from VLCs that can be applied to support the design of distributed communities of practice (DCoPs) in higher education (HE). Why? Because at the heart of it, both are concerned with learning, both are built on the assumption that collaboration is critical to their existence, and both face the difficult challenge of nurturing learning in artificial and sometimes hostile contexts.

The purpose here is not to take the reader through an exhaustive comparison of the two types of communities. Instead, this chapter will proffer an abbreviated discussion of their similar features, and then explore what it means for practitioners. What can be taken from an understanding of VLCs that can be directly applied to building and maintaining DCoPs in HE?

Theoretical Underpinnings

The observations offered in this chapter are largely drawn from a 5-year research program that investigated the fundamental characteristics of formal VLCs—the kinds of communities most often associated with online courses in universities. The research program employed a wide array of methods to isolate catalysts, emphases, and elements exhibited by online learning communities, as they emerged in graduate courses and seminars, as well as in problem-based learning environments. At various stages, the research used grounded theory transcript analysis of structured online discussions and e-mail, an array of social network analysis tools, Thurstone analysis and Bayesian belief network analysis and modeling in an attempt to build a reliable map of the characteristics of online communities in formal learning environments, and to begin the process of validating the model (Marra, Moore, & Klimczak, 2004; Mazur, 2004; Rourke & Anderson, 2004; Schwier & Daniel, 2007; Strauss & Corbin, 1998; Thurstone, 1927).

For the purpose of this discussion, a community is a group of people who relate socially to each other to achieve some common goals (Cox & Osguthorpe, 2003). These relationships often reinforce one another, and they are neither serial nor isolated. Fundamental to this notion of community is a measure of commitment to a set of shared values, norms, and meanings, a shared history and identification within a particular culture. A virtual community can also be compared to a temporal community. A temporal community resides in a fixed location and its members usually meet, talk, and develop knowledge of each other. A virtual community, on the other hand, is a composite of people, the space where they interact, their goals, and the technologies that they use to communicate, collaborate, and work together to achieve their goals as a community. In a virtual community, members might not even be aware of each other's backgrounds.

In practice, there has not been widespread adoption of learning communities in online courses in HE. Traditional pedagogy appears to drive the design of courses, making it difficult to determine the actual contributions of collaboration in VLCs (Naidu, 2003). E-courses have not necessarily included the kind of deliberate and sustained collaboration needed for communities to emerge, as they are often constrained by presumptions of traditional face-to-face pedagogy and by the structures imposed by commercial course management systems, among many other constraining factors (Reeves, Herrington, & Oliver, 2004; Romiszowski, 2004). At the same time, there is growing attention in the literature to the design of collaborative online learning environments (e.g., Cox & Osguthorpe, 2003; Hung & Chen, 2002; Kirschner, Strijbos, Kreijns, & Beers, 2004; Milheim, 2006; Uribe, Klein, & Sullivan, 2003) and to theory and models for specific learning contexts (e.g., Barab & Duffy, 2000; Garrison, Anderson, & Archer, 2003; Gunawardena, Ortegano-Layne, Carabajal, Frechette, Lindemann, & Jennings, 2006; Hiltz & Goldman, 2005). But to date, the research in VLCs, and distance learning generally has not yielded a coherent understanding of formal online learning environments, at least partly due to the paucity of quality research from which to draw valid conclusions (Bernard, Abrami, Lou, & Borokhovski, 2004).

Virtual Learning Communities and Distributed Communities of Practice

Virtual communities take various forms, most of which are organized around temporal community models. There are fundamentally two kinds of virtual communities considered here—VLCs and DCoPs. These two kinds of virtual communities share certain elements in common, such as common goals, shared understanding, trust and adherence to a common set of social protocols and so forth. The remainder of this chapter will concentrate on shared features of VLCs and DCoPs. A VLC is a group of people who gather in cyberspace with the intention of pursuing learning goals, while a DCoP refers to a group of geographically distributed individuals who are informally bound together by shared expertise and shared interests or work (Daniel, O'Brien, & Sarkar, 2003). Such individuals depend on information and communication technologies (ICTs) to connect to each other. One difference between DCoPs and VLCs

is the nature of membership identity. Individuals in VLCs in HE are often brought together in formal environments that are externally defined and the common area of interest is assigned to the participants, whereas the identities of individuals in DCoPs are defined to a greater extent by their shared interest and expertise. Although all virtual communities have an element of learning in them, not every community can be referred to as a learning community. A learning community implies that members have explicit goals involving learning. One assumption is that a community taken as a whole is greater than the sum of its parts (i.e., highly skilled or knowledgeable individuals in a community are a necessary but not a sufficient condition for a community to become a "learning community"). Knowledgeable or experienced individuals in a learning community join those who are less knowledgeable so that members grow mutually as a community.

Successful DCoPs are organized around the needs of their members and as such, exhibit a wide range of sizes, structures, and means of communication. The notion of DCoPs used here is built upon the

Table 17.1.   Key Features of Virtual Learning Communities and Distributed Communities of Practice

Virtual Learning Communities (VLCs)	Distributed Communities of Practice (DCoP)
Membership is explicit and identities are generally known	Membership may or may not be made explicit
Participation is often required	Participation is often voluntary
High degree of individual awareness(who is registered in the course or activity)	Low degree of individual awareness
Explicit set of social protocols for interaction	Implicit and implied set of social protocols for interactions
Formal learning goals	Informal learning goals
Possibly diverse backgrounds	Common subject-matter
Low shared understanding of domain	High shared understanding of domain
Loose sense of identity	Strong sense of identity
Strict distribution of responsibilities	Less formal distribution of responsibilities
Easily disbanded once established	Less easily disbanded once established
Low level of trust	Reasonable level of trust
Life span determined by extent to which goals are achieved, or externally defined by an educational institution	Life span determined by the instrumental/expressive value the community provides to its members
Preplanned enterprise and fixed goals	A joint enterprise as understood and continually renegotiated by its members

understanding of the Lave and Wenger (1991) theory of CoPs. While traditional learning communities are situation specific and tend to have clearly defined memberships, DCoP are task and goal focused and people normally engage in discourse as a need arises (Johnson, 2001).

DCoP in HE are not well researched but they are becoming critical in promoting and sustaining effective interdisciplinary collaboration in HE and building partnerships between HE and other sectors such as government and the private sector, which are often important to enhancing research and institutional development. DCoP in HE essentially emphasize the fading boundaries between traditional HE and distance education contexts and breaking down the distinctions between formal and informal learning environments. Evidence of DCoPs in HE in this regard can be seen in flexible learning models, blended learning environments and computer-mediated informal learning groups adopted in many institutions of higher learning around the world.

Unlike other kinds of learning communities, DCoPs can be easily supported in HE with existing and emerging technologies for learning and research, especially technologies such as social software and other kinds of groupware that are used for group communications and collaborative activities in the learning and teaching process. Since members of a DCoP can be geographically distributed and diverse in both individual and organizational cultures, various technologies can help them connect with each other. In addition, initial face-to-face meetings are often beneficial for initiating interpersonal engagement, and helping members become aware of the diversity of the group and build rapport to lubricate collaboration and learning.

DCoPs can serve as a baseline for connecting people with similar interests, and they often draw individuals from different training and professional backgrounds, and who are distributed in terms of time and space. DCoPs are bounded, but may be exclusively virtual or blended to included distributed and occasional interpersonal engagement. In either case, for a DCoP to evolve it requires individuals who are geographically, organizationally, culturally distributed to become aware of each other and build connections among members of the group. Such individuals normally share common interests and are interested in connecting to others through the use of ICT. The fundamental benefits of DCoPs can be described as follows:

- sharing data, information, and knowledge
- connecting people-to-people, people-to-systems, and systems-to-systems to help people do their work more efficiently and effectively regardless of time and space

- creating individual and organizational awareness of members' identities, members' knowledge, and members' awareness of which members possess valuable knowledge
- facilitating the creation of a community knowledge repository and tools for engagement, knowledge deliberations, and negotiation, stimulating the capture of new ideas and finding of information
- helping individuals build useful social networks with others in their fields of interest
- helping link isolated geographical, organizational, professional, and linguistics cultures
- ensuring that knowledge is easily accessible to those who need it and can act on it effectively and efficiently to produce desirable results

These benefits enable participants to systematically share data, information and knowledge and also build tools to enhance knowledge collection, aggregation and dissemination under distributed circumstances. In addition, the notion of DCoPs provides techniques, tools and processes for identifying knowledge gaps, and leveraging existing knowledge. With the application of DCoPs in business organizations and learning communities, a web of social networks can emerge that can sharpen the flow of information and knowledge within a community and promote the development of social capital.

VLCs are closely related to DCoPs in many ways. For example, both emphasize a social constructivist epistemology and they may both have learning goals. However, VLCs and DCoPs also have considerable differences in membership, goals and social norms (see Table 17.1). Ultimately, it can be suggested that the most important characteristic shared by VLCs and DCoPs is collaboration. Studies have demonstrated that collaborative learning enhances active exchange of ideas within small groups and increases interest among the participants while also promoting critical thinking (Garrison, 1997; Hiltz, 1998). Heinrichs (2003) observed that learning environments with rich interaction and collaboration increase the chances for deep learning. Such environments will create meaningful learning environments by sharing and employing what students know in the assessment of learning (Pellegrino, 2001).

A MODEL OF VIRTUAL LEARNING COMMUNITIES

This chapter presents a brief overview of a model of VLCs in HE that has been developed and tested over several years. The chapter emphasizes the implications of the model for practice, but does not elaborate on the details of the model.[1]

The VLC model is divided into three separate areas of concern: catalysts, emphases, and elements of community. The center feature of the model of VLCs, labeled "catalysts," underscores the fundamental importance of communication to virtual communities (Figure 17.1). As a catalyst, communication serves to energize each of the characteristics of communities and interactions among them. Communication is the central concern of virtual communities, and communities only exist so long as communication is available to participants. As prerequisite to meaningful communication, participants must first be aware of others in the group, and this is typically accomplished through interaction and observation. But for community to emerge, the group must move beyond simple awareness and interaction to engagement and alignment (after Wenger, 1998). In a VLC engagement may vary dramatically among members, however to become a contributing member of a community, some kind of engagement has to happen. When individuals engage a virtual community and as commitment to the group increases, some measure of alignment occurs. Individuals align personal, private purposes with the collective, public purposes of the community. But personal and community alignment is reciprocal. An individual's personal intentions influence the community, and the community influences the personal intentions of individuals.

The model also describes various emphases that can exist or coexist in VLCs. VLCs might emphasize building interpersonal connections among people (relationship), create an online version of a geographic location (place), provide a place for reflection and self-examination (reflection), provide a gathering place to conduct or support ritual (ceremony), or emphasize sharing knowledge and opinion (ideas). These emphases overlap in practice; any particular VLC might feature more than one emphasis.

Thirteen elements of community encircle the catalysts and emphases: history, identity, mutuality, plurality, autonomy, participation, trajectory, technology, reflection, intensity, learning, trust, and social protocols. These 13 elements (see Figure 17.1) illustrate the idea that communities are complex and multidimensional, and each element carries corresponding implications for supporting learning in virtual learning environments (VLEs).

IMPLICATIONS OF THE VLC MODEL FOR BUILDING DISTRIBUTED COMMUNITIES OF PRACTICE

The VLC model was originally built to try to understand how communities function in formal learning environments. The research that informs

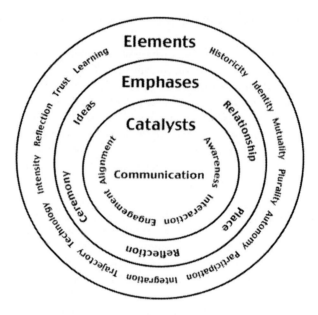

Figure 17.1.   Model of formal virtual learning
communities.

the model was conducted in postgraduate courses in HE exclusively. It can be argued that the model maps onto informal learning environments and DCoPs fairly closely, but support for this argument is intuitive rather than empirical. There are more similarities than differences between DCoPs and VLCs; in fact, from a finer-grained analysis and classification, one can argue that a DCoP is actually one type of VLC. In addition, both environments confront collaborative learning among adults, an elusive yet powerful construct. Given these assumptions, the following section offers advice on building communities, managing communities as they evolve, and taking advantage of the characteristics of communities we identified in the model to build DCoPs in HE.

Advice for Building Communities

It is probably folly to think that we can actually build a community—construct it out of the whole cloth of a formal class or a group of employees—any more than we can create a forest by planting some trees. But it is possible to deliberately put things in place that will encourage communities to spring up, and to nurture them once they do. Bryce-Davis

(2001) identified five critical features for building VLCs that she called rules, roles, rounds, rituals, and ringers and each makes an important contribution to DCoPs. Rules and roles are transparent. Learning communities require the establishment of rules to govern the operation of the community and articulate protocols for engagement with others. How restrictive the rules of engagement are will probably significantly influence the personality of the community. Similarly, roles help define the activities carried out in learning communities and set out expectations for participation.

The notions of rounds, ringers, and rituals are important but often overlooked pedagogical elements for developing effective learning environments of any type, but particularly for DCoPs. Rounds refer to the iterations of events in the community. In a course, for example, it might be useful to set up several events that follow a common pattern, and because there are "rounds" of communication, it permits participants to develop skill and comfort with this type of interaction. It is often the case that participants require several events before they learned how to perform successfully in online learning environments. Similarly, in DCoPs, it is important to make learning events routine expectations, and allow the practice of eliciting and sharing tacit knowledge to become part of the normal course of events in a work environment. In effect, by using several rounds of events in online learning communities, it allows time for rituals to be developed and used. Rituals can be thought of as the ceremony around the routines in learning communities, and they can be as simple as the way people are greeted when they enter a virtual space or as complex as a set of procedures for moderating a planned event. Rituals are the ways we make what we do familiar, comforting and predictable, so they play a very important part in all communities. One useful ritual in HE courses is to have a participant take responsibility for conducting a discussion, summarize each topic when the discussion is completed, and to post the notes to the group in a public Wiki. Then, each member of the class is encouraged to review the summary and edit it. This happens every week, and always on the same days. This little ritual has the effect of making the discussions transparent, promoting reflection, and also propelling the class from one topic to the next throughout the entire term.

The notion of ringers in courses has also proved to be useful. Ringers are the surprise events, the small rocks tossed into the glassy surface of smoothly operating communities. A fresh, unexpected or unusual activity can also disrupt the established patterns and expectations just enough to renew interest. For example, a surprise guest in a chat room can be a ringer, as can a contentious statement from a participant. Using ringers reinforces the idea that complacency is a natural enemy of successful communities. If participants become tired or lazy in DCoPs, the community quickly loses its vitality. Ringers can be planned or serendipitous, but in either case, they keep a virtual community awake. Ringers can be most effective if they flow naturally from the activities of the group, rather than feel contrived and artificial. Participants may feel manipulated by artificial ringers, and may feel resentful, so attention should be paid to building interventions that are authentic to the task or purpose of the group.

Advice for Dealing With Communities Over Time

Communities are not static; they shift, morph, and undulate, sometimes in unpredictable ways. But they do also move through a fairly predictable series of changes over time, and it is useful to think about how the evolution of communities can influence how we operate with them. Misanchuk, Anderson, Craner, Eddy, and Smith (2000) suggested that learning communities evolve from simple cohorts by employing "increasing levels of student interaction and commitment" (p. 1). In DCoPs, this interaction is characterized by different ways of working together, and participants move through discussion to cooperation and collaboration as the community takes form.

Essentially, communities seem to move through stages of growth, maturation, and disintegration. Architects of DCoPs should plan to be more directive during the earlier stages of community growth, and relax control as the community matures. After several meetings and opportunities for engagement and after comfort levels among participants start to rise, the community will begin to make its own rules, revise protocols to fit its needs and monitor the environment without the intervention of an external leader/moderator. But a leader also needs to plan for communities to die (Gongla & Rizzuto, 2004). How does one disassemble a community that has been vibrant, and that has become an important part of the lives of participants? In formal VLCs, this is typically handled very abruptly. A class comes to an end, and participants are ushered out of the community unceremoniously following a final examination. But in DCoPs, the process seldom has a predicted end date; therefore, the process of bringing an end to a community will require the deliberate intervention of a leader. This process should be managed sensitively. In learning communities, participants can often grieve the loss of connection with other participants, and even build alternative methods to keep relationships alive long after the community has died (or has been killed).

The formative stage in the life of a VLC is characterized by the attraction of new members. During the formative stage, the identity of the community is malleable, and participants are typically somewhat tentative as they try out communicating and making connections with other community members. A mature stage of life in the virtual community is ultimately achieved once the purpose, shape, and operation of the community are settled. At this point, the leader does not have to play a central a role in negotiating the purpose and monitoring the activities of members. Ultimately, most virtual communities will be challenged to undertake a metamorphosis and become a new entity with a focus that is different from the original conception of what the VLC would become. As a DCoP passes through these various stages, it is reasonable to expect that the strategies appropriate for intentionally using them for learning will also change.

Advice for Taking Advantage of Community Elements

Each of the elements identified in the model has implications for designing DCoPs that emphasize learning. The remainder of this chapter will consider each of these elements in turn, and discuss some of the practical notions that correspond with each.

Historicity

Communities are stronger when they share history and culture. Conversely, they are weak when they are based on general interests and abstract ideas. The quality of participation depends on individual and shared commitment or relevance of the substance of the community. Commitment depends on shared values in the community. At minimum, the strength of the commitment need only be sufficient to maintain participation in the group, but stronger commitment generally leads to the development of stronger communities. To foster historicity, a leader should pay attention to individual contributions, and even keep notes on them. Later, the leader can make specific references to what participants have done in the past, and make their stories part of the community culture. Explicit mention of the culture, value, and context of the virtual community is important in order to shape the perception of the participants and to help them appreciate that they are members of something significant. Where possible, it is also important to make public the history of the community. If a repository or library of resources is built from what is learned from participants, a public record can be made available that acknowledges individual contributions.

Identity

Communities foster a sense of shared identity. Successful VLCs need to have boundaries—an identity or recognized focus. Use team-building exercises, develop community logos, and offer paraphernalia to members, and publicly acknowledge accomplishments by the group and individual members within the community. Periodically review the focus or purpose of the community, and outline the requirements and rituals accompanying membership in the community.

Mutuality

Communities emerge and are maintained by interdependence and reciprocity. While virtual communities are built around central themes, ideas or purposes, the organizing principles are not externally imposed. Participants often construct purposes, intentions, and the protocol for interaction and if this is to happen, a leader must encourage and facilitate the group decisions without taking over responsibility for them. A leader can include group exercises, assignments, and activities that require each member to contribute to a final product. Ask leading questions that encourage members of the community to invest in concerns held by other members, and to share ideas and possible solutions.

Plurality

Communities draw much of their vitality from "intermediate associations" such as families, schools, clubs, churches, and other peripheral groups. Encourage membership and participation from, and association with, groups related to the learning focus of the organization. These might include business associations, professional associations, community service groups, or online discussion groups in other countries exploring similar issues. The purpose is to expand the collective field of experience on which the CoP can draw.

Autonomy

Within the emphasis on group identity, particularly in corporate settings, it is important that communities respect and protect individual identity. Individuals should interact with each other and have the capacity to conduct discourse freely and meaningfully, or withdraw from discourse without penalty. In DCoPs, there may be a corporate expectation, or even a requirement, that members participate in developing a CoP. At the same time, interaction should be based on influence among participants rather than power relationships, in order to create an open community and promote the level of candor and trust necessary to create a robust community. A leader should foster individual expression and comment explicitly on its value. One approach is to establish a protocol for respectful communication and reach consensus in the group about how engagement will be conducted. It is also possible to create strategies for settling disputes or inappropriate behavior collectively, prior to any infractions.

Participation

Communities are by their very nature social entities. Social participation in the community, especially participation that promotes self-determination, supports autonomy and sustains the community should be encouraged. Participants can be encouraged to think about the level of intimacy appropriate for any relationship with another participant or with the group. Anonymity is possible, but as the sense of community develops, it is unlikely that a participant would choose to remain anonymous, and ultimately anonymity does not advance the agenda of a CoP. Members of the group should be encouraged to shape agendas, give guidance to new community members, and promote opportunities for established members to go outside the boundaries of the learning event or focus.

Trajectory

Learning communities are not static; they create movement in a direction. Learning communities "open trajectories of participation that place engagement in its practice in the context of a valued future" (Wenger, 1998, p. 215). In order to employ trajectory of participation, identify the direction of learning in the group and make it public, so that members can measure their participation against the expected outcomes of the group. Ask participants to describe ways they will use what they have learned in the community in the future. Conduct "visioning" exercises to determine new initiatives to be undertaken by the community.

It is important to note that every member of a community may exhibit a different trajectory of participation, and any individual's trajectory may change dramatically over time. From the organization's point of view, it is the collective trajectory of the CoP that holds the most interest, and it is a composite metric of the individual participants in the group

Technology

In virtual communities, technology facilitates the development of community, but it can also inhibit its growth. Technology is the means for bringing together individuals who might otherwise not engage one another. It acts as the conduit for discourse among participants, and it is the medium of engagement that binds the community together. At the same time, technology can be a barrier to communication and can exclude some people from the community who cannot afford or use communications technology. It is important in a DCoP to employ technology that allows meaningful and authentic communication, and which is easy for participants to use. IP-based video media allow for synchronous communication that is engaging and inexpensive, but a variety of synchronous media permit relatively uninhibited conversations to happen that feel natural to participants.

Learning

Learning is a central element of VLCs and DCoPs of practice, although the nature of the learning can be broadly defined and contextual. For the purpose of defining elements of community, it is not important whether learning is focused, lasting, substantial, educationally sound, associated with any particular curricula, or entirely serendipitous. The point is that people in a virtual community want to learn, and the purposes to which that learning may be put are irrelevant to the legitimacy of the community. That is not to say that learning in a VLC or DCoP is not purposeful; it should be, but users can define the purposes and the purposes may not fit traditional ideas of what constitutes acceptable learning. In a recent work, we have elaborated our understanding of learning in the context of VLCs (Daniel, Schwier, & Ross, 2007); however, the large grain of learning as a key element of VLCs is sufficient to inform this discussion. A community moderator should remind participants of learning intentions, and intervene when interaction drifts too far away from the learning focus. The leader can also encourage individuals on the periphery of the community to contribute their tacit knowledge to the explicit knowledge of the community.

Reflection

Communities' exhibit conversational "flow" and later conversations often make reference to earlier conversations and interactions. Reflection is evidenced when participants ground current discussions in previous events, discussions or experiences. A skilled moderator can look for linkages in conversations over time, and ask participants to comment on how a current conversation relates to something previously mentioned. For participants to make original and important contributions, it is also important to give them the time and environment to reflect on their own performance and contributions.

Intensity

Strong communities exude a sense of urgency—that involvement in the community is purposeful and meaningful. Intensity in DCoPs is made manifest by active engagement, open discourse, and a sense of importance in discussion, critique, and argumentation. Introduce provocative or significant organizational or social issues related to topics of conversation to provide context and authenticity for online conversations, and to ignite debate in the community.

Trust

In this context, trust refers to the level of certainty or confidence that one community member uses to assess the action of another member of the community. When people build communities, they commit themselves to each other through trusting social relationships. A sense of belonging and the concrete experience of social networks can produce trust, but trust is reciprocal and complex, and it shares variance with other intermediate variables, such as understanding, awareness, reputation, and coreliance. Trust reinforces an expectation of reciprocity. Provide opportunities for participants to collaborate on small activities in the community. Simple, noncompetitive activities, such as comoderating discussions, can promote the development of trust among individuals. As part of these activities, an element of coreliance is important, such that the success of the pair or team depends on the participation of everyone in the group.

Social Protocols

Conventions and rules of engagement are usually prescribed in formal learning environments, but even in informal learning environments such as DCoPs, participants follow conventional patterns of interaction. These conventions may be culturally bound and participants may engage each other online in ways they have become used to in other parts of their lives. This introduces potential for conflict in communities when different cultural traditions (e.g., age-related traditions of communication) are brought into a single learning environment. Establish clear rules and expectations for engagement, especially for setting the acceptable and unacceptable ways of behaving in a community. As the sense of community grows, the group can review existing protocols and be given responsibility for monitoring engagement in the community.

Communication: Awareness, Interaction, Engagement, and Alignment

With open, vibrant communication, communities flourish; when communication stops, communities cease to exist. Promote awareness by posting and regularly updating profiles of each participant. Also it may be possible to use virtual "introduction" exercises, where one member of the community interviews another one, and introduces that person to the rest of the group, but such ice-breaking activities can be time consuming and inappropriate for some groups. To promote interaction, explicitly ask people to respond to postings by others. We have noticed that some participants are more eager than others to participate and that too much interaction from one participant can be interpreted as overbearing or annoying by other participants. An attentive leader will watch for levels of engagement, encouraging reluctant participants to interact with others on specific topics, and by encouraging overenthusiastic participants to temper their interactions. Authentic engagement is often difficult to achieve in a group. Members are often tentative and cautious, particularly in the early stages of community development. To foster engagement, groups can be encouraged to challenge each other—critiques or intellectual jousting exercises. Moot courts and authentic problem-solving exercises can also be used as devices to stimulate engagement, but all of these require the light touch and skill of a facilitator to be effective. As for alignment, the group leader should take the pulse of the group regularly on key issues and track coherence. Gravitation toward consensus is a mark of a cohesive group (not necessarily an indication of strong learning). The most learning and growth in a CoP will happen when there is diversity, but the community will build trust and coherence when there is more commonality. A leader should balance these two competing variables to draw the best from a group, but the process is additive, not subtractive. One can promote greater diversity on key issues while simultaneously calling attention to ideas and values the participants have in common.

Face-to-Face Issues

Wherever possible, build in actual face-to-face meetings among participants and the leader(s). While communities can exist without actual meetings, the communities are strengthened and enlivened by gatherings. This is also true of DCoPs (Daniel, Brien, & Sarkar, 2003). Mentis, Ryba, and Annan (2001) suggested that learning communities, whether face-to-face or virtual, are brought closer through commonality and interdependence. This commonality in the case of DCoPs is more easily initiated in face-to-face settings.

In DCoPs and VLCs alike, there is an important potential benefit to be derived from combining actual interpersonal contact with the virtual contact among participants. Face-to-face communication can be thought of as the way that members of a DCoP achieve the necessary level of engagement to develop their identities, relationships, and learning. In fact, most studies of the ways that people engage with each other to build strong sense of community have focused primarily on face-to-face communication (Lesser & Storck, 2001). While participants can conduct business and communicate effectively in distributed environments, interpersonal contact is extremely valuable to the development of trust and depth in relationships.

CONCLUSION

DCoPs are similar to VLCs, but they tend to focus on exchange of data and information among professionals across different domains, geography, and organizational boundaries. DCoP members are often drawn from professionally diverse organizations and individuals, with different prior training backgrounds, and who are often engaged in using different approaches and tools to solve shared problems. These communities are similar to VLCs in many respects. Drawing from research into VLCs, this chapter has presented a model of VLCs and the fundamental elements underlying it.

The main contribution of this chapter is to enhance the understanding of the fundamental elements of VLCs which can in turn help provide instructors, instructional designers, researchers, and community architects with better insights for designing strategies, processes, and tools to support engagement and learning in VLCs. Knowledge drawn from this understanding can help support the design and sustainability of DCoPs.

ACKNOWLEDGEMENT

This research was supported by a grant from the Social Sciences and Humanities Research Council of Canada

NOTES

1. A list of background publications that offer a comprehensive treatment of the model and its development can be found at http://www.vlcresearch.ca

REFERENCES

Barab S. A., & Duffy, T. M. (2000). From practice fields to communities of practice. In D. Jonassen & S. Land (Eds.), *Theoretical foundations of learning environments*. Mahwah NJ: Erlbaum. Retrieved August 29, 2006, from http://crlt.indiana.edu/publications/complete.pdf

Bernard, R. M., Abrami, P. C., Lou, Y., & Borokhovski, E. (2004). A methodological morass? How we can improve quantitative research in distance education. *Distance Education, 25*(2), 175-198.

Bryce-Davis, H. (2001, August). *Virtual learning communities*. Paper presented at the Multimedia in the Home Conference, TRLabs, Saskatoon, Saskatchewan.

Cox, S., & Osguthorpe, R. (2003). Building an online instructional design community: Origin, development, and the future. *Educational Technology, 43*(5), 44-48.

Daniel, B. K., O'Brien, D., & Sarkar, A. (2003). A design approach for a Canadian distributed community of practice on governance and international development: A preliminary report. In R. M.Verburg & J. A. De Ridder

(Eds.), *Knowledge sharing under distributed circumstances* (pp. 19-24). Enschede: Ipskamps.

Daniel. B., Schwier, R. A., & Ross, H. (2007). Synthesis of the process of learning through discourse in a formal virtual learning community. *Journal of Interactive Learning Research, 18*(4), 461-477.

Garrison, D. R. (1997). Computer conferencing: The post-industrial age of distance education. *Open Learning, 12*(2), 3-11.

Garrison, D. R., Anderson, T., & Archer, W. (2003). A theory of critical inquiry in online distance education. In M. G. Moore & W. G. Anderson (Eds.), *Handbook of distance education* (pp. 113-127). Mahwah, NJ: Erlbaum.

Gongla, P., & Rizzuto, C. (2004). Where did that community go? Communities of practice that "disappear." In Hildreth P. & Kimble C. (Eds.), *Knowledge networks: Innovation through communities of practice* (pp. 295-307). Hershey, PA: Idea Group.

Gunawardena, C. N., Ortegano-Layne, L., Carabajal, K., Frechette, C., Lindemann, K., & Jennings, B. (2006). New model, new strategies: Instructional design for building online wisdom communities. *Distance Education, 27*(2), 217-232.

Heinrichs, R. J. (2003). Computer science, meet learning science. *Computing Research Association.* Retrieved May 14, 2006, from http://www.cra.org/CRN/articles/may03/hinrichs.html#17

Hiltz, S. R. (1998, November). *Collaborative learning in asynchronous learning networks: Building learning.* Paper presented at WebNet 98', World Conference of the WWW and the Internet. Retrieved October 6, 2007, from http://www.eric.ed.gov:80/ERICWebPortal/custom/portlets/recordDetails/detailmini.jsp?_nfpb=true&_&ERICExtSearch_SearchValue_0=ED427705&ERICExtSearch_SearchType_0=eric_accno&accno=ED427705

Hiltz, S. R., & Goldman, R. (2005). *Learning together online: Research on asynchronous learning networks.* Mahwah, NJ: Erlbaum.

Hung, D., & Chen, D. T. (2002). Understanding how thriving internet quasi-communities work: Distinguishing between learning about and learning to be. *Educational Technology, 42*(1), 23-27.

Johnson, C. (2001). A survey of current research on online communities of practice. *Internet and Higher Education, 4,* 45-60.

Kirschner, P., Strijbos, J. W., Kreijns, K., & Beers, P. J. (2004). Designing electronic collaborative learning environments. *Educational Technology Research and Development, 52*(3), 47-66.

Lave, J., & Wenger, E. (1991). *Situated learning: Legitimate peripheral participation.* New York: Cambridge University Press.

Lesser, E. L., & Storck, J. (2001). Communities of practice and organizational performance. *IBM System Journal of Knowledge Management, 40*(4), 83. Retrieved January 18, 2007, from http://www.research.ibm.com/journal/sj/404/lesser.html

Marra, R. M., Moore, J. L., & Klimczak, A. K. (2004). Content analysis of online discussion forums: A comparative analysis of protocols. *Educational Technology Research and Development, 52*(2), 23-40.

Mazur, J. (2004). Conversation analysis for educational technologists: Theoretical and methodological issues for researching the structures, processes and meaning of on-line talk. In D. H. Jonassen (Ed.), *Handbook for research in educational communications and technology* (2nd ed., pp. 1073-1098). Mahwah, NJ: Erlbaum.

Mentis, M., Ryba,, K., & Annan, J. (2001). *Creating authentic on-line communities of professional practice.* Paper presented at the Australian Association for Research in Education Conference. Retrieved January 19, 2007, from http://www.usq.edu.au/electpub/e-jist/docs/html2002/mentis_frame.html

Milheim, W. D. (2006). Strategies for the design and delivery of blended learning courses. *Educational Technology, 46*(6), 44-47.

Misanchuk, M., Anderson, T., Craner, J., Eddy, P., & Smith, C. L. (2000, October). *Strategies for creating and supporting a community of learners.* Annual proceedings of selected research and development papers presented at the 23rd annual National Convention of the Association for Educational Communications and Technology (Vol. 1-2). Denver, CO. (ERIC Document Reproduction No. ED455785)

Naidu, S. (2003). Designing instruction for e-learning environments. In M. G. Moore & W. G. Anderson (Eds.), *Handbook of distance education* (pp. 349-365). Mahwah, NJ: Erlbaum.

Pellegrino, J. W. (2001). Knowing what students know: The science and design of educational assessment. *National Academy Press.* Retrieved August 13, 2006, from http://www.nap.edu/catalog/10019.html

Reeves, T. C., Herrington, J., & Oliver, R. (2004). A development research agenda for online collaborative learning. *Educational Technology Research and Development, 52*(4), 53-65.

Romiszowski, A. J. (2004). How's the e-learning baby? Factors leading to the success or failure of an educational technology innovation. *Educational Technology, 44*(1), 5-27.

Rourke, L., & Anderson, T. (2004). Validity in quantitative content analysis. *Educational Technology Research and Development, 52*(1), 5-18.

Schwier, R. A., & Daniel, B. K. (2007). Did we become a community? Multiple methods for identifying community and its constituent elements in formal online learning environments. In N. Lambropoulos & P. Zaphiris (Eds.), *User-evaluation and online communities* (pp. 29-53). Hershey, PA: Idea Group.

Strauss, A., & Corbin, J. (1998). *Basics of qualitative research: Techniques and procedures for developing grounded theory* (2nd ed.). Thousand Oaks, CA: Sage.

Thurstone, L. L. (1927). A law of comparative judgment. *Psychological Review, 34,* 273-286.

Uribe, D., Klein, J. D., Sullivan, H. (2003). The effect of computer-mediated collaborative learning on solving ill-defined problems. *Educational Technology Research and Development, 51*(1), 5-20.

Wenger, E. (1998). *Communities of practice: Learning meaning and identity.* London: Cambridge University Press.

CHAPTER 18

ONLINE CoPs

Towards the Next Generation

Leonie Ramondt

This chapter is set in the context of the online communities of practice (CoPs) developed by the Ultralab facilitation team for the National College of School Leaderships (NCSL) in England. First, the background and philosophy are briefly explored along with elements of facilitation that enable CoPs to thrive. Next, the impact participation had on practice, from the individual to the systemic, is described along with Fullan's (2005) assertion that sustainable capacity building requires a tri-level solution. It is then suggested that members of CoPs are becoming increasingly e-mature and that embedding key performance indicators into online practice for feedback and self-evaluation can empower members to effectively co-facilitate their communities as well as generate a range of outputs including system indicators, policy measures, and rapid feedback. Finally, some features of current Web-based technologies are described along with ways these might be integrated into a holistic framework. The aim is to stimulate a discussion of strategies and tools that might help the next generation of CoPs to realize more fully their potential.

Communities of Practice: Creating Learning Environments for Educators,
Volume 2, pp. 367–393

INTRODUCTION AND BACKGROUND

Between January 2000 and December 2003, Anglia Ruskin University's Learning Technology Research Center, Ultralab, researched and developed online learning communities and CoPs for English school leaders for and with the NCSL. The full-time team of 23 online learning facilitators developed methodologies to assist 38,000 school leaders to integrate formal and informal online learning communities into their professional practice.

The first of the communities funded by the Department for Education and Skills (DfES) in advance of the NCSL was Talking Heads, an online learning community piloted for 1,200 headteachers and ably facilitated by 12 senior educationalists. Feedback from a representative sample of headteachers ensured that the Talking Heads community was scaled up for all 24,000 English headteachers. This work also catalyzed the development of online communities for headteachers in other countries including Heads Together in Scotland, Principals Electronic Network in New Zealand and Pen i Ben in Wales. This pilot research project allowed many different forms of community to be developed and tested as requested by these head educators. Some of these developed into CoPs. Talking Heads provided the blueprint for other online communities developed with the NCSL, who after the project handover, extended online communities to 70,000 English school leaders.

A philosophy of empowerment underlay this work, based in social constructivism (Vygotsky, 1934/1986) and Senge's (1990) model of the learning organization. Many educators have been inspired by the vision of learning that is constructive, active, complex, intentional, collaborative, and where knowledge is pooled within an authentic context, conversations are frequently reflective (Jonassen, 1995).

Although these elements lie at the heart of all online learning communities, CoPs as described in this chapter also generated (Bradshaw, Chapman, Powell, Ramondt, & Terrell, 2002),

- A shared agreement to actively explore and learn more about a well defined professional topic or domain
- A commitment to a specific group of peers within a private workspace
- A sense of ownership and active levels of participation

Successful online CoPs are a testimony to the quality and depth of the conversation under these conditions (Chapman, Ramondt, & Smiley, 2005).

Peter Senge (1990) has long recognized dialogue to be at the heart of learning organizations. He defines these as,

> organizations where people continually expand their capacity to create the results they truly desire, where new and expansive patterns of thinking are nurtured, where collective aspiration is set free, and where people are continually learning to see the whole together. (Senge, 1990, p. 3)

Characteristics to which a CoP might aspire. Wenger (1998) also identifies ownership as central to CoPs, and it became apparent from Talking Heads that this ownership drives the outcomes of participation. It also became apparent that when people think together, their combined knowledge and experience could cast a new light on their professional practice (Bradshaw et al., 2002; Torbert, 2004). The power of timely pooling knowledge is illustrated by the following case study.

Case Study—HIV Student Discussion

An urgent question was raised by a headteacher who has in his school a HIV positive child with educational and behavioral disorder (EBD) who frequently tried to bite staff and students. The parent threatened to sue the educator if her child's health status was revealed. A dynamic and supportive conversation ensued between the CoPs members, where the participants extended each other's knowledge by pooling information from their experience as well as from official sources. A summary of their advice follows.

- All students are potential infectious disease carriers (e.g., HIV and hepatitis) and therefore every student should be treated the same way
- Following from this, a school needs to establish clear policies and procedures for first aid and sterile procedure, for example, dealing with bodily fluids
- Reassure and train staff to be able to de-escalate volatile situations, and to use self-protection such as long sleeved clothing and holding techniques
- Consult all interested parties, that is, local authorities and the unions regarding health and safety and legal issues, without revealing the child's identity
- Inform the parents of the school's policies and explain that the child must behave within those parameters

- Enlist the support of the parents in developing the protocols, reassuring them their child is not being singled out
- Do not put your staff or students at risk

This generic and comprehensive advice consequently informed school policy.

Although there is no guarantee that the knowledge generated in CoPs is as comprehensive as a textbook, its grounding in first-hand experience ensures currency, resonance and "fit."

METHODOLOGY FOR ESTABLISHING ONLINE CoPs AND ENCOURAGING PARTICIPATION

Talking Heads as a DfES funded voluntary headteacher online learning community, acted as an umbrella for scores of communities. As mentioned previously, among these large more generic communities, a number of CoPs cohered to focus on a variety of specific issues, for example, pupil behavior management or domains, for example, small schools and schools in special measures. Some were set up by headteachers to bring together colleagues in a region, or to provide an online environment for a preexisting group. All these groups were purposeful, required a degree of privacy, and generated a strong sense of ownership, cohesion, and empathy, marking them as CoPs (Bradshaw et al., 2002).

The members of these CoPs benefited from the support of professional online facilitators who undertook a wide range of tasks to ensure the CoPs were vibrant, relevant, and effective (Bradshaw et al., 2002). Among tasks such as administering the communities, signposting information, summarizing, and supporting individuals, they also assisted members to network effectively, and as far as possible, to "appropriate" the technology to meet their own needs and circumstances. Initially there were numbers of instances where members were enthusiastic to set up their own CoP but failed to attract active participants. After a number of false starts, a methodology evolved that was more robust. This methodology was adapted according to the requirements of the specific group.

High success rates occurred when there was a group of "hero innovators" or "champions" (on average five) who were liked and respected among their colleagues and who agreed on a clear purpose and undertook to design the Web-based environment collaboratively. They shared the responsibility for planning events and activities, seeded the environment, and refined and tested it. They then evaluated their efforts at an agreed time. When ready, they "launched" the community to their wider community of peers, clearly publicizing the purpose and agreements for participation (Bradshaw et al., 2002).

There are also a number of strategies for engaging members that apply to educator CoPs. These were reported in the Talking Heads short report (Ramondt, Chapman, & Powell, 2002) and have been adapted here.

Be Clear About the Purpose of Your Community

The NCSL communities' overarching purpose was generic. These were to,

- Communicate with peers to share ideas and experiences
- Reduce isolation and develop a sense of community
- Access to up to date information and useful resources such as policy documents, assembly ideas and colleagues' key web links
- Discuss topical issues with colleagues and policymakers

Purpose statements for CoPs are more specific although the purpose of a CoP may develop over time.

Seeking feedback from members via focus groups, questionnaires, online conversations and performance indicators (see below) allows the online environment to evolve in alignment with members' needs.

To strengthen the purpose, consider integrating the technologies into the CoPs practices, for example, developing meeting agendas collaboratively, with everyone posting key information in advance of the meeting for prereading.

As Far As Possible, Centralize Communication

As a general principle, resist the temptation to make unnecessary private spaces. The fewer separate spaces to post, the greater the pooling of knowledge, and the quicker questions can be answered. One of the bigger challenges has been to generate an ethos where members ask queries of the group instead of an individual. One effective remedy was to ask all members to post messages only to the group.

Once members are active however, the next challenge is discernment: in a wealth of communication, which messages are key? A strategy commonly used is to read the first message of a thread, but changes in topic within the thread are easily missed unless signified in the title. Quick scanning can be supported by developing conventions agreed among the group to make use of the features of specific software. For example, in Think.com, the facilitation team developed a bulletin board where red text signified urgent please help, black—information please read, blue—current work, purple—tasks carried over from yesterday and green—off task social. This color coding significantly enhanced scanning and responsiveness.

Match the Rhythm and Pace of the School Year

Once key topics and themes are established, schedule, and publicize a calendar of events that fits the school year so that members can plan their participation into their diary and working schedule. Ensure that conversations are timed to match and enhance the activities of the school year.

Expect holiday periods to be quiet, a catch up and recreational time, while pre- and postholidays teachers will generally be especially focused on in-school activities. Immediately postholidays, teachers will mostly seek access to relevant resources such as lesson plans and policies. The key exception is a "burning issues" item where teachers can quickly tap into the experience of colleagues (see HIV case study) as they face new situations in the class room, as for example how to include a new autistic student. A good time to hold the first online events or key conversation is when a school is back a few weeks. This can help to reestablish the routine of participation.

Be Proactive

Educators are very busy and most need regular reminders to log in. Whether members are automatically notified via e-mail that someone has contributed to a topic of interest; agreements are made between members regarding a particular pattern of participation or a weekly e-mail newsletter is sent out that provides URLs to key topics, expect to actively remind members to participate. Fifty-five percent of respondents to the NCSL communities' questionnaire indicated that they appreciated being reminded to participate.

Create a Clear Sense of Audience and Voice

To help professionals share their uncertainties in online communities, they need to know who the audience is, how secure the environment is, what the agreements are about confidentiality and participation, and to have places where they can speak informally and socially.

As one headteacher indicated, posting online is a public act.

> First time you participate, you wonder if you've done the right thing, and it requires some confidence to do this, especially when members haven't developed a routine and the audience is not known to the individual ... it is largely confidence in being able to speak freely ... I think heads are also shy about floating good ideas ... on a national platform.

A "Footprints in the Sand" item can invite otherwise invisible members (who might otherwise become lurkers) to contribute their thoughts. Encouraging an ethos of contribution by having a place for all members to post their first reactions, general queries, and serendipitous finds assists the community to remain fresh, lively, and topical.

Keep It Useable, Relevant, and Topical

Use devices to make topics easy to find such as "site maps" or topic calendars, and develop conventions such as clear titles. If it is useful to establish the tone of the community, "seed" topics by contributing to them and inviting key individuals to do so too.

It is also useful to adapt the open space technology (Owen, 1997) approach by encouraging members to generate a list of key topics of interest. These can then be scheduled into the rhythm of the school year.

Ask Good Questions for the Group Size

In the larger NCSL communities, general questions that stimulate most responses are clear, concise, open (not yes/no) and topical. "Successful specific questions tend to be topical, focused and contain enough information and emotion to resonate with colleagues" (Bradshaw et al., 2002, p. 72).

It was found that specific questions were more likely to be answered in large communities as the audience were more likely to have the range of expertise required to answer them unless of course the question is specific to the expertise or focus of a small group e.g. support, advice, experience. "Unanswered questions tended to share a profile of length, complexity and asking more than one question" (Bradshaw et al., 2002, p. 72).

Create a Social, Informal, and Fun Climate

Sociability is a key factor in generating a sense of community. Informality and openness generate the rapport and disclosure that is fundamental to the sharing of professional uncertainties and the emergence of new ideas (Chapman, Ramondt, & Smiley, 2005).

It has also been found in Talking Heads that there is a strong and fairly constant ratio between social and task focused messages. "Across the communities, on average 55% of messages are task focused, 25% are social/emotional and 20% of messages are both task and socially focused" (Bradshaw et al., 2002, p. 72). Analysis indicates that sociability is not restricted to small communities; it also flourishes in large communities.

Informality can be generated using greetings, expressions of thanks, giving supportive feedback, self-disclosure, and the use of first names. When members begin to use "we," arrange to share information, initiate discussions, mentor each other informally, suggest further collaboration, and begin to lobby each other on specific issues, the community can be seen to be emerging (Bradshaw et al., 2002).

Media, humor, photo galleries, role-play scenario events, off-topic threads, and competitions can add an element of fun.

It is also important to know the members. Time is a key issue and some people are simply not very sociable or willing to read more than a few lines of online text. This is less true of teachers however as written communication tends to be their strength. Designing the environment with the active participation of members ensures a fitness for purpose.

Be Explicit About Collaborative and Generative Philosophy

Collaboration, transparency, reciprocity, the power of learning together is not within everyone's experience, yet these are the lifeblood of effective CoPs. Many schools still rely on hierarchical systems because the staff have no experience with other ways of working. CoPs, as communities of peers, have an opportunity to forge systemic change by giving people experience with collaborative methodologies that build engagement, prove the power of learning organizations and build capacity for distributed leadership.

Issues of power and control within the group therefore need to be addressed. How are decisions made? Is there transparency? Does everyone have the right to post new topics and to edit pages? If so, is this easy to do, and what are the agreements regarding community use so that the space remains effective? Are there roles that people can adopt for a specific time (summarizing for example, or facilitating the weekly bulletin board) and then pass on the skills to the next volunteer?

Innovate and Agitate!

One innovation that has been very popular is the "hotseat" (see chapter 12). This allows a key proponent or personality to answer questions or respond to statements from members regarding a topic over a period (2 weeks is ideal for a busy membership). In advance of the hotseat, a "thought piece" is posted. The hotseat is then begun with a provocative statement or question to members.

In October 2003 the late Professor Ted Wragg, then the director of education at the University of Essex and celebrated columnist, posted the following provocation in the "NCSL in Dialogue" community,

> Politicians will not really shut down Ofsted and start again, of course, even though it would be the right thing to do. They could not handle any flak, so they are more likely to run stark naked round and round Piccadilly, ranting on about "our standards agenda," until the last disaffected teacher has quit.

This spawned about 50 pages of lively, humorous, and thoughtful conversation.

IMPACT

With so much investment of resource and time, it is important to establish if a CoP is having a genuine impact. However, impact can be very difficult to evaluate because it frequently occurs later and members rarely think to report it, even if they have cause to reflect on where the catalyst for an intervention or innovation originated. Nevertheless, it is evidence of impact that funding agencies most require.

In order to meet the accountability requirements of the NCSL, the Ultralab facilitation team researched the evidence of impact of the online communities (Bradshaw et al., 2002) by analyzing the data generated by headteachers in response to two online questionnaires, plus online conversations and interviews. A series of impact categories were identified. It is recognized that the quotes may fit within several categories.

Personal Support

Reducing isolation through community "Communicating with others in dark moments"

Professional Development

"Much of the expertise most valuable to you has been hard won by your peers"

Topicality "Getting information about performance management, from both the horse's mouth and from other heads."

Learning new skills and knowledge "I have learnt new management skills relating to budget planning, policy formation, and new approaches to behavior."

Using the experience of other headteachers "Often a decision I was hesitating over has been confirmed or discarded by seeing other head's ways of dealing with issues, e.g., managing an uncooperative member of SMT."

Reflection on practice "The ability to look at other people's points of view on current issues, particularly before a recent Ofsted (school) inspection at the end of my first year."

Researching colleagues' views "I have found the debate tool very useful, particularly when researching attitudes towards writing in the NLS, and the deployment of teaching assistants."

Increased professionalism "Developing a more open-minded approach to managing the constraints of a small budget in a small school."

Impact on the School, Colleagues, and Pupils

Flow of information to colleagues "Being able to bring a range of ideas to discussions with staff."

Contributing to "school improvement" In Talking Heads this meant building a capacity for continuous change to improve the achievements of children. Key concepts of professional development, creating learning organizations, and developing distributed leadership were discussed along with innovations in learning.

Table continued on next page.

| Building capacity through local groups | Building local networks at a local level and dealing with local issues—"Sharing the expertise of staff across a cluster or pair of schools." |
| Building connections between research and practice | Linking specialists and researchers to the teaching community via hotseats and consultation communities. |

Systemic Impact

Fullan (1996) describes systemic change as the mobilization of large numbers of people in new directions. He argues it takes around 6 years for an initiative to make a systemic impact. The following examples capture the early cultural changes that participating in collaborative communities affords.

| Producing a generation of "wired" head-teachers | "I recently attended a training day as a senior member of staff in the LEA Behavior Support Service We set ourselves the task of redrafting referrals, admissions, and outreach policy and I was able to DTP the amendments as we discussed them." "We are hoping to develop a school Web site and to place a wide range of information to support parents, staff, and pupils." |
| Future ICT planning | "Greater urgency in getting all staff access to ICT for admin without fighting over the staff room computer." |

Longer-term systemic impact is also evidenced by an increase in collaboration, empowerment, transparency, and reflective conversations on and offline in the participants' schools and interschool networks.

Impact on Policy

The "DfES in Dialogue" community was established alongside the Talking Heads community to provide a direct interface between policy makers and school leaders. The occasionally confrontational tone became more collaborative as both groups recognized the authenticity of each other's good will. A watershed point was reached when government policy advisors began to consult with headteachers before policy was written.

| Impact on government policy through access to government policy makers | "Debates/hotseat discussions—good to hear what government "gurus" think and be able to contribute." |

IMPLICATIONS FOR EDUCATORS

It is tempting to assume that systemic change is beyond the scope of teachers' CoPs. Fullan (2005) however found that individual learning communities (including CoPs) will remain as transitory phenomena unless the whole system of education is examined and improved. His model of "tri-level development" encompasses the school/community level, the district/regional level, and the state or national policy level. Along with the need to refine ideas and practices constantly, he identifies a need to,

> Foster greater cohesion and a shared commitment toward a higher purpose (the moral imperative). When all three levels ... are engaged in this agenda, it will be possible to make substantial progress. Huge accomplishments literally become more within our reach. But they can only become doable if we make them system-wide pursuits. In the absence of tri-level participation, professional learning communities on any scale will be impossible to achieve. Professional learning communities writ large is everyone's agenda across the tri-levels. (p. 223)

Fullan (2005) states that schools need to pursue cultures of learning and that the district needs to develop infrastructures to support this as well as link at a national policy and strategy level. Fortunately, Internet technology and professional practice is reaching a level of maturity that may soon assist his vision to be realized.

The new Web technologies provide tools that can fundamentally change the educator's role, setting them free from numerous routine tasks to focus on the creative work of facilitating learning: inspiring, challenging, identifying faulty conceptualization, and remediating it with a key task or question for example. This streamlining of routine tasks also applies to CoPs as illustrated later in this chapter.

Professional knowledge can be readily shared, extended, tested, and evidenced with authenticity and depth via collaborative online dialogue when there is a sense of community (Chapman, Ramondt, & Smiley, 2005).

Reflective practice as the "Active, persistent, and careful consideration of any belief or supposed form of knowledge in the light of the grounds that support it, and the further conclusions to which it tends" (Dewey, 1933, p. 6) remains a central tenet of quality work. The ability to reflect in action is a skill that has significant impact on practice. For example, research has shown that a teacher's conscious control over thoughts and responses has a 40% impact on pupil behavior for effective classroom management. This is an effect greater than any other single intervention (Petty, 2006).

So what can help practitioners to achieve this level of self-awareness when the pressure is on? Torbert (2004) has shown that reflective practice can be greatly enhanced by action inquiry "a timely discipline to exercise because its purpose is always in part to discover, whether coldly and precisely or warmly and stumblingly, what action is timely" (Torbert, 2004, p. 13). When a CoP is available online to support action inquiry, a new immediacy and responsiveness becomes possible. The online CoPs can support educators to share and extend their knowledge together in a "just-in-time" environment so that support and advice is available as a new situation or key event arises.

Of course, this immediacy can also become distracting and time consuming when participation becomes an end in itself; if for example, participants use participation to avoid work or to build a reputation. Online CoPs can also become labyrinths of information and chatter that require far too much time to negotiate and therefore exasperate the initiated members when the novice asks the same questions again that have been answered repeatedly before.

The following section will therefore explore some of the elements of future online CoPs for educators that might help them to build capacity for insight and effective practice, and assist them to develop their professional self-direction and reflection.

LEVERAGING THE NEXT GENERATION OF CoPs

As the wireless internet becomes ubiquitous, online communication is coming of age. People are growing increasingly accustomed to the new degrees of transparency afforded by the Internet; new ways of leveraging knowledge; and new nonhierarchical or flat models of organizing. The philosophy of empowerment is replacing concepts of moderation and mediation with that of facilitation, and increasingly, with member cofacilitation. Wikipedia and Linux are both examples of "Commons-based peer production" (Benkler, 2005) projects where skilled people contribute voluntarily to large meaningful projects. As Internet technologies assist people to bypass traditional corporate media control, participation and ownership are becoming the norm. Online blogs and Wikis are so widely accepted that they are being integrated into news and corporate Web sites, while online Web tools allow people to publish their photographs and videos for their friends and/or the world at large.

Although Prensky (2001) suggests that the younger generation are "digital natives." the UK e-strategy (DfES, 2005) has identified that e-maturity is a characteristic that is developing among people of all ages. The appropriation of Internet technology is not restricted to the young.

Educators are well served to develop alacrity with the use of Web technologies, both to empower themselves and to allow them to challenge their digitally native students to remain engaged in learning.

Characteristics of E-Maturity

The British Educational Communications and Technology Agency (Becta, 2006) suggests that e-maturity is not determined or limited by age or even experience, being instead stimulated by context and purpose. The following characteristics have been observed in e-mature individuals. (Ramondt, 2006)

Self-Direction
That is, the ability to be proactive, to use trial and error, to initiate experiments, and establish what works and what does not.

Confidence
The confidence that if technology breaks it can be fixed; a "can do" attitude and willingness to explore what is possible, what does not work, and why.

Experience
Sufficient experience with effective use of technology and with problem solving and troubleshooting when problems arise.

Philosophy
E-maturity is about empowerment. This is where the real impact of technology lies. A multiplicity of voices can challenge and reframe traditional power structures. If a company does not deliver on a service, it is possible for consumers to make their protest public via a blog. An e-mature youth can have an equal status to a 40 year old.

Discernment
E-maturity understands that everyone potentially has a voice, but not everyone is honest or wise. Information literacy strategies (November, 2005) need to be developed for establishing the veracity of claims. Ideally, there is also an understanding of how careers are furthered and beliefs are forged (Jha, 2005), to support the ability to evaluate claims and attitudes.

Creativity
That is, the ability to imagine new, innovative and/or valuable uses for the new technologies.

Maturity

Maturity, in the sense of emotional intelligence (Goleman, 1998) including the ability to see the big picture. The fiscal notion of maturity is useful here, in that it describes the point an investment begins to pay dividends.

As e-maturity increases, the potential exists for Teachers' CoPs to aspire to new heights such as those Peter Senge (1990) describes as being achieved by great teams.

When you ask people about what it is like being part of a great team, what is most striking is the meaningfulness of the experience. People talk about being part of something larger than themselves, of being connected, of being generative. It becomes quite clear that, for many, their experiences as part of truly great teams stand out as singular periods of life lived to the fullest. Some spend the rest of their lives looking for ways to recapture that spirit (Senge, 1990, p. 13).

Empowering Self-Evaluation

Evaluation is a systematic effort to learn from experience. It is a common human activity, one that enables us to make sense of the world and our impact on it. The understanding that comes from careful evaluation empowers us to act more effectively. (Elliott, Pearson d'Estrée, & Kaufman, 2003)

The process of evaluating the effectiveness of the NCSL communities in an environment of reflective practice (Schön, 1991) and action research, highlighted the opportunities for using digital data generated by practitioners in the course of their participation. For example, it was possible to evidence the shift of login times from out-of-hours to work-time as online dialogue became integrated into headteacher professional practice (Bradshaw et al., 2002). This began to occur as headteachers realized that they were able to save time through using the community and/or extend their perspective on key issues such as remodeling the curriculum. The effectiveness and vibrancy of these communities was in part due to the efforts of the dedicated facilitation team.

As most CoPs do not have the benefit of full-time facilitation, the need arises to design the online environment to be as effective as possible for busy teachers. The following section explores ways this may be achieved. The advantage of online conversations is that they can be captured and tagged for easy retrieval and that all activity in the community provides accurate and immediate information regarding the health of the community. This data can be used as key performance indicators to provide feedback for action, a reporting mechanism and a powerful knowledge base. Where the software is designed to empower the community, a large amount of the facilitation load can be removed leaving teacher free to focus on sharing knowledge and reflecting on the impact of their online CoP.

The power of integrating self-evaluation into practice was recognized by Hargreaves, Hopkins, Leask, Connolly, and Robinson (1989). They developed an approach that integrated judicious self-evaluation into a school's development plan. Wilcox (1992) pointed out that self-evaluation generally requires substantial energy, time, resources, and open communication in a context of professional development and esteem. Might it be however, that today's technologies are finally ripe to enhance, augment and simplify these procedures so that they can become a genuine tool for empowerment?

Innes and Booher (2000) offer some ideas that may transfer to education. These town planners found "that cities can be self-organizing learning systems that can be creative and sustainable" (p. 183) and that citizens can develop distributed intelligence or the ability to respond effectively to current circumstance. Knowing in advance for example that a particular arterial road is blocked, people will choose alternate routes and adapt their route according to traffic flow.

Innes and Booher (2000) also suggest that people from a variety of backgrounds are able to learn jointly and respond innovatively to environmental feedback through conversations that generate shared meaning (dialogue) and the use of technologies that provide strategic information.

> It is this distributed intelligence which allows players in a community to anticipate and constructively address both individually and collectively the systemic problems the community continually faces and to deal with the threats and opportunities of natural and man-made disasters, the shifting global economy, and the inequitable distributions of resources. (p. 178)

As the 2006, Hurricane Katrina in New Orleans highlighted, identifying and communicating relevant information (performance indicators by another name) is a skill that members of the public may require without notice. Having pertinent information can mean the difference between disempowerment and effective action. Knowing how to understand and successfully respond to performance indicators is a skill that educators will impart more effectively once they have experience of it themselves (Schön, 1991)

In the context of generating sustainable communities in towns and cities, Innes and Booher (2000) suggest that indicators should be selected and developed by those who will use and learn from them. They outline three tiers of indicators: (a) system performance indicators (e.g., Gross

National Product, Ultra Violet levels) that give feedback to the public regarding the overall health of a community or region, (b) policy and program measures to provide policy makers with feedback (e.g., service usage, satisfaction levels, monthly maintenance costs), and (c) rapid feedback indicators that assist individuals and organizations to make more sustainable decisions on a just-in-time basis (e.g., power usage, traffic conditions, school league tables). These three tiers of indicators also map to Fullan's (2005) tri-levels development of local, regional, and national policy levels of education management.

Citing complexity theory, Innes and Booher (2000) suggest that complex behaviors (based on studies of flocks of birds) can be simulated with simple algorithms, so that elements of a system "can work together effectively so long as they get feedback and so long as they have a capacity to respond" (p. 179). To become complex adaptive self-sustaining learning systems they also need to "share a general purpose, get feedback from their actions, and then act differently" (p. 179).

They warn that some indicators such as those on crime rates seldom assist enlightened action to reduce it, as they only report what happens, not why or how. This confirms Yin's (1989) assertion that insight into the why and how of a matter requires qualitative data, reinforcing the point that performance indicators are most effective when grounded in practice. Innes and Booher (2000) have found that it is the learning involved in collaboratively designing indicators that informs effective policy, design and action. Indicators only become influential when "they become part of the thinking and ordinary decision making of the players" (p. 178). Further, they argue "this only happens if the players were involved in developing them so they can relate them to their own contexts and perspectives" (p. 178) and that they need to be linked directly to policy. In their experience, it takes considerable time for effective indicators to be developed. Clearly, the measures themselves need to be holistic ("Sustainable Measures," 2005) and linked directly to the purpose of the CoP.

So how might this be achieved? The Innes and Booher (2000) article was written at a time when synchronous and interactive Web 2.0 technologies were not yet available and pervasive asynchronous conversations were less commonplace. Might performance indicators be combined with online database technologies to be honed and utilized with more alacrity and immediacy now?

EMBEDDING PERFORMANCE INDICATORS

The Internet is a vast searchable database that provides mechanisms for privacy as well as dissemination. Embedding mechanisms to capture and organize both quantitative and qualitative data generated by participants as key performance indicators can provide a window onto a CoP's processes. The transparency and continual feedback this provides members can assist self-organization and serve a variety of purposes. At the same time, anonymized data can be aggregated to inform regional and national development. The following list is explained further below.

Embedded performance indicators presented via well-designed software tools can provide,

- A sense of ownership through foregrounding members' interests and celebrating exemplary contributions and new insights
- Just in time feedback from peers' ratings to allow participants to increase the effectiveness of their contributions
- A framework for reflection in action by linking contributions to members' personal journals and by allowing pivotal contributions to be flagged for future feedback
- An audit trail for allowing contributions that provide new information or insight to be tracked to future feedback regarding their impact on practice
- Personal portfolios that aggregate each member's contributions and their impact as evidence towards accreditation or appraisal
- Ongoing progress updates to inform decision making
- A workflow or project management framework through linking the indicators to an action plan and outcomes aggregator
- A reporting template and methodology with automated collation, formatting and charting so that a formal report needs only to be edited into fluency
- The basis for dissemination of the best contributions or of summaries of conversations via the internet or for publication
- Transparent just-in-time accountability for stakeholders, who can gain quick insight, for example, regarding current issues arising as well as anonymous participation data
- Aggregate statistics for benchmarking against like groups
- Just in time feedback to regional and national bodies to inform policy, staff development and future planning

How Might Performance Indicators Be Integrated Into Online CoPs?

Yalom (1995) recognized that dynamic feedback was,

most effective when it stemmed from here-and-now observations, when it followed the generating event as closely as possible, and when the recipient checked with other group members to establish its validity and reduce perceptual distortion. (p. 489)

Online communication provides a wealth of qualitative data. The notion of linking feedback to contributions naturalizes the peer review process. Current online forum and virtual learning environment (VLE) technologies also provide a wealth of statistics that traditionally were used by system administrators. These can be made available as anonymous aggregates to the tri-level partners (Fullan, 2005) in the categories outlined by Innes and Booher (2000) to provide them with feedback and inform further action.

1. System performance indicators regarding the overall health of the CoPs, for example, levels of participation, degree of communication between CoPs, benchmarking data.
2. Policy and program measures for example, evidence of impact, key topics arising.
- Rapid feedback for example, topical issues, contributions that receive the highest ratings, what is new.

Performance indicators can be readily built into community activity. The Internet is burgeoning with social software and peer-to-peer technologies. Increasingly the ability to provide feedback is being integrated into Web pages. Best known are the online auction Web site eBay with the ability to rate sellers, and the giant online bookstore Amazon, with the ability to review books and rate the usefulness of these reviews.

Integrating a rating scale into online communication has been refined by a number of online communities. Slashdot, an online community for ICT specialists, has integrated ratings into all their online contributions. Their suitably colloquial scale ranges across normal, off-topic, flame-bait, troll, redundant, insightful, interesting, informative, funny, overrated, and underrated.

Talking Heads, using Oracle's Think.com software, implemented a very simple model in one community using something Oracle termed the "debate" tool. This tool allowed members to assign their own label to a color. A tool such as this would allow a community to use Bloom's taxonomy to classify contributions or simply begin with,

- Useful information
- Extends my understanding
- I will try this out

- Insightful
- Feels like community

Where community members can chose the categories linked to the purpose of the CoP, statements like these can easily function as performance indicators. If the software tracks this feedback by linking it to members' online personal journal or workspace, they can revisit it in the future. This allows them to append information about how they applied what they learned in their professional practice, some months later, thereby providing evidence of impact. Each of these would aggregate under the key overarching objectives for example: personal support, professional development, impact on the school, colleagues, pupils, and their subcategories as required.

Every participant would also have their contributions listed in their workspace, along with the community's ratings. If a member receives

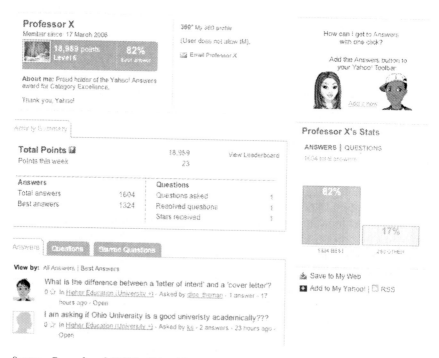

Source: Reproduced 2007 by Yahoo! Inc. YAHOO! and the with permission of Yahoo! Inc. YAHOO! logo are trademarks of Yahoo! Inc.

Figure 18.1.   Eighty-two percent of this member's answers were rated as "Best" by members.

feedback that some of their contributions were seen as insightful and/or impacted on the practice of their colleagues, this could provide evidence for their professional portfolio. Yahoo Answers is a useful example showing how members can be rated and profiled by their contributions.

TOWARDS A HOLISTIC FRAMEWORK

Barrett's (2006a) holistic model for organizational consciousness may be a useful tool to consider in the search for some helpful performance indicators. He states that a number of dimensions are required to ensure that an organization is robust, healthy, and socially beneficial. It can be argued, that in developing awareness of how these apply to their CoP, participants may also begin to generalize this awareness to their school environment.

Barrett (2006b) indicates that an organization can aim to build positive values at each level, although those up to and including transformation have to be in place first. Being aware of the dimensions can assist a CoP to build mechanisms that either implicitly or explicitly integrate these dimensions into their online community practices and/or use them as a framework to examine the impact of their participation in the online CoP on their professional practices and thereby their students, schools, and wider community.

If a CoP was to adopt Barrett's (2006a) model as their holistic framework, they might begin with Table 18.2.

Further Possibilities

Web sites such as Pledgebank encourage members to take action on an issue if enough people agree. It takes little imagination to adapt this practice to a collaborative action research project where members subscribe to research a specific intervention in their practice and contribute both qualitative and quantitative data for example assessing the impact of different interventions on classroom behavior. In this manner, practices can be easily compared, contrasted, tested, and expanded. Yahoo Answers rewards members for contributing by increasing their rating. The person who asked the question identifies the best answer. The names of members who have high ratings for giving the best answers are placed on an honor roll. Another interesting device they use to encourage participation occurs when a member submits an

Table 18.1.   Barrett's (2006a) Holistic Model for Organizational Consciousness

Dimension	Keywords
Survival	health, safety, financial stability, (framework/control) CoP participation, agreements, guidelines
Relationships	harmony, good communication, conflict resolution, openness, student service, loyalty, respect, friendship
Self-esteem	high performance systems, performance measuring metrics, excellence, productivity, quality, professionalism, pride
Transformation	improvement, learning, adaptability, personal growth, empowerment and diversity, innovation, overcoming fear, courage, challenge, risk taking
Internal cohesion	shared vision and shared values, healthy internal community, trust, integrity, honesty, strong commitment, people looking for meaning, alignment between individuals and their CoP
Making a difference	mentoring and coaching, strategic alliances and partnerships, fulfilment, integration with other communities, community involvement, and environmental awareness
Service	social responsibility, ethics, human rights, impact on future generations, ecology and sustainability, recognition of interconnectedness, compassion and wisdom

Table 18.2.   Barrett's (2006a) Holistic Model Applied to a CoP

Dimension	Keywords	Performance Indicators
Survival	Financially sustainable, participation, agreements/guidelines	Transparent accounting, site statistics mission statement/code of practice
Relationships	Good communication, openness	Social/task mix, disclosure
Self-esteem	Performance measuring metrics, excellence, productivity	Evaluation framework, personal profiles valued, vibrancy and "useful information" ratings
Transformation	Learning, innovation, risk taking	Conversation ratings that promote evidence for these
Internal cohesion	Healthy internal community	Evidence of dialogue, engagement, alignment
Making a difference	Mentoring and coaching, integration with other communities	Formal or informal mentoring dissemination and networking
Service	Social responsibility, impact on future generations	An integrated mechanism for dissemination evidence of impact

answer. The contributor is thanked and given a friendly invitation to respond to other topics in the domain of the person's expertise or interest.

Software can also be used to assist members to network more effectively with others across communities. Members can develop their own "Folksonomy" (Vanderwal, 2005) by collaboratively developing keywords to categorize their content. This would allow them to search on a variety of terms to find project partners or mentors, or gain access to resources. Projects such as ecademy (www.ecademy.com) and the Family Support Network (http://www.familynetwork.org) have developed useful technologies to optimize the skill and resource networking processes.

Software on its own will not engender reflective practice. How a CoP might evolve into a community of inquiry where members engage in double loop (Argyris as cited Smith, 2001) and triple loop (Torbert, 2004) reflection is worthy of consideration.

Torbert (1978, 1991, 2004) found that self-direction, shared purpose, and quality work need to be developed actively. With colleagues, he developed a "Liberating Structure" that challenged his business school students (1978) and middle managers (1991) to engage in complex experiential tasks that disconfirmed their expectations. When they dealt with conflict successfully, they came to experiment increasingly with self-correcting task achievement, more authentic communication, and took more ownership of the organizational purposes, processes, and tasks. Perhaps this model can assist online CoPs actively to transform into communities of inquiry (Torbert, 2004).

DRAWING IT TOGETHER

This chapter explores a variety of elements that might be integrated into online CoPs to help synergize the members to achieve excellence.

To assist in visualizing this, imagine an attractive and customizable interface that allows members to type in their group and/or personal purpose, intended impact, and assign actions to each one. These are linked via a holistic framework to key performance indicators, providing a window onto the pulse and health of the community.

As the conversations progress, members easily rate and flag key items for future use. This feedback encourages participants to hone their responses for effectiveness and quality, with the best contributions being saved to personal portfolios, reflective journals, and/or shared spaces. These can later be used to evaluate impact, as evidence for appraisal and for reporting and public dissemination (unless the contents are commercially sensitive). At the same time, persistently effective contributors are recognized.

Editable templates aggregate the key performance indicators and contributions into a variety of formats including, reports that provide charts for key statistics as well as summaries of key topics, their impact and/or issues arising; as well as articles for publication to Web pages or print. The tagging system allows members to find relevant information, questions, and events easily.

Project groups track their tasks, actions, and topics, creating an audit trail and key topics are scheduled for an optimal time, as determined by the school and individual calendars. Key data valuable for benchmarking is extracted as anonymous aggregates. A variety of other outcomes are pursued as members reconfigure the software to support projects such as collaborative action research and staff development. Effective tri-level communication ensures that professional development and policy measures are designed with and for the education community.

In a truly transparent environment, an external evaluator might engage in a critical review with participants, perhaps even taking the role of expert coach and mentor.

Discussion

The new online technologies provide a range of opportunities for collaboration and knowledge building not previously afforded. Evidence of progress can be collated in a manner that is SMART (specific, measurable, attainable, realistic, timely) and streamlined. Where this process is owned by participants, great power is afforded for intelligent action.

Where this process is owned by the few, there is great power for surveillance and control. It is therefore fortunate that the new technologies are grounded in a philosophy of personal empowerment, flat hierarchies, and collaboration. Were the system to be imposed however and ownership not experienced, it is equally possible for members to subvert the system; for example by agreeing to give each other positive ratings.

Care also needs to be given to the holistic nature of the design. Giving members kudos only for answering questions may shift the focus away from dialogue and collaborative knowledge creation for example.

The success and power of this combination of technologies comes from members realizing the potential of CoPs and seizing the tools to help them achieve authentic outcomes in their practice for their students. Where the new technologies are collaboratively developed with system-wide stakeholders to empower professional practice in a no blame culture, Fullan's (2005) vision of huge accomplishments may well be realized.

Summary

This chapter outlines the Talking Heads and NCSL online community project development and philosophy, and the facilitation and impact of online CoPs for educators. It then explores the issue of systemic change via reflective practice and deep learning as a tri-level development; what the new Web 2.0 software platforms might offer an e-mature self-facilitating community. A holistic model for self-evaluation is proposed, to provide just-in-time feedback, reflective practice, and empower intelligent responsiveness. The issue of how performance indicators can be easily tracked and extracted for a variety of purposes is explored, and how they might be used for a range of purposes including benchmarking and policy design. It is also suggested that collaborative action research across CoPs might be achieved, and that tagging can allow members of this broader community to locate the elements and resources relevant to them easily. It is finally suggested that a culture of empowerment can be achieved across the whole sector, from the local to the national.

ACKNOWLEDGMENTS

The preparation of this chapter was supported by the AHRC research project Practical Design for Social Action, part of the Design for the 21st Century Program.

REFERENCES

Barrett, R. (2006a). *The seven levels of corporate consciousness.* Retrieved March, 16, 2007, from http://www.valuescentre.com/business/slorgpresentation.htm

Barrett, R. (2006b). *The seven levels of corporate consciousness.* Retrieved March, 16, 2007, from http://www.valuescentre.com/business

Becta. (2006, June 14). *The e-mature learner workshop.* London: Victoria Plaza Hotel.

Benkler, Y. (2005). *Common wisdom: Peer production of educational materials.* Logan, UT: COSL Press.

Bradshaw, P., Chapman, C., Powell, S., Ramondt, L., & Terrell, I. (Eds). (2002). *Talking Heads: Two years of research reflections.* Unpublished report to the National College of School Leadership, NCSL, Nottingham.

Chapman C., Ramondt L., & Smiley G. (2005). Strong community, deep learning: Exploring the link. *Innovations in Education and Teaching International, 42*(3), 217-230.

Dewey, J. (1933) *How we think.* Chicago: Henry Regnery.

Department for Education and Skill. (2005). *The e-Strategy: Harnessing technology learning and children's services*. Retrieved March, 16, 2007, from http://www.dfes.gov.uk/publications/e-strategy/

Elliott M., Pearson d'Estrée T., & Kaufman S. (2003). Evaluation as a tool for reflection. Beyond intractability. In G. Burgess & H. Burgess (Eds.), *Conflict Research Consortium*. Boulder: University of Colorado. Retrieved March, 16, 2007, from http://www.beyondintractability.org/essay/Evaluation_Reflection

Fullan, M. G. (1996). Turning systemic thinking on its head. *Phi Delta Kappa, 77*.

Fullan, M. G. (2005). Professional learning communities writ large in Dafour. In R. Dufour, R. Eaker, & R. DuFour (Eds.), *On common ground* (pp. 203-223). Bloomington, IN: National Education Services.

Goleman, D. (1998). *Working with emotional intelligence*. New York: Bantam Books.

Hargreaves, D. H., Hopkins, D., Leask, M., Connolly, J., & Robinson, P. (1989). *Planning for school development: Advice to governors, headteachers and teachers*. London: DFES.

Innes, J. E., & Booher, D. E. (2000). Indicators for sustainable communities: A strategy building on complexity theory and distributed intelligence. *Planning Theory & Practice, 1*(2), 173-186.

Jha, A. (2005). Where belief is born. *Guardian Unlimited Science*. Retrieved June 30, 2005, from http://www.guardian.co.uk/life/feature/story/0,13026,1517186,00.html

Jonassen, D. H. (1995, July-August). Supporting communities of learners with technology: A vision for integrating technology with learning in schools. *Educational technology*, 60-63.

November, A. (2005). *Information literacy*. Retrieved from http://novemberlearning.com/

Owen, H. (1997). *Open space technology: A user's guide*. San Francisco: Berrett-Koehler.

Petty, G. (2006). *Evidence based teaching: A practical approach*. Cheltenham: Nelson Thornes

Prensky, M. (2005-6). Listen to the Natives: Educational leadership. *Learning in the Digital Age, 63*(4), 8-13. Retrieved November, 1, 2007, from http://www.ascd.org/authors/ed_lead/el200512_prensky.html

Ramondt, L. (2006). *The e-mature learner, Becta invited think piece*. Retrieved November 1, 2007 from tre.ngfl.gov.uk/uploads/materials/24872/ematurity_ultralab.doc

Ramondt, L., Chapman, C., & Powell, S. (Eds.). (2002). *The Talking Heads Short Report*. Retrieved from http://intra.ultralab.net/~leonie/cothsreport02/index.html

Schön, D. (1991). *Educating the reflective practitioner*. San Francisco: Jossey-Bass.

Senge, P. (1990). *The fifth discipline: The art and practice of the learning organization*, New York: Doubleday.

Smith, M. K. (2001). Chris Argyris: theories of action, double-loop learning and organizational learning. *The Encyclopaedia of Informal Education*. Retrieved January 28, 2005, from www.infed.org/thinkers/argyris.htm

Sustainable Measures. (2005). Retrieved from at http://www.sustainablemeasures.com/

Torbert, W. R. (1978). Educating to toward shared purpose, self-direction direction and quality work: The theory and practice of liberating structure. *Journal of Higher Education*, 49(2), 109-135.

Torbert, W. R. (1991). *The power of balance: Transforming self, society and scientific inquiry.* Thousand Oaks CA: Sage.

Torbert, W. R., & Associates. (2004). *Action inquiry: The secret of timely and transforming leadership.* San Francisco: Berrett-Koehler.

Vanderwal, T. (2005). *Explaining and showing broad and narrow Folksonomies.* Retrieved from http://www.personalinfocloud.com/2005/02/explaining_and_.html

Vygotsky, L. S. (1986). *Thought and language.* Cambridge, MA: Harvard University Press. (Original work published in 1934, foreword to the 1986 edition by A. Kozulin)

Wenger, E. (1998) *Communities of practice: Learning, meaning and identity.* London: Cambridge University Press

Wilcox, B. (1992). *Time-constrained evaluation: A practical approach for LEAs and Schools*: London: Routledge.

Yalom, I. D. (1995) The theory and practice of group psychotherapy (4 ed.). New York: Basic Books. In M. K. Smith (Ed.), *Kurt Lewin, groups, experiential learning and action research: The Encyclopaedia of Informal Education.* Retrieved March, 16, 2007, from http://www.infed.org/thinkers/et-lewin.htm

Yin, R. (1989). *Case studies research: Design and methods.* Newbury Park, CA: Sage.

CHAPTER 19

GENDER AND MODERATION

The Style's The Thing!

Valentina Dodge and Sheila Vine

The chapter offers an approach for improving student participation in virtual or distributed communities of practice (vCoPs or dCoPs) through changes in the style of moderation. It describes some research into the possible effect of gender-bias on the duration and success of communities. Examples of male and female discourse styles and similar gender-influenced behavior in computer mediated communication (CMC) are given, and a classification of these is advanced. The research method involves a case-history analysis of the monitoring of four selected vCoPs, concluding that, in this type of environment (dispersed, CMC, and extended over a period), participants are more encouraged to learn from e-moderators who have been trained in, and understand, the importance of recognizing male and female styles of moderating.

Communities of Practice: Creating Learning Environments for Educators,
Volume 2, pp. 395–415
Copyright © 2008 by Information Age Publishing

INTRODUCTION

Terminology

A CoP is defined by Wegner, McDermott, and Snyder (2002) as a group of people who share a concern about a set of problems or a passion about a topic and who deepen their knowledge and expertise by interacting on an ongoing basis.

Distributed Community of Practice

A dCoP as defined by Wegner, McDermott, and Snyder (2002) is a CoP that is geographically dispersed, and so cannot rely on face-to-face communication as its primary form of participation. Most of the exchanges in such a group rely on CMC, assisted by one of the array of software items now available such as Yahoo! Group, chatrooms like those offered to educators at Tapped In® or Learning Times or even Voice over Internet Protocol (VoIP) tools such as Skype. A vCoP is more or less synonymous with a dCoP, except that members are more unlikely to have any "real" contacts. Both terms are used in this chapter (depending on the group being discussed).

Aims and Starting Point

The research described in this chapter was triggered by an article by Joyce and Kraut, (2006). A sentence in the abstract of that document states, "Surprisingly, the quality of the response they received—its emotional tone and whether it answered a newcomer's question—did not influence the likelihood of the newcomer's posting again." This observation was the opposite of our professional experience: that people respond to the messages they receive (e.g., if people do something for us, we will do something for them, with exchanges not necessarily being equal). This latter observation also appears in Skinner's model (Ferster & Skinner, 1957), and is echoed in Gouldner's (1960) reciprocity model. However, in 1957 and 1960, the Web did not exist, let alone allow people to communicate with each other across the world at any time of the day or night, free of charge, but it may be assumed that these 1960 precepts are still valid in a world "going virtual." With the birth of the Web, more and more new tools of communication, especially multimedia tools, are being used for learning purposes. It seems likely that their management will benefit from keeping earlier knowledge on good teaching styles in mind.

A vCoP, which had recently been started, provided the vehicle for a program of investigation. We were practicing what we were already preaching in the classroom and ensured we used a personal tone and female lexis when moderating. Take-up of the project had, however, been disappointingly slow. We wondered if style, among all the other variables affecting success, mattered as much as we believed. It was decided to see whether the Joyce and Kraut (2006) findings for newsgroups were duplicated in the education-based newsgroups of which we were members. This would be carried out through case histories of four such groups, with the aim of producing a classification of moderating styles and techniques that would serve as guidelines for the teachers we were already training. A secondary aim was to discover ways of improving moderating techniques.

Design

The first stage was to explore the existing literature, starting with the Joyce and Kraut's (2006) research. Second, a list of questions about gender-bias in e-moderators of vCoPs (fourth section) was collated. This provided a set of hypotheses that would be tested.

The next stage was the design of a piece of action research (fifth section). Unfortunately, this was to some degree limited by time and budget constraints. It was intended to investigate female and male discourse styles and to study their effect on participation in four selected vCoP. The research results were collected. These led to some conclusions that may hopefully be of use to future e-moderators (sixth and seventh sections).

LITERATURE REVIEW

There is a considerable body of literature on the subject of building successful CoPs, however it is surprising how little of it touches on the gender roles of moderators in virtual, education-based groups. Despite this, some points emerge with a possible bearing on the question:

Joyce and Kraut's (2006) findings, mentioned in the introduction, seemed to contradict the research of others in the field particularly that of Herring (2000). She states that female groups have more strictly enforced posting rules than men, who see rules as imposing restrictions on their freedom. Giving a welcoming response to a newcomer's first message is seen to be a trait of a female-biased moderator, along with other female discourse patterns, such as thanking, showing appreciation, or apologizing. These patterns are evident even when an attempt at disguise is made by moderators using a neuter pseudonym. Male gender traits, Herring claims, tend to inhibit women participants, who are less likely to persist in posting when their messages receive no response or a negative one. These findings were obtained in studies on newsgroups, whereas the research reported in this chapter focussed on the moderation style in education-centred vCoPs using Yahoo! Group software.

Johnson (2005) explains that, as organic entities, CoPs are constantly in flux between extremes or trade-offs. He states that if CoPs drift too much towards the ends of these extremes they become endangered. We feel it is possible to align some of the trade-offs described by Johnson with Herring's (2000) theories, by asking some questions about gender effects in three specific areas.

Is There too Much or too Little Leadership?

Too much management can hinder learning, while lack of leadership leads to chaos. According to Herring's (1992, 2000) work, a heavily authoritarian setting would be discouraging for males; on the other hand, females would not be comfortable working in a loose setting. Lave and Wenger (1991) believed that CoPs needed to be cultivated, not dominated. These two authors supported the idea contained in the trade-off between rules to reassure the hesitant and more permissiveness to foster creativity and independence. They considered that order, uniformity and perceived efficiency can stifle both creativity and identification within a virtual community; they apparently favored a male-biased style.

Is There a Gender Connection Between Core Membership and Boundary Activity?

The core participants establish and are at the heart of the CoP but innovation is often contributed by new members. Too much emphasis on the core causes a stagnation problem. In a learning community, new member contribution is more likely to be female as it is more of a female trait to admit to not understanding and therefore producing a new iteration. It is common for core members not to notice the development of new ideas. Core and new membership are both essential for an organic group.

Does Familiarity Lead to Fragmentation?

Female participants are more likely to form subgroups. These can be useful for expertise, specialization, and social exchange, but tend towards splinter group formation, as the women in the vCoP start to create a space where they, not the men, are in control (and there they linger!). So too much subgroup activity can end in fragmentation and finally to the breakdown of the group

Johnson (2005) states that clearly defined roles for participants are vital for virtual community success. He contrasts this with a recognition that too much defining of roles can make for stagnation in the group as it prevents the novice moving towards the expert. Johnson postulates that in many researchers' opinion moderators are not identified with the role of "boss" but seen rather just as another member. This, followed by Storck and Storck's (2004) findings that facilitators should deal with relationship development, shows clear agreement with the findings of Brown and Duguid as long ago as 1991. They argued that recognition and nurturing —two female traits—are valued in CoP theory. This kind of concern for establishing relationships would not be evident or clearly visible in male-dominant groups.

Johnson (2005) next brings in the concept of trust and quotes various other researchers who agree that this concept is central to a well-functioning CoP (Johnston, 2005).

The suggestion is that for an efficient exchange of information to occur, an environment of safety and trust must emerge (Herrington, Herrington, & Oliver, 1999). Social ease and experience in collaboration makes higher order thinking more efficient. Teams with a high degree of safety and trust are more innovative and productive (Lipnack & Stamps, 2000). Almost by definition, networking is based on trust. Hierarchical and bureaucratic measures do not work with virtual teams. Ardichvili, Page, and Wentling (2002) cited lack of trust as well as fear of ridicule or nonacceptance by peers as barriers to trust in CoPs. If this is so, virtual collaboration will not develop. It will be impeded, at least between the sexes, if the prevailing ethos allows members to be ridiculed, harassed, teased, and criticized by others (which occurs often in a male-biased CoP (Johnson, 2005). Trust will be hard to gain and easy to lose in such a situation. Lee and Neff (2004) go so far as to say that the social aspects of a CoP are more important than its technology.

Herring (2000) concentrates on one particular social aspect in her reviewing the place of gender in CMC. She sets her study in the Internet time frame, starting in the 1980s, when there was general optimism about gender-neutral internet. Perhaps those were still the days when politeness was a necessary part of nearly all social discourse! Alternatively, because men were majority users of the Internet there was no reason for them to feel threatened into using gender-biased communication.

This optimism has not been supported in later research. As more females entered the previously male province, surveys began to show that gender-free equality did not exist. Selfe and Meyer (1991) found that males and participants with high off-line status dominated the interaction. In further studies, men were reported as using aggressive tactics in CMC discussion groups sometimes targeting women (Herring, 1992, 1993).

Again, Herring (2000) states that gender-bias is reflected in the two discourse styles. Group participants themselves may not be aware of what is taking place, although in a virtual setting, gender is usually clearly signalled even when noms de plume are used: looking at the text of the discourse is enough for most people to guess gender accurately. (This does not mean that all males or all females communicate in exactly the same way: for a variety of reasons beyond the scope of the chapter, males do act like males, and females like females, most of the time. This is one of the factors to consider when seeking equality in learning.)

Male discourse, according to Herring (1992), usually features the adoption of adversarial positions, longer message posts, and the assertion of opinions as facts. Females use shorter messages and express support even when in disagreement with each other. They feel much happier when they can achieve consensus. They also tend to be more polite, justify their assertions and apologize. Women seem to prefer rules about posting which are clearly expressed and properly observed. Men, on the other hand, both indulge in themselves and tolerate the breaking of rules by others, claiming that the use of rules inhibits their personal freedom. These gender differences tend to disadvantage women, who, because they may be in a minority in the groups, seldom have the chance to control the topic or have their contributions recognized.

Some evidence suggests that women do have more influence when the moderator insists on a "well-mannered" environment, free from the threat of disruption and harassment (Herring, 1992). Women-centered groups whose moderators place restrictions on the number or nature of messages tend to flourish with large active memberships. On the other hand, with male-style moderating, if the moderator does not exercise control, then a permissive atmosphere plays into the hands of the most aggressive individuals, who are usually male.

There is evidence[1] that the minority gender in an online community gradually adapts its communicative behavior until it is copying the majority gender: survival of the fittest, perhaps? The bigger an online group, the greater the influence the predominating gender will have on shared discourse patterns.

Cherny (1994) and Herring (2000) give other examples of the differences in discourse style: for example, females will use neutral and affectionate words such as "hugs," while males favor more violent verbs (reference is even made to verbs such as "kill"). Females produced 3 times as many similes as men while the gender ratio was reversed for aggressive and insulting speech acts. Herring's conclusions were that Internet users display their culturally learned gender styles and that these gender differences work to the disadvantage of women.

Collins (2003) talks of moderators' roles having changed over the years and a new category of host/hostess being added. She states that when moderators use this approach, they find their tasks to be a source of personal satisfaction and relaxation. Their motivation enables them to make interpersonal connections, fosters professional development, and knowledge sharing, helps them in creating a community and gaining personal and professional recognition.

Soukup (1999) supports Herring's (2000) statements. He discusses patterns of discourse in computer mediated chatrooms. Through participant observation, he discovered that the traditional discourse forms dominate there. Regarding the study of CoPs, he interestingly describes male discourse as power-orientated, in other words, tending to the authoritarian side of the leadership trade off. He describes the female discourse pattern as relationship-and intimacy-dominated, but warns that this may end up in weaker leadership, at the far end of the spectrum. However, if this were set beside what Herring says about females appreciating the sense of safety provided by following rules, it would seem that these two styles could balance each other and produce a good climate for discussions. In other words, if rules are set for posting, allowing women to make contributions, they are less likely to show overdependence on female relationship patterns and a drift towards chaos.

Fredrick (1999) analyzes language use in two newsgroups and points out the way in which sarcastic questioning, strong assertions, sexist comments, or accusatory disagreements can create a hostile and noninclusive ethos. It is women who are most affected, but shy men or people from other cultures than the Western model may also find this behavior intolerable.

The most important skills that online teachers need to be taught in order to become e-moderators, according to Salmon (2003), are flexibility and creativity in working and a willingness to be trained and developed. Among the necessary skills or attributes needed by e-moderators she mentions confidence, ability to build trust and act as a catalyst, ability to encourage others, ability to value diversity with cultural sensitivity, ability to engage with people, rather than with software, and ability to communicate authority in a sensitive, positive, and knowledgeable manner. It is in the acquisition of the last two skills mentioned that awareness of gender-bias can be most helpful.

Wegner, McDermott, and Snyder (2002) discuss the principles for cultivating CoPs and suggest that, because of their voluntary nature, success often depends on the ability of moderators to generate enough excitement, relevance, and value to attract and retain members. In these authors' view, aliveness, the essential ingredient, is fostered by interaction and organic growth within the group. The dynamic nature of CoPs is vital for their evolution: if they start to stagnate, they might as well not exist. Two other important elements, as these authors see them, are the building of trust and the creation of a "rhythm" in the progress of the community. These aspects are both connected with gender-bias awareness.

They lay out suggestions for an approach built on their seven principles: evolution, openness, levels, spaces, value, familiarity coupled with excitement, and rhythm. When studying most of these areas, novice moderators will find that an awareness of the effect of gender-bias will be an asset, however this area is unfortunately rarely discussed in the literature. It may be that it is considered irrelevant by many researchers but there is another reason why attitudes in this area need to change. As a result of the demand for learning, more and more teaching will be done in virtual or dispersed settings, aided by the huge development of the tools available. More and more learners from the latest generation will be entering the virtual classroom. These people, the future, were weaned off traditional toys and onto computer toys by the age of five and are already highly skilled in certain types of virtual assembly. Although valuable work has been done on making vCoPs successful and viable, the topic of gender-bias in moderating has so far been neglected. This might be a good moment for investing it with more importance.

METHODOLOGY

Research questions

The list of questions emerging from the literature as discussed above is as follows:

- Is there evidence of gender-bias in the discourse styles of moderators of vCoPs?
- Do moderators take account of their own gender and that of their members in the style of their moderating?
- Is a female moderating style welcoming and hence encouraging to females in the group? Is it also successful in encouraging positive male participation? Does this affect posts?
- Does a male moderating style elicit initial and durable enthusiasm from male group members? Does it have the same effect on female participation? Does this affect posts?

Research Methods

The research was designed to study the effects of gender-bias in the moderating styles adopted in four vCoPs. The particular groups were chosen because: (a) we had personal experience of them; (b) they qualified as dCoPs (according to Wegner, McDermott, and Snyder, 2002) and (c) initial approaches indicated that many of their members would collaborate willingly with the research.

The qualitative data was collected following the requirements suggested by Lofland (1971), namely, close personal knowledge of the subjects; collection of perceived facts, that is, actual data and notes on interviews, descriptions of backgrounds, and direct quotations.

Where available, quantitative data was also collected and analyzed, though it was clear that there would be limits to its usefulness, given the unavoidably heterogeneous profiles (e.g., size, purpose) of the groups chosen.

The case studies were carried out between March 1, 2006 and August 31, 2006. The month of May was selected for the detailed lexical study. Postings were scrutinized on a daily basis. Gender-bias was identified by key words and the discourse style features suggested by Herring (2000) and other researchers [see literature review]. Their frequency was analyzed using Microsoft and Yahoo! Group software. Some of the characteristic features of the differing gender styles are given in Table 19.1.

In addition to these quantitative case studies, other research activities included an initial survey, a follow-up survey and interviews. Members of the participating groups were made aware of the survey by e-mail, at the

Table 19.1.   Some Characteristic Features of Differing Gender Styles

Female	*Male*
Social, welcoming, encouraging	On task, to the point
Rule-based	More authoritarian/high status figures
Innovative—allows boundary activity	Resisting boundary activity
Recognition and nurturing	Apt to ridicule what is seen as less important
Encourage trust-relationship concern	Relationships unimportant
Social ease & collaboration	Criticism rife
Discourse features	Libertarianism
Short messages	Long messages
Similes	Spreading the word
Creating a community	
Sensitivity	

outset. The initial questionnaires were set up using Survey Monkey software, which ensures total anonymity.

Characteristics of Groups Studied

All four groups are run via Yahoo! Groups and draw their membership worldwide. They are listed below, with their own descriptions of the groups.

WebHeads in Action (WiA)

WIA (http://groups.yahoo.com/group/evonline2002_webheads/) was set up and moderated by Vance Stevens in November 2001.

> This group comprises participants in events convened under the auspices of TESOL EVOnline (Electronic Village). Participants meet informally throughout the year but more formally between January and March to help each other learn about forming and maintaining robust online communities through hands-on practice with synchronous and nonsynchronous text and multimedia CMC tools.

Learning With Computers (LwC)

LwC   (http://groups.yahoo.com/group/learningwithcomputers/)   was started by Gladys Baya in November 2005; moderated by Gladys Baya, Maria Claudia Bellusci, and Mary Hillis.

> All (first, second, or foreign) language teachers are here invited to get together to learn how we can start integrating computers into our teaching. Join others, learn and share what you know! Make this your place!

EFLTU

EFLTU (http://groups.yahoo.com/group/efltu/) was started in March 2005 and moderated by Dennis Newson/Andrea MacLeod.

> A group formed to gather information on and struggle to improve the pay and conditions of foreign language teachers (including teachers of EFL/ESL/ESOL) as well as pensions, sick pay, holiday pay, contracts, cost of travel to take up post and any other relevant issues that may arise from time to time—and to liaise with local teachers' unions.
>
> EFLTU exists as a forum not only for discussion but also for the coordinating and planning of appropriate action for teachers of all foreign languages, including English as a Foreign or Second Language, English for Speakers of Other Languages. Membership is open to all foreign language teachers (not just native speakers of the language taught) regardless of gender, nationality or creed.

This group has worldwide membership even though its main base is in Germany; its main objective is as stated above. Since its foundation, the leadership of the group has changed from the founder only to a committee structure with various members.

Dogme

Dogme (http://groups.yahoo.com/group/dogme/) was started in March/April 2000and moderated by Scott Thornby and Graham Hall.

> Are a mix of teachers, trainers, and writers working in a wide range of contexts, who are committed to a belief that language learning is both socially motivated and socially constructed, and to this end we are seeking alternatives to models of instruction that are mediated primarily through materials and whose objective is the delivery of "Grammar McNuggets." We are looking for ways of exploiting the learning opportunities offered by the raw material of the classroom, which is the language that emerges from the needs, interests, concerns, and desires of the people in the room.

RESULTS: GENDER BIAS OF MODERATORS

To assess bias the messages posted in each vCoP for the period of the research period (March 1, 2006 to August 31, 2006) were studied. In addition, the data for the month of May 2006 were analyzed in more depth, as this allowed the youngest group LwC time to start up. For that month, all posts, and all moderators' posts were noted and where possible, the male/female proportions of moderators' posts to members.

Our analysis for each of the groups follows.

WebHeads in Action

In the period under investigation (May 2006) there were 261 posts to the group, of which 21 or 8% were from the moderator. Fifteen of these posts were in response to other participants. The tone of the posts was clearly welcoming and encouraging to members, with plenty of inclusive language. Expressions like "let's, can't wait, interesting, wow! Well done! Thanks, please, what I need is ..." were frequently used by the moderator. This language is an example of the nurturing language common to female posters or trained/experienced facilitators.

On the other hand, it was found that moderator posts to individual members were inclined to "long-windedness," usually indicative of a male message. (The average post length is 173 words, an average skewed in this case because of a handful of short posts, 37-52 words in length. Without this distortion, the wordiness would have been even more noticeable). It can be concluded that the moderator is highly skilled in moderation and in encouraging the members of his group to contribute, yet evincing male traits as far as post length is concerned.

Of the 261 May posts (Figure 19.1), 95 are clearly from male participants, so females post twice as many times as males. Membership of this group is high (521 members subscribed—as of August 31, 2006), and the gender ratio is relatively evenly mixed. However, as not all members have revealed their gender in the membership list the data cannot be used for extrapolation. The core/active members of WiA are mostly female so a mixed gender result could have been expected; clearly, from the longevity and vitality of the group and its success in providing support, a great deal of moderation skill has been exercised.

Learning With Computers (LwC)

During May 2006 there were 255 posts to the LwC Yahoo! Group. (This group also uses a number of other social software options such as a blog and Wiki for member participation but our study could not include it). Of these 255 posts, 67 (26%) were by the main female moderator. Of these moderator posts, 49 (73%) were responses to member posts. Six out of the total 67 moderator posts (almost 9%) were welcome messages to a new member. This welcoming is a clear characteristic of the group and

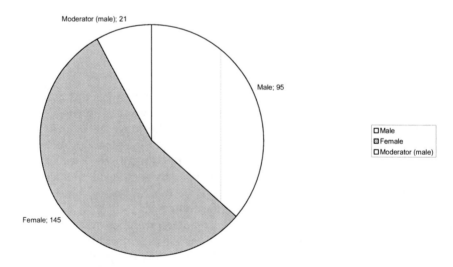

Figure 19.1.   Distribution of gender in posts for WiA May 2006.

illustrates the early stages in its development. The moderator's other posts were self-initiated, mainly in connection with the group's weekly tasks, social software or calling for shared moderation.

The posting length of the moderator's messages is high (95 words), though not as high as most male moderators'. In this group, most of the moderator's postings related to other learning technologies being used by the group. This is a good example of female rule-orientated moderation. Since its inception, the moderators have guided its members through a group of clearly defined tasks including the creation of these other features. Members know what the group is aiming to do at any one time and are guided to complete certain tasks. Female members feel safe to contribute. Another female trait is sharing moderation across the whole group. This group is developing very early along these lines. The more expert and active members are invited to take on support roles and many of the 67 moderator postings contained questions to members asking for direct participation or advice. This is a clear two-way style of maintaining the group.

Selfe and Meyer (1991) lead to an expectation that high status males are more active in message sending, and this was visible, even in this generally female-orientated group. Yet the few male members, a clear minority, appear to exert considerable influence on the group and are active participants (see Figure 19.2).

Another point observed was some evidence of active male participants changing their behavior patterns to a more female "hugs" mode. This is in sharp contrast to postings on all of the other groups. The group has 142 members (as of August 31, 2006) of whom 72 are clearly female, 23 clearly male, with the rest not revealing their gender. Further data would

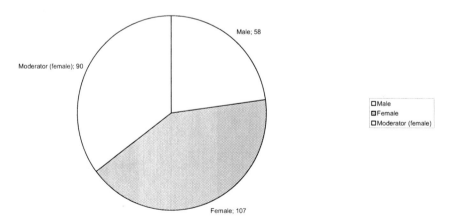

Figure 19.2.   Distribution of gender in posts for LwC May 2006.

be interesting: one third of the group's 142 strong membership did not reveal their gender. If all of these were male, the conclusions would have to have been different.

EFLTU

In May 2006, this Yahoo! Group only made 60 posts (noticeably fewer owing to the make-up of the group and its aims). Of these, 24 (40%) were by the male moderator, the female moderator rarely appearing on the group. The average length of the moderator's posts was 80 words with actual posts breaking down as follows: 12 posts in response to a members post, 8 self-initiated posts, 3 references to learning technologies groups and 2 "invitations" to members of the group to become more involved. Welcome messages are not a general characteristic of this group. The group has 182 members (as of August 31, 2006) of whom 73 are clearly male and 35 clearly female, the gender of the rest of the group unknown. The gender ratio of 2.1 was not reflected in May postings: of the 60 posts, 56 were by male members or the moderator (see Figure 19.3).

It was concluded that the high status male moderator seemed to dominate the group and appeared to exert a strong male influence in it. It is possible, therefore, that female members were in some way inhibited from posting. No evidence of male aggressive language was found and the numerical dominance shown in the data could be interpreted as a benign

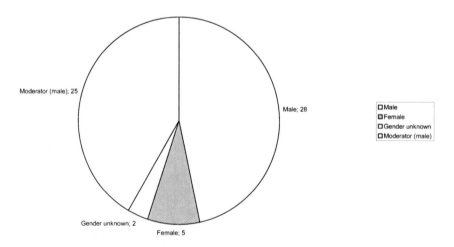

Figure 19.3.   Distribution of gender in posts for EFLTU May 2006.

attempt to enliven and strengthen the group. Here again, the large number of "genderless" members prohibits any valid conclusion.

Dogme

In May 2006 there were 121 messages posted in Dogme: only four of them were from the moderator and these were all in response to a comment from a contributor. There was an absence of self-initiated posts and welcome messages to new members. (The latter are not a characteristic of this group.) Very light moderator control is observed in the data, but when the moderator does contribute, posts are long (average: 318 words). This length of posts and the "light-control" style are markers for masculine style. Looking at the ratio of male to female posts in the month the vast majority were from male contributors. The gender ratio of members was investigated but this figure was unusable, as many did not reveal their gender, making any serious statistical comparison impossible.

Dogme seems to be a group with strong male-biased moderation. When approached with the request that they participate in the survey aspect of this research, neither moderators nor members replied. This would indicate a different group ethos in the group from the ones we know. It might be significant that the request was made by a female long-term member of the group. The same lack of acknowledgement was noted whether the requests had been on-list or off-list.

The 6-month scrutiny of this group's Yahoo! posts reveals that new ideas from the outside are less relevant than to the other three groups because of the group's specific focus.

RESULTS OF THE SURVEYS

A total of 104 responses to our surveys were received from members of the various groups that were encouraged to take part. There were 54 respondents to Part 1 of Survey 1 and 50 to Part 2 of Survey 1. The second survey received very few responses. A total of 15, as moderators were the principal target. With so few respondents and a lack of clarity in their answers it was impossible to draw a clear picture of the situation, however much of value was learned from the wide contact with practitioners in different corners of the field. These insights have been used in drawing up the seventh section, the advice for novice vCoP moderators.

Were similar research to be carried out in future, it should be based on better collection data. However, even in this research many encouraging comments were received from moderators and other participants. A female respondent commented that she finds those groups where the leaders are cheerleaders—helpful, friendly, full of praise for even small accomplishments—thrive best. The research described in this chapter would suggest that this is indeed the case.

CONCLUSIONS

This study was primarily a qualitative one leading on from the theories of Joyce and Kraut (2006), and of Herring (2000, 1992, 1993). Personal opinions were collected and analyzed in the hope of extrapolation to a larger frame. Despite the limitations in the extrapolation of data over the 6 months, the analysis provides the following answers to the questions posed in the section heading "WebHeads in Action (WiA)."

Is there evidence of gender bias in the discourse style of vCoP (or dCoP) moderating?

> Answer: All of the moderators, knowingly or not, gave evidence of some gender bias, but this was over a very wide spectrum of acceptability.

> Do moderators take account of their own gender and that of their group in the style of their moderating?

> Answer: If taking account of gender style in VCoP moderating and learning can be judged by a successful group result, then some of the moderators had obviously paid it due attention.

> Is a female moderating style welcoming and hence encouraging to females in the group? Is it also successful in encouraging positive male participation? Does this affect the number of posts?

> Answer: Yes, to all three questions.

> Does a male moderating style elicit initial and durable enthusiasm from male group members?

> Does it have the same effect on female participation? Does this affect the number of posts?

> Answer: Yes, whether males are in the majority in the group or not. Females do not seem to respond so well to male moderating styles and contribute fewer posts.

This research study had set out to investigate gender-bias in moderators' style. Examples have been studied both in the literature and in four case histories, and lead to the conclusion that it occurs often, but that moderators give it a low priority in their planning. Our recommendation is that it should be taken into account right from the start by any professional committing to the idea of education in a vCoP. This is the principal conclusion.

IDEAS FOR MODERATORS

In conclusion, we offer you these (female!) key points as recommendations (quotes from a range of female moderators.)

Preparation

Prepare the launch of your vCoP. Have clear aims from the start of who your target members will be. Anticipate the development and set yearly goals. Be prepared, but stay flexible enough to change your plan.

Focus on new members—don't want to get more advanced, encourage unintended members to try other communities, avoid moving on to a level of expertise that alienates newcomers. (Gladys Baya)

Inclusion

Be inclusive. Allow for free-flow of membership, core to peripheral circularity. Share and rotate moderation when possible or appropriate. Do not be surprised if the majority of people are takers and not givers but understand that entry and engagement processes help members to become active participants.

"Be supportive but live and let lurk! (Hockly, 2003)

Trust and Interweaving

To build up trust, express frequent support, offer areas for sociability and accept the fact that a heterogeneous group will call for special understanding and patience. Diversity in learning style, culture, and personal styles can be constructive and hasten learning, but first there must be trust.

Socialization is essential—as important as "content." We don't have a special environment—but we have clear moments when [socialization] is emphasized—a week called "extension"—replying to people who have written to you, contacting those who have fallen behind. I think this is very important otherwise you don't join a community, you just play with the tools on your own. (Gladys Baya)

Media Richness and Social Software

The choice of media can engage participants further but the focus needs to be on giving members a reason to use them and creating systems that enhance knowledge sharing rather than impeding it. Collaborative use of blogs, Wikis, Skypecasts, and social bookmarking spaces are ways of overcoming barriers of text-based IT for transfer of knowledge. Task-oriented dCoPs move forward faster. Many dCoPs start out as Yahoo! Groups and evolve to include other sharing knowledge platforms. Flexibility and meeting specific aims is essential. Respect your users—keep them informed and provide tutorials or support to help members embrace the tools your group uses. From passwords to real-time sessions, ensure electronic retrieval of files and shared knowledge is logical and accessible. Each tool serves a certain use better.

A Wiki is great for collecting info, blog helps for reflection [on what we have achieved], Yahoo! Posts for daily discussion, social bookmarking serves as an archive and reference tool. (Gladys Baya)

Back to Basics

Remember people will be joining at the bottom of the pyramid all the time as well as jumping on the top. Recycling by deepening discussions can be beneficial to new members as well as the more experienced. Encourage peer-to-peer support networks as the group moves on in order for newcomers to feel networked. Male members find this more irritating —so plan activities and tasks that will ensure you do not lose them.

Avoid the feeling that you are contacting machines. (Gladys Baya)

Manage

Successful groups are "managed" groups. A sole moderator can be ill or go on holiday so a fallback system is needed. If you want to increase female participation, display female rule observing tactics but be aware of a possible backlash from male members who may find a strengthened female cohort unsettling. There is no point in increasing female presence if you lose all the males. Swap roles: have joint moderators, one of each gender.

We bring our own individual styles to the COP and its moderation. (Sheila Vine)

Time

Be prepared to commit a great deal of time to this project. The reward may not be measurable but it will be worthwhile.

I spend at least 5-hours a week. (Gladys Baya)

Troubleshooting

Establish guidelines, query members on their views. Be prepared to deal with flaming or storming between members. Sort out copyright and accountability agreements. Create a group "policy" that is transparent, adapt and model the agreement yourself.

Into every community a little rain must fall. (Nancy White, 2000)

Language

The moderators' words are what participants get: no body language, eye contact, dropping of voice, or broad smiles (unless VoIP chatrooms are being used). So they must be chosen with care. Female and male words may differ and may deter or foster participation. The moderator's style has practical implications for female participation. New ideas will evolve and be contributed faster in an environment that is nonthreatening and where roles are changing.

At the beginning, it all depends on the moderators!! They make the wheels run when a VCoP starts, and it has to start with a good purpose, an objective and interest. Then, the participants take over the reins, but the moderators should always be there, behind the scenes, watching, leading, tutoring and moderating! (Female survey respondent)

NOTES

1. The evidence in this case comes from the postings of individuals in the different communities, for example, the use of "hugs" as an initially female only expression gradually taken up by a male member.

REFERENCES

Ardichvili, A., Page, V., & Wentling, T. (2002). Motivation and barriers to participation in virtual knowledge-sharing communities of practice. *Proceedings OKLO 2002 Conference,* Athens, Greece.

Brown, J., & Duiguid, P. (1991). Organisational learning and communities of practice: towards a unified view or working, learning and innovation. *Organisational Science, 2*(1), 40-57.

Cherny, L. (1994). *Gender differences in text based virtual reality.* Paper presented at the 3rd Berkeley Conference on Women and Language.

Collins, M. P. (2003). *Invisible adult educators public online discussion group moderators' perception of their roles tasks and responsibilities.* Unpublished doctoral dissertation, Pennsylvania State University Retrieved August 15, 2006, from http://etda.libraries.psu.edu/theses/approved/WorldWideIndex/ETD-370/index.html

Ferster, C. B., & Skinner, B.F. (1957). *Schedules of reinforcement.* New York: Appleton-Century-Crofts.

Fredrick, C. A. N. (1999). *Feminist rhetoric in cyberspace: The ethos of Feminist Usenet Newsgroups.* Retrieved August 15th 2006, from http://www.indiana.edu/~tisj/readers/abstracts/15/15-3%20Fredrick.html

Gouldner, A. W. (1960). The norm of reciprocity: A preliminary statement. *American Sociological Review, 25*(2), 161-178.

Herring, S. (1993). *Gender and democracy in computer-mediated communication online.* Retrieved August 15, 2006, from http://ella.slis.indiana.edu/~herring/ejc.txt

Herring, S. C. (1992) *Gender and participation in computer mediated linguistic discourse* (Document No. ED 345552). Washington DC: ERIC ClearingHouse on Languages and Linguistics. Retrieved August 15, 2006, from http://cade.athabascau.ca/vol17.1/fahy.html

Herring, S.C. (2000). Gender differences in CMC: Findings and implications. *CPSR Newsletter.* Retrieved August 15, 2006, from http://www.cpsr.org/issues/womenintech/herring/

Herrington, A., Herrington, J., & Oliver, R. (1999). Providing reflective on-line support for pre-service teachers on professional practice in schools. In B. Collis & R. Oliver (Eds.), *Proceedings of the 11th World Conference on Educational Multimedia, Hypermedia and Telecommunications* (pp. 166-171). Chesapeake, VA: Association for the Advancement of Computers in Education

Hockly, N. (2003). Live and let lurk. *IATEFL Newsletter, 173,* 8.

Johnson, C. M. (2005). *Establishing an online community of practice for instructors of English as a foreign language.* Unpublished doctoral dissertation, Graduate School of Computer and Information Sciences Nova Southeastern University.

Joyce, E., & Kraut, R. E. (2006). Predicting continued participation in newsgroups. *Journal of Computer-Mediated Communication, 11*(3), 3. Retrieved August 15, 2006, from http://jcmc.indiana.edu/vol11/issue3/joyce.html

Lave, J., & Wegner, E. (1991). *Situated learning: Legitimate peripheral participation.* London. Cambridge University Press.

Lee, L., & Neff, M. (2004) How information technologies can help build and sustain an organizations CoP: Spanning the socio-technical divide? In P. Hildreth & C. Kimble (Eds.), *Knowledge networks: Innovation through communities of practice*. Hershey, PA: Idea Group.

Lipnack, J., & Stamps, J. (2000) *Virtual teams: People working across boundaries with technology* (2nd ed.) New York: Wiley.

Lofland, J. (1971) *Analyzing Social settings*: Belmot, CA: Wadsworth

Salmon, G., (2003). *The march of the moderator.* Retrieved August 15, 2006, from http://www.heacademy.ac.uk/embedded_object.asp?id=21663&filename=Salmon

Selfe, C. L., & Meyer, P. R. (1991). Testing claims for online conferences. *Written Communications, 8*(2),163-192.

Soukup, C. (1999). *The gendered interactional patterns of computer-mediated chatrooms: A critical ethnographic study.* Retrieved August 15, 2006, from http://www.indiana.edu/~tisj/readers/toc/15.html

Storck, J., & Storck, L. (2004). Trusting the knowledge of large online communities: Strategies for learning from behind. In P. Hildreth & C. Kimble (Eds.), *Knowledge networks: Innovation through communities of practice* (pp. 243-255). Hershey, PA: Idea Group.

Wegner, E., McDermott. R., & Snyder, W. M. (2002). *Cultivating communities of practice*. Cambridge, MA: Harvard Business School Press.

White, N. (2000). *Facilitating and hosting a virtual community.* Retrieved August 15, 2006, from http://www.fullcirc.com/community/communityfacilitation.htm

ABOUT THE CONTRIBUTORS

Debbie Bergholdt holds a master's of education from Old Dominion University, in Norfolk, Virginia, and a bachelor of arts from the University of Minnesota in Minneapolis, Minnesota. She has 13 years of experience in adult education and training. Debbie is currently the state GED administrator for the Virginia Department of Education, Office of Adult Education and Literacy, in Richmond, Virginia. Prior to this, she served as program development specialist with the Virginia Adult Learning Resource Center in Richmond, chief GED examiner with Hampton Public Schools in Hampton, Virginia, and adult education program manager for York County, Virginia. Debbie has extensive experience in program improvement, strategic planning, group facilitation, and online professional development planning and delivery.

Dr. Beverly Bickel is the director of the English Language Center at the University of Maryland, Baltimore County (UMBC) and assistant research professor in the language, literacy. and culture doctoral program. Working with international teams, she has developed and taught globalized communication courses and developed online professional development courses for English teachers and English language learners. Her research is in globalized communication and how the public space of the Internet supports transformational dialogue and knowledge projects.

Chris Blackmore is a senior lecturer in environmental and development systems in the Open Systems Research Group at the UK's Open University. Her current research and teaching is about systems approaches to environmental decision making, with particular interest in learning systems and communities of practice. She develops open learning course material and has worked on several European research projects. Her background was originally in environmental sciences/education, later sustainable development education. Before joining the Open University, she worked in Nigeria, Lesotho, and Sierra Leone.

Mélanie Ciussi Bos is in charge of eLearning at CERAM Business School since 2002. She is also a researcher at University Aix Marseille I (psychology and education sciences). Her PhD was specifically on networks and communities of learning in a virtual campus. Another domain of expertise is educational simulation games for children, which she worked on for 2 years as head of this project for the French ministry of research. She studied economics, has a master's degree in marketing (1996) and in multimedia (2002). Before moving into research, she worked for Marks and Spencer for 3 years as assistant personnel manager across Scotland and Belgium.

Ben K. Daniel, is a PhD candidate at the University of Saskatchewan and has a broad interdisciplinary research interests, mainly in applied artificial intelligence in education (AIED). Currently his active research foci are on the application of Bayesian belief network in ill-defined areas and imprecise data sets and analysis of complex social software systems, discourse analysis of online interactions, virtual learning communities, distributed communities of practice and knowledge management. Ben is the senior research associate in the Virtual Learning Communities Research Laboratory in the College of Education and a member of the ARIES Research Group in the Department of Computer Science.

Valentina Dodge is a teacher, teacher trainer, and online moderator. She works part-time at the University of Naples and comanages a consultancy specializing in tailor-made business courses in the Salerno area. Having worked in education for over 20 years, and as a consultant for local and European projects for the past 5 years. She is involved in setting up, running, and mentoring transnational projects at secondary school level involving ICT and developing educational material for international exchanges. Together with Sheila Vine she has codesigned/moderated online courses for German companies via their online company www.worldwide-webquests.com, worked online on the award wining "ICT in the Classroom" courses and developed and copresented the e-moderator's exchange www.echatbox.com at the IATEFL International Conference.

Dr. Judi Fusco is a research scientist in SRI International's Center for Technology in Learning, and specializes in researching and developing online communities, technologies, and resources. For the past 5 years, she has directed the community development of Tapped In®, an online community for teacher professional development. While developing the community, she has worked with master teachers from all over the world; and organizations like, NCREL, PBS, Pepperdine University, and Los Angeles County Office of Education. She has helped grow Tapped In® from 300 teachers to over 21,000 and has helped many organizations learn to work online. Dr. Fusco's research on the community involves examining social and technical supports necessary for online community, individual and group readiness, investigating models for online professional development, understanding the nature of local K-12 education communities of practice, and analyzing and applying social network analysis (SNA) techniques to data gathered in communities.

Fernand Gervais is a professor from the faculty of education at Laval University, Canada. His research interests are in the area of Teacher Education more specifically in learning and cognition. His expertise is in situated learning, sociocultural perspectives on cognition, social theories of learning and ethnomethodology. Recently, he has participated in a few research projects involving virtual communities of practice. His contribution has been in the development of a coherent theoretical framework to investigate communities of practice.

Michael Hartley worked in the Scottish secondary sector in a variety of teaching (geography) and in school management (middle and senior) posts. Before joining Ultralab at Anglia Ruskin University in 2000, Michael was working in special educational with primary/secondary pupils with severe & profound learning difficulties. His recent projects include: "TescoSchoolnet," 2000 Project; "Talking Heads," an online community for Head Teachers in England; "Heads Together," an online community for headteachers in Scotland; "Ultraversity," an online, content free degree. He is now a freelance learning technology consultant.

Kathy Hibbert is the director of continuing teacher education, faculty of education, and the director of the Center of Education, Diagnostic Radiology and Nuclear Medicine, Schulich School of Medicine and Dentistry, University of Western Ontario, London, Ontario Canada. Her more than 20 years in education have fostered research interests in the following areas: investigating scholarship in medical education, language and literacy teaching and learning, professional development, virtual learning environments and professional communities of practice. In particular, her interests lie in looking at policies/decisions/practices surrounding learning environments that stimulate and engage teachers' intellectual curiosity in ways that inform classroom practices. She teaches graduate courses in virtual learning environments, pedagogic discourse, research methods and curriculum. She recently published in *The International Handbook of Virtual Learning Environments* (Kluwer Academic).

Anne Hewling is presently working as an e-learning specialist in the Library and Learning Resources Center at the UK Open University having previously worked as project officer for the PROWE project that was based there. She is an educationalist who began her working life teaching face-to-face but subsequently moved into open and distance and then online learning. She has a PhD in educational technology for which she investigated how culture impacts the online class. Most recently, she has taught online courses in use of new technologies and in development and global citizenship for universities in the UK, Australia, and Canada.

Erik Jacobson is an assistant professor in the Early Childhood, Elementary and Literacy Education Department at Montclair State University (New Jersey, United States of America). He worked in community based adult education for 10 years, teaching in a variety of programs (e.g., English as a second language, citizenship, family literacy). For the last 5 years he has been involved in professional development at the individual, program, and statewide level. During this time he has become increasingly interested in the role that technology can play in helping educators develop and share their professional wisdom.

Brenda Kaulback is communities coordinator with Knowledge in the Public Interest (kpublic.com), a strategy consulting firm specializing in the development and deployment of virtual communities for social innovation (VCSI) and focused on new models of organization leadership and learning for the nonprofit, public, and philanthropic sectors. For the past 10 years, she has consulted in cross-systems work, assisting people and institutions to reach out across boundaries and work together. Her clients have included leading public and private agencies. She has held senior leadership positions in state government in education, employment, and training and social services, and taught secondary school and college. She received her master's in teaching from the University of Maine and her BA in English from Bates College, in Lewiston, Maine.

Melissa Koch designs and implements educational learning environments for teachers and youth. She specializes in the development of online collaborative technologies and technology-based curricula for learning in and out of school. She also designs and implements teacher professional development programs to support teachers in integrating technology into their practice. As senior educational developer at SRI International's Center for Technology in Learning, she coleads the design and management of NSF's CLTNet and Tapped In®. At RealCommunities, she led the development of Applications of Purpose, including a mentoring application, to be used in a variety of online environments to enable community members to learn from one another. She has developed several Internet products for the K-12 education market while working with organizations such as Computer Curriculum Corporation, The Learning Company, PBS, The Edison Project, and O'Reilly & Associates.

Thérèse Laferrière is full professor of pedagogy at Laval University. Her research activities focus on networked learning environments and especially participants' online interactions in networked communities (learning communities, communities of practice and knowledge building communities). She served as president of the Canadian Association for Teacher Education (CA TE/CSSE), and was the president of the Canadian Education Association (2001-2002). She was dean of education at Laval University (1987-1995) as well as president of the association francophone des doyennes et doyens, directeurs et directrices d'education du Canada. She is the current coordinator of CATE SIG Technology and Teacher Education.

Sabine Little currently works for CILASS, (Center for Inquiry-based Learning in the Arts and Social Sciences), a center for excellence in teaching and learning at the University of Sheffield, UK. As a learning development and research associate for Networked Learning, she supports projects using technologies to facilitate inquiry-based learning. Prior to this, she worked in the school of education, where she facilitated an MEd as part of the school's Caribbean program. She is particularly interested in the concept of peer cognizance, that is, the ways in which groups collaborate and develop a mutual sense of responsibility and stake in outcomes, and how this process can be facilitated, either face-to-face or online.

Dr Janet Macdonald is learning and teaching coordinator for the Open University in Scotland. She has first hand experience of being both a distance student and tutor, and now provides staff development for others. She has a doctorate in online course design and assessment, and has directed a variety of studies in the use of online communities for supporting distance tutors.

Eric M. Meyers is a doctoral student and research associate at the Information School of the University of Washington, where he studies youth information behavior and information literacy instruction in formal and informal contexts. He holds master's degrees in information and education from the University of Michigan and Stanford University respectively. Formerly a teacher, school librarian, and technologist, he consults with school professionals on information services, library spaces, and technology curriculum.

Lisa P. Nathan is a doctoral candidate and research associate at the Information School of the University of Washington. Her doctoral dissertation research addresses ways in which social and cultural values influence information and communication technology (ICT) appropriation. She holds a master's degree in library and information science from Simmons College. Her other research interests include information behavior, social informatics, and ethnography. She has been a teacher and a public librarian.

Dr. Linda Polin holds the Davidson Endowed Professorship in education and technology at Pepperdine University's Graduate School of Education and Psychology where she teaches graduate courses in learning, technology, and design, as well as in action research methods. Dr. Polin consults with school districts, universities, and software developers. Her current research interests focus on knowledge coconstruction and sharing, that is, learning, in informal online communities. She is studying informal yet self-organized learning communities in massively multiplayer online gaming and literature-based role-playing communities on the Web. Her most recent publications include "Dialogue With a Practicing Community," in Duffy and Kirkley (Eds.), *Learner Centered Theory and Practice in Distance Education,* LEA, 2003; and with Margaret Riel, "Models of Community Learning and Online Learning in Communities," in Barab, Kling, & Gray (Eds.), *Designing Virtual Communities in the Service of Learning,* Cambridge University Press, 2004. Dr. Polin also writes occasional pieces for the district administrator magazine blog, *The Pulse* (www.districtadministration.com/pulse/)

Leonie Ramondt worked at Ultralab for 9 years and in 1997-978 piloted the Online Learning Network for educationalists in advance of the University for Industry. In 1998-99 she designed and facilitated the EU funded SMILE project for engineers in the automotive and aerospace industries. From 2000, she headed up the research and development of Talking Heads and other online communities for the English National College of School Leadership (NCSL). She currently works for Inspire at

Anglia Ruskin University and is a research partner in the Design in the 21st Century funded PRADSA—Practical Design for Social Action Project.

Susan Restler is cofounder with Diana Woolis of Knowledge in the Public Interest (kpublic.com), a strategy consulting firm specializing in the development and deployment of virtual communities for social innovation (VCSI) and focused on new models of organization leadership and learning for the nonprofit, public, and philanthropic sectors. Ms Restler is a business strategist with particular expertise in marketing. Her background includes market research and Internet-based marketing. She was a managing director of JP Morgan and holds an AB degree from Harvard University and an MBA from Columbia University.

Gillian Rosner is coordinator of language teaching at CERAM Business School where she is also responsible for EFL programs. Before joining CERAM, she worked extensively in the EFL field, both in academia (University of Nice) and in companies (IBM). She has been collaborating on various e-projects with Melanie Ciussi Bos and Marc Augier ever since they set up the online learning platform at the business school. She is very interested in transferring communicative pedagogical approaches from the traditional classroom to online situations. She studied sociology at Sussex University, and has an MA in applied linguistics from the University of Surrey.

Johann Sarmiento is a doctoral candidate in the College of Information Science and Technology at Drexel University. His areas of interest include social computing, computer-supported collaborative learning, and human-computer interaction. His forthcoming dissertation, *Bridging Mechanisms in Team-Based Online Problem Solving: Continuity in Collaborative Knowledge Building*, investigates from an interactional perspective issues of continuity and cross-team collaboration as part of the knowledge building activity of small groups in the virtual math teams project—a research project at the Math Forum. Prior to starting his doctoral studies, he worked as a senior research associate at the Center for Research in Human Development and Education (CRHDE) at Temple University, conducting research and development work on the application of advanced technologies for learning.

Matthew L. Saxton is an assistant professor in the Information School of the University of Washington. His primary research interest is in question-answering behavior, intermediation, and the evaluation of library and information services. His book, *Understanding Reference Transactions* (2002), applies hierarchical linear modeling to investigate the factors that contribute to success in responding to reference questions in public libraries. He received the 1997 ALISE Methodology Award.

Richard. A. Schwier is a professor of educational communications and technology at the University of Saskatchewan, where he coordinates the graduate program in educational technology. He is the principal investigator in the virtual learning communities research laboratory, which is currently studying the characteristics of formal online learning communities. Professor Schwier's other research interests include instructional design and social change agency.

Joan Kang Shin is a full-time lecturer in the Education Department at the University of Maryland, Baltimore County (UMBC). She is the coordinator of online and off-campus programs in the ESOL/bilingual education master's program. In addition, she is also a doctoral candidate in the language, literacy, and culture doctoral program at UMBC. As a teacher trainer in the field of teaching english to Speakers of other languages (TESOL), Joan embraces both online and face-to-face teaching environments. Her current research revolves around building successful virtual communities of practice (vCoPs) for TESOL teaching professionals around the world.

Wesley Shumar is a cultural anthropologist at Drexel University whose research focuses on virtual community, higher education, and ethnographic evaluation in education. Since 1997 he has worked as an ethnographer at the Math Forum, a virtual math education community and resource center. He is co-pi on the virtual math teams (VMT) project, a 5-year NSF project at the Math Forum that is investigating the dynamics of online and face-to face collaborative problem solving and problem creation. He is also co-pi on Leadership Development for Technology Integration: Developing an Effective NSDL Teacher Workshop Model. This project is a 3-year NSF project to develop and refine a hybrid workshop model that supports teachers to integrate National Science Digital Library (NSDL) resources and technologies into their classrooms.

Yvonne Thayer is a career public educator having worked in school districts and a state Department of Education in the United States. Currently she is with the Southern regional education board as director of leadership development. Her work has focused on school improvement, and her publications direct school leaders on actions to improve the instructional programme. As director of adult education for the Commonwealth of Virginia, she refocused statewide professional development from traditional meetings and workshops to a community of practice using synchronous and asynchronous technologies. She holds a doctorate in adult education from Columbia University and an MA in curriculum and instruction from Virginia Tech.

Kevin Thompson worked in the Scottish secondary sector in a variety of teaching and management posts teaching chemistry and computer science. He has a variety of computing books published. Kevin joined Ultralab at Anglia Ruskin University, in 2000. His recent projects include: "Not school" a community for disaffected youngsters; "Talking Heads" an online community for headteachers in England; "Heads Together" an online community for Scottish Head teachers; and "Ultraversity" an online, content free degree. He is now in the faculty of education at Anglia Ruskin and a frequent guest speaker at conferences.

Sheila Vine is a freelance teacher, teacher trainer, and online moderator, working part-time for the University of Applied Sciences in Germany. She also works as a freelance business English teacher and worked in training in various business fields in the United Kingdom, including credit management. Together with Valentina Dodge, she has developed and copresented the e-moderator's exchange www.echatbox.com at the IATEFL International Conference (UK) April 2006, and coauthored articles for EFL journals and virtual magazines, for example, *Humanizing Language Teaching* online, *Pilgrim's Publication, English Teaching Professional, Voices and English Teaching Matters*. Sheila also codesigned/moderated online courses for German companies via their online Web quest company www.worldwide-webquests.com and worked online for The Consultants-E.com on the award wining "ICT in the Classroom" courses.

Diana D. Woolis is cofounder with Susan Restler of Knowledge in the Public Interest (kpublic.com) a strategy consulting firm specializing in the development and deployment of virtual communities for social innovation (VCSI) and focused on new models of organization leadership and learning for the nonprofit, public, and philanthropic sectors. Dr. Woolis has served in executive positions in government, nonprofits, and education. She holds a master's and doctorate in education from Columbia University, has published in both popular and academic journals and has been recognized for her work on issues of equity and access. She wrote one of the first doctoral dissertations exploring public sector learning organizations.

Lightning Source UK Ltd.
Milton Keynes UK
24 October 2009

145330UK00001B/8/A